New Perspectives in Monetary Macroeconomics

Explorations in the Tradition of Hyman P. Minsky

edited by
Gary Dymski and Robert Pollin

Ann Arbor

THE UNIVERSITY OF MICHIGAN PRESS

1997   1996   1995   1994   4   3   2   1

Library of Congress Cataloging-in-Publication Data

New perspectives in monetary macroeconomics : explorations in the
    tradition of Hyman P. Minsky / edited by Gary Dymski and Robert
    Pollin.
        p.   cm.
    Includes bibliographical references and index.
    ISBN 0-472-10472-1 (alk. paper)
        1. International finance.   2. Monetary policy.   3. Uncertainty.
    4. Macroeconomics.   5. Minsky, Hyman P.   6. Marx, Karl, 1818–1950.
    7. Schumpeter, Joseph Alois, 1883–1950.   8. Sraffa, Piero.
    I. Minsky, Hyman P.   II. Dymski, Gary.   III. Pollin, Robert.
    HG3881 N414   1993
    332.4—dc20   93-45596
                                                                        CIP

Contents

Acknowledgments

This volume builds from the contributions of Prof. Hyman Minsky, and it is to his intellectual leadership, of course, that the book is most indebted. But Minsky teaches that debts have a way of accumulating quickly once one becomes accustomed to relying on them. We have depended on several very capable people in seeing the book through to publication: Colin Day, Director of the University of Michigan Press and his associates Laurie Ham and Lorrie LeJeune; Jenya Weinreb, our manuscript editor; Joan Tenma Noguera of the Economics Department staff at University of California-Riverside; and Paul Woodburne, a graduate student at UC-Riverside, who compiled the index. Just as in the Minsky model, we now find ourselves unable to adequately repay the debt of thanks we owe to each of them. We also are grateful to the UC-Riverside Committee on Research for its financial support.

−The Editors

CHAPTER 1

Introduction

Gary Dymski and Robert Pollin

Joseph Schumpeter, in his great *History of Economic Analysis*, describes David Ricardo as "the horse that will take hold of the bit, put out its nose, and gallop for what it is worth." Hyman Minsky, whose life's work as an economist we honor with this volume, possesses that same Ricardian energy—a mind that strives purposefully for definite and meaningful conclusions.[1] Through his work, he has provided a powerful demonstration of why economics is an important and exciting discipline—and, in particular, of why someone who cares about the betterment of human-well being would dare plunge into the forbidding bramble bush of monetary macroeconomics.

Why indeed? Let us pursue this question by considering Minsky's contributions in both their historic and analytic context.

1. Spheres of Theory and Reality

The defining characteristic of the monetary and financial systems of the capitalist economies since the early 1960s has been persistent and fundamental change.[2] Considering the U.S. economy, financial markets were highly regulated in the early 1960s, and the regulations created sharply segmented markets among various intermediaries. By the early 1990s, the regulatory system had been almost entirely abandoned, either through formal repeal of laws or the circumvention of remaining rules through innovation.

Interest rates were relatively stable and low in real terms in the early 1960s, partially because of regulations establishing ceiling rates but also because of the general stability and constraints on competition in the market.

---

1. We wish to call attention to another collection of essays published in Minsky's honor (Fazzari and Papadimitriou 1992). That book includes most of the features of a traditional Feschrift volume, including personal testimonials by colleagues; a survey article on Minsky's career (written by the editors of the current volume); and a bibliography of Minsky's principal publications. The aim of the current volume, as its subtitle suggests, is thus more focused on expanding the frontier of thinking in the tradition to which Minsky has contributed.

2. This section draws substantially from Pollin 1993.

By the 1990s, interest rates had long been freed from regulation. Rates became much more volatile from the 1970s onward, and, over the 1980s, they rose to and maintained a level that was unprecedented at least since the 1920s.

The dollar was still the official reserve currency for international transactions through the 1960s, and its exchange rate was fixed relative to other major currencies through Bretton Woods. At the same time, U.S. credit markets were largely self-sufficient in the 1960s, as, on average, only 1 percent of credit market funds came from foreign sources. Currency markets became highly volatile after the demise of Bretton Woods, and exchange rate fluctuations became a major factor in setting U.S. monetary policy, especially since the contribution of foreign sources to U.S. credit markets rose to an average of 6.5 percent over the 1980s.

The reality of a fundamentally changing financial structure is also evident from more formal measures of macrofinancial activity. The velocity of money, as measured by M1, rose from a value of 3.67 in 1967—meaning roughly that each dollar of currency and transaction accounts purchased $3.67 of GNP—to 6.64 in 1989. Similarly, the ratio of aggregate net borrowing by domestic nonfinancial sectors rose from 6.6 percent of GNP in 1960 to over 13 percent by 1989. Moreover, much of the increase in private sector borrowing—indeed nearly all the borrowing growth by the nonfinancial corporate sector—was used to finance speculative activity such as mergers and takeovers.

These structural changes were accompanied by increasingly frequent and severe bouts of financial instability. No serious financial dislocations had occurred from the end of World War II to the mid-1960s, and indeed, in the 1960s high noon of macroeconomic finetuning, such phenomena were considered as relics of a bygone era. By the early 1990s, financial crises had become a regular feature of the financial landscape, from the credit crunch of 1966 to the Wall Street crash in 1987 and the collapse of the Savings and Loan industry in 1990. The unexpectedly long recession and sluggish recovery of the early 1990s were also largely due to the excessive levels of private indebtedness incurred in the 1980s.[3]

---

3. Anna Schwartz (1986) claims that "no financial crisis has occurred in the United States since 1933 and none has occurred in the United Kingdom since 1866. All the phenomena of recent years that have been characterized as financial crisis—a decline in asset prices of equity stocks or real estate commodities; depreciation of the exchange value of a national currency; financial distress of a large non-financial firm, a large municipality, a financial industry, or sovereign debtors—are pseudo-financial crises." These are pseudocrises according to Schwartz because they have not produced an economy-wide cataclysm on the order of the 1930s Depression. But the fact that this hasn't happened does not mean that the effects of financial dislocations on macro performance have been insignificant. Moreover, as Minsky stresses, understanding the reasons that a 1930s-style collapse hasn't happened is central to an understanding of the trajectory of modern advanced economies.

The ramifications of persistent structural changes over the past thirty years have been felt most severely not in the United States or other advanced economies, but in the less developed economies, especially Latin America. Financed through foreign credits, the massive debt buildup in Latin America in the 1970s and subsequent collapse in the early 1980s produced a depression in that region more severe than that of the 1930s. Mass living standards and life opportunities fell dramatically. It is also most unlikely that the free market restructuring strategies being pursued in the early 1990s will establish a new equitable and sustainable growth path for the region.

Remarkably, amid such profound changes in the sphere of money and finance and their implications for broad economic well-being, the sphere of *theorizing* about money and finance has largely neglected these developments. Indeed, as the forces of change in the financial system gathered momentum from the mid-1960s onward, the economics profession increasingly came to embrace theoretical approaches in which financial markets and private institutions play essentially no role in explaining economic outcomes. The very idea of systemically generated destabilizing forces was beyond the pale of discussion.

We refer first, of course, to the dramatic ascendence of monetarist theory advanced by Milton Friedman and associates. Regarded initially in the 1950s as a negligible rehash of pre-Keynesian quantity theory, by the 1980s it represented a preeminent orthodox position throughout the world.

According to monetarism, the only channel through which financial forces affect the aggregate economy is via the money supply, and significant changes in the money supply are generated not by market forces but by central banks—that is, they are exogenous to the private economy. Money demand, according to monetarism, is a stable function of permanent income, and, as such, the velocity of money is also stable within any short-term period (Friedman argued that long-term velocity should fall because money is a luxury good). Fluctuations in the supply and demand for credit merely reflect the more fundamental changes in money growth—they are "supporting players", according to Friedman, in a drama in which the money supply is the headliner (1969, p. 189). It therefore follows that financial institutions, and the role of historical change in the financial system, carry almost no importance in the monetarist system; this, despite the massive researches into the history of U.K. and especially U.S. monetary institutions conducted by Friedman and Schwartz (1963a, 1970, 1982).

But monetarists are not the only postwar school that cast aside institutional considerations in its theoretical models. Orthodox Keynesians, following the IS-LM framework initiated by Hicks, accepted that financial institutions and market forces could be adequately characterized within a model that focused only on money supply and demand rather than on a broader array of institutional variables. The Keynesians' primary dispute with monetarists here was over the degree of interest elasticity of the money demand function. The subsequent debates over the slope of the money demand curve only weakly established any independent influence for private market forces in determining aggregate activity. Beyond this, orthodox Keynesians accepted Modigliani and Miller's conclusion (1958) that financial structures were "irrelevant" for the valuation of nonfinancial firms, and, by implication, for broader macroeconomic outcomes as well.

Most economists' interest in incorporating institutional and historical realities into their models eroded further because of the influence of the general equilibrium model developed by Arrow, Debreu, and others in the 1950s and 1960s. This model showed how, under idealized conditions including perfectly coordinated markets, individual self-interested behavior would achieve an optimal allocation of economic resources. The monetarist agenda, which was closer than its Keynesian rival to the notion that unregulated market activity generated social optima, was given renewed vigor by several technical breakthroughs that extended the scope for institution-free theorizing within monetary macroeconomics. The rational expectations hypothesis, the real business cycle model, and the overlapping generations model all contributed methodological ammunition for those who sought to show that money— and indeed government policy—doesn't matter.

2. Minsky and the Alternative Tradition

It is not surprising, of course, that economists using these theoretical approaches have encountered severe difficulties in explaining the dramatic changes that have occurred over the past thirty years. It should also not be surprising that a large number of economists, seeking to explain these real-world issues as well as to formulate effective and equitable policies for resolving them, have developed alternative theoretical approaches in which financial institutions, structural change, and instability are the central features of the analytic agenda.

Hyman Minsky has been the single most important figure in developing this modern alternative tradition. Through an academic career that has spanned forty years and scores of important publications, Minsky has developed an approach to monetary macroeconomics that he alternatively calls the "financial instability hypothesis" or the "Wall Street paradigm." This approach to macroeconomics has allowed him to systematically pursue a range of crucial questions: a "financial" interpretation of Keynes, an attack on mainstream macroeconomics, a theory of investment and endogenous financial instability, an endogenous theory of money and analysis of contemporary stabilization policies, and most important, an original and fruitful analysis of the problems afflicting contemporary capitalist economies.

Minsky describes his approach as follows:

> The financial instability hypothesis was advanced as an interpretation of Keynes' *General Theory.* . . . The conceit is that Keynes was aware of the great contraction and wholesale collapse of the financial and economic system of 1929–33 as he was developing the *General Theory.* In particular, I assumed that Fisher's debt-deflation theory of great depressions was known to Keynes.
>
> The financial instability hypothesis is addressed to this economy rather than an abstract economy. Our economy is taken to be a capital-using capitalist economy with complex, sophisticated and ever-evolving financial institutions and usages. The model focuses on the relations between finance, asset values, and investment. It can be characterized as a Wall Street view of the world: the principal players are profit-seeking bankers and businessmen (1991, p. 158).

Minsky's approach leads in many directions over the macroeconomic landscape. Yet it also leads to one central result that is fundamentally at odds with the mainstream view: Capitalist economies are inherently unstable, and disequilibrium and unemployment are their normal state of affairs. Minsky writes, "The capitalist market mechanism is flawed in the sense that it does not lead to stable price-full employment equilibrium, and that the basis of the flaw resides in the financial system" (1974, p. 267).

In short, Minsky belongs to the tradition of thinkers Keynes praised as his predecessors in the concluding section of his *General Theory* as those who "prefer to see the truth imperfectly rather than to maintain error reached with clearness and consistency and by easy logic but on hypotheses inappropriate to the facts," (1936, p. 371). The heterodox pantheon in monetary macroeconomics actually has a long and honored tradition in economic thought, beginning at least a century before Keynes with the work in the 1840s of Thomas Tooke.

Tooke developed a "credit theory of money" in debates with the proponents of the "currency school," the predecessors of contemporary orthodoxy. Against this approach, Tooke advanced two primary arguments that carry relevance today: there is a fundamental identity between different financial instruments, so that theory needs to focus on the array of instruments rather than on any single one; and the creation of credit by intermediaries takes place only because the nonbank public *demands* its creation.

Thus, from Tooke, we begin to develop a theoretical framework in which broad credit conditions rather than narrow monetary aggregates are the focus of concern and in which demand forces, relative to supply, are given at least as important if not more prominent a role in determining financial market behavior. In short, Tooke opened the door to the very type of institutional analysis that appears so appropriate for the present.

This approach resurfaced in many subsequent incarnations: in the work of Marx in volume 3 of *Capital*, where he seeks to specify both the financial and nonfinancial sources of instability and crisis; Wicksell, in his discussions on institutional forces determining velocity change; and Schumpeter, in his attempts to "bring money in on the ground floor" in his *Theory of Economic Development*.

The legacy from Keynes is powerful but mixed. In his *Treatise on Money*, Keynes brings great insight to describing the structural complexity of modern financial systems and shows how aggregate investment decisions can be substantially independent of prior aggregate saving. But Keynes shifted his focus in the *General Theory* to the problem of unstable effective demand resulting from the volatility of investment spending and left his complex analysis of financial market interactions to one side. This created an opening for the development of more mild versions of Keynesianism in which financial markets and institutions play a negligible role.

Nevertheless, important efforts were made in the 1950s and early 1960s to develop monetary macroeconomics within a broad financial market approach. Major contributors included John Gurley and Edward Shaw, James Tobin, and the Radcliffe Commission in Britain, led by Nicholas Kaldor. Minsky's earliest writings were within this stream of thought, though there were significant differences in the approaches taken by these various authors. One of the great puzzles of contemporary economics is why this approach, which appeared so promising in the early 1960s, was completely disregarded thereafter by mainstream economists, during precisely the period when the reality of a rapidly changing financial system emerged before our eyes.[4]

Recently, some important steps toward a financial market approach to monetary macroeconomics have been made by mainstream economists such as Benjamin Friedman, Alan Blinder, Joseph Stiglitz, and Ben Bernanke. Building from the theory of imperfect information in financial markets, they have embraced the argument that the availability of credit and the quality of balance sheets are important determinants of the rate of investment. Moreover, they accept the view that the money supply is not a key quantity in the determination of the price level and output. They recognize that, through

---

4. See Pollin and Justice (this volume, note 3) for a discussion based on Earley's (1985) explanation as to why the financial market approach to monetary macroeconomics never developed within the mainstream literature.

increasing velocity, the financial system is sufficiently flexible to generate as much credit as might be needed to finance any given level of activity.[5]

How compatible is this new mainstream perspective with the heterodox tradition led by Minsky? Useful links have been developed, and are explored in some of the papers included in this volume. But the degree of basic compatibility remains an open question. Meanwhile, the Minskian framework is making important advances, both in developing its theoretical foundation and in applying this approach to addressing many of the pressing economic questions facing the world today.

3. Finance, Uncertainty, and Investment Volatility

The essays in this volume range widely, demonstrating the vibrancy of thinking inspired by Minsky's career. The first section of the book includes four theoretical papers. The first two develop macroeconomic models of economic dynamics, and the third and fourth explore microfoundational questions in understanding macrofinancial behavior.

Lance Taylor's paper seeks to establish specific conditions through which financial fragility can lead to destabilizing speculation and output shocks. His aim is to define an "etiology" of financial fragility comparable to an etiology of disease in medicine, whereby the basic relationship of cause and origins of destabilizing finance can be made apparent and thereby more tractable for policy practitioners.

According to Taylor, financial fragility occurs when positive feedback emerges between the level of some financial variable and its own rate of growth. For example, in his initial model, positive profit expectations cause wealth holders to increase their willingness to supply credit. The increase in credit supply generates a decline in interest rates, which feeds back on the positive profit expectations. The upward momentum is then reversed when the deterioration of interest coverage ratios established in the upswing becomes apparent.

Taylor then shows how this same dynamic feedback situation may arise within different types of structural situations—through borrowing and lending among real-sector firms, speculation on financial assets based on anticipated capital gains, and firms' decisions to hold nonproductive assets such as real estate.

---

5. In summarizing this new mainstream approach, Blanchard and Fischer write, "The basic argument is that the capital markets not only intermediate in a mechanical way between savers and investors but in addition deal with a variety of problems that arise from asymmetric information about investment projects between borrower and lender. These informational problems both shape capital market institutions and debt instruments and affect the way in which policy actions are transmitted to the goods markets" (1989, p. 479).

One especially interesting case modeled by Taylor involves foreign asset speculation in developing countries in the wake of implementation of orthodox adjustment policies of reducing government spending and subsidies, while liberalizing trade and finance. Part of the scenario involves freezing the upward movement of the nominal exchange rate in an effort to improve the trade balance. But this policy brings a reduction in the return on foreign assets relative to domestic assets, which increases the supply of domestically held cash reserves. As a result, domestic interest rates fall, encouraging domestic activity. The net effect is therefore to worsen the trade balance and increase the exchange rate. This situation, of course, is unsustainable, leading to a new round of capital flight and domestic instability.

The point of departure for the paper by Delli Gatti, Gallegati, and Gardini is the sharp rise in indebtedness by U.S. corporations during the 1980s. According to the mainstream tradition following from Modigliani and Miller, a rise in corporate leverage should have no impact on either the market valuation of firms or on the macrostability of the financial structure. This view, of course, is completely at variance with the Minsky approach. In recent years, the Modigliani-Miller view has been strongly challenged by new Keynesians working from the postulate of asymmetric information. Delli Gatti et al. seek to build from both the Minsky framework—which they call the "debt deflation" school, including contributions by Irving Fischer (1933) and Charles Kindleberger (1978) as well as Minsky—and the new Keynesian framework in constructing a model that demonstrates the destablizing effects of excessive corporate leverage.

The model they develop generates three types of dynamic behavior: When investment plans are financed primarily through internally generated funds, so that the need for external finance is negligible, the system converges to steady-state stable equilibrium. When the propensity to invest rises to a level where external funds represent a significant amount of the total financing, then the dynamic behavior of the model is chaotic. But when the propensity to invest increases to an extent that it is primarily financed through external funds, the model follows divergent trajectories, which Delli Gatti et al. interpret as a path to financial crisis. They are able to specify a cyclical path for the economy that moves from a financially robust expansion (income growing, debt falling) to a fragile expansion (income and debt growing) to a fragile recession (debt growing, income shrinking) and finally to a robust recession (debt falling, income shrinking).

Gary Dymski develops a more critical perspective on the relationship between new Keynesian developments and the Minsky tradition within post-Keynesian theory. Minsky grounded his views about the centrality of financial structures in the famous chapter 12 of Keynes's *General Theory*, focusing on the nature of uncertainty of investment decisions. Dymski's paper distinguishes three sources of instability: asymmetric information, probabalistic risk, and Keynesian (chapter 12) uncertainty. But the concept of asymmetric information, as formulated by new Keynesians and employed by Delli Gatti et al., has become the tool of choice in Keynesian theory. Theorists such as Bernanke and Stiglitz have shown how financial structure "matters" in investment because of asymmetric information in the credit market. Does this mean that chapter 12 uncertainty, a mainstay of post-Keynesian monetary theorists, is an extraneous analytical conceit?

Dymski shows that asymmetric information alone is necessary and sufficient for credit rationing. Conversely, when risk alone exists, financial structure has no important effect on economic outcomes. However, credit rationing can arise under Keynesian uncertainty even if information is not asymmetric. Further, Keynesian uncertainty leads to an additional reason, overlooked in new Keynesian models, that financial structure matters: it can generate stock/flow imbalances, and hence unstable dynamics ruled out in models that allow only for risk.

James Crotty explores the theme of uncertainty further in his paper, focusing on its implications for the theory of investment. According to Keynes, the notion that private investment decisions are necessarily made on the basis of uncertainty is the basic reason why investment is volatile and, in turn, capitalist economies are unstable. In the theoretical work following Keynes, there is a sharp divergence of views as to the viability of Keynes's notion of investment uncertainty. Mainstream Keynesian theorists, including recent new Keynesian authors, believe that investors do have the information necessary to make optimal decisions. Post-Keynesians such as Minsky have followed Keynes in assuming they do not. Crotty advances a post-Keynesian perspective on this question.

Crotty argues that for decentralized agent choice to generate stable macroequilibria, agents must be assumed to have correct expectations about a future equilibrium. This is an untenable assumption for what Shackle calls "crucial" decisions, which are unique, nonrepeatable, and reversible only at substantial cost. In other words, there is simply no way for investors to acquire correct information about a future that their own investments, and that of other market participants, will themselves create.

But does this mean that there cannot be any general theory for understanding how agents make investment decisions? Crotty argues that how agents incorporate information is itself subject to change, depending on historical circumstances—"the relation between agent and social environment is dialectical and interactive." Agents themselves may recognize that the circumstances under which they make decisions are unstable. This is why investors develop a "conventional" process of expectations and confidence formation. Crotty briefly enumerates the institutional devices by which conventional judgments are formed and the degree of uncertainty reduced, including forward contracts, regulation of competition, and policies to stabilize financial markets and the macroeconomy.

For Crotty, agents are willing to make investment decisions only because they believe in conventional forecasts. But this also means that when events contradict agents' prior conventional judgments, such as when government policy interventions are incapable of delivering the anticipated degree of stability, investors' confidence will suffer a double-pronged disillusion: they will lose confidence both in what to expect and in their ability to re-create a new set of conventional judgments. The conventional belief in the future—"the main anchor of expectations formation"—is thereby lost. Following Crotty, any theory of investment that does not understand both this process of conventional judgment formation and its fragility is incapable of explaining why capitalist economies are subject to persistent and sometimes severe volatility.

4. Financial Globalization and Latin American Debt

Two essays focus on the international dimensions of financial instability. The paper by Peter and Jean Gray suggests a conceptual framework for understanding financial instability within an open international system. Then David Felix investigates how both "moral lapses and failures of policy analysis" have engendered the hardships associated with the Latin American debt crisis.

Peter and Jean Gray argue that the internationalization of financial markets has increased the likelihood of financial instability. They argue that shocks are more likely in an integrated international system than in a purely national one simply because the system is bigger and thereby more exposed to disruptive events. Thus, creating effective stabilizing measures becomes increasingly difficult as international financial integration proceeds.

For example, a cross-border loan is more fragile than an intraborder loan, both because a new political dimension affects the likelihood of repayment and because any refinancing required is contingent on conditions in international as well as domestic markets. Thus, they argue, "the weakest national system can now serve as the source of disturbance, which launches its own crisis," endangering the systems of other countries.

Further, foreign exchange markets are themselves a source of instability. Price fluctuations in these markets are dominated by speculators, and the markets will move quickly among currencies depending on their assessment of economic conditions in various countries. The foreign exchange markets thereby exercise substantial power over the pursuit of domestic policy within any given country. In addition, each country becomes exposed to the rumors, guesses, and conventional wisdom that can rapidly move the financial markets among countries.

Gray and Gray go on to discuss how the stability of the international system can be enhanced. Their analytic point is that an approach that works from Minskian fundamentals will be more successful in creating effective stabilizing mechanisms in a global context than the approaches pursued thus far, which rely on orthodox theories of macrofinance.

Similarly, Felix contends that policies that were pursued in Latin America since 1982—often under coercion from private international lenders and the International Monetary Fund and World Bank—were doomed to failure because they operated from neoclassical analytic premises. Policy makers disregarded the institutional realities of the Latin American economies and instead worked from the orthodox assumption that by liberalizing and cutting government spending, market forces would be strengthened. This itself was meant to bring both short-term recovery and a path to sustainable growth. In fact, the orthodox remedy led to a spiral of inflationary finance, devaluation, and capital exporting—i.e. scenarios similar to those modeled in Lance Taylor's paper.

Felix argues that the short-run tradeoff that got the economies through the depths of crisis in 1982—the exchange of ex post government guarantees on private sector debt—had the longer-run consequence of adding to the fiscal and debt burdens of the debtor nations. Moreover, Felix points out that the burdens of adjustment fell most harshly on the working class and poor, since they paid the immediate price of cuts in government services while assuming the burden of the government's guarantees of private debt. Finally, whereas both the domestic and foreign liabilities of the private sectors were socialized through these adjustment policies, the foreign assets of the Latin wealthy were not. Thus, foreign assets held by Latins were roughly equivalent to if not greater than foreign liabilities—that is, the debt crisis could have been resolved through the simple mechanism of eliminating domestic capital flight.

Felix writes that the policies pursued "needlessly intensified inflation, production decline, physical and human decapitalization, and income inequality" in most of the region, and he concludes that these could have been avoided through both a Minskian-type understanding of macrodynamic instabilities and—perhaps the far greater challenge—greater pressures for equitable burden sharing.

5. Conflict, Finance and Instability in Advanced Economies

In the first of three empirical papers focusing on advanced economies, Dorene Isenberg considers the usefulness of a Minskian framework for understanding the 1930s Depression in the United States. Her particular focus is the 1920s, a period associated with widespread speculative finance. One might reasonably expect to see a pattern of rising leverage ratios during this period. A Minskian theory of the Depression would emphasize the role of such overleveraging in the 1920s, yielding a fragile financial structure in the 1930s that was vulnerable to external shocks and interactive deflations.

Thus far, researchers of the Depression, including those who have considered the role of financial forces, have not seriously examined the extent to which financial fragility contributed to the Depression. Friedman and Schwartz, for example, focus on errors in monetary policy but never consider the impact of endogenous destabilizing forces in the financial sector. More recently, both Bernanke and Bernstein do contend that credit markets were important channels for propagating the impact of the 1929 crash throughout the economy. But they disregard the role of increasing leverage and similar indicators of systemic instability in creating the preconditions for both the crash and long deflationary decline.

Isenberg reviews previous studies on the debt buildup of the 1920s, which generally show that firms' leverage ratios in the industrial sector did not rise through this period. This would certainly be contrary to what Minsky's financial fragility hypothesis would anticipate.

But Isenberg then decomposes firm balance sheet data by firm size and growth rate and discovers a rising leverage ratio for the faster-growing and larger firms over the 1920s. In addition, she also finds that the reason leverage ratios did not rise in the aggregate was that firms to an increasing extent issued equity to raise external funds. This meant that other sectors—including households and the financial sector—were increasing their debt in order to acquire these new equity issues. Thus, rising financial fragility was present in the 1920s. But the burden of increased leverage was displaced from the industrial to nonindustrial sectors.

One of Minsky's most important contributions has been toward the development of an endogenous theory of money (see Wray 1990, 1992; Pollin 1991, 1993). According to Minsky, the flexibility inherent in well-developed, sophisticated financial markets means that central bank efforts to constrain either the availability or cost of reserves—and thereby credit availability and interest rates—are inhibited by the financial markets' capacity to circumvent these restrictions. Gerald Epstein's paper acknowledges the significance of this Minskian position but then goes on to argue that one important piece of the endogeneity argument is missing. That is the role of political forces in the formulation of central bank policy.

What are the political forces acting on central banks? Mainstream analysts provide two answers: the "social welfare" approach, which argues that central banks, like the state in general, make policy in the interests of society as a whole; and the "bureaucratic" approach, which argues that central banks make policy in their own narrow bureaucratic interests. But neither of these approaches is adequate in Epstein's view.

As an alternative, Epstein proposes a "contested exchange" model of central banking. This approach is based on two principles. First, it views the state, and therefore the central bank, as a terrain of both class and intraclass struggle. And second, policy is constrained by structural factors, including the structure of capital and labor markets, the position of the domestic economy in the world economy, and the dynamics and contradictions of capital accumulation itself. This last element encompasses the financial market structural questions that are central in Minsky's work.

Epstein develops an econometric model to test the contested terrain approach, examining the interaction of four key variables in the determination of central bank policy: the structure of labor markets, the connections between finance and industry, the position of the economy in the world economy, and the position of the central bank in the state apparatus. Considering large OECD economies, Epstein finds that the configuration of political forces is an important determinant of both central bank reaction functions and the impact of central bank policy on the macroeconomy.

All of Keynes's basic arguments in the field of macrofinance stem from the idea that "finance"—by which he meant the ability of private intermediaries and the central bank to supply credit—was largely independent of prior or concurrent saving flows. This means that once entrepreneurs' animal spirits were inflamed, they would not be inhibited by the availability of savings as they pursued investment opportunities. But this fundamental Keynesian idea has been challenged in recent years, and not only by mainstream economists. In particular, from a post-Keynesian perspective, Asimakoupoulis mounted a significant critique of Keynes and Kalecki on this question, which launched an extended debate. However, none of the contributors to the debate attempted to specify the issue in a manner amenable to empirical testing. Working with data from the U.S. economy, Robert Pollin and Craig Justice attempt just such a formal specification and set of empirical tests.

The specification builds in part from Minsky's work on the endogeneity of the money supply in financial markets capable of rapid and substantial innovation; Pollin and Justice wish to explore the link between the concept of money supply endogeneity and the saving/finance nexus. The results of the empirical work lead to a middle ground between Keynes and Asimakoupoulis, in which finance is not completely independent of saving but the constraint exercised by saving on finance is empirically weak. This result supports the notion that the structure of financial markets does matter—and indeed is usually decisive—in determining the flow of funds to finance investment and the rate of interest at which the funds are obtainable.

6. Sraffa, Schumpeter, and Marx

The next section of the book explores the various facets of the heterodox tradition in monetary economics. The influence of Keynes on Minsky is evident. But the papers by Arnon, Earley, and Nell consider less familiar connections—with Marx, Schumpeter, and the classical Sraffian school.

One lively point of tension in the intellectual development of modern nonneoclassical economics is the split between post-Keynesian monetary theory, as represented by people such as Minsky, and the surplus approach following from the work of Piero Sraffa. Minsky, for his part, has little regard for the Sraffian tradition because it abstracts from finance and therefore from anything resembling the real world. Indeed, Minsky says that Sraffian analysis is just as "irrelevant to the understanding of modern capitalist economies" as neoclassical theory, since both ignore finance in their models (1988, p. 1). Yet an aggrieved Sraffian might respond that Minsky's model, focused almost entirely on finance, neglects the relationships of production and distribution.

Edward Nell's paper explores in depth the roots of this conflict in an effort to see where fruitful linkages may be established. Nell argues that there are several differences between the Sraffian approach and that of Minsky, but the most important one is over the status of long- versus short-run analysis. The Sraffians determine prices and the rate of profit in a long-period equilibrium that abstracts from demand. As such, their notion of equilibrium abstracts from the factors that preoccupy Minsky: finance, uncertainty, and dynamic change, all elements whose influence operates in the short period, but are assumed away in long-period models. As Nell writes, "What the classical equations supposedly describe, a long-period equilibrium, cannot exist in a Keynesian world."

Of course, the classical model introduces the long-period notion to explore relationships of distribution that exist independently of short-term fluctuations. As Nell writes, "Sraffa's equations could be understood as the abstract, normal form of the system, showing how the parts would be related, abstracting from money and demand." The purpose of this approach is to reveal interconnections and dependencies, but not to analyze actual behavior. The central point, however, is that the actual behavioral patterns studied by Minsky and other post-Keynesians take place "in the context whose structure is presented in Sraffa's equations."

Joseph Schumpeter is another figure whose connections with Minsky are significant, though not apparent. Minsky initially came to Harvard to work under Schumpeter, but Schumpeter unfortunately died before any personal relationship could develop. But Schumpeter's ideas about institutional change and long waves in capitalist development are echoed in Minsky's ideas about financial development and the long-term tendency toward increasing fragility. (see Minsky 1964).

In addition, Schumpeter's thinking on monetary theory actually was quite compatible with Minsky's approach, though, as James S. Earley explores, Schumpeter was never able to give a systematic, coherent accounting of his views on monetary theory. Earley views Schumpeter, along with Minsky, as a "creditist," by which he means one who approaches macroeconomics "by dealing with the motion of a pecuniary economy rather than its equilibrium positions" and who views credit as the fundamental financial variable determining macroeconomic behavior. But whereas Minsky is an unreconstructed creditist, Earley writes that Schumpeter remained a "frustrated creditist" throughout his career.

Earley describes Schumpeter's long struggle with fundamental questions about the nature of money. This struggle centered on his never-completed manuscript on money. Earley argues that Schumpeter's hesitancy in finishing his manuscript on monetary theory stemmed from his inability to free himself from the static monetary conceptions of Leon Walras, his acknowledged theoretical master. For Walras, the circulation of money through the economy facilitated its functioning, but money per se—and implicitly credit—played no role in the dynamic evolution of the economy. The crux of Schumpeter's dilemma thus lay in the tension between the restricted role for money in the static Walrasian model and the central role for credit in Schumpeter's own dynamic model of growth, as presented in his initial theoretical foray, *Theory of Economic Development*, and throughout his career thereafter. Drawing on his own contributions to a "credit theory of money," Earley shows how Schumpeter could have overcome his dilemma.

Are there fruitful intellectual connections between Marx and Minsky? Or, as Arie Arnon asks in the introduction to his essay, are we essentially revisiting such burning matters as "The Elephant and the Jewish Question" by even posing the issue? Arnon's essay does develop some important linkages.

The first link is in the area of monetary theory itself. As Arnon points out, Marxian economists in the 1930s, Minsky's formative years, focused almost entirely on the "real" side of Marx's work. However, Marx himself developed a much broader analytical framework, which included a sophisticated analysis of the interaction between real and monetary forces in capitalism. In fact, as Arnon explores further, both Marx and Minsky can be placed within the monetary theory tradition beginning with Tooke and the Banking School.

Closely related to their views on money, a central idea in work of both Marx and Minsky is that capitalist economies are systemically unstable. For Minsky, the sources of instability reside within the financial sphere exclusively. Marx, on the other hand, stresses real factors in explaining instability. Marx however, did also take great care—especially in volume 3 of *Capital*—to show the interactions between real and financial forces in the propagation of instability.

Finally, Arnon writes that Minsky does have important attachments to the socialist tradition in economics, which are not well known. Minsky's early intellectual development was strongly influenced by Oscar Lange and Abba Lerner, two thinkers who made major contributions to the formulation of market socialist ideas. And while Lange and Lerner both rejected central tenets of Marxism, such as the labor theory of value, they both also embraced Marxian ideas about class conflict and the dismal future of capitalism. Lange and Lerner's efforts to build a model of market socialism are reflected in Minsky's efforts to specify Keynes's notion of socializing investment.

7. A Framework for New Macro-Policies?

The "Minsky paradox," to which the volume's concluding paper by Pollin and Dymski refers, is as follows: Minsky argues that advanced capitalist economies become increasingly fragile, and thus susceptible to financial crises over time; and yet, in Minsky's view, financial crisis on the scale of 1929–32 cannot happen again. The creation of "big government" capitalism after the Depression and World War II—and in particular the exercise of federal deficit spending and lender-of-last-resort central banking policies—is the reason depressions won't happen again. Nevertheless, whereas big government policies are quite adept at avoiding depressions, they are incapable of eliminating altogether the symptoms of systemic instability. Thus, these symptoms must emerge in other forms.

This paper first asks whether we can actually observe the outlines of the Minsky hypothesis in the long-run behavior of the U.S. macroeconomy. Answering in the affirmative, it then asks what the policy implications are at the present conjuncture, in which we have solved the problem of depression prevention but not the problem of systemic instability. Our argument is that the 1980s represented a new historical phase, in which government policies had become less capable of acting as a stabilizer but in which no alternative, superior approach to stabilization was available either within the mainstream economic literature or on the political landscape. The paper ends by arguing that policy options have sharpened in the contemporary period through the weakening of traditional big government policies but the non-viability of small government, free market approaches.

Minsky's work helps us see the need for new approaches, based on the principles of rigging markets and socializing investment. Our success in developing a new framework for macroeconomic policy—and thus a more productive, stable, equitable, and sustainable economic future—will depend in significant measure on our ability to appropriate the insights of Professor Minsky's contributions.

REFERENCES

Blanchard, Olivier and Stanley Fischer (1989). *Lectures on Macroeconomics*, Cambridge, MA: MIT Press.

Earley, James S. (1985). "Money, Credit, and Financial Intermediation: the Need for a New 'New View'", unpublished ms., Department of Economics, University of California, Riverside.

Fazzari, Steven and Dimitri B. Papadimitriou, eds. (1992). *Financial Conditions and Macroeconomic Performance: Essays in Honor of Hyman P. Minsky*. Armonk, NY: M.E. Sharpe.

Fisher, Irving (1933). "The Debt Deflation Theory of Great Depressions," *Econometrica* 1: 337–57.

Friedman, Milton (1969). *The Optimum Quantity of Money and Other Essays*. Chicago: Aldine Publishing Company.

Friedman, Milton and Anna J. Schwartz (1963a). *A Monetary History of the United States*. Princeton, NJ: Princeton University Press.

——— (1963b). "Money and Business Cycles," *Review of Economics and Statistics*, 45(1).

——— (1970). *Monetary Statistics in the United States* New York: National Bureau of Economic Research.

——— (1982) *Monetary Trends in the US and the UK* Chicago: University of Chicago Press.

Keynes, John Maynard (1936). *The General Theory of Employment, Interest, and Money*. New York: Harcourt Brace.

Kindleberger, Charles P. (1977). *Manias, Panics, and Crashes*. New York: Basic Books.

Minsky, Hyman (1964). "Longer Waves in Financial Relations: Financial Factors in the More Severe Depressions," *American Economic Review Papers and Proceedings* 54 (May): 324–32.

——— (1974). "The Modeling of Financial Instability: An Introduction." *Modelling and Simulation 5* (Proceedings of the Fifth Annual Pittsburgh Conference, Instrument Society of America).

——— (1988). Sraffa and Keynes: Effective Demand in the Long Run. Working Paper no. 126 (November), Washington University.

——— (1991). "The Financial Instability Hypothesis: A Clarification," in M. Feldstein, ed., *The Risk of Financial Crisis* Chicago: University of Chicago Press.

Modigliani, Franco and Merton Miller (1958). "The Cost of Capital, Corporate Finance and the Theory of Investment, *American Economic Review*, 48 (June): 261–95.

Pollin, Robert (1991). "Two Theories of Money Supply Endogeneity," *Journal of Post Keynesian Economics*, 13(3): 366–96.

——— (1993) "Money Supply Endogeneity: What Are the Questions and Why Do They Matter?" forthcoming in Nell and Deleplace, eds., *Money in Motion: The Circulation and Post Keynesian Approaches*, New York: Macmillan.

Schwartz, Anna (1986). "Real and Pseudo-financial Crises," in F. Capie and G. Wood, eds., *Financial Crises and the World Banking System*, New York: St. Martins.

Wray, L. Randall (1990. *Money and Credit in Capitalist Economies: The Endogenous Money Approach* Brookfield, VT: Edward Elgar.

——— (1992). "Minsky's Financial Instability Hypothesis and the Endogeneity of Money," in Fazzari and Papadimitriou, eds., *Financial Conditions and Macroeconomic Performance* Armonk, NY: M. E. Sharpe.

Part I
Theoretical Papers

CHAPTER 2

Financial Fragility: Is An Etiology at Hand?

*Lance Taylor**

Etiology refers to the assignment of causes and origins; doctors use the word a lot. As policy practitioners, economists need such a science, especially in the poorly understood domain where financial fragility can lead to destabilizing speculation and output shocks. Fragility is widely but vaguely discussed, provoking an obvious question: Can Minsky's (1975, 1986) metaphor become an etiology prosaic enough to be used by someone who is not a genius at deciphering financial systems?

This paper reports on different approaches to fragility, in models based on institutional specification of the relationships between the real and financial sides of the economy. Whether the models go very far in telling us about observed financial excursions is left as an open question, but some progress does seem to have been made in describing stylized cycles and bursts. As a first step toward causal analysis, a taxonomy of potential instabilities is presented here. Six cases are outlined in the paper's major sections.

First, existing crisis models hinge on a positive feedback (often transmitted via the real side of the economy) between the level of some financial variable and its own rate of growth. In the version of Minsky's theory set out by Taylor and O'Connell (1985), for example, an increase in expected future profits causes desired loans from wealth holders to firms to rise. This shift in portfolio preferences *reduces* the interest rate, which in turn leads observed and expected profits to grow faster. A downward-sloping LM curve enters this process in the short run, combining with surges of investor animal spirits (stimulated by low interest rates) to make cycles or divergent behavior possible over time. Cycles arise when the unstable profit dynamics are stabilized by the evolving capital/money ratio, a general indicator of "intermediation" or coverage of the real side of the economy by non-speculative financial claims.

In passing, it bears emphasis that Minsky-style dynamics of the foregoing sort differ from mainstream models of asset price bubbles, although they too involve positive feedback. An example is arbitrage between the return to a

---

* Suggestions from Gary Dymski were very helpful in organizing this paper.

riskless asset and the sum of dividends and capital gains expected from holding a share. Either the share price turns out to be the discounted sum of future dividends, or else it can diverge exponentially in a bubble blown up by expected capital gains (Blanchard and Fischer, 1989). In higher dimensions, bubbles are nonsaddlepath solutions to the standard dynamic optimization exercises. Our first case already shows that a typical model of financial fragility need not produce bubbles. Rather, it is "dynamically" unstable since its differential equations generate oscillations due to complex characteristic roots of the linearized system instead of the "static" instability demonstrated by a saddlepoint, with its real characteristic roots.[1]

A second case shows how cycles can be generated not only by portfolio decisions of wealth-holders "outside" the sphere of production, but also "inside" it by firms lending and borrowing among themselves (Foley, 1987). Liquidity expansion via inter-enterprise loans stimulates investment during an upswing but also generates the (possibly) stabilizing increase of the financial to real asset ratio that is characteristic of booms.

Third, financial wealth may expand if the price of a speculative asset— real estate, shares, or collectables—jumps up in anticipation of capital gains. In historical examples, there have been bursts of speculation when real investment opportunities were low and potential saving rose in response to regressive income redistribution, leading desired portfolios to switch from assets linked to production. Bubble-type divergence or cyclical convergence of the real/financial system to equilibrium can result, depending on cross-dynamics between the speculative asset price and other state variables.

Fourth, there can also be "inside" decisions by firms to hold nonproductive assets, such as real estate that serves as a loan collateral for South Korean businesses. As with cycles in firms' liquidity, destabilizing speculation may or may not be offset by other real and financial fluctuations.

Fifth, in scenarios painfully common in developing countries, foreign assets may become the object of speculation, with destabilizing capital movements responding to interest rates and expected real exchange depreciation (Frenkel, 1983).

Sixth, regardless of whether positive feedbacks arise with regard to speculative or nonspeculative assets, are induced by actors inside or outside the productive system, or are stabilized or exacerbated by other interactions, the dynamics of real/financial models can be complicated and quite possibly chaotic, even in low-dimensional systems. Etiology is essential to advances in

---

1. The static/dynamic distinction in talking about unstable systems is drawn by engineers, for example to describe buckling beams and the galloping Tacoma Narrows Bridge, respectively (Thompson and Stewart, 1986). Divergent saddlepaths and cycles are the equivalents in economic models.

the macroeconomics of finance, but with mathematical chaos potentially present, it may prove empirically difficult to pursue.

1. Portfolio Shifts and Animal Spirits

Following Taylor (1991), we begin with financial instability in a Kaleckian macromodel, which will be modified later to bring in different financial structures. Asset markets are sketched first, then the real side.

1.1 Asset Markets

Table 1 presents a simplified set of national balance sheets of the type that might be observed in semi-industrialized countries, which will be at the focus of the discussion. The banking system dominates the picture: its assets are base money H (which in a closed economy essentially takes the form of government liabilities placed with the banks) and loans to firms L_b. Deposits (D) held by the public compose the banks' liabilities.

In a one-sector model, let K stand for the capital stock (as a proxy for capacity or potential output, *pace* Cambridge controversies), and let P be the price level, assumed to be set as a mark-up over variable cost, i.e. $P = (1 + \tau)wb$, where w is the money wage, b the labor-output ratio, and τ the mark-up rate. Firms are assumed to finance their holdings of capital stock PK by borrowing from either banks (L_b) or the public (L_p). The public holds its wealth W only in the form of loans to firms and deposits, since there are no markets for equity or government obligations.[2] By consolidating entries in Table 1, one can see that private wealth is the sum of the value of the capital stock and base money:

$$W = PK + H. \tag{1}$$

Since wealth-holders have only two assets, their portfolio choice is described by a single market equilibrium condition. We use the one stating that excess demand for deposits should equal zero,

$$\delta(PK + H) - \xi H = 0,$$

---

2. Only a few developing economies have managed to develop active markets for equity and/or government securities (Taylor, 1988). One consequence is that the state basically finances its deficits by borrowing from the banking system or abroad. Implications of private foreign borrowing are taken up in section 5. A stock market could easily be added to the present model along the lines suggested by Taylor and O'Connell (1985); the effects they stress are built into the deposit demand function discussed in the text.

TABLE 1. Financial Structure

Banking System			
Base Money	H	D	Deposits from the public
Bank loans	L_b		

Firms			
Capital stock	PK	L_b	Loans from banks
		L_p	Loans from the public

The Public			
Bank deposits	D	W	Wealth
Loans to firms	L_p		

in which δ is the fraction of wealth held as deposits and ξ is the deposit/base money ratio, controlled by the monetary authorities as their policy tool.

The deposit equilibrium can be rewritten as an LM curve,

$$\delta(i, u)(V + 1) - \xi = 0, \qquad (2)$$

in which $V = PK/H$ is the "velocity" of base money with respect to the value of the capital stock. We will use V as a state variable in dynamic analysis below; in the short run it is predetermined since its components P, K, and H all come from history. The arguments of δ are the nominal interest rate i and the output/capital ratio $u = X/K$ as an index of economic activity. We consider the signs of the impacts of changes in i and u in turn.

The interest rate varies to clear the loan (and implicitly, deposit) market. Typically, the partial derivative $\partial\delta/\partial i$ is assumed negative: an increase in the interest rate paid by firms for loans pulls wealth holders from deposits. From (2), the sign of this response implies that in partial equilibrium, a less restrictive monetary policy in the form of an increase in ξ will raise total deposits and reduce i. Higher velocity, a signal of financial disintermediation in the sense that there is less monetary "coverage" of the capital stock, has the opposite effect.

With regard to the output/capital ratio (or "capacity use"), the usual hypothesis is that when u increases then so does transactions demand for money, meaning that δ goes up. To restore financial equilibrium, i has to rise. But alternatively, company profits increase along with u. The wealth-holding public may then view firms as more promising investments; their portfolio preferences shift from deposits to loans. In that event, i would decline. These two possibilities respectively represent "crowding-out" and "crowding-in" of loans to producing firms by higher output; as we will see, crowding in can lead to financial instability along Minskian lines.[3]

1.2 The Commodity Market

Investment theories popular since about 1980 postulate that capital formation rises in response to an increase in P_k or the price of capital-in-place, defined as the capitalized value (over an infinite future, for simplicity) of expected future profits per unit of capital stock:

$$P_k = Pr/i$$

where we take the current real interest and profit rates (i/P and r, respectively) as proxies for their expected future values. Such a formulation appears in Minsky (1975) and underlies mainstream "Q" investment theory as proposed by Tobin (1969). In convenient notation, Minsky's theory asserts that $g^i = I/K$ or the ratio of investment to capital stock (the capital stock growth rate, in the absence of depreciation) depends on the premium of P_k over the cost of new capital goods P. Linearizing this profitability linkage and bringing in a direct effect of capacity utilization on investment along lines suggested by Kaldor (1940) and Steindl (1952) gives the following relationships:

$$g^i = g_0 \,(\rho) + \alpha r + \beta u - \theta i$$

$$= g_0 \,(\rho) + (\alpha \pi + \beta)u - \theta i \tag{3}$$

where π stands for the profit share, and the second line incorporates the identity $r = \pi u$. The argument ρ of the intercept term g_0 is a proxy for investors' confidence (or "animal spirits") which will also be discussed.

The aggregate saving function can be written as

$$g^s = \text{Saving/Value of capital stock}$$

$$= [s_\pi \pi + s_w(1 - \pi)]u = s(\pi)u, \tag{4}$$

where s_π and s_w are saving rates from profit and wage income, respectively. If real government dissaving per unit of capital is γ, then the economy's IS schedule or the sum of demand injections minus leakages is

---

3. Crowding in can also take place through the stock market, as in Taylor and O'Connell (1985).

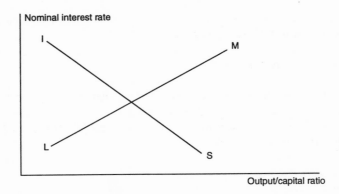

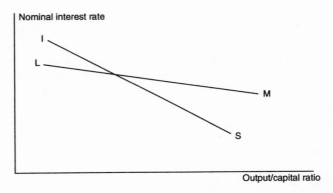

Fig. 1. Financial crowding out (upper diagram) and crowding in (lower diagram) in an IS/LM system

$$\gamma + g_0(\rho) + (\alpha\pi + \beta)u - \theta i - s(\pi)u = 0, \tag{5}$$

which can be solved with the LM curve (2) to give short-run equilibrium.

1.3 Comparative Statics in the Short Run

Figure 1 illustrates the crowding effects previously mentioned. In the upper diagram, a rightward shift of the IS curve (from livelier animal spirits or more government dissaving, for example) makes both output and the interest rate rise. The interest rate response is the standard financial crowding-out effect of higher economic activity.

Financial crowding in is illustrated in the lower diagram of figure 1, in which higher capacity utilization stimulates loans to firms, making the interest rate decline. The LM curve has a negative slope, so that higher aggregate demand increases u and reduces i. From the investment function (3), the capital stock growth rate correspondingly speeds up. A big enough increase in g^i can stabilize divergent confidence dynamics.

1.4 Velocity and Confidence Dynamics

The growth rate of velocity follows from its definition: $V = PK/H$ and therefore $\hat{V} = \hat{P} + \hat{K} - \hat{H}$, where the "hats" over the variables stand for their growth rates. We abstract from wage inflation and productivity growth, and assume a constant mark-up rate so that $\hat{P} = 0$. Any increase in base money comes from government dissaving ($H = dH/dt = \gamma PK$). The equation for $\hat{V}$ becomes

$$\hat{V} = g^i - \gamma V, \tag{6}$$

To generate real/financial fluctuations, we have to combine (6) with an equation for investors' confidence. When there is financial crowding-in as in the lower diagram of figure 1, a destabilizing investment response is a possibility in a demand-driven economy. This is one interpretation of Minsky's financial instability hypothesis, illustrated formally here.

The easiest way to tell the story is through the confidence variable ρ, representing investors' animal spirits. It is reasonable to assume that confidence rises when actual profit rates are high or real interest rates low. With crowding in, the two events run together, so we settle for a simple differential equation of the form

$$\dot{\rho} = \phi(i^* - i), \tag{7}$$

where $\dot{\rho} = d\rho/dt$, and i^* is a reference interest rate.

When there is financial crowding in, the lower diagram of figure 1 suggests that an increase in ρ will stimulate investment demand and shift the IS schedule to the right. The nominal interest rate will fall as wealth-holders' desired portfolios tilt toward loans to firms. From (7), $\dot{\rho}$ rises, that is there is positive feedback of ρ into its own growth rate, and potential dynamic instability. Will it lead to economic divergence, or will fluctuations in ρ somehow be tamed by V?

The dynamics of the two state variables are illustrated in figure 2, in which the "finance" locus corresponds to $\hat{V} = 0$ and the "animal spirits" schedule to $\dot{\rho} = 0$. In the upper diagram, an initial adverse shock to confidence leads ρ to jump down, leading the interest rate to rise from the lower picture in figure 1. From equation (7), $\dot{\rho}$ turns negative and investment con-

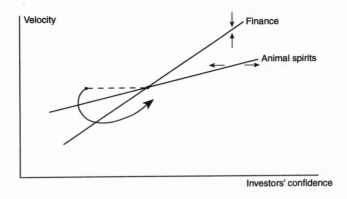

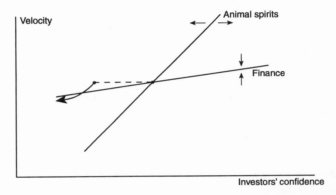

Fig. 2. Potentially stable (upper diagram) and unstable (lower diagram) dynamics in an economy with animal spirits responding to a lower interest rate and financial crowding in

tinues downward. But slow capital stock growth means that velocity starts to decline, ultimately easing monetary tightness enough to let the interest rate fall. After a time, $\dot{\rho}$ turns positive as the trajectory crosses the animal spirits curve, and as the figure is drawn, equilibrium is gradually restored.

In the lower diagram, the growth rate g^i is not very sensitive to ρ, so the slope of the Finance schedule is shallow. Now the initial decrease in confidence is not offset over time by growing monetary cover of capital (or "intermediation"), and the economy demonstrates saddlepoint instability—it cannot recover from an adverse (or favorable) shock to ρ.

With nonlinear dynamics, elementary catastrophe theory suggests a potential outcome besides cyclical convergence and outright divergence, respectively illustrated in the upper and lower diagrams. In the upper figure, if $\partial\dot{p}/\partial p$ is increased parametrically from a value permitting cyclical convergence through the point at which $\partial\dot{p}/\partial p + \partial\hat{V}/\partial V = 0$ (where the trace of the Jacobian of (6) and (7) vanishes at equilibrium as the real parts of its two complex roots go to zero), there could be a Hopf bifurcation to a limit cycle with permanent, bounded fluctuations of p and V. The existence of such an attracting cycle "between" stable and unstable spiral trajectories depends on nonlinearities in the system (6)–(7) that could damp its divergent tendencies. Such cycles are explored further in the following sections.

2. Liquidity Cycles "Inside" the Productive Sector

The foregoing model can be restated to allow financial transactions among firms to generate liquidity-profit cycles of the sort discussed by Foley (1987). Table 2 extends table 1 to permit loans L_f within the enterprise sector. Total borrowing $L = L_b + L_p + L_f$ is assumed to be fixed at any time, while interfirm credit L_f evolves in response to financial market signals to be discussed shortly.

Loan dynamics are most easily analyzed using a new state variable, the credit/capital ratio $C = L/PK$. Positive feedback on the real side of the economy can occur if investment responds *positively* to a higher debt ratio, so that (3) is modified to the form

$$g^i = g_0 + (\alpha\pi + \beta)u - \theta i + \mu C.$$

In the financial crowding in case of the lower diagram of figure 1, a higher C shifts the IS curve upward, leading the profit rate r to rise and the interest rate i to fall. Such movements can stimulate additional interfirm borrowing ac-

TABLE 2.   Financial Structure

		Banking System	
Base Money	H	D	Deposits from the public
Bank loans	L_b		
		Firms	
Capital stock	PK	L_b	Loans from banks
Loans to firms	L_f	L_p	Loans from the public
		L_f	Interfirm loans
		The Public	
Bank deposits	D	W	Wealth
Loans to firms	L_p		

cording to a relationship such as $\dot{L}_f = \rho(r, i)PK$, with partial derivatives $\partial\rho/\partial r$ > 0 and $\partial\rho/\partial i$ < 0. Dynamics of C become

$$\dot{C} = \rho(r, i) - Cg^i. \tag{8}$$

Signs of the entries in the Jacobian matrix of (6) and (8) are as follows:

$\partial\hat{V}/\partial V$ < 0: Velocity is self-stabilizing.
$\partial\hat{V}/\partial C$ > 0: A higher value of C increases investment g^i, raising the growth rate of velocity.
$\partial\dot{C}/\partial V$ < 0: Higher velocity increases the interest rate, reducing new interfirm credit transactions.
$\partial\dot{C}/\partial C$ ambiguous: A higher C increases both components of the term Cg^i in (8), but on the other hand also increases $\rho(r, i)$ under financial crowding-in (and even under crowding out if $\partial\rho/\partial r$ substantially exceeds $|\partial\rho/\partial i|$).

If $\partial\dot{C}/\partial C$ > 0, the dynamics of (6) and (8) are the same as in Figure 2, with the "animal spirits" loci corresponding to (8). As already noted, there can be convergent or divergent spirals, or a limit cycle. For example, at the bottom of the cycle (when both V and C are low), the interest rate will also be low. Interfirm credit transactions are stimulated, so that C begins to increase. As firms become more liquid, investment rises; velocity grows as well. After a time, the higher V increases the interest rate and at the top of the cycle cuts back on profits and investment demand.

As in the example of section 1, overall stability depends on parameter values. In Foley's (1987) words, "The role of the elasticity of borrowing with respect to the profit rate-interest rate differential as the stability parameter of this model [that is, in the present formulation the nature of the $\rho(r, i)$ function in (8)] is an example of Minsky's idea that a boom is accompanied by qualitative changes in financial practices that create financial fragility. A stable economy could be destabilized into a limit cycle by a rise in the propensity to borrow as a function of the profit rate-interest rate differential or by an increase in the sensitivity of capital outlays to the current profit rate."

3. A Speculative Asset and Financial Fragility

Regressive income redistribution or windfall gains in wealth can cause output stagnation and a surge in speculative finance. Tight monetary policy can make these outcomes worse. As discussed in Taylor (1991), episodes in the United States in the 1920s, and in Chile, Kuwait, and Argentina ten to fifteen years ago can broadly be described under the following headings:

The Real Side of the Economy

There were regressive income redistributions in all four cases, for a variety of reasons. One consequence was that the level of economic activity fell. The simplest rationale is that real wage cuts make consumption decline. Investment demand, driven by an accelerator as in (3), drops off at the same time as potential saving rises from an increased profit share π in (4). Idle funds find their outlet in speculation. High interest rates from tight money can amplify these shifts.

The Financial Side

Prices of the speculative assets rise as desired portfolios switch from productive ends. Financial means are found to bid up speculative demands and prices further, making nominal wealth endogenous in the short run. Deregulation of the financial system—practiced during all four episodes—can help make speculation and/or chicanery more attractive. Disintermediation in the form of increasing velocity and a rising ratio of speculative to productive assets may follow, especially if money is tight.

Dynamics

A cumulative process based on growing speculation and increasingly fragile enterprise balance sheets unfolds until disintermediation surpasses feasible bounds. There can be limit cycles or chaotic dynamics. Other possibilities include a crash or cyclical convergence to a new equilibrium, even perhaps on a faster growth path where speculative gains boost domestic demand, accelerating investment to absorb higher potential saving. The outcomes depend on how strongly an increase in velocity or the shifts in the portfolio shares of real and speculative assets accentuate or reduce confidence in nonproductive holdings.

A model based on the one in section 1 can be used to analyze these developments. As before, we begin with the financial side of the economy.

3.1 Financial Structure

Table 3 expands on table 1 in showing the economy's balance sheets, in which two groups of households made up of rentiers and workers (who receive profit and wage incomes respectively) undertake transactions with firms and banks. In the first panel, the banks' assets are base money and loans to firms; they accept deposits from both sorts of households. As before, we do not consider equity holdings and posit that firms finance their capital by borrowing from banks and rentiers.

The main difference from section 1 is that wealth owners now have access to a third asset. Besides their loans and deposits, they also hold a

TABLE 3.   Financial Structure

Banking System

Base Money	H	D_π	Deposits from rentiers
Bank loans	L_b	D_w	Deposits from workers

Firms

Capital stock	PK	L_b	Loans from banks
		$L\pi$	Loans from rentiers

Rentier Households

Bank deposits	$D\pi$	W_π	Wealth of rentiers
Loans to firms	L_π		
Value of speculative asset ("gold")	$P_z Z$		

Worker Households

Bank deposits	D_w	W_w	Wealth of workers

speculative good Z which has a market-clearing prize P_z. It can be thought of as comprising objects such as foreign exchange, collectables, real estate or shopping malls as in the recent American S&L crisis, and speculative shares—we will call Z "gold." Workers are more cautious than rentiers with their wealth—they put it only in banks. This assumption is consistent with the two-class income division. Less affluent people have a high share of their incomes coming from wages and typically hold wealth in unsophisticated forms.

For the bulk of the discussion, we will set workers' wealth to zero to keep the algebra in hand; Taylor (1991) shows that the results that follow carry over to the general case. With only rentiers holding wealth, the sum of asset market excess demands (equal to zero in equilibrium) is

$$(\delta W_\pi - \xi H) + [(\xi - 1)H + \lambda W_\pi - PK] + (\zeta W_\pi - P_z Z) = 0. \qquad (9)$$

In this equation, rentiers' wealth W_π is split among deposits, loans to firms, and gold in the proportions δ, λ, and ζ respectively—the restriction $\delta + \lambda + \zeta = 1$ on these functions is required for market balance. Monetary policy takes the form of controlling the deposit/base money ratio ξ. In the absence of excess reserves, the supply of loans from banks is $(\xi - 1)H$.

Cancelling terms in (9) gives the wealth "identity" in this model as

$$W_\pi - H - PK - P_z Z = 0, \qquad (10)$$

so that the primary assets are base money, the value of the capital stock, and the value of gold. From (9), we need only specify two asset excess demand functions explicitly. It is easiest to work with deposits and gold. The equations are

$$\delta(i, u, \rho)W_\pi - \xi H = 0, \tag{11}$$

and

$$\zeta(i, u, \rho)W_\pi - P_z Z = 0. \tag{12}$$

The arguments in the demand functions are the interest rate i that firms pay for short-term loans, the output-capital ratio u as an indicator of the level of economic activity, and the expected return ρ to holding gold (with ρ redefined from its meaning in previous sections).

The first thing to note from these equations is that rentiers' wealth W_π need not evolve steadily in response to their saving but can jump in the short run. If ρ increases, meaning that speculation suddenly becomes more attractive, the gold price P_z rises to clear the market in (12). But then from (10), the value of wealth itself goes up. Speculation is self-propelling because it makes people feel richer. Nominal wealth expansion also provides room in the financial system for loans within a bank/industry group, post-dated checks, or excessive margin accounts such as those that appeared during the booms in Chile, Kuwait, and the United States. These novel financial vehicles intermediate between increases in $P_z Z$ and W_π, creating the unhealthy financial "layering" that crisis theorists such as Minsky stress. At the same time there can also be non-speculative wealth expansion,[4] but we ignore this channel for the moment.

Solving (10) and (12) together gives a reduced form for wealth,

$$W_\pi = \frac{H + PK}{1 - \zeta}, \tag{13}$$

and plugging (13) into (11) does the same for deposit demand,

$$\frac{\delta(i, u, \rho)}{1 - \zeta(i, u, \rho)} (1 + V) - \xi = 0 \tag{14}$$

where again $V = PK/H$ is the velocity of base money with respect to the value of the capital stock.

Equation (14) amounts to an LM curve, more complicated than (2) because of the endogeneity of W_π. Using subscripts to denote partial deriva-

---

4. An example is the late 1970s expansion of bank reserves and loans due to capital inflows in Argentina, as modeled in section 5.

tives, we assume that δ_i and δ_ρ are negative while δ_u is positive. In the gold demand function, $\zeta_i < 0$, $\zeta_u < 0$ (if higher transactions balances are drawn in part from hedge assets), and $\zeta_\rho > 0$.

3.2 The Real Side

The real part of the economy is modeled as in section 1, with a stable money wage rate and mark-up pricing; the output/capital ratio u is the adjusting macroeconomic variable. The growth rate of the capital stock is g^i, determined by the investment function (3), and saving behavior is described by (4). The IS curve (5)—with g_0 now assumed to be unaffected by the confidence level ρ—shows that u is an increasing function of γ.

The sign of $\partial u / \partial \pi$ turns out to be positive if $\alpha - (s_\pi - s_w) > 0$. By ignoring workers' wealth, we are already assuming that s_w is negligible. Given the usual econometric finding that profitability effects in investment demand are weak, we assume that $\partial u / \partial \pi < 0$, that is output responds in wage-led fashion to income redistribution in the short run. This hypothesis has been widely discussed in recent years (Rowthorn, 1982; Dutt, 1984); it rationalizes the observation made above that regressive redistribution may be associated with recession and a shift in portfolios toward speculative financial holdings in the absence of vibrant real investment demand.

3.3 Comparative Statics

Equations (5) and (14) constitute an IS/LM system in u and i, illustrated by the upper diagram in figure 1. A leftward shift in the IS curve would result from an increased profit share π or lower public spending γ. An upward shift in LM could come from contractionary monetary policy (a lower ξ) or disintermediation in the form of higher velocity V. All these changes reduce the level of activity u, and tight money plus redistribution could well increase i. With a big accelerator term β, growth will also slow from (3).

With regard to gold, a lower u reduces deposit demand and makes ζ rise. The outcome is a higher speculative price P_z, especially if gold and loans to firms are *not* close portfolio substitutes. An increase in ρ, the expected return to holding gold, decreases the ratio $\delta / (1 - \zeta)$ in (14) when

$$\delta(\zeta_\rho + \delta_\rho) + \lambda \delta_\rho < 0.$$

If deposits and gold are close subsitutes, ζ_ρ and $-\delta_\rho$ will be nearly equal, i.e. the second term will dominate and deposit demand will fall. The LM curve shifts downward, meaning that happy speculation reduces the interest rate and increases growth along with capacity use. Of course, easy substitution between money and gold is an empirical hypothesis, and need not always hold; however, facile shifts among specific speculative and non-speculative assets underlie many models of financial crisis, not least the one in Minsky (1975).[5]

3.4 A Confidence Boom

Now we have to specify dynamics for ρ, the expected return to holding the speculative asset. In practice, wealth-holders' confidence depends on myriad factors—the credibility of government promises about key variables such as the exchange rate, the overall political situation, anticipated actions of power-ful entities outside the country such as international banks, and the attitude of regulatory authorities toward veiled swindlers (as in the recent Savings and Loan crisis in the United States) are only a few. But, for holding "gold," one of the major motivations is surely the expected capital gain. A reasonable proxy is the current rate of gold price increase $\hat{P}_z$ (where as usual a "hat" over a variable signifies its growth rate). We assume that

$$\rho = \rho(\hat{P}_z) \tag{15}$$

and denote the positive derivative by ρ'.

Now from (12) and (13), P_z itself is given by

$$P_z = \phi(i, u, \rho)(1 + V)Q, \tag{16}$$

where the new symbols are $\phi = \zeta/(1 - \zeta)$ and $Q = H/Z$. From (15) and (16), it is easy to see that P_z and its growth rate $\hat{P}_z$ are positively related. This linkage can be the source of "dynamic" or oscillatory financial instability of the sort discussed in sections 1 and 2. A key question is whether the rest of the financial system will tame speculation in gold.

In differential form, $\hat{P}_z$ depends on P_z and other variables as follows:

$$d\hat{P}_z = \frac{1}{\phi_\rho \rho'} \left[\frac{dP_z}{Q(1 + V)} - (\phi_i di + \phi_u du) \right.$$

$$\left. - \phi \left(\frac{dQ}{Q} + \frac{dV}{1 + V} \right) \right]. \tag{17}$$

For an instantaneously given gold price P_z, a regressive redistribution/tight money experiment will accelerate its rate of inflation $\hat{P}_z$ by increasing i and

---

5. Or at least, easy asset substitution is the key to Taylor and O'Connell's (1985) formaliza-tion of Minsky's discussion of the political economy of financial fragility and crisis.

reducing u. The story is that the expected gold return rises to meet the new economic situation. Disintermediation, or a higher V, has the same positive effect on $\hat{P}_z$ through i and u, but its direct impact in (17) is clearly negative. A higher V is more likely to slow $\hat{P}_z$ when V itself is small, that is, when the degree of financial intermediation is high. An increase in the money/gold ratio Q reduces $\hat{P}_z$. All these effects as well as the positive feedback of P_z into $\hat{P}_z$ will be stronger when gold demand is relatively insensitive to ρ, or ρ to $\hat{P}_z$.

In a full dynamic specification, we must also consider the evolution of the ratio variables V and Q. Equation (6) still holds for $\hat{V}$, and it remains likely that $\partial \hat{V}/\partial V < 0$ (a certainty around a steady state at which $V = g^i/\gamma$). Since regressive redistribution and tight money both reduce investment g^i, they also make $\hat{V}$ decline. Finally, a higher gold price P_z and a lower money/gold ratio Q increase $\hat{P}_z$ and ρ, raising g^i and thereby $\hat{V}$.

The money/gold ratio Q is a nuisance state variable that will largely be ignored in the informal stability analysis that follows; however, we should indicate its dynamics briefly. We want to analyze a steady state in which no state variable goes to zero or infinity. Growth in the economy is determined by capital accumulation, so to keep the gold supply from diverging we assume that it is created (by real estate developers, artists, and imaginative financiers) in proportion to the capital stock, that is, $\dot{Z} = \sigma K$. This formula leads to the differential equation

$$\dot{Q} = Q(V/P)(\gamma P - \sigma Q). \tag{18}$$

At a steady state where $Q = \gamma P/\sigma$, $\partial \dot{Q}/\partial Q$ is clearly negative and $\dot{Q}$ is unaffected by P_z and V.

Around a steady state, the 3×3 equation system made up of (17), (6), and (18) has partial derivatives signed as follows:

	P_z	V	Q
$\hat{P}_z$	$+$	$\pm$	$-$
$\hat{V}$	$+$	$-$	$-$
$\dot{Q}$	0	0	$-$

Application of Routh-Hurwitz criteria suggest that the system will be stable when equations (17) and (6) for $\hat{P}_z$ and $\hat{V}$ are well-behaved. Hence, we concentrate on this subsystem. Figure 3 illustrates the possibilities, with the "velocity" and "gold price" schedules respectively representing the loci along which $\hat{V} = 0$ and $\hat{P}_z = 0$.

In the upper diagram, the effect of V on $\hat{P}_z$ in (17) is positive, and the equations demonstrate the saddlepoint instability of the mainstream literature on bubbles: The gold price increases exponentially on the basis of expected

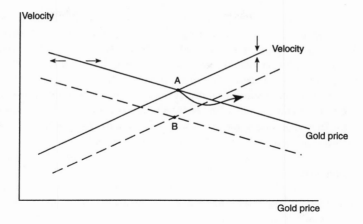

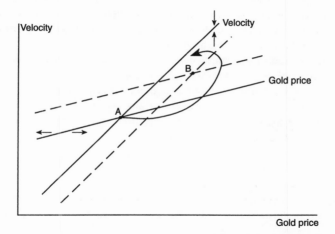

Fig. 3. Unstable (upper diagram) and possibly stable (lower diagram) adjustment in a model with rentier speculation

capital gains, triggered by a regressive shock that reduces output and drives up the interest rate, shifting the steady state point from A to B. Initially, P_z rises while slow output growth makes $\hat{V} < 0$. When the trajectory crosses the shifted Velocity schedule, both variables diverge—disintermediation and a gold boom go hand-in-hand until the model has to change. A jump of P_z to reach the negatively-sloped saddlepath through B (not shown) is conceivable but implausible under reasonable institutional assumptions.

In the lower diagram, higher velocity slows the increase in the price of gold, basically by driving down the return ρ in (12) for a given P_z. The spiral path may be diverging or converging (or may lead to a limit cycle), depending on the strength of the positive feedback of P_z into its own growth rate. If stable, the economy may come to the new equilibrium B with faster potential output growth. Disintermediation ultimately cools speculative fever, and the gains in wealth that speculation creates can stimulate investment demand and growth performance. Although this finale is possible, it seems a remote contingency in a financially fragile system. The boom-and-crash fluctuations en route to the new, improved steady state could be extreme.

4. A Speculative Investment Boom

As described in Taylor (1988), productive enterprises can also play speculative games. Chilean conglomerates that borrowed from banks they controlled to bid up their own industrial companies' shares in a self-manufactured stock market boom during the late 1970s are one example; Korean firms which hold real estate as collateral for bank loans are another. A higher gold price may lead firms to invest more, in turn forcing them to try to buy more gold as they seek collateral, igniting a surge in borrowing. To work out the details, we need a revised set of balance sheets, shown in table 4. The main difference from table 3 is the shift of $P_z Z$ from rentiers' to firms' portfolios.

The modified financial accounting means that we also have to restate IS and LM relationships. Since rentiers now hold only deposits and loans to firms, the LM equation can be written as

$$\delta(i, u)[(1/V) + 1 + P_z D] - (1/V)\xi = 0, \tag{19}$$

in which D (for "debt") stands for Z/PK, the ratio of gold to productive capital that firms ultimately finance by borrowing. Equation (19) differs from (14) in

TABLE 4.   Financial Structure

	Banking System	
Base Money H	D_π	Deposits from rentiers
Bank loans L_b		
	Firms	
Capital stock PK	L_b	Loans from banks
Value of speculative	$L\pi$	Loans from rentiers
asset ("gold") $P_z Z$		
	Rentier Households	
Bank deposits $D\pi$	W_π	Wealth of rentiers
Loans to firms L_π		

that rentiers' wealth W_π is normalized by PK instead of H and gold's expected return ρ and portfolio share ζ have been dropped. Also, W_π is no longer a jump variable. Speculative asset changes will now be represented by smooth changes in firms' balance sheets.

In place of (3), we write the investment function as

$$g^i = g_0 + (\alpha\pi + \beta)u - \theta i + \epsilon P_z D,$$

in which the last term shows that firms' capital formation is stimulated by an increased value of their speculative holdings. Just as higher corporate liquidity was assumed to spur capital formation in the model of section 2, we now postulate that higher loan collaterals can do the same thing.

Adding government dissaving γ and subtracting saving (4) from the investment equation give the IS curve as

$$\gamma + g_0 + (\alpha\pi + \beta)u + \epsilon P_z D - \theta i - s(\pi)u = 0, \tag{20}$$

replacing (5). The IS/LM system is still represented by the upper diagram in figure 1. The additional comparative static result is that an increase in $P_z D$ shifts the LM curve upward and the IS to the right. The outcomes are a higher interest rate and an ambiguous change in capacity use.

Rather than letting $\hat{P}_z$ jump to meet changes in other variables as it does in (17), we now follow the approach in section 2 by assuming that $\dot{P}_z$ varies to meet evolutionary movements in the demand and supply of gold. Total enterprise borrowing L (the sum of L_b and L_π) grows according to a behavioral equation to be presented shortly. With L, PK, and Z all fixed at a point in time, P_z must be given by $P_z = (L - PK)/Z$ from the consolidated balance sheets of all firms. Its change over time becomes

$$\dot{P}_z = (1/Z)[\dot{L} - (Pg^i + P_z\sigma)K], \tag{21}$$

since $\dot{K} = g^i K$ and $\dot{Z} = \sigma K$.

Firms increase their debt to pay for new capital formation and acquisition of speculative assets. The investment function has already been specified. We now assume that demand for gold rises in response to its expected capital gain and also when firms have a high cash flow (this latter effect can also be included in the investment demand function without changing the model's results). Let λ stand for cash flow relative to capital stock:

$$\lambda = \frac{\pi PX - i(PK + P_z Z)}{PK} = \pi u - (1 + P_z D)i. \tag{22}$$

Then we write the change in total borrowing of firms as

$$\dot{L} = Pg^iK + [\phi(\dot{P}_z/P_z) + \psi\lambda]P_zZ - \upsilon L, \tag{23}$$

in which ϕ and ψ are coefficients for the effects of expected capital gains and high cash flow on firms' desired increases in speculative holdings. New loan demand $\dot{L}$ is also assumed to increase less rapidly when the total loan stock L is high, reflecting credit rationing by banks or the firms' own prudent behavior.

Equations (21)-(23) can be solved simultaneously for $\dot{P}_z$ and $\dot{L}$. Either P_z or L/PK could be used as a state variable along with V and D to determine the evolution of the economy. For comparison with the model of section 3, we choose P_z. Its differential equation is

$$\dot{P}_z = \frac{1}{(1 - \phi)D} \left\{ P_z \left[(\psi\lambda - \upsilon)D - \frac{\sigma}{P} \right] - \upsilon \right\}, \tag{24}$$

and for the system to make sense we assume $\phi < 1$. Near a steady state where $\dot{P}_z$ vanishes, (24) shows that P_z grows more rapidly when cash flow λ, the gold/capital ratio D, and its own level are high. The latter two results depend on a sufficiently high value of $\psi\lambda$, and indeed the condition $\psi\lambda > \upsilon + g^i$ is also necessary for P_z to take on a positive value at steady state.

More generally, behavior of $\dot{P}_z$ depends on how λ responds to shifts in the state variables. From (22), λ declines when i and P_zD rise, or when u falls. The IS/LM equations show that cash flow is lower with higher values of P_z, D, and V, unless the parameter ϵ giving the response of investment demand g^i to a higher value of P_zD is improbably large. Moreover, the partial derivatives of λ with respect to P_z and D become more negative as these variables increase. Hence, from (24), $\dot{P}_z$ behaves quadratically—it may respond positively and then negatively to P_z as the gold price becomes larger. In the discussion that follows, we assume that this sign shift does in fact occur.

The differential equation for the gold/capital ratio D is

$$\dot{D} = (1/P)(\sigma - Dg^i). \tag{25}$$

Equations (24), (25), and (6) form a simultaneous system for P_z, D, and V with the signs of the Jacobian matrix as follows:

	P_z	D	V
$\hat{\dot{P}}_z$	$\pm$	$+$	$-$
$\dot{D}$	$-$	$-$	$+$
$\hat{V}$	$+$	$-$	$-$

Velocity here on the whole exerts a stabilizing influence, so we do not consider it explicitly in analyzing how the model behaves.

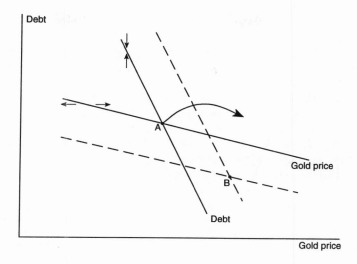

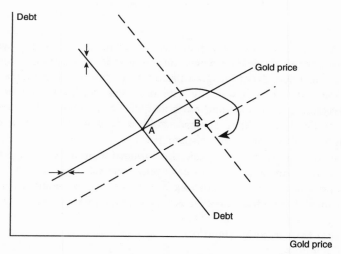

Fig. 4. Unstable (upper diagram) and stable (lower diagram) dynamics in the model in which firms speculate

The upper diagram in figure 4 shows the unstable case in which $\partial \dot{P}_z / \partial P_z$ is positive. The gold price and debt loci respectively correspond to the conditions $\dot{P}_z = 0$ and $\dot{D} = 0$. An initial regressive shock at point A increases both $\dot{P}_z$ and $\dot{D}$. Hence, in a new steady state, P_z must fall and D rise. After the shock, the gold price begins a speculative increase and $\dot{D}$ is also positive because investment g^i declines. From (25), the increase in D (plus higher

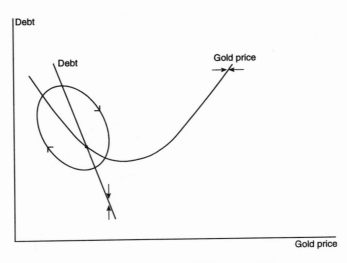

Fig. 5. A limit cycle when firms speculate

investment from a higher P_z) finally makes $\dot{D}$ negative, but the system is unstable and never reaches a new equilibrium at B. In the stable case (lower diagram) an upward-sloping gold price locus "catches" the trajectory and brings the system to a new steady state at B—the cyclical convergence rests on alternating gold booms and busts as cash flows rise and fall. As in the model of the last section, a higher gold price may stimulate investment enough to lead to a faster growth rate at B.

The sign shift of $\partial \dot{P}_z / \partial P_z$ can also produce a limit cycle, as shown in Figure 5. Here, the alternation of cash flow increases, speculation, and then increasing debt leading to retrenchment never ceases; the sequence is similar to the "inside" liquidity fluctuations of the Foley-style model of section 2.

5. Foreign Exchange Speculation

Entire textbooks are written about devaluation, the trade balance, and capital flows. That is not the intention here. The emphasis is on one issue of great policy relevance: destabilizing foreign asset speculation in the wake of over-valuation, following Frenkel (1983). Two topics are addressed: the real and asset market effects of slowing exchange rate devaluation when there is ongoing inflation in an "active" crawling peg aimed at reducing the rate of price increase, and how these effects may cumulate over time to upset this "ortho-dox shock" stabilization strategy.

Table 5 sets out the financial structure for a three-asset model like the one in section 3. Instead of gold, wealth owners now hold foreign assets with a domestic value of eY (e is the peso/dollar exchange rate) in addition to loans to firms and deposits. The banking system also has foreign reserves in the amount eR. Total public wealth is

$$W = PK + e(Y + R) + H = PK + eJ + H,$$

where J stands for total foreign assets of the nation. The total J *cannot* change in the short run, since foreign asset stocks accumulate or decumulate on a flow basis only, through the current account of the balance of payments. If the public reduces its foreign holdings then bank reserves must jump upward, and *vice versa.*

Asset market equilibrium is determined when two of the public's three excess demand functions are equal to zero:

$$\delta(i, \sigma, u)[V + A + 1] - \xi[1 + A - (eY/H)] = 0 \qquad (26)$$

and

$$\chi(i, \sigma, u)[V + A + 1] - eY/H = 0. \qquad (27)$$

In these expressions, $\xi = D/(H + eR)$ is the credit multiplier controlled by the monetary authorities, $V = PK/H$ is the velocity of the domestic component H of base money (coming from fiscal deficit spending) with respect to capital stock, and $A = eJ/H$ is the ratio of total foreign asset value to the monetized fiscal debt.

In the asset demand functions δ and χ, the usual arguments appear along

TABLE 5. Financial Structure

	Banking System		
Base Money	H	D	Deposits
Bank loans	L_b		
Foreign reserves	eR		
	Firms		
Capital stock	PK	L_b	Loans from banks
		L_p	Loans from the public
	The Public		
Bank deposits	D	W	Wealth
Loans to firms	L_p		
Foreign assets	eY		

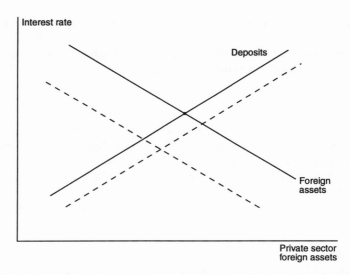

Fig. 6. Asset market responses to a slower pace of nominal devaluation

with σ which stands for the expected return to holding foreign assets. We can set $\sigma = j + \hat{e} + \rho$, where j is the foreign real interest rate, $\hat{e}$ is the expected (-actual) rate of exchange rate devaluation, and ρ is a confidence-based expected extra return from holding Y. The nominal interest rate i is the variable that adjusts to satisfy (26), while Y itself shifts in (27) when the exchange rate is pegged.

As recounted by Diaz-Alejandro (1981) and Frenkel (1983), the stabilization strategy in vogue in South America's Southern Cone in the late 1970s was based on freezing (or drastically reducing the rate of depreciation of) the nominal exchange rate. Through the law of one price in commodity markets and also via "rational" expectations, this policy move was supposed to slow inflation drastically. Inflation turned out to have cost-based, structural causes, and the policy failed to hit its major target. It also strongly destabilized the real sides of the economies in which it was tried (Argentina, Chile, and Uruguay). It is interesting to use the model just sketched to spell out the reasons why.

Figure 6 illustrates equilibrium in asset markets, with the "deposits" schedule corresponding to equation (26), and the "foreign assets" schedule to (27). The shifts in the curves result from credibly reducing the rate of depreciation $\hat{e}$,[6] so that the return σ to holding foreign assets falls.

---

6. The exchange rate was simply frozen in Chile, while "tablitas" of preannounced reductions in the crawl rate were issued by the authorities in Argentina and Uruguay.

The Deposits locus in the diagram slopes upward since an increase in Y must reflect itself into reduced bank reserves in the short run. Deposit supply $\xi(H + eR)$ contracts, leading the interest rate to rise. In the market for foreign assets, a higher interest rate reduces demand and Y declines, explaining the negative slope of that schedule.

When $\hat{e}$ is decreased, two main reactions transpire. Desired asset portfolios shift toward the domestic market, and the interest rate declines (as might also be expected from the tendency of i to line itself up with the foreign asset return $\sigma = (j + \hat{e} + \rho)$. In the diagram, the deposits curve shifts downward. Moreover, foreign holdings are also cut back, so that since $R + Y = J =$ constant in the short run, the money supply goes up. Therefore, the interest rate is also reduced by a leftward shift of the foreign assets schedule.

The consequence is that in the short run, slowing $\hat{e}$ is likely to stimulate the domestic economy by relaxing credit tightness. Moreover, with a cost-based structural inflation underway, ongoing wage increases mean that inflation will not drop off as rapidly as the exchange rate, that is, there will also be real appreciation. Depreciation has regressive redistributional effects that often reduce the level of economic activity in developing economies (Krugman and Taylor, 1978); one implication is that appreciation must work the other way.[7] After the crawling peg is slowed, changes in both the interest and exchange rates make the level of economic activity rise.

This short-run response can set off dynamic instability, via the lower σ leading to its own further decline. In other words, reducing the return to foreign assets stimulates the economy, but then the improved domestic situation may reduce the expected return further still. A positive feedback of local euphoria into itself is the classic signal for financial fragility, as the discussions in previous sections have pointed out.

A model is easy to set up in terms of the expected extra return to holding foreign assets ρ (which directly pushes up the overall return σ) and the state variable $A = eJ/H$. The evolution of σ over time will be discussed informally. The equation for $\hat{A}$ is

$$\hat{A} = \hat{e} + (t/J) + j - \gamma V, \tag{28}$$

where t is the trade balance relative to the value of the capital stock. The steady state solution at $\hat{A} = 0$ and $A > 0$ is

$$J = t/(\gamma V - \hat{e} - j), \tag{29}$$

---

7. The Krugman-Taylor model of the real side of the economy underlying the assertion in the text relies on mark-up pricing based on costs of labor and imported intermediate inputs, in an obvious extension of the specification in section 1.

showing that sustainable foreign assets rise with the trade balance, the pace of devaluation, and the foreign interest rate, and decline with the growth rate of fiscal debt, $\hat{H} = \gamma V$.

Formally speaking, we should work with three state variables: σ, A, and V. As usual, velocity stabilizes the system (possibly in chaotic fashion), and the gist of the story is preserved if it is told in terms of σ and A. Changes in these state variables affect their rates of increase as follows:

$\partial \dot{\sigma} / \partial \sigma > 0$: The initial downward jump in $\sigma \, (= j + \rho + \hat{e})$ from slowing the crawl increases bank reserves R and stimulates domestic activity. The expected incremental return ρ declines, as national financial assets look increasingly attractive. The process reverses when the trade balance declines, leading to reserve loss, higher internal interest rates, and lower activity.

$\partial \dot{\sigma} / \partial A < 0$: Higher foreign assets from any source make their expected return decline.

$\partial \dot{A} / \partial \sigma > 0$: An increase in σ pulls the public toward foreign holdings, reversing the adjustment in Figure 6. Interest rates increase, activity decreases, and the trade surplus t goes up. From (28), $\hat{A}$ rises.

$\partial \dot{A} / \partial A < 0$: Higher foreign assets mean more reserves R and monetary expansion. The resulting increase in economic activity reduces the trade surplus and $\hat{A}$.

The phase diagram for A and σ appears in figure 7. Slowing a crawling peg makes σ jump down from an initial steady state; from (29), the steady state value of J (and therefore A) declines, as shown by the dashed line. After the policy change, foreign assets begin to fall immediately since greater economic activity makes the trade surplus decrease. Nonetheless, because of the portfolio switch discussed in connection with figure 6, bank reserves R go up as private foreign holdings Y jump down—the authorities see no need to be apprehensive and continue to let the currency grow stronger.

For a time, the return to foreign assets keeps falling even though the trade surplus is declining and the exchange rate is becoming increasingly overvalued. At some point, the widening trade deficit becomes handwriting on the wall as the trajectory crosses the "return" schedule along which $\dot{\sigma} = 0$, and σ begins to rise. Capital flight in the form of portfolio switches toward foreign assets ensues, leading to output contraction and perhaps accelerating price increases that limit aggregate demand via forced saving and the inflation tax as the foreign exchange constraint on domestic supply commences to bind. The likely outcome is a period of stagflation before foreign asset stocks start to rebuild as contraction produces a trade surplus; lagged export responses can complicate this process.

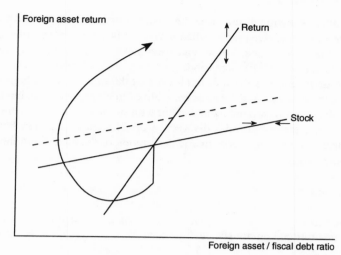

Fig. 7. Potentially unstable dynamics of the return to foreign assets

In practice, the agony may be cut short by a maxidevaluation before the trajectory reaches the "stock" schedule above which *A* starts to rise. The maxi amply rewards the speculators and, with good luck, assets held abroad may begin to flow home. With bad luck, "hysteresis" in the form of declining confidence in the national project on the part of the bourgeoisie may hold national asset stakes down in the very long run. As of the early 1990s, repatriation was possibly beginning in Mexico but was still out of the question in Argentina even though capital had been flying out of both countries for more than ten years.

6. Chaos

The examples discussed so far can all produce stretching of differential equation trajectories in a plane, such as the divergent spirals in the variables σ and *A* in the model of last section, ρ and *V* in the model of section 1, and so on. If fluctuations in another variable fold these trajectories over one another in a third dimension, we have a recipe for chaotic dynamics of the sort produced by an olde English toffee machine, or a Rössler Band (Thompson and Stewart, 1986).

As described in Taylor (1991), one example could come from the model of section 1, when beside the dynamics already discussed (1) real wage increases raise output along the lines discussed here, and (2) higher output in turn feeds back into real wage growth along Philips curve lines. Alternatively, in the model of section 4, the three-dimensional system in P_z, D, and V could demonstrate chaotic dynamics. When $\partial \dot{P}_z / \partial P_z$ is positive, trajectories tend to spread in the (P_z, D) plane. These separating flows could be folded by velocity changes, again as in a Rössler band.

The implication of these examples is that the rather tedious limit cycles discussed in sections 2 and 4 can be generalized to give much more interesting dynamic fluctuations around a chaotic attractor in three or more dimensions.[8] Unfortunately, the exponential divergence of differential equation flowlines under chaos would make econometric description of the underlying model an impossible task.

7. Conclusions

To recapitulate, the models suggest that financial excursions can occur in diverse institutional circumstances:

1. They can be provoked by portfolio shifts toward real assets with feedbacks into investment demand (sections 1 and 2), speculative assets with bubblelike prices (sections 3 and 4), or an asset such as foreign exchange with a price made "wrong" by misguided policy under a controlled rate system (section 5).

2. The dynamic instabilities can involve actors inside (sections 2 and 4) or outside (sections 1, 3, and 5) the productive sector. Although the idea is not developed formally here, Harris (1989) rightly points out that the contingent relationships of banks (or S&Ls!) with productive lending can also provoke financial fragility.

3. The models emphasize that cross-dynamics between a financial variable subject to positive self-feedback and other real or financial indicators evolving over time are crucial in determining whether the overall system will be frankly unstable or will generate cyclical or chaotic fluctuations. "Static" instability of the price bubble or buckling beam variety is not intrinsic to the stories set out here; "dynamic" fluctuations around an investment-driven growth path certainly are. Small shifts in key parameters—representing qualitative changes in financial practices—can switch the system among cyclically stable, oscillating, unstable, and chaotic regimes.

4. Finally, it is worth recalling that economics is a historical science, oriented toward learning about the past and making contingent projec-

---

8. In continuous time, the Poincaré-Bendixson theorem essentially rules out chaotic dynamics in one- or two-dimensional differential equation systems, c.f. Thompson and Stewart (1986).

tions regarding the future. At the level of abstraction of the models herein, in 1991 it would not be hard to set out a description of the S&L crisis in the United States. Price increases for speculative assets (junk bonds, shopping malls) combined with credit expansion by the S&Ls to provoke an "outside" speculative boom with ample endogenous expansion of wealth. The underlying parameter shifts may well have been triggered by declining standards of prudence and regressive income redistribution in general and passage of the Garn–St. Germain Act in particular. But this sort of story is not so easy to write in advance, either institutionally or in the form of the models developed here.[9] Despite a few modeling steps, we still lack an etiology of how financial systems fall apart in historical time—often causing great social and fiscal distress.

REFERENCES

Blanchard, Olivier Jean, and Stanley Fischer (1989) *Lectures on Macroeconomics*, Cambridge MA: MIT Press

Diaz-Alejandro, Carlos F. (1981) "Southern Cone Stabilization Plans," in Cline, William, and Weintraub, Sidney (eds.), *Economic Stabilization in Developing Countries*, Washington DC: Brookings Institution

Dutt, Amitava K. (1984) "Stagnation, Income Distribution, and Monopoly Power," *Cambridge Journal of Economics*, vol. 8, pp. 25–40

Foley, Duncan K. (1987) "Liquidity-Profit Rate Cycles in a Capitalist Economy," *Journal of Economic Behavior and Organization*, vol. 8, pp. 363–376

Frenkel, Roberto (1983) "Mercado Financiero, Expectativas Cambiales, y Movimientos de Capital," *El Trimestre Economico*, vol. 50, pp. 2041–2076

Harris, Laurence (1989) "Structuralist Monetary Theory," Milton Keynes: Financial Studies Group, The Open University

Kaldor, Nicholas (1940) "A Model of the Trade Cycle," *Economic Journal*, vol. 50, pp. 78–92

Krugman, Paul, and Lance Taylor (1978) "Contractionary Effects of Devaluation," *Journal of International Economics*, vol. 8, pp. 445–456

Mayer, Martin (1990) *The Greatest-Ever Bank Robbery: The Collapse of the Savings and Loan Industry*, New York: Scribner's

Minsky, Hyman P. (1975) *John Maynard Keynes*, New York: Columbia University Press

Minsky, Hyman P. (1986) *Stabilizing an Unstable Economy*, New Haven CT: Yale University Press

---

9. There is also the Cassandra phenomenon to be taken into account. Mayer (1990) reprints a 1982 op-ed piece he wrote in the wake of Garn-St. Germain, predicting much of the crisis that would transpire. Prophets are rarely honored in their own time.

Rowthorn, Bob (1982) "Demand, Real Wages, and Economic Growth," *Studi Economici*, vol. 18, pp. 2–53

Steindl, Josef (1952) *Maturity and Stagnation in American Capitalism*, Oxford: Basil Blackwell

Taylor, Lance (1988) *Varieties of Stabilization Experience*, Oxford: Clarendon Press

Taylor, Lance (1991) *Income Distribution, Inflation, and Growth*, Cambridge MA: MIT Press

Taylor, Lance, and O'Connell, Stephen (1985) "A Minsky Crisis," *Quarterly Journal of Economics*, vol. 100, pp. 871–885

Thompson, J. M. T., and H. B. Stewart (1986) *Nonlinear Dynamics and Chaos*, New York: John Wiley and Sons

Tobin, James (1969) "A General Equilibrium Approach to Monetary Theory," *Journal of Money, Credit, and Banking*, vol. 1, pp. 15–29

CHAPTER 3

Complex Dynamics in a Simple Macroeconomic Model with Financing Constraints

Domenico Delli Gatti, Mauro Gallegati, and Laura Gardini*

1. Introduction

For the past decade, the gloomy prospect of a major breakdown of the financial system—that is, the risk of imminent financial crisis—has attracted widespread attention and concern. At first glance, increased financial fragility seems to have resulted from a sequence of shocks to capital markets in the 1980s, including the LDC debt crisis and its repercussions for the banking system, the stock market crash of 1987, and the S&L insolvency crisis. From this point of view, the financial system as a whole is not instability prone: instead, unfortunate occurrences are to blame for the increasing weakness of financial institutions.

But this view substantially underestimates the extent of the process of increasing financial fragility currently underway, and misconstrues its nature. Crises popping up here and there in capital markets are only symptoms of a deeper financial malaise. This malaise has occurred under similar circumstances in the past and is bound to occur again in the future; it is a built-in feature of the system.

The stability of the financial system is threatened primarily by the huge increase in corporate indebtedness since the mid-1980s (Friedman, 1986,

* We thank H. Minsky, R. Day, W. Godley, W. Semmler, J. Crotty, G. Dymski, J. Caskey, S. Fazzari, J. Veitch, P. Skott, and the participants in seminars held at the University of Southern California and the Jerome Levy Economics Institute of Bard College for comments and criticisms that have helped to improve the paper substantially. Of course the usual disclaimer applies. The paper stems from the joint effort of the authors; however, Domenico Delli Gatti wrote sections 1, 2.3, 3.1, and 3.2; Mauro Gallegati wrote sections 2.1, 2.2, 4, and 5; and Laura Gardini wrote section 3.3.

1990; Kaufman, 1986; Bernanke and Campbell, 1988), which has taxed the capacity of overextended borrowers to meet their obligations. If and when banks find their corporate clients unable to repay their loans, defaults and bankruptcies will spread both in the financial and nonfinancial sectors of the economy. In the absence of a resolute intervention of the central bank as lender of last resort, the financial system would collapse and a financial crisis ensue.

However, central bankers have learned the lessons of the Great Depression:[1] they are ready to inject liquidity to prevent the spread of financial panic. Monetary authorities face a trade-off between *monetary stability*, that is, stability of the price level, and *financial stability*, that is, the orderly activity of financial markets and institutions. B. Friedman (1990) has recently focused on this policy dilemma and has strongly emphasized the inflationary risks of monetary policy when it aims at preventing a financial crisis.

So far the real effects of financial instability—that is, the relationships between financial market turbulence and business cycle fluctuations—have been neglected in macroeconomic models because of the widespread acceptance of the Modigliani-Miller irrelevance theorem. In the 1970s, only the so-called debt-deflation school, rooted in the seminal contribution of Fisher (1933) and revisited by Kindleberger (1978) and Minsky (1975, 1982, 1986), emphasized the role of financial factors in business cycle fluctuations.[2]

Beginning with the 1980s, renewed attention has been paid to the real effects of the changing financial structure of the economy (B. Friedman, 1986, 1990; Bernanke, 1983; Blinder, 1987; Bernanke and Blinder, 1988; Gertler, 1988; Gertler and Hubbard, 1988). This New Keynesian line of research has been fostered by the burgeoning literature on asymmetric information in capital markets (pioneered by Stiglitz and Weiss (1981)), which has convincingly challenged the Modigliani-Miller irrelevance proposition (Fazzari, Hubbard, and Petersen, 1988).

The macroeconomic implications of informational imperfections in labor and capital markets rank first in the New Keynesian research agenda.[3] So far,

---

1. M. Friedman and A. J. Schwartz (1963) have emphasized monetary mismanagement—that is, a liquidity squeeze in a period of falling prices and financial distress—as the main cause of the Great Depression, whereas Kindleberger (1986) has downplayed the role of monetary policy. A restrictive monetary stance may have not been the main cause of the Great Depression, but it surely helped to bring it about. This is also the opinion of the late John Hicks (1989, p. 100).

2. The macroeconomic effects of credit availability, however, have been explored also outside the debt deflation school. A remarkable example is Brunner and Meltzer's version of monetarism (Brunner and Meltzer 1968, 1974, and 1976).

3. Asymmetric information on the labor market is the root of the efficiency-wage hypothesis, which can be thought of as a rational foundation of involuntary unemployment. Asymmetric information on the market for bank loans can bring about credit rationing (and underinvestment). Fundamental contributions in this line of research are surveyed in Stiglitz 1987. A second strand

however, no attempt has been made to build a full-fledged New Keynesian macroeconomic model, with the notable exception of the theoretical framework of Greenwald and Stiglitz (1988a, 1988b), in which nominal shocks affect real output through their impact on firms' net worth. However, their model does not explicitly investigate investment behavior.

In this paper we explore the macrodynamic implications of asymmetric information in capital markets when it affects investment activity. To focus on macroeconomic fluctuations, we outline a simple model whose aggregate behavioral relations have a distinct New Keynesian mark, even if they are not explicitly derived from "first principles" as in Greenwald and Stiglitz (1988a, 1988b). In particular, financial variables such as retained earnings and debt commitments play a prominent role in investment determination because of the uneven distribution of information about the reliability of borrowers and the performance of managers among participants in the credit and stock markets, respectively.

In this type of economy, financing constraints are crucial in determining the volume and direction of investment activity, which in turn is the prime mover of the business cycle, since it is at the root of the process of income and profit determination. Equilibrium in the markets for goods, bank loans, and equities defines the dynamic paths of income and corporate debt, which in turn endogenously determine the dynamics of the interest rate and the price of capital assets.

Depending on the value of the propensity to invest, the model can generate a wide range of dynamic processes: convergence to the steady state, chaotic behavior, and "financial crises." In other words, starting from the assumption of asymmetric information on the credit and equity markets, we are led to link the endogenous dynamics of the system to the closely-intertwined laws of motion of income and debt.

This approach bears a close resemblance to the theoretical perspective on business cycle fluctuations of the debt deflation school. By working out the implications of asymmetric information on capital markets, the New Keynesian literature sheds new light on the economy's financially determined endogenous dynamics, as emphasized in the Fisher-Kindleberger-Minsky line of thought.

This paper is organized as follows. In section 2 we outline the model and discuss the interrelations of the goods, equity, and credit markets in turn. In section 3 we derive a system of two nonlinear difference equations that yield the dynamics of income and corporate debt. Section 4 is devoted to a verbal

---

of new Keynesian literature is concerned with the macroeconomic implications of imperfect competition and coordination failure. This second line of research is surveyed in Gordon 1990. For a succinct overview of new Keynesian economics see the introduction of the editors in Mankiw and Romer 1991.

analysis of business cycle fluctuations. In section 5 we summarize the model and draw some conclusions.

2. The Model

We consider a closed economy consisting of households, firms, and banks. Households supply labor and demand consumption goods, money (deposits), and equities. Firms supply goods, bank assets (loans), and equities, and demand labor and investment goods. Banks supply liabilities (deposits) and demand assets (loans and reserves). The balance sheets of the private agents in our economy are summarized in Table 1.

To avoid unnecessary complications, we largely ignore the public sector. Taxation and government expenditure do not show up in the model. As a result, we cannot introduce high-powered money through the monetization of budget deficits, as is usual in macroeconomic models. Instead, we assume there is a central bank whose role is to supply reserves as bank assets—the only type of base money in our framework. Of course, this is no more than a simplifying short cut, since this liability to the banking system has no counterpart on the asset side of the central bank's balance sheet.

Households' portfolio consists of money (deposits) and equities. In our framework, the stock of equities outstanding is given and constant (as discussed in section 2.2). Therefore, household wealth changes with changes in either the money stock or the stock price.

Turning to firms, internal funds have been ignored for the sake of clarity in Table 1. In this case *corporate net worth*—that is, the difference between the stock of capital at book value and the stock of debt owed to the banking system—coincides with the value of equities outstanding. However, the model does explicitly take *internal financing* into account, so that net worth

TABLE 1. Agents, Assets, and Liabilities

	Agents			
	Households	*Firms*	*Banks*	*Total*
(Net) Assets:				
Money	M		$-M$	0
Equities	EV	$-EV$		0
Loans		$-L$	L	0
Reserves			H	H
Capital		PK		PK
Total	W	0	0	$H + PK$

Legend: M = deposits; E = equities; V = stock price; W = households' wealth; L = bank loans; P = book value of capital goods; K = capital stock; H = bank reserves.

must be thought of as the sum of share values plus internal financial resources—that is, as the cumulative value of retained profits generated in the past, net of debt commitments.

As usual in short-run macroeconomic models, we hold capacity utilization approximately constant even though we allow explicitly for investment activity; that is, we assume that additions to the capital stock (net investment) are of negligible size compared to its prior level.

Bank liabilities coincide with households' deposits (money). Banks hold reserves at the central bank and extend loans to corporate clients. Therefore, given the stock of bank reserves, the supply of money is endogenous inasmuch as the supply of bank loans is endogenous.

Our economy consists of five markets: goods, labor, money (deposits), credit (bank loans), and equities. Following Keynesian tradition, the labor market is residual. On the assumption that wages and prices are approximately constant, employment is an increasing function of output, which in turn is determined by effective demand. In this framework, therefore, the real wage has no equilibrating role to play: we rule out full employment and assume that excess supply of labor always prevails. We will leave the labor market in the background and ignore it in the formal analysis that follows.

Thanks to Walras' law, in equilibrium we can neglect one of the remaining four markets. Contrary to the usual procedure, we will abstract from the market for money. Therefore, we are left with three markets: goods, equities, and credit. This procedure aims at bringing the financial decisions of firms to the fore. In turn, the key role for investment and income determination of firms' decisions about their liability structures stems from the presence of asymmetric information in the capital markets.

2.1 Equilibrium in the Goods Market: The GG Locus

To simplify the argument, we ignore wealth effects and model consumption as a linear function of current and lagged income:

$$C_t = c_0 + c_1 Y_t + c_2 Y_{t-1} \tag{1}$$

where c_0 is autonomous consumption and c_1 and c_2 are the propensities to consume out of current and lagged income respectively.

Equation (1) is consistent with the life-cycle and permanent-income hypotheses.[4] The Robertsonian lag in equation (1), however, can be explained

---

4. "Broadly speaking, all of these theories postulate lag mechanisms which mediate the response of C_t to changes in Y_t," (Davidson et al. 1978).

by wage earners' receiving their share of income during the production period, whereas dividends are distributed with a one-period lag. Therefore, the propensity to consume out of current income can be defined as follows:

$$c_1 = c_w (1 - \pi)$$

where c_w equals the propensity to consume out of the wage bill and π equals the share of profits in national income, with $0 < c_w < 1$ and $0 < \pi < 1$. The propensity to consume out of lagged income then equals:

$$c_2 = c_d (1 - \theta)\pi$$

where c_d is the propensity to consume out of dividends, θ is the retention ratio, and $(1 - \theta)$ is the dividend payout ration, with $0 < c_d < 1$ and $0 < \theta < 1$. In sum, the marginal propensities to consume out of current and lagged income (c^w, c^d) are polynomials of parameters describing consumption patterns out of different types of income (c_w, c_d), income distribution (π), and corporate financial strategy (θ). This interpretation of equation (1) has the advantage of linking the consumption function to the investment function through the income distribution and corporate financial strategy parameters.

The core of the real side of the model is the investment equation

$$I_t = aV_t + bIF_t \tag{2}$$

where V is the price of capital assets and IF equals internal finance. The first component in equation (2) incorporates Tobin's q effect. Given the price of current output (which we assume to be uniform across sectors and therefore to coincide with the price of investment goods), changes in the price of capital assets are equivalent to changes in the relative price of the "representative machine" in use with respect to the newly produced machine.

The second component in equation (2) is proportional to internal finance, defined as retained profits (lagged one period) net of debt service:

$$IF_t = \theta\pi Y_{t-1} - r_{t-1} L_{t-1}$$

where r equals the interest rate and L the stock of corporate debt. In a world of asymmetric information, internal finance ranks first in the *financing hierarchy* (or pecking order) of corporate resources allocated to investment activity. Moreover, it summarizes the past performance of the firm. Therefore banks take into account the volume of internally generated funds when they make a decision about the financing of an investment project. So from this point of view, internal financing is a proxy for collateral. The theoretical underpinnings of equation (2) are discussed at length by Fazzari, Hubbard, and Petersen (1988), who also test alternative econometric specifications for U.S. data.[5]

The parameter b, referred to hereafter as the *propensity to invest*, plays a crucial role in determining the volume and direction of investment activity. In Keynes' terminology, it incorporates both borrower's and lender's risk. In modern New Keynesian jargon, it is an "adverse selection" parameter. The lower the risk of adverse selection perceived by banks, the higher the perceived quality of borrowers (firms), the higher the value of the parameter b, and hence the higher is investment activity.

We will explore the dynamic implications of alternative specifications of b, all of which can be nested, so to speak, in the following functional form:

$$b = b_0 + b_1 Y_{t-1}$$

where $b_0 > 0$, $b_1 = b_2 \pi$, and $b_2 > 0$. The rationale for a procyclical propensity to invest is that during the expansion (recession), the growing (shrinking) flow of profits, by increasing (decreasing) internal finance, reduces (increases) the riskiness of the average investment project and lowers (increases) the level of adverse selection perceived by banks, stimulating (depressing) investment activity. This is a well-known "stylized fact" in the Fisher-Kindleberger-Minsky line of thought.

The equilibrium condition on the goods market is

$$Y_t = C_t + I_t. \tag{3}$$

By substituting equations (1) and (2) into (3), and taking into account the definitions of b and IF_t, we get

$$Y_t = \left[\frac{1}{(1 - c_1)} \right] \left[c_0 + c_2 Y_{t-1} + a V_t + b IF_t \right]$$

$$= \left[\frac{1}{(1 - c_1)} \right] \left[c_0 + (c_2 + b_0 \theta \pi - b_1 r_{t-1} L_{t-1}) Y_{t-1} \right. \tag{GG}$$

$$\left. + b_1 \theta \pi Y_{t-1}^2 + a V_t - b_0 r_{t-1} L_{t-1} \right]$$

that is, a relationship linking Y_t, Y_{t-1}, V_t, r_{t-1}, and L_{t-1}, which is referred to hereafter as the GG *locus*.

---

5. For the sake of precision, however, we notice that the magnitudes that show up in Fazzari's investment equations are rates of growth or ratios, whereas in equation (2) they are flows or levels.

2.2 Equilibrium in the Equities Market: The EE Locus

According to portfolio theory, the share of equities in households' wealth is an increasing function of the rate of return on equities,[6] which in turn is the sum of the dividend yield and the expected (percentage) capital gain:

$$E \frac{V_t}{W_t} = e \left(\frac{(1 - \theta)\pi Y_{t-1}}{V_t} + \frac{V^e - V_t}{V_t} \right)$$

where $\left((1 - \theta)\pi Y_{t-1})/V_t\right)$ is the *dividend yield*, that is, the ratio of the flow of dividends to the current stock price; $(V^e - V_t)/V_t$ is the *expected percentage capital gain*, that is, the ratio of the expected capital gain to the current stock price; and $e(\cdot)$ is a generic increasing function.

To keep the analysis as simple as possible, we ignore the expected capital gain; so the rate of return on equities boils down to the dividend yield. Moreover, we assume that $e(\cdot)$ is linear in its argument; so e represents a positive constant magnitude. As a consequence, the demand for equities can be written as

$$E^d = \left(\frac{W_t e}{V_t} \right) \left(\frac{(1 - \theta)\pi Y_{t-1}}{V_t} \right).$$

Finally, we assume that the demand for equities is a linear function of the dividend yield, that is

$$E^d = d \left(\frac{(1 - \theta)\pi Y_{t-1}}{V_t} \right) \tag{4}$$

where $d > 0$. Equation (4) implies that $W_t e/V_t = d$ or $W_t/V_t = d/e$; that is, this equation implicitly assumes a constant ratio of wealth to the stock price.

According to equation (4), the demand for equities increases with the dividend yield; that is, it increases with income and decreases with the stock price. Since households' portfolio consists solely of money and equities, this implies that the share of money in total wealth $(1 - e)$ decreases with income and increases with the stock price.

Given the dividend payout ratio, when income goes up the stream of dividends goes up and makes portfolio composition change in favor of equities, so that the demand for money decreases, other things being equal. This is

---

6. It is also a decreasing function of the rates of return on alternative assets. In our framework, there is only one other asset, namely money (bank deposits), whose rate of return is assumed to be zero so that we can ignore it in modeling the demand for equities.

Blanchard's *good news effect* (Blanchard, 1981). In our model, therefore, the positive relationship between income and the transactions demand for money is weak enough to be offset by the good news effect.

To simplify the argument, we assume that equity rationing (Leland and Pyle, 1977; Myers and Majluf, 1984) prevents firms from issuing new equities to finance investment. Therefore, we can take the supply of equities (E^s) as given and constant:

$$E^s = E. \tag{5}$$

Substituting equations (4) and (5) into the equilibrium condition

$$E^d = E^s \tag{6}$$

and rearranging, we get

$$V = \frac{d(1 - \theta)\pi\, Y_{t-1}}{E}. \tag{EE}$$

EE is the locus of equilibrium pairs (Y_{t-1}, V_t) for the stock market. To maintain equilibrium, lagged income and the price of capital assets are positively correlated: an increase in the current stock price brings about an excess supply of equities, and thus must also be associated with an increase in income, which stimulates demand.

2.3 Equilibrium in the Credit Market: The LL Locus

The demand for bank loans (L^d) is the sum of the stock of debt inherited from the past (L_{t-1}) and the need for external finance (EF_t), defined as the difference between planned investment expenditure and internal finance. Equity rationing prevents firms from issuing new equities to fund their investment. Given the definitions of these variables, the demand for bank loans can be written as follows:

$$L^d = L_{t-1} + EF_t = L_{t-1} + I_t - IF_t = L_{t-1} + aV_t + (b-1)\, IF_t$$

$$= L_{t-1} + aV_t + \left((b_0 - 1)\, \theta\pi - b_1\, r_{t-1}\, L_{t-1}\right)Y_{t-1} +$$

$$b_1 \theta\pi Y_{t-1}^2 + (1 - b_0)r_{t-1}L_{t-1}. \tag{7}$$

The demand for bank loans is a function of the stock price, income, and the interest rate. Although a change in the price of capital assets changes the demand for bank loans in the same direction ($L_V^d \equiv \partial L^d / \partial V = a > 0$),[7] the partial derivatives of the demand for loans with respect to (lagged) income and the interest rate can be either positive or negative.

The partial derivative of the demand for loans with respect to internal finance is $L_{IF}^d = b - 1$. If $b > 1$, then $L_{IF}^d > 1$: firms then behave as bold and sanguine borrowers, increasing their exposures when cash flows become more abundant as properity boosts their animal spirits and strengthens their confidence in the possibility of repaying debt. This characterization of the demand for loans, when it arises, can be termed a *euphoric regime*. Behavior in this regime is consistent with Minsky's financial instability hypothesis, according to which *financial fragility* escalates during prosperous times. But if, instead, $b < 1$, then $L_{IF}^d < 1$: firms are cautious and responsible borrowers who reduce their demand for loans when internal finance goes up. This is a regime of *wary expectations* with respect to the future.

The partial derivatives of the demand for loans with respect to (lagged) income and the interest rate are

$$L_Y^d = b_Y \, IF + L_{IF}^d \, IF_Y$$

$$L_r^d = L_{IF}^d \, IF_r$$

where $b_Y = b_1$, $IF_Y = \theta\pi$, and $IF_r = -L_{t-1}$. If $L_{IF}^d > 0$, then $L_Y^d > 0$ and $L_r^d < 0$. On the other hand, if $L_{IF}^d < 0$, then $L_r^d > 0$, but L_Y^d is sign-indefinite. In the latter case, in fact, an increase in income affects the demand for loans in opposite directions. On one hand, it boosts investment and the need for external financing, through its impact on the propensity to invest; on the other hand, it stimulates cash flows and leads cautious firms to reduce their indebtedness.

Given the supply of reserves, the supply of loans is

$$L^s = H\mu r_t \tag{8}$$

since the credit multiplier is an increasing function of the rate of interest (μr). Equation (8) can be conceived of as an interest-rate equation:

$$r_t = L^s / H\mu. \tag{8'}$$

The credit multiplier is bounded by the reserve requirements established by the central bank. Therefore there exists a threshold level of the rate of interest,

---

7. In order to save on notation, hereafter the partial derivative of a generic function $f(.)$ with respect to the argument x will be indicated by fx.

say $\hat{r}$, such that if $r < \hat{r}$, the multiplier is μr and the supply of bank loans is represented by (8), whereas if $r > \hat{r}$, the multiplier is μ_{max} and the supply of bank loans is $L = H\mu_{max}$.

Substituting equations (7) and (8) into the equilibrium condition for the credit market,

$$L^d = L^s, \tag{9}$$

and rearranging, we get

$$H\mu r_t = L_{t-1} + aV_t + [(b_0 - 1)\theta\pi - b_1 r_{t-1} L_{t-1}]Y_{t-1}$$

$$+ b_1\theta\pi Y_{t-1}^2 + (1 - b_0)r_{t-1}L_{t-1}, \tag{LL}$$

that is, a relationship linking r_t, Y_{t-1}, V_t, r_{t-1}, and L_{t-1}, that will be referred to hereafter as the LL locus.

3. The Dynamic Paths of Income and Debt

Solving the system of equations (GG) (EE) (LL), we get the triple (Y_t^*, V_t^*, r_t^*), which brings about equilibrium in the goods, equities, and credit markets given L_{t-1}, Y_{t-1}, and r_{t-1}. The system is recursive. The (EE) locus maps V_t into Y_{t-1}, which can be substituted into (GG) and (LL) to obtain a system of two equations in Y_t and r_t, given L_{t-1}, Y_{t-1}, and r_{t-1}. Moreover

$$L_t = L^s = H\mu r_t, \tag{10}$$

that is, the feasible debt of the corporate sector is equal to the credit supply. Equation (10), which maps r_t into L_t, can be substituted into the (GG)(LL) loci; this forms a system of two nonlinear difference equations in the level of output and the stock of debt, which we will label map F:

$$Y_t = \frac{1}{1 - c_1}\left(c_0 + (c_2 + \Gamma)Y_{t-1} + b\left[\pi(1 - \theta)Y_{t-1} - \frac{L_{t-1}^2}{H\mu}\right]\right)$$

$$L_t = L_{t-1} + \Gamma Y_{t-1} + (b - 1)\left[\pi(1 - \theta)Y_{t-1} - \frac{L_{t-1}^2}{H\mu}\right]$$

where $\Gamma = ad\pi(1 - \theta)/E$ and $b = b_0 + b_1 Y_{t-1}$.

The system is characterized by two types of nonlinearity. The first nonlinearity arises because interest payments are defined as the product of the interest rate, lagged one period—as defined by equation (8')—times the stock of debt inherited from the past. The second nonlinearity arises because the propensity to invest, which multiplies the flow of internally generated funds, is procyclical. The analysis of the dynamic behavior of a system of two nonlinear difference equations is no easy task. To bring the macroeconomic implications of the dynamic analysis to the fore, we will first discuss some special cases that allow significant simplifications of map F.

3.1 Debt Neutrality

When the Modigliani-Miller proposition holds true, the availability of internally generated funds doesn't constrain investment activity and therefore can be ignored in specifying the investment function. In our framework, this case arises when $b = 0$, which implies $I = aV$: investment activity is entirely determined by the ratio of the (flexible) stock price to the (given) price of current output in the investment goods sector.

When $b = 0$, map F can be simplified as follows:

$$Y_t = \frac{1}{1 - c_1}(c_0 + (c_2 + \Gamma)Y_{t-1})$$

$$L_t = L_{t-1} + (\Gamma - \pi\theta)Y_{t-1} + \frac{L_{t-1}^2}{H\mu}$$

that is, to a system of two linear difference equations. The first equation is the reduced form of the (GG)(EE) system, which can be solved for the dynamic path of income. Once the first equation is solved, the law of motion of income can be plugged into the (EE) locus to determine the dynamic path of the stock price.

In other words, equilibrium in the goods, equities, and money markets isn't affected by developments in the credit market. This is a regime of *debt neutrality*. Of course the converse is not true: developments on the goods, equities, and money markets do have effects on the equilibrium in the market for bank loans. In fact, the dynamics of income are needed to solve to second difference equation, which determines the dynamics of corporate debt (and therefore of the interest rate).

Debt neutrality does not necessarily imply money neutrality. If monetary policy affects households, portfolio decisions and the stock price, it can influence investment decisions. On the other hand, no real repercussions will follow from changes in monetary policy that affect the interest rate and the accumulation of corporate debt: the transmission mechanism based on credit availability is ineffective. Of course, this result rests on the implicit assumption according to which, in the short run, changes in the interest rate on banks' loans are not necessarily parallel to changes in the rate of return on equities.

The steady-state level of income derived from the first difference equation is

$$Y^* = \frac{c_0}{1 - c_1 - c_2 - \Gamma}$$

where $1/(1 - c_1 - c_2 - \Gamma)$ is the multiplier. The dynamic path of income converges to the steady state (that is, equilibrium is stable) if $c_1 + c_2 + \Gamma < 1$. Of course, when this condition is satisfied, the multiplier is finite and equilibrium income is positive. In our framework the multiplier is a complex polynomial composed of parameters for income distribution (π), corporate financial policy (θ), consumption patterns (c_w, c_d), investment decisions (a), and the demand for and supply of equities (d and E respectively). A quick inspection of these parameters shows that stability is enhanced by thriftiness (low propensity to consume), a restrictive dividend policy (a low dividend payout rate), cautious investment decisions (a low sensitivity of investment to the stock price), a dividend-inelastic demand for equities, and an abundant supply of equities (a "thick" stock market).

The repercussions for equilibrium of changes in income distribution (that is, changes in π) are uncertain. *Ceteris paribus*, a higher share of profits in national income depresses consumption out of the wage bill, but boosts both investment—since the demand for equities and hence the stock price are both driven upward—and consumption out of dividends. Note that changes in income distribution or in dividend policy have a direct impact on consumption expenditure and only an indirect impact on investment expenditure (through the stock market); in a regime of debt neutrality, these shifts do not exert any *direct* influence on investment activity.

From the second equation in map F we get the dynamic path of corporate debt, which in turn can be substituted into equation (8') to derive the law of motion of the interest rate. Developments in the goods, equities, and money markets do have repercussions on debt accumulation through the dynamic path of income. An increasing level of income exerts a positive impact on the accumulation of corporate debt if $\Gamma > \theta\pi$, that is if $(ad/E) > ((\theta/1 - \theta))$. The lower the retention ratio, the more likely is a positive correlation between the growth of income and the accumulation of debt. The second equation in map F shows that in this case a cumulative process of debt accumulation occurs.

An increasing level of income affects the accumulation of corporate debt negatively if $\Gamma < \theta\pi$, this is, if $(ad/E) < [\theta/(1 - \theta)]$. In this case the steady state stock of debt is

$$L^* = \left(H\mu(\theta\pi - \Gamma)Y^*\right)^{1/2}.$$

The dynamic path of corporate debt does not converge to the steady state (the equilibrium is unstable).

In our framework, the second equation of map F plays the role of disclosing the hidden dynamics of debt embedded in the (GG)(EE) macro model. The dynamics of debt do not converge to a stationary value, even if the macroeconomic equilibrium—that is, the pair (V^*, Y^*), which clears the goods and money markets—is stable. In a regime of debt neutrality, in fact, firms do not take into account their capital structure when deciding investment expenditure. Nevertheless, they must find external funds to fill the financing gap. Therefore, even if the equilibrium is stable, corporate debt grows because of debt commitments:

$$L_t = (1 + r_{t-1})L_{t-1} + aV^* - \theta\pi Y^*.$$

The accumulation of debt goes on until banks are able and willing to accommodate firms' demand for loans.

3.2 Financial Autarchy

Although the flow of internally generated funds is irrelevant in the case of debt neutrality, we can imagine a regime of financial autarchy in which firms' expenditure on capital goods is constrained by the availability of internal finance. To assess the macroeconomic implications of this regime, we set $a = 0$, $b_0 = 1$, and $b_1 = 0$. Therefore the investment and loan demand equations must be rewritten, respectively, as follows:

$$I_t = IF_t = \theta\pi Y_{t-1} - r_{t-1} L_{t-1} \tag{2'}$$

$$L^* = L_{t-1} \tag{7'}$$

Using equations (2') and (7') instead of (2) and (7), map F can be rewritten as follows:

$$Y_t = \frac{1}{1 - c_1}\left[c_0 + (c_2 + \theta\pi)Y_{t-1} - \frac{L_{t-1}^2}{H\mu} \right]$$

$$L_t = L_{t-1}.$$

In a regime of financial autarchy, the banking system has no role to play by construction. The second equation in map F says that the stock of corporate debt is constant. For the sake of simplicity and without loss of generality, we can set $L_t = L_{t-1} = 0$. In this case, map F boils down to the following equation:

$$Y_t = \frac{1}{1 - c_1} [c_0 + (c_2 + \theta\pi)Y_{t-1}].$$

Therefore the steady state level of income is

$$Y* = \frac{c_0}{1 - c_1 - c_2 - \theta\pi},$$

where $1/(1 - c_1 - c_2 - \theta\pi)$ is the multiplier. The dynamic path of income converges to the steady state (that is, equilibrium is stable) if $c_1 + c_2 + \theta\pi < 1$. Of course, when this condition is satisfied, the multiplier is finite and equilibrium income is positive.

In this case the multiplier is a polynomial of parameters involving income distribution (π), corporate financial policy (θ), and consumption patterns (c_w, c_d). Parameters and exogenous variables related to the demand for and supply of equities do not show up in the multiplier because the stock price is irrelevant in investment decision making. The repercussions of changes in income distribution (captured by changes in c) on the nature of equilibrium are uncertain. Other things equal, an increasing share of profits in national income boosts consumption out of dividends and positively affects investment through its impact on internal finance, while depressing consumption out of the wage bill.

Changes in dividend policy affect consumption and investment in opposite directions. An increasing retention ratio reduces consumption out of dividends but boosts investment by generating a larger flow of internal funds. Since the positive impact on investment is greater than the negative impact on consumption, all in all an increase in the retention ratio stimulates aggregate demand. This is a major difference from the case of debt neutrality. In a regime of debt neutrality, in fact, the higher the retention ratio, the lower is consumption out of dividends and aggregate demand.

3.3 Nonlinear Dynamics

So far, we have dealt with special cases. We now turn to the study of map F in its most general form. To simplify the analysis, we proceed in two steps. We first analyze the dynamic behavior of the system when $b_0 > 0$ and $b_1 = 0$. By setting $b_1 = 0$, we are implicitly assuming that the propensity to invest is given and constant. In this case map F assumes the following form:

$$Y_t = \Phi_0 + \Phi_1 Y_{t-1} - \Phi_2 L_{t-1}^2$$

$$L_t = L_{t-1} + \Omega_1 Y_{t-1} - \Omega_2 L_{t-1}^2$$

where

$$\Phi_0 = c_0/(1 - c_1) > 0,$$

$$\Phi_1 = [(c_2 + \Gamma) + b_0 (1 - \theta)\pi]/(1 - c_1) > 0,$$

$$\Phi_2 = b_0/H\mu > 0,$$

$$\Omega_1 = \Gamma + (b_0 - 1)(1 - \theta)\pi, \text{ and}$$

$$\Omega_2 = (b_0 - 1)/H\mu;$$

this will be labelled map F_0 for convenience.

We can now derive the conditions for the existence of a feasible stationary point $E = (Y^*, L^*)$, that is, a fixed point of map F in the positive quadrant of the (Y,L) plane. Map F has two steady states:

$$E_1 = Y^*, (\Phi_1 Y^*/\Phi_2)^{1/2}$$

$$E_2 = Y^*, - (\Phi_1 Y^*/\Phi_2)^{1/2}$$

where $Y^* = (\Phi_0\Omega_2)/(\Omega_2 + \Phi_2\Omega_1 - \Phi_1\Omega_2) - c_0(b_0 - 1)/((b_0 - 1)(1 - c_1 - c_2) + \Gamma)$.

The fixed point E_2 is nonfeasible ($L^* < 0$), while the fixed point E_1 is economically feasible if $b_0 > 1$. To perform the local stability analysis of E_1, we denote by $P(.)$ the characteristic polynomial of the Jacobian matrix of map F evaluated at the fixed point. We recall (see Gandolfo, 1983) that necessary and sufficient conditions for the local asymptotic stability of E_1 are the following:

$$P(1) = 2L^* (\Omega_2 + \Phi_2\Omega_1 - \Phi_1\Omega_2) > 0$$

$$P(-1) = 2(1 + \Phi_1 - 2\Omega_2 L^*) + 2L^* (\Omega_2 + \Phi_2\Omega_1 - \Phi_1\Omega_2) > 0$$

$$P(0) = \Phi_1 + 2L^* (\Phi_2\Omega_1 - \Phi_1\Omega_2) < 1$$

The stationary point E_1 may be positive even if $b_0 < 1$. In this case, however, $P(1) < 0$: the equilibrium point is unstable (the eigenvalues of the Jacobian matrix are real and one of them is greater than one) and no other stable attractor has been numerically observed in the positive quadrant of the (Y,L) plane. Therefore, in the analysis that follows we assume $b_0 > 1$, which yields $P(1) > 0$: the first condition for local asymptotic stability is satisfied.

The second condition $(P(-1) > 0)$ is satisfied whenever $L^* < (1 + \Phi_1)/2\Omega_2$; that is, when $Y^* < (1 + \Phi_1)^2 H\mu/4(b_0 - 1)(\Gamma + (b_0 - 1)(1 - \theta)\pi)$, which may be considered a reasonable assumption.

Thus the crucial condition is the third one: $P(0) < 1$. The polynomial $\Phi_2\Omega_1 - \Phi_1\Omega_2 = (\Gamma - c_2(b_0 - 1))((1 - c_1)H\mu)$ is a "small number," the leading term of which is the coefficient Γ_1. The value of Γ_1 increases with the value of b_0. A range of values of b_0, say $b_0 < b_0^*$, can be numerically detected such that the third condition is satisfied and the steady state E_1 is locally stable. Changes (increases) in b_0 do not violate the first and second conditions for local stability, which are always satisfied: the stable equilibrium point E_1 can neither become a saddle point (through a real eigenvalue greater than 1) nor become unstable via flip birfucation (through an eigenvalue equal to -1). Thus only a Hopf bifurcation can occur (E_1 may become an unstable focus: Guckenheimer and Holmes, 1983; Iooss, 1979; Lorenz, 1989).

The second step in our analysis consists of relaxing the restrictive assumption $b_1 = 0$ in order to deal with the most general form of map F. The dynamics of map F will be studied by means of numerical simulations. Of course, the set of fixed points of map F is different from the set of fixed points of map F_0. It is worth noting, however, that a steady state of map F, say E, which is quite "close to" the (feasible) steady state E_I of map F_0, can be detected. E is the feasible steady state of map F.

We have simulated the dynamic behavior of map F for several different sets of values of the parameters, generating a sequence of values of the endogenous variables analogous to the one we will describe below, which is associated with the following set of parameters: $a = 0.1$, $\theta = 0.25$, $\pi = 0.5$, $c_1 = 0.5$, $c_2 = 0.4$, $d = 0.2$, $b_1 = 0.001$, $c_0 = 800$, $E = 1000$, $H\mu = 2000$. At low values of b_0, such that $b = b_0 + b_1 Y^*$ belongs to the interval $(1,2)$, the fixed point $E = (Y^*,L^*)$ "close to" $E_1 = (1330, 1000)$ is locally stable. A bifurcation occurs when b_0 falls in the interval $(0.65, 0.70)$, which means that b falls in the interval $(1.98, 2.00)$. E becomes unstable via a supercritical Hopf bifurcation, and a closed invariant locally attractive curve (γ) appears, on which orbits are periodic or quasi-periodic: at least locally, the trajectories are bounded and asymptotically cyclic.

The dimension of γ increases with b_0: in Figure 1 the attractive curve g is depicted by an orbit when $b_0 = 0.9$ so that $b = b_0 + b_1 Y$ falls in the interval $(1.35, 3.47)$. As suggested by several examples of plane nonlinear maps

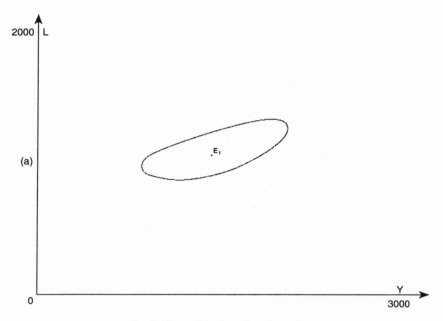

Fig. 1. The orbit of g when b_0 = 0.9

(Gumowski and Mira, 1980; Mira, 1987; Gallegati and Gardini, 1990), the invariant attractive curve γ may disappear because of changes in b_0, and other bounded attractors (periodic orbits, strange attractors, attracting sets) may appear.

Indeed, several periodic orbits have been detected. For example, a period-6 orbit exists for $b_0 \in (1.21, 1.215)$, which is followed by a cascade of period-doubling bifurcations. Figure 2 represents the periodic orbit associated with $b_0 = 1.21$, which implies $b \in (1.35, 3.76)$. Figure 3a depicts a strange attractor associated with $b_0 = 1.22$—that is, $b \in (1.26, 3.82)$; the magnification in Figure 3b shows some structure for this attractor. When the value of b_0 goes beyond that threshold, the strange attractor changes its shape (two examples are reported in Figures 4a and 4b) until a critical value is reached (here, $b_0 = 1.3$), at which point the attractor disappears, probably following a global bifurcation of catastrophic character (Thompson and Stewart, 1987).

4. Financial Instability and Business Cycle Fluctuations

In sum, this model generates three types of dynamic behavior:

1. When investment plans are financed primarily through internally generated funds, so that the need for external finance is negligible, the system converges to the steady state (equilibrium is stable);

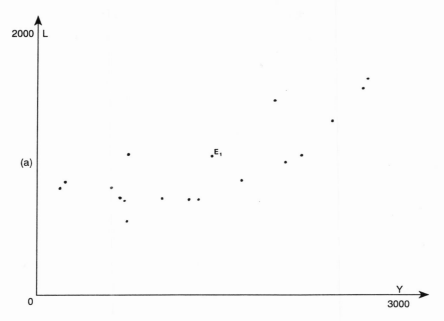

Fig. 2. The orbit of g when b_0 = 1.21

2. When the propensity to invest is neither too high nor too low, the dynamic behavior is chaotic;
3. Finally, when the propensity to invest goes beyond a specified critical value, the system follows divergent trajectories, a dynamic behavior that we will associate with a financial crisis.

The solution of systems of nonlinear difference equations that generate supercritical Hopf bifurcations is characterized by closed orbits of unpredictable periodicity. Even if the system is deterministic, each fluctuation has its own story and shape, which won't be replicated in any predictable way. The endogenously determined dynamic path is somehow bounded but highly irregular and is therefore observationally equivalent to the dynamic behavior of the time series generated by stochastic perturbations of the steady state.

It is extremely difficult, if not impossible, to account for the interplay of economic factors behind the scenes of these complex dynamics. Therefore we apply the macroeconomic relationships outlined in section 2 to a closed invariant locally attractive curve on the debt-income plane, such as γ in Figure 1, to describe the economic determinants of business fluctuations in our framework.

At the beginning of a recovery, income is low; the same is true of the propensity to invest. During the recovery, income increases through the

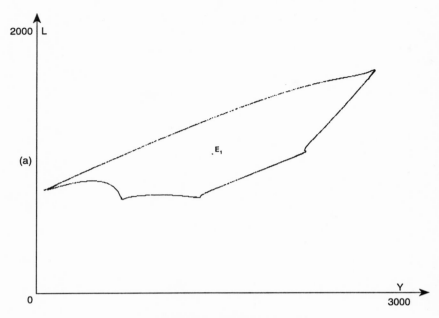

Fig. 3a. The orbit of g when $b_0 = 1.22$

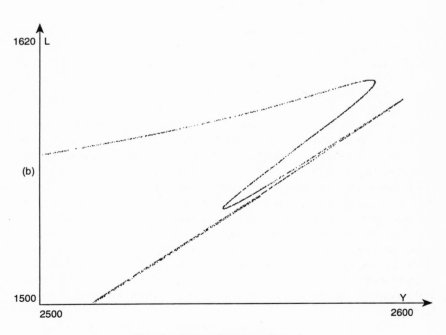

Fig. 3b. A Magnification of Fig. 3a

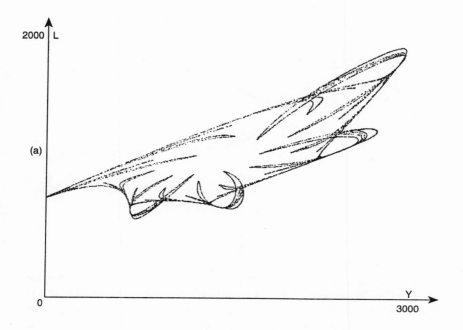

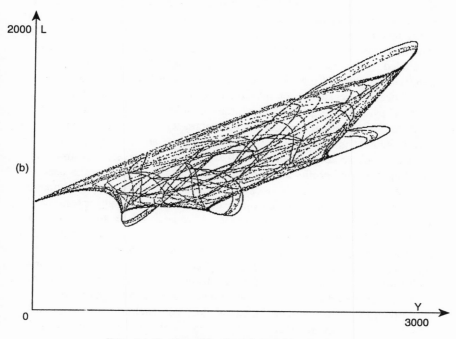

Figs. 4a, 4b. An orbit of g when $1.22 < b_0 < 1.3$

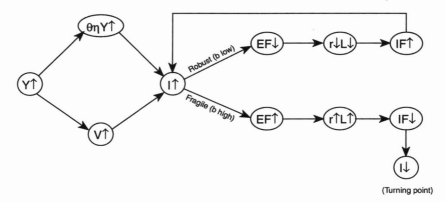

Fig. 5. An orbit of g when $1.22 < b_0 < 1.3$

Keynesian multiplier and boosts retained profits, which in turn have a positive feedback on investment. If the configuration of behavioral parameters is such that the propensity to save and the retention ratio are greater than the propensity to invest, retained earnings and households' savings increase more than investment expenditure, reducing the need for external finance. A decrease of the interest rate ensues, and the burden of debt commitments becomes lighter. In the market for equities, the positive impact of the increase in dividends on the return to equities pushes up demand and the price of capital assets. The growth of investment, income, cash flows, and the price of capital assets is paralleled by declines in the interest rate, the stock of debt, and debt commitments. We will label this virtuous circle a *financially robust expansion*.

Since the sensitivity of investment to cash flow, as measured by the financial parameter b, is procyclical, during the recovery we can trace out the transition to a different configuration of parameters wherein the propensity to invest becomes greater than the propensity to save and the retention ratio. In this case, income keeps rising through ever-increasing excess investment in a spiraling boom of profits and capital accumulation. Therefore the need for external finance goes up, as does the interest rate. Moreover, the booming price of capital assets strengthens investment and the demand for bank loans. This scenario describes a vicious circle of growing indebtedness, which we term a *fragile expansion*, paralleling the growth of investment, income, and the price of equities. A fragile expansion is the counterpart in a fix-price framework of the credit inflation discussed at length in the monetary literature on business cycle fluctuations of the 1920s and 1930s. Figure 5 can help us visualize the evolution of the variables involved over the expansion.

When the flow of retained earnings does not catch up with the growing burden of debt commitments, a turning point in the business cycle is likely. The recession is characterized by the decline in investment, income, and the price of capital assets. Profits fall more quickly than investment, so the need for external finance increases, together with the stock of corporate debt, the interest rate, and debt commitments. Since it is procyclical, the propensity to invest decreases in the recession even if the configuration of parameters—that is, the relative magnitudes of the propensity to invest, the propensity to save, and the retention ratio—is the same as in the final stage of the expansion.

The drop in b signals a change in the attitude of entrepreneurs with far-reaching and paradoxical implications: by adopting a more cautious investment strategy so as to reduce indebtedness, entrepreneurs worsen the financial situation of their firms. This scenario describes what could be called a *fragile recession*. A fragile recession is the counterpart in a fix-price framework of the "debt-deflation" discussed by Fisher (1933).

To break the evil circuit of shrinking cash flows and booming debt, the propensity to invest must become smaller than the propensity to save and the retention ratio. Only when income reaches a sufficiently low level will this condition be satisfied. In this case investment falls more rapidly than profit, and the need for external finance decreases, together with the stock of corporate debt, the interest rate, and debt commitments. This is the scenario of a *robust recession*. Eventually the lower turning point of the cycle occurs, and the system is ready to start a robust expansion. If the propensity to invest becomes too high, the dynamic behavior of the system leads to a financial crisis—that is, an explosive growth of debt commitments occurs.

A few remarks are in order at this point about the role of monetary policy in preventing or halting a financial crisis. Monetary authorities can inject liquidity into the system (through an increase in banks' reserves). A reduction in the interest rate follows; this, in turn, makes the burden of debt commitments lighter and stimulates investment because of the increasing cash flow. This *direct* transmission mechanism of monetary policy in our framework is based on credit availability. If income was growing, it will grow even faster; if it was falling, there will most likely be an upturn. The increasing flow of dividends will force a portfolio change in favor of equities, which boosts the stock price and fuels investment expenditure. This *indirect* transmission mechanism of monetary policy is based on portfolio choice.

5. Conclusions

We have presented and discussed a macroeconomic model with financial constraints that generates complex dynamics of income and corporate debt. Asymmetric information in capital markets yields a financing hierarchy in which the flow of internal finance ranks first, having a cost advantage over bank loans and new equity issues. Therefore retained earnings and debt commitments play a crucial role in investment and income determination.

From the equilibrium conditions in the goods, equities, and credit markets we derive a system of two nonlinear difference equations in the level of income and the stock of corporate debt, whose solution endogenously determines the dynamic paths of income, debt, the interest rate, and the price of capital assets. If the procyclical propensity to invest is close to zero, the steady state is stable. If it is neither too low nor too high, the macroeconomic system shows chaotic dynamic behavior. Finally, if the propensity to invest becomes too high, the system becomes dynamically unstable and prone to financial crisis.

The nature of business cycle fluctuations is determined in our model by the interaction between retained earnings and debt commitments. We have devised a tentative taxonomy of business cycle fluctuations in which a financially robust recovery is followed by a fragile boom and a fragile recession is followed by a financially robust depression. Further research should investigate the implications of stochastic shocks to aggregate demand. Our analysis of business cycle fluctuations is based on the lack of a central coordinating mechanism capable of preventing the rate of debt accumulation from overcoming that of capital. In this context, income and unemployment fluctuations cannot be conceived of as reactions of an otherwise stable system to exogenous impulses. On the contrary, such fluctuations represent the normal functioning of a decentralized economy with capital and debt accumulation.

REFERENCES

Akerlof, G., and Yellen, J. 1985. "A Near-Rational Model of the Business Cycle with Wage and Price Inertia," *Quarterly Journal of Economics*, vol. 100, no. 5, pp. 823–838.

Ball, L., Mankiw, G., and Romer, D. 1988. "The New Keynesian Economics and the Output-Inflation Trade-off," *Brookings Papers on Economic Activity*, no.1, pp. 1–65.

Bernanke, B. 1983. "Nonmonetary Effects of the Financial Crisis in the Propagation of the Great Depression," *American Economic Review*, vol. 73, no. 3, pp. 257–276.

Bernanke, B., and Blinder, A. 1988. "Credit, Money and Aggregate Demand," *American Economic Review*, vol. 78, no. 2, pp. 435–439.

Bernanke, B. S., and Campbell, J. Y. 1988. "Is There a Corporate Debt Crisis?" *Brookings Papers on Economic Activity*, no. 1, pp. 83–140.

Blanchard, O. 1981. "Output, the Stock Market and Interest Rates," *American Economic Review*, vol. 71, no. 1, pp. 132–143.

Blinder, A. 1987. "Credit Rationing and Effective Demand Failures," *Economic Journal*, vol. 97, no. 386, pp. 327–352.

Brunner, K., and Meltzer, A. H. 1968. "Liquidity Traps for Money, Bank Credit and Interest Rates," *Journal of Political Economy*, vol. 76, no. 1, pp. 1–38.

Brunner, K. and Meltzer, A. H. 1972. "Money, Debt and Economic Activity," *Journal of Political Economy*, vol. 80, no. 5, pp. 951–977.

Brunner, K. and Meltzer, A. H. 1976. "An Aggregative Theory for a Closed Economy," in J. Stein, ed., *Monetarism*, Amsterdam: North-Holland.

Davidson, J. E. H., Hendry, D. F., Srba, F., and Yeo, S. 1978. "Econometric Modelling of the Aggregate Time-Series Relationship Between Consumers' Expenditure and Income in the United Kingdom," *Economic Journal*, vol. 88, no. 352, pp. 661–692.

Delli, Gatti, D., and Gallegati, M. 1992. "Imperfect Information, Corporate Finance, Debt Commitments and Business Fluctuations," in S. Fazzari and D. Papadimitriou, eds., *Financial Conditions and Macroeconomic Performance*. Armonk, NY: M. E. Sharpe, Inc. Pp. 133–160.

Fazzari, S., Hubbard, G., and Petersen, B. 1988. "Financing Constraints and Corporate Investment," *Brookings Paper on Economic Activity*, no. 1, pp. 141–206.

Federal Reserve Bank of Kansas City. 1986. *Debt, Financial Stability and Public Policy*, Kansas City.

Federal Reserve Bank of Kansas City. 1988. *Financial Market Volatility*, Kansas City.

Fisher, I. 1933. "The Debt-Deflation Theory of Great Depressions," *Econometrica*, vol. 1, no. 4, pp. 337–357.

Friedman, B. M. 1986. "Increasing Indebtedness and Financial Stability in the United States," in Federal Reserve Bank of Kansas City, *Debt, Financial Stability and Public Policy*.

Friedman, B. M. 1990. "Implications of Corporate Indebtedness for Monetary Policy," NBER Working Paper no. 3266.

Friedman, M. and Schwartz, A. J. 1963. *A Monetary History of the United States*, Princeton: Princeton University Press.

Gallegati, M., and Gardini, L. 1991. "A Nonlinear Model of the Business Cycle with Money and Finance," *Metroeconomica*, vol. 42, no. 1, pp. 1–32.

Gandolfo, G. 1983. *Economic Dynamics: Methods and Models*, Amsterdam: North-Holland.

Gertler, M. 1988. "Financial Structure and Aggregate Economic Activity," *Journal of Money, Credit and Banking*, vol. 20, no. 3 (part 2), pp. 559–588.

Gertler, M. and Hubbard, R. G. 1988. "Financial Factors in Business Fluctuations," in Federal Reserve Bank of Kansas City, *Financial Market Volatility*.

Gordon, R. 1990. "What is New-Keynesian Economics?" *Journal of Economic Literature*, vol. 28, no. 3, pp. 1115–1171.

Greenwald, B., and Stiglitz, J. 1988a. "Financial Market Imperfections and Business Cycles," NBER working paper no. 2494.

Greenwald, B., and Stiglitz, J. 1988b. "Imperfect Information, Finance Constraints, and Business Fluctuation," in Kohn, M., and Tsiang, S. (1988).

Greenwald, B., and Stiglitz, J. (1988c), "Money, Imperfect Information and Economic Fluctuations," in Kohn, M. and Tsiang, S., *Finance Constraints, Expectations and Macroeconomics*, Oxford: Oxford University Press.

Greenwald, B., Stiglitz, J. and Weiss, A. 1984. "Informational Imperfections in the Capital Market and Macroeconomic Fluctuations," *American Economic Review*, vol. 74, no. 2, pp. 194–200.

Guckenheimer, J., and Holmes, P. H. 1983. *Nonlinear Oscillations, Dynamical Systems and Bifurcation of Vector Fields*, New York: Springer-Verlag.

Gumowski, I., and Mira, C. 1980. *Dinamique Caotique*, Toulouse: Cepadues.

Hicks, J. R. 1989. *A Market Theory of Money*, London: Basil Blackwell.

Iooss, G. 1979. *Bifurcation of Maps and Applications*, Amsterdam: North-Holland.

Kaufman, H. 1986. "Debt: The Threat to Economic and Financial Stability," in Federal Reserve Bank of Kansas City, *Debt, Financial Stability and Public Policy*.

Kindleberger, C. P. 1978. *Manias, Panics and Crashes*, New York: Basic Books.

Kindleberger, C. P. 1986. *The World in Depression 1929–1939*, revised edition, Berkeley: University of California Press.

Kohn, M., and Tsiang, S. 1988. *Finance Constraints, Expectations and Macroeconomics*, Oxford: Oxford University Press.

Leland, H., and Pyle, D. 1977. "Information Asymmetries, Financial Structure, and Financial Intermediation," *Journal of Finance*, vo. 32, no. 2, pp. 371–387.

Lorenz, H. W. 1989. *Nonlinear Dynamical Economic and Chaotic Motion*, New York: Springer-Verlag.

Mankiw, G., and Romer, D., eds. 1991. *New Keynesian Economics*, Cambridge: MIT Press.

Miller, M. 1988. "The Modigliani-Miller Propositions after Thirty Years," *Journal of Economic Perspectives*, vol. 2, no. 4, pp. 99–120.

Minsky, H. 1975. *John Maynard Keynes*, New York: Columbia University Press.

Minsky, H. 1982. *Can "It" Happen Again?* Armonk, NY: M. E. Sharpe.

Minsky, H. 1986. *Stabilizing an Unstable Economy*, New Haven: Yale University Press.

Mira, C. 1987. *Chaotic Dynamics*, Singapore: World Scientific.

Myers, S. and Majluf, N. 1984. "Corporate Financing and Investment Decisions When Firms Have Information Investors Do Not Have," *Journal of Financial Economics*, vol. 13, no. 2, pp. 187–222.

Rotemberg, J. 1987. "The New Keynesian Microfoundations," *NBER Macroeconomics Annual*. Cambridge: MIT Press.

Stiglitz, J. 1987. "The Causes and Consequences of the Dependence of Quality on Price," *Journal of Economic Literature*, vol. 25, no. 1, pp. 1–48.

Stiglitz, J. and Weiss, A. 1981. "Credit Rationing in Markets with Imperfect Information," *American Economic Review*, vol. 71, no. 3, pp. 393–410.

Thompson, J. M. T. and Stewart, H. B. 1987. *Nonlinear Dynamics and Chaos*. New York: John Wiley.

CHAPTER 4

Asymmetric Information, Uncertainty, and Financial Structure: "New" versus "Post-" Keynesian Microfoundations

*Gary Dymski**

> Most new Keynesian models combine rational expectations with maximizing behavior at the level of the individual agent. Any attempt to build a model based upon irrational behavior or submaximizing behavior is viewed as cheating . . . So the game is to tease a failure of macro markets to clear from a starting point of rational expectations and the maximization of profits and individual welfare at the micro level.
>
> —Robert J. Gordon

1. Introduction: Why Financial Structure Matters

Momentous recent events such as the LDC debt crisis, the thrift fiasco, and the build up of corporate indebtedness have renewed interest among Keynesians—that is, among economists for whom "economic fluctuations reflect . . . market failure on a grand scale" (Mankiw, 1990: 1654)—in the idea that financial structures affect real outcomes.

Post-Keynesian economists have long asserted that financial relations crucially affect the economy. Shackle (1974) and Davidson (1978), building on chapter 12 of Keynes's *General Theory*, provided the microfoundation: decisions to finance irreversible, illiquid assets must be made under *Keynesian uncertainty*—that is, without knowing either the range of possible outcomes or the proper weights to assign to any thinkable outcome. Minsky (1975,

* The author would like to acknowledge comments by seminar participants at the University of Southern California; the University of California, Riverside; and the University of Massachusetts, Amherst; and very helpful suggestions by Sam Bowles, Domenico Delli Gatti, David Fairris, Jeff Frieden, Mauro Gallegati, Herb Gintis, Timur Kuran, Marcus Noland, Robert Pollin, and two anonymous referees. The ideas expressed herein are solely the author's own. The author also acknowledges gratefully his many hours of discussion on the paper's themes with Jim Crotty, Steve Fazzari, Michael Magill, Martine Quinzii, and John Veitch.

1986) used these insights to show how financial structure matters in investment: as the firm's reliance on external financing grows, its marginal cost of funds rises both because its subjective assessment of the likely return from investment falls and because lenders grow more cautious. Minsky's financial instability hypothesis argues that as firms become more dependent on external finance, their financial structures shift from "robust" to "fragile" and become more susceptible to shocks that will evaporate their cash flows and be propagated throughout the economy.[1]

More recently, a "new" Keynesian approach to financial structure has developed. Unlike the post-Keynesian framework, it emphasizes asymmetric information in credit markets. Borrowers are better informed about their credit worthiness than are their creditors, but these two parties' incentives are incompatible. So creditors either ration credit to borrowers or engage in costly monitoring of their post contract behavior. Second-best outcomes are achieved.[2]

The rapid spread of this newer information-based Keynesian approach raises a question: has it superseded the older approach? In a provocative paper, Fazzari (1992) uses *asymmetric* information to explain why, in Minsky's theory of investment, borrower's risk and lender's risk rise and limit investment volume as external finance increases. If lenders and borrowers have the same information, he argues, they would agree about any borrower's investment prospects. But then financing *constraints* would never limit real investment: for rational lenders would not prevent rational borrowers from undertaking investment projects about which both parties have symmetric information. In sum, "*imperfect* information (in the sense of uncertainty) does not provide adequate foundations for financial constraints, one needs *asymmetric* information." (Fazzari 1992, 125)

So in Fazzari's view, a microfoundational model based on asymmetric information provides a satisfactory means of capturing Minsky's notion of finance-constrained investment. Further, this story has an inherent advantage over Minsky's story: it pertains to the very structure of information and markets, not to the use that agents make of any given set of information and markets.[3] Minsky's characterization of investment relies on the idea that agents' subjective assessment of investment prospects is a function of the

---

1. Dymski and Pollin (1992) provide a systematic account of Minsky's ideas. Minsky himself has always resorted to Keynes's chapter-12 uncertainty to explain these phenomena.

2. Gertler (1988) reviews new Keynesian literature on financial structure. Rationing as defined here occurs when quantity demanded exceeds quantity supplied at the market price.

3. Fazzari writes: " . . . from a post-Keynesian perspective, asymmetric information may seem to be no more than a minor flaw, incapable of supporting the pervasive critique of orthodoxy associated with the Keynesian revolution. . . . [But t]hese asymmetries are not just minor wrinkles in an otherwise smoothly functioning system, nor are they arbitrary, 'ad hoc' assumptions. They are inherent characteristics of decentralized market production" (1992, 126–127).

investing firm's reliance on external finance. But this violates a deep assumption of equilibrium theory, characterized as the *Harsanyi doctrine* by Kreps: "Any difference in subjective probability assessment must be the result of differences in information" (Kreps 1990, 111). Subjective probability assessments should not, according to this doctrine, be sensitive to the extent of exposure of cash flows.

It seems that in Minsky's approach, then, investors' ability to perceive the true state of investment prospects can be distorted by their financing position. Bernanke (1983), in developing his collateral-based new Keynesian model of credit, remarks that Minsky relies on agent *irrationality*. What he means is that agents in Minsky's story are irrational because they systematically misjudge the true state of the world. (Also see Gordon's quote at the beginning of this chapter.) So it would seem in these authors' view that the Keynesian revolution should be reignited with new Keynesian analytical tools. Asymmetric information allows one to play the "game," as Gordon terms it, whereas a resort to subjective probability distortions places one on the sidelines.

This paper takes up Fazzari's—and to a lesser extent Bernanke's—new Keynesian analytical challenge to the adequacy of the post-Keynesian view about why financial structure matters. In this paper, financial structure "matters" when principals and agents involved in external financing relations cannot reach the outcomes they could attain if all their activities were internally financed. My approach is to explore and contrast the new and post-Keynesian microfoundations of financial structure. In so doing, I emphasize the implications of different assumptions about information for conclusions about how information structure affects financial structure and, in turn, economic outcomes.

This investigation clarifies analytical differences between the two approaches. In both approaches, financial structure matters because markets and information are *incomplete*. Agents cannot precontract for every outcome and cannot know in advance which outcome will be drawn. Informationally disadvantaged agents must make costly adjustments that would be unnecessary if they knew everything ex ante and could contract for any future state. The adjustments they make, and the ways in which financial structure matters, depend on the sort of uncertainty they face.[4]

In the new Keynesian framework, the central problem with information is its unequal distribution. This gives rise to endogenous uncertainty in the sense that outcomes depend on what the better-informed agents within the

---

4. Debreu (1959, chapter 7) shows that even if multiple future states may occur, a competitive economy achieves an optimum if there is a market for each possibility in each feasible state. Violating this condition introduces missing markets into an analysis. A situation of incomplete information is logically equivalent to one of missing markets.

model do. In the post-Keynesian framework, the overriding informational problem in any economy is agents' common ignorance about the outcomes of at least some actions. For new Keynesians, this "Keynesian uncertainty" is just an extreme case of exogenous uncertainty, wherein "the probabilities of the states do not depend on the act chosen" by any of the agents involved (Kreps 1990, 101). New Keynesians admit that exogenous uncertainty per se exists, but they treat it as involving simply *risk*. Risk entails situations in which *both* range and likelihood of outcomes are known or at least discoverable, and consequently probability distributions over outcomes can be developed with confidence.

This paper shows first that when risk alone exists, financial structure has no important effects on economic outcomes. But endogenous uncertainty taken by itself is necessary and sufficient for financial structure to "matter." If this endogenous uncertainty arises because of adverse selection in the credit market, then credit rationing—finance constraints on investment—arises in equilibrium. If it arises because of moral hazard, then lenders must engage in costly monitoring. Either way, the existence of external (as opposed to internal) financing affects which equilibria can be reached. Fazzari's argument goes through, in that these results obtain when exogenous uncertainty in *any* form is absent.

But Fazzari's claim that asymmetric information is required to microfound credit rationing goes through only if exogenous uncertainty takes the form of risk. If exogenous uncertainty instead involves Keynesian uncertainty, credit can be rationed even if information is not asymmetric. The presence of Keynesian uncertainty in an economy creates a situation in which information must be constructed; it cannot be conceptualized as pregiven. The Harsanyi doctrine is more likely to be violated than to hold in this sort of world. Further, financial structure matters not just because it leads to credit rationing or to costly adjustments by lenders but also because it can generate stock/flow imbalances and hence unstable dynamic paths that are ruled out in models that allow only for risk.

So the post- and new Keynesian microfoundations are independent and very different approaches to establishing why financial structure matters. Both (new Keynesian) endogenous and (post-) Keynesian uncertainty involve tension between *ex ante* anticipations and *ex post* results, and either can lead to outcomes wherein financial structures "matter." In this sense, neither type of uncertainty is *categorically* deeper than the other. But if its presence in the economy is acknowledged, Keynesian uncertainty *is* deeper than asymmetric information. New Keynesian models assume agents know more about their economic environment than they can know in a post-Keynesian world. Asymmetric information is not inconsistent with Keynesian uncertainty in principle, but clearly the informational parameters that appear in new Keynesian models must be reinterpreted once they are implanted into a Keynesian uncertain world.

2. Production and Finance under Certainty

This section develops a simple model peopled only by "owners" and "entrepreneurs," with a built-in role for external finance. Owners have capital but cannot produce efficiently. Entrepreneurs have no capital, but they own efficient nontransferable production technologies that can be operated only with capital. So a credit market in owners' capital must open before entrepreneurs can produce using this model's socially efficient technologies. In this credit market, the owner is a principal and entrepreneurs are the owner's agents.

Ensuing sections explore how the amount of information, and its distribution, affects the outcomes that principal and agents reach in their credit market. This section introduces this model under perfect information.

Owners are endowed by nature with a stock of productive capital, K, in each time period. K depreciates completely after one period. Owners can use it in two ways: they can lend it to entrepreneurs or they can invest it in a costless, publicly available reservation technology. Either way, the return takes the form of a homogeneous, perishable consumption good, Q. The reservation technology yields a fixed return R for the K^R units invested therein. Owners must expend some effort to make loans to entrepreneurs. Each entrepreneur has one unit of time to allocate each period between leisure, S^o, and loan-making work, W^o, where $S^o + W^o = 1$; in effect, $W^o = W^o(K^e)$, where K^e represents capital lent to entrepreneurs. Owners value their leisure, S^o, and their consumption, Q^o: so their utility functions equal $U^o = U^o(Q^o, S^o)$. U^o is concave in Q^o and S^o.

Entrepreneurs' endowments consist of nontransferable production technologies for producing Q. The amount of Q entrepreneurs generate depends on how much capital, K^e, they obtain from owners. So production is finance constrained. Production also requires entrepreneurial work, W^e, whose amount varies directly with K^e. We can thus write the production function

$$Q = Q(K^e, (W^e(K^e)))$$ (1)

where $Q_i > 0$, $Q_{ij} < 0$, for $i, j = 1, 2$.[5] Entrepreneurs' utility functions are of the same form as owners': $U^e = U^e(Q^e, S^e)$.

---

5. Throughout this chapter, for any function F, F_i equals the derivative of F with respect to its ith argument, while F_{ij} indicates the second derivative of F with respect to i and j..

The transfer of K^e from owner to entrepreneur constitutes a one-period loan, with principal and interest paid off at period's end. So the amount loaned to any entrepreneur equals some L^e such that $L^e = (P^K/P^Q)(1+r)K^e$, where r denotes the one-period interest rate and (P^K/P^Q) the price of K expressed in units of Q. Note that the entrepreneur's decision to accept a loan represents an irreversible investment commitment within the restricted one-period framework of this model. Once entrepreneurs have accepted some K, they cannot return it or sell it on a secondary market; they must hold it until its effective lifespan is extinguished.

The prices of the consumption and capital goods are set competitively, and the consumption good price is used as a numeraire; however, the credit market is imperfectly competitive: each owner faces a given number (N) of entrepreneurs and sets her own optimal loan rate given her endowment of K in each period.

This model clearly abstracts from numerous issues in the real economy. To cite two glaring simplifications: endowing agents with capital each period eliminates the problem of accumulation and consumption over time; and production involves no class relations. Further, most of the trappings of a competitive equilibrium situation with conventionally rational agents are adopted without comment. In particular, no false trading occurs because market decisions are auctioneered. The use of these simplifications and assumptions does not represent an endorsement: rather, these conventions appear here because they are commonplace in new Keynesian models. In effect, with its "representative agent" microfoundational emphasis, the model developed here sets up the "game" as new Keynesians have played it (see Gordon's quote) in making claims about aggregate outcomes.

Allowing for price setting in the loan market also leads to a deviation from the case of pure competition and does not allow the model to find its competitive Pareto optimum. This deviation is not necessary but is used here because it is a standard feature of asymmetric information models; so including it allows maximum comparability between this benchmark case and the imperfect information cases that follow.[6]

The entrepreneur's maximand then is given by Λ^e:

$$\Lambda^e = U^e(Q^e,(1 - W^e(K^e)) \quad \text{where} \quad Q^e = Q(K^e, W^e(K^e))$$

$$- r^{PK}K^e$$

---

6. The principal's ability to set the price is fundamental in asymmetric information models. The reason is obvious: if "principals" could trust price signals to accurately convey information about both quantity and quality, agents would be completely reliable and the principal/agent problem would disappear.

and where $(1 - W^e)$ has been substituted for S^e in U^e. The entrepreneur's first-order condition over her choice variable K^e equals:

$$Q_1 - Q_2 = rP^K + (U_2^e/U_1^e)W_{K^e}^e. \tag{2}$$

The concavity of U and Q guarantees that second-order conditions are satisfied. Equation (2) specifies that K is taken until its marginal consumption benefits are just offset by its cost added to the marginal cost of surrendering leisure time. Varying r leads the entrepreneur to choose different levels of K, thus determining the entrepreneur's loan demand schedule.

Denote the summed loan demand from all entrepreneurs in any owner's market area as NK^e; NK^e is a function of the owner's choice variable r. After substituting $(1 - W^o)$ for S^o in U^o as above, the owner's maximand then equals Λ^o:

$$\Lambda^o = U^o(Q^o,(1 - W^o(NK^e))) + \lambda_1(NK^e + K^R - K)$$

where $Q^o = rP^KNK^e + R(K^R)$.

If the adding-up constraint is used to eliminate the term K^R, this maximand can be reexpressed as $\Lambda^o = U^o(rP^KNK^e + R(K - NK^e), (1 - W^o(NK^e)))$ where $NK^e = NK^e(r)$ and clearly, $NK_r^e < 0$. The owner's first-order condition for its choice variable r then equals

$$rP^K(\epsilon_r^{-1} + 1) = R + (U_2^o/U_1^o) W_{NK^e}^o, \qquad \epsilon_r = NK_r^e(r/NK:ece). \tag{3}$$

The return to entrepreneurial loans must equal the return from the reservation technology plus the marginal disutility due to the cost of making this marginal loan.

Given the assumptions we have made about technology and preferences, a unique equilibrium clearly exists for owners and entrepreneurs. This solution is Pareto optimal save for the distortion caused by having a monopolistic lender. Credit is not rationed. Ex ante plans and ex post realizations do not differ: all agents' revenue flows are well defined in advance for every level of prices and interest rates. Production takes "time," but time holds no terrors.

So financial structure itself—the fact that production is externally financed—does not matter; it has no effect on equilibrium. If owners and entrepreneurs exchanged capital and consumption goods in competitive markets, the solution of this model would be indistinguishable from the case of internally-financed production. To see this, consider two scenarios. In both scenarios, suppose that owners and entrepreneurs have identical utility functions. In the first scenario, owners both receive capital-good endowments and produce consumption goods or sell capital goods, based on their leisure/consumption preferences. In the second scenario, the situation is the same except that prices are precoordinated and set competitively. Given that information acquisition and market transactions are costless, the two scenarios generate an identical equilibrium.[7]

3. Probabilistic Risk and Financial Structure

We now abstract from asymmetric information and consider how exogenous uncertainty in the "weak" form of risk, taken on its own, affects the link between financial structure and economic outcomes.

Risk is introduced as follows. Neither owners nor entrepreneurs know in advance of production precisely how much consumption-good output will result from the application of entrepreneurial effort and capital. To simplify matters, one of two possible levels of output may result: $\bar{Q}(K^e, W^e(K^e))$ or $\underline{Q}(K^e, W^e(K^e))$, where $\bar{Q}(K^e, W^e(K^e)) > \underline{Q}(K^e, W^e(K^e))$ for any K^e. Associated with these respective outcomes are the publicly-known probabilities α and $(1 - \alpha)$, where $0 < \alpha < 1$.

It is important to specify what *risk* entails. A stochastic shock creates risk when

1. This shock can be understood accurately as generated by a stable probability distribution.
2. All agents have ready, costless knowledge of this distribution (or it is equally costly for all agents to learn about it), independent of each agent's previous actions and endowment.
3. The probability of the shock is independent of any agent's actions.
4. The uncertainty created for individual agents by the stochastic shock is eliminated within the economy as a whole, via either aggregation across agents or repeated draws through time—that is, "systemic risk" is ruled out.

Entrepreneurs now maximize expected utility, $EU^e = U(EQ^e, (1 - W^e(K^e)))$, where $EQ^e = EQ(K^e, W^e(K^e)) - P^K K^e(1 + r)$. But entrepreneurs can readily identify the expectation of $Q(K^e)$ as the "average" Q outcome, $\hat{Q}$, where $\hat{Q}(K^e) = \alpha \underline{Q}(K^e, W^e(K^e)) + (1 - \alpha)\hat{Q}(K^e, W^e(K^e))$. While the precise outcome ex ante is uncertain, there is sufficient information available about

---

7. If owners' and entrepreneurs' utility functions differ, then these agents cannot transfer resources as they would if they were solitary planners. But agents' "loss" from interacting with other agents with different utility functions is due not to the addition of a credit relation but to the shift from centralized to decentralized resource allocation.

the stochastic term to allow its reexpression in this deterministic form. To have any other expectation under the circumstances would be myopic. The entrepreneur's first-order condition for K^e then equals

$$\bar{Q}_1 - \alpha(\bar{Q}_1 - \underline{Q}_1) - Q_2 W_{K^e}^e = \bar{P}^K (1 + r) + (U_2^e/U_1^e)W_{K^e}^e. \tag{4}$$

Here the deterministic variable P^K is replaced by the expectation of P^K, $\hat{P}^K$, where $\hat{P}^K = P^K(\alpha\bar{Q} + (1 - \alpha)\underline{Q})$. The optimal values of K^e and Q^e may be larger or smaller than in the perfect-information case, depending on the magnitude of α.

The shock to Q may affect owners, depending on whether the owner faces enough entrepreneur borrowers that any systemic risk is eliminated. For convenience, owners face no systemic risk and thus maximize knowing precisely the Q that will be drawn on average across their borrower pool. The owners' maximization problem remains as in section 2 and their first-order condition over r again equals (3), with one exception: the price of the capital good, P^K, is now replaced by its ex ante expectation, $\hat{P}^K$. This does not affect the *form* of the equilibrium condition, however. Again, the owner's equilibrium relative to the certainty case depends on α.[8]

As in section 2, this model achieves an optimum that is "first best" given the information available (and given monopoly in the lending market). As Radner put it in considering "Equilibrium under Uncertainty," the term " 'optimum' here must be interpreted as optimum relative to a given structure of information in the economy," (1968: 45). Financial structure—the fact of borrowing and lending—clearly has no effect on this optimum, as in section 2. Agents may have differing degrees of risk aversion, just as they may have differing leisure/consumption preferences; and these differences will have an impact on relative prices in the credit market. But the credit market is merely an incidental mechanism for sorting out differential risk preferences; any market that opened between agents with different risk preferences would yield prices reflecting this differential.

The key to this scenario is that the use of subjective probabilities eliminates any effects of uncertainty per se on decision making. The uncertain technology is made certainty equivalent by parameterizing its behavior. Obviously, the assertion that agents know the possible states of the world and the likelihood of each assumes these agents are operating in a stable decisional environment. Implicitly, decisions are made repetitively, so that prior experi-

---

8. If each owner were *not* exactly sure ex ante what the magnitude of Q in her market area would be, little would change. If a proportion of $\bar{Q}$ other than α is drawn, the ex post relative price of the capital good, P^K, will differ from that anticipated. This ex ante/ex post deviation can, in turn, be eliminated through aggregation over a large enough number of owners. Again, an insurance market for owners can be imagined that eliminates their systemic risk completely.

ence serves as an error-correction mechanism. The firm under probabilistic risk thus uses realizations to make ex ante uncertain outcomes predictable in the limit.

What behavioral consequences does risk have for owner and entrepreneur? Risk creates the possibility of a wedge between ex ante anticipations and ex post realizations. Ex post outcomes may yield either windfalls or shortfalls. But ex ante/ex post differences have no impact, because risk is insurable in this model. Risk is an individual, not aggregate, phenomenon; so insurance arrangements can be worked out among the model's agents on the basis of the (accurately) anticipated Q. Markets do not span all outcome possibilities; but contingent contracts can fill in gaps in the market ranks. Welfare losses are entailed (compared to the certainty case) only to the extent that insurance contracts are costly. By the same logic, irreversibility plays no role herein because there is no regret.

So thus far Fazzari's argument holds up. Risk can be insured against, allowing agents to treat ex ante expected equilibria as effectively deterministic. The coordination of resources achieved under external financing differs from that possible with internal finance only to the extent that agents' utility functions differ, save for the deadweight loss due to the cost of writing insurance contracts.

4. Asymmetric Information and New Keynesian Credit Rationing

We now add asymmetric information to the model of section 2. At the same time, we allow for no exogenous uncertainty. This allows us to demonstrate that endogenous uncertainty alone is sufficient for financial structure to matter. So while risk often appears in new Keynesian models, it is not analytically essential. We first generate an adverse selection example like Fazzari's, and then we consider moral hazard.

We change the assumption set of section 2 in three ways. First, individual entrepreneurs differ behaviorally ex post—that is, better or worse, from owners' perspective as creditors—after they have signed contracts. Second, entrepreneurs' behavioral differences—whether rooted in capacity or in effort—are "private information," not costlessly and publicly observable. This assumption implies asymmetric information, since some agents do not know what other agents know.[9] These two assumptions of differential agent behavior that cannot be readily observed interact with a feature already embedded in this model—divergent interests between owner and entrepreneurs—to create a principal/agent "problem."

---

9. Useful introductions to asymmetric information are Arrow 1986 and Rasmusen 1989.

A third shift from section 2 is required: we must posit that it is costly to make contracts and hence to use markets. If it were not, then the principal could eliminate behavioral indeterminacy simply by writing extremely specific contracts. Efficient arms-length contracts could then be written, as when (in principle) compensating wage differentials are deployed in labor contracts. But if it is costly to make contracts behaviorally specific, then beyond some point the return from eliminating residual indeterminacy is exceeded by the cost of closing the behavioral gap further. We assume here that arms-length contracts eliminating the principal/agent problem cannot be written.

There are two root causes of variable ex post entrepreneur (agent) behavior and hence two independent problems of asymmetric information: differences in agents' ability levels—that is, in agent *type*; and differences in intensity of work, holding agent type fixed. If agents are of different types, and if agents of a "lesser" type are less desired by principals, then these agents have an incentive to hide their type from principals. Under adverse selection, price increases will not cause the lesser-type agents to self-selectively leave the market: the price mechanism thus malfunctions. By contrast, moral hazard arises when agents' capacity to perform ex post—after the contract is signed—differs, even if ex ante these agents' performance capabilities are equal.

In the presence of either adverse selection or moral hazard, then, arms-length contracts are imperfect devices for social coordination. Principals are not helpless: they can limit their risk exposure when faced with adverse selection and can reduce moral hazard by either inducing or compelling desired performance. But these adjustments by principals would be unnecessary under symmetric information.

4.1 Adverse Selection and Financial Structure

Adverse selection may arise whenever a principal must choose from among agents of different, but indistinguishable ex ante, types. The principal's problem is to sift through an excess supply of agents to find those with superior quality, but the usual response of raising the prevailing price will, given adverse selection, reduce the average quality of agents and hence expected return.

To introduce the notion of entrepreneurial type, suppose that output for any given level of capital and entrepreneurial effort varies according to each entrepreneur's competence level. This competence is captured by an index number μ. So output equals $\mu Q(K^e, W^e)$. Entrepreneurs' μ levels in any period are unobservable; and any given owner's μ in one period is independent of its value in another.

Now the owner would like to avoid lending to entrepreneurs with low μ

values. A number of strategies available to owners in this situation have been suggested, including signaling and screening. Here, however, we assume that owners may only set prices and accept loan applications; they cannot bar low-μ entrepreneurs from their credit market. So the owner has no way out of this adverse selection problem.

The owner receives loan demand from numerous entrepreneurs. These entrepreneurs' μ levels differ, but they are indistinguishable to the owner ex ante. The average level of μ for all entrepreneurs demanding loans from any owner is given by $\bar{\mu}$. All entrepreneurs, even incompetent ones (those with low μ), would rather obtain capital and produce no matter what interest rate they are charged, even if they will be unable to repay the owner. We need this stark assumption because we have completely ruled out exogenous uncertainty. To motivate the assumption, suppose entrepreneurs first consume their own portion of Q^e before turning over the remainder—a residual, in effect— to the owner from whom they have borrowed. Then a low μ will jeopardize the consumption enjoyment and utility of the owner before it begins to reduce that of the entrepreneur in question. Let entrepreneurs' default rate as a proportion of all borrowers be given by δ.

A final assumption must be made for adverse selection to crop up here. That is, suppose some entrepreneurs have access to the reserve technology; this access is correlated positively but imperfectly with μ. So the owner does not know which entrepreneurs have this access but does know that μ and this access are correlated. By implication, $\bar{\mu} = \bar{\mu}(r)$, where $\bar{\mu}_r < 0$; and $\delta = \delta(\bar{\mu}(r))$, where $\delta_{\bar{\mu}} < 0$.

Now we can reconsider the owner's loan-market behavior. The owner no longer earns r with certainty but instead anticipates an expected r, wherein $Er = r - \hat{\delta}(\bar{\mu}(r))$ and $\hat{\delta}$ is the expected level of δ. There are several approaches to finding equilibrium in this type of situation; see Stiglitz 1987. Under one plausible approach,[10] the owner's first-order condition over its choice variable r equals

$$\left(r - \hat{\delta}(\bar{\mu}(r))\right)P^K(\epsilon_r^{-1} + 1) = R + (U_S^o/U_Q^o)W_{NK^e}^o \tag{5}$$

That is, the expected marginal return from loans to entrepreneurs is set equal to the marginal return from using the residual technology, including the utility

---

10. Specifically, the owner first determines the loan rate that maximizes expected return per dollar of loan. This simply involves differentiating $Er = r - \hat{\delta}(\bar{\mu}(r))$ by r, setting the resulting expression to zero, and rearranging to find $r = \hat{\delta}_{\bar{\mu}}\bar{\mu}_r$. The owner then substitutes the resulting optimum-return loan rate, r^*, into its expected profit equation and chooses a profit-maximizing loan level. The owner's maximand thus equals $U^o(Q^o, S^o(NK^e))$, where Q^o is now given by $Q^o = (r^* - \hat{\delta}(\bar{\mu}(l^*)))P^KNK^e + R(K^R)$. This maximization occurs subject to the condition that the resulting loan volume, L, is no greater than the level of loan demand given r^*, that is, $L(r^*)$. As long as this condition is not binding, the owner's first-order condition is given by condition (5).

gain from additional leisure. The marginal return from loans takes into account the average quality of entrepreneurs that will demand credit given the loan rate set by the owner.

The effect of adverse selection on the equilibrium loan rate is indeterminate; if we compare conditions (3) and (5), we see that this effect depends on whether the equilibrium r under perfect information generates too high a level of defaults, and hence too low a net return, compared with a lower r. When credit demand exceeds credit supply at this r, credit is rationed in equilibrium. The loan rate is then "sticky"—insensitive to changes in loan demand—because of optimizing owner behavior in the presence of asymmetric information. In any static equilibrium, otherwise-creditworthy borrowers may be denied credit.

Financial structure matters in this case because external finance leads to credit rationing; this outcome clearly would not occur if agents were self-financing. By contrast with the scenario of section 3, at least some of the risk to which principals are exposed here is uninsurable. The owner cannot obtain insurance, because an insurance contract cannot be priced until the quantity of insurance provided is known.[11]

4.2 Moral Hazard and Financial Structure

We inject moral hazard into the perfect-information case of section 2 by assuming that entrepreneurs' "work" no longer depends simply on the hours on the job, but instead, "work" equals the product of two distinct variables: effort per hour on the job, e; and hours worked, H^e. In effect, $W^e = eH^e$. Ceteris paribus, an increase in e will increase total output Q. As before, entrepreneurs' hours on the job plus their hours idle sum to one. But leisure and hence utility is greater, the less is work; in effect, U^o decreases in e and in H^e separately. Suppose hours worked, H^e, is determined exclusively by K^e. If entrepreneurs can choose their own e level—which we term e^*—then S^e remains as under perfect information. But to the extent that entrepreneurs expend any other e, their utility is reduced. This can be depicted formally by redefining S^e in entrepreneurs' utility function as $(1 - H^e - (e - e^*)H^e)$.

Moral hazard arises if (1) entrepreneurs' degree of work effort is not prespecified by the terms of the loan contract itself, and (2) entrepreneurs do not work as hard as owners think they should under the terms of the loan contract. In effect, the ex ante terms of the contract do not lock in the ex post performance of agents whose goals conflict at least partially with the principal's goal.

---

11. Feasible insurance contracts would have to specify both a price and a quantity—but then, by definition, the owner could not purchase as much insurance as she needed at a given price. The classic treatment of this problem is Rothschild and Stiglitz 1976.

A principal/agent *problem* arises when owners want more effort than entrepreneurs will freely put forth. Analytically, there is a missing market for entrepreneurial effort. Owners derive more total return, Q^o, when entrepreneurs are working extra hard than when entrepreneurs are working at their own pace. This gain in the owner's total return is explained by the rise in P^K, the relative price of capital goods, as more consumer goods are produced.

The question for the owner is how to extract additional effort from entrepreneurs. In general, principals can induce and/or coerce agents into going along with their preferences. Here, the owner coerces agents into harder work by (1) offering the inducement of a higher consumption level, and (2) monitoring entrepreneurs' work effort to browbeat them into higher effort. These two elements are linked: the more intensively entrepreneurs are monitored, the more effort they expend and the more consumption output they produce, and hence the more output there is to distribute. Let the monitoring level be given by m; the owner's m depends on how much the owner works at monitoring. This suggests that we redefine the owner's "work" function as $W^o = W^o(NK^e, m)$.

The owner "moves" first. In so doing, the owner is assumed to know entrepreneurs' reaction function—that is, how much effort will rise as monitoring intensity increases. Here, we simply write $e = e(m)$ and assume the owner knows this function exactly. This function is convex—$e_m > 0$ and $e_{mm} < 0$.

Assuming an interior solution, the owner's maximand over the choice variables r and m can be written as follows:

$$\Lambda^o = U^o\big((rP^K(e(m)))NK^e + R(K - NK^e), 1 - W^o(NK^e, m)\big).$$

The owner's first-order conditions are

$$rP^K(e(m))(\epsilon_r^{-1} + 1) = R + (U_2^o/U_1^o)W_{NK^e}^o \tag{6}$$

$$rNK^e P_e^K e_m = (U_2^o/U_1^o)W_m^o \tag{7}$$

Note that the owner's optimal r condition, though identical in form to the case of perfect information, represents a different equilibrium since P^K under perfect information differs from the $P^K(e(m))$ obtained under asymmetric information.

We can combine (6) and (7) into the owner's condition:

$$rP^K(\epsilon_r^{-1} + 1) = R + rNK^e P_e^K e_m \frac{W_{NK^e}^0}{W_m^0}$$

This combined condition can be contrasted with the owner's equilibrium condition in the perfect-information case (condition (3)). The only difference arises in the last term on the right-hand side, reflecting the additional cost of ensuring that entrepreneurs perform as the owner wishes.

Now consider entrepreneurs' optimum. The owners' offer to entrepreneurs must be just sweet enough to induce the amount of effort they want entrepreneurs to expend given the monitoring effort the owners are making. This *incentive compatibility* constraint forces owners to increase entrepreneurs' income share as the tradeoff for more agent effort.[12] Then entrepreneurs' first-order conditions over choice variable K^e and over their incentive compatibility constraint are

$$Q_1 - Q_2 eH_{K^e}^e + \lambda_2\big(H_{K^e}^e (e(m) - e^*)\big) =$$

$$rP^K + (U_2^e/U_1^e)\big(eH_{K^e}^e + \lambda_2(e(m) - e^*)\big) \tag{8}$$

$$U^e\big(Q(K^e, e(m)H^e(K^e)), (1 - H^e(K^e)(e(m) - e^*) - H^e(K^e)) -$$

$$rP^K e(m)K^e\big) \geq U^e\big(Q(K^e, e^* H^e(K^e)),$$

$$(1 - H^e(K^e)) - rP^K(e^*)K^e\big) \tag{9}$$

Equation (9) depicts the incentive compatibility constraint: it demonstrates that entrepreneurs' utility from behaving as the owner wants them to must at least equal their utility from behaving as they would given no monitoring of their effort.

As in the previous scenarios, a solution can be developed on the basis of equations (6)–(9). The specifics of this solution remain unimportant. The main points for the relationship between moral hazard and financial structure are these. The owners do not ration credit, since in the absence of exogenous uncertainty they can determine ex ante whether entrepreneurs are creditworthy and can then monitor those who are awarded credit ex post. Financial structure matters here because owners now engage in costly monitoring. The presence of this additional cost for owners ensures that the equilibrium loan rate will be higher than under perfect information. This in turn implies a lower loan volume than before. So financial structure matters in that moral hazard

---

12. Entrepreneurs' maximand in this case follows: $\Lambda^e = U^e(Q(K^e, eH^e(K^e)) - rP^K K^e$, $(1 - H^e - (e - e^*)H^e)) + \lambda_2(U^e(Q(K^e, eH^e(K^e)), (1 - H^e(K^e)(e - e^*) - H^e(K^e)) - rP^K eK^e - U^e(Q(K^e, e^* H^e(K^e)), (1 - H^e(K^e))) - rP^K(e^*)K^e)$.

induces owners to reduce loan volume and hence the level of economic activity.

5. Asymmetric Information plus Risk

This section injects risk, as portrayed in section 3, into the adverse-selection and moral-hazard scenarios of sections 4.1 and 4.2. We will see this "narrow" exogenous uncertainty has a marginal impact—changing its quantitative but not its qualitative nature—on the "pure" asymmetric-information equilibria reached in section 4.

5.1 Adverse Selection plus Risk

In the adverse-selection scenario of section 4.1, entrepreneurs' creditworthiness depended on their competence, captured in the index number μ; the owner did not know any entrepreneur's μ but knew the average competence level (and hence default risk) of the entrepreneurial borrower pool for any given loan rate.

Now suppose that entrepreneurial output depends not just on entrepreneurs' capital volume and competence levels but on a shock to Q. As in section 2, Q takes on just two values, either $\bar{Q}$ or $\underline{Q}$, with respective probabilities α and $(1 - \alpha)$. The occurrence of either Q is independent of the value of μ.

The precise effect of the random shock to Q on the principal/agent equilibrium depends on when its magnitude becomes known. We suppose here that actual Q is revealed only after both the owner principal and agent entrepreneurs have made binding contractual commitments. Then entrepreneurs' choice problem is precisely the same as under risk alone (section 3) except that their expected return is composed of the two prospective returns $\mu\bar{Q}(K^e, W^e(K^e))$ and $\mu\underline{Q}(K^e, W^e(K^e))$, weighted by α and $(1 - \alpha)$, respectively. Apart from the μ term, the remainder of the problem remains as before. The entrepreneur's first-order condition now equals

$$\mu\bar{Q}_1 - \alpha\mu(\bar{Q}_1 - \underline{Q}_1) + Q_2 W_{K^e}^e = \hat{P}^K (1 + r) + (U_5^c/U_1^c)W_{K^e}^e. \quad (10)$$

If $(\mu(\bar{Q}_1 - \alpha(\bar{Q}_1 - \underline{Q}_1)) < \mu Q_1$, then the entrepreneur's relative utility from working is lower compared to the pure adverse-selection case.

The owner, in turn, rations credit here as under adverse selection. The difference with risk is that μ becomes an anticipated μ based on the weighted sum of $\bar{Q}$ and $\underline{Q}$. If $(\mu(\bar{Q}_1 - \alpha(\bar{Q}_1 - \underline{Q}_1)) < \mu Q_1$, then the anticipated default rate, $\hat{\delta}$, is higher than when adverse selection alone exists; so the owner lends less, at a lower rate, than when risk was not considered. The amount of rationing in the loan market increases pari passu. In effect, risk for the owner still comes from nature, but it now takes two forms: each agent draws a Q from nature, no matter what the agent's type; and each agent draws a μ, a type. The owner knows neither the state of nature that will later prevail (Q) nor the agent type.

Clearly, financial structure matters here because credit is rationed in equilibrium, as in section 4.1. Recall that under risk alone, financial structure did not matter because risk to market participants was insurable; and under pure adverse selection, competitive insurance contracts could not be written. Is risk insurable here? In principle, an insurance contract for the *owner* can be written as long as the owner faces no systemic risk. But insurance contracts for *entrepreneurs* cannot be written. The reason is that entrepreneurial "type" is an unobservable. So it would be impossible to determine for any entrepreneur, ex post, whether a low Q outcome was due to inferior entrepreneurial "type" or to a bad random draw. Every entrepreneur would have an incentive to lie if asked the result on her stochastic shock. So the agent with private information cannot insure against a bad draw because perverse incentive effects and revelation problems scare off insurers. And because the good is not storable, there is no way to hedge by hoarding in "fat" periods against the occurrence of "lean" periods.

So the combination of adverse selection with risk forces agents, but not principals, to fully absorb the effect of a bad draw from nature. Ex ante, this will cause entrepreneurs (the agents) to shift closer to leisure as they compare the tradeoff between consumption (and production) and leisure. Ex post, what happens to entrepreneurs depends on what Q they draw. If they get a high Q, they will have a windfall; if a low Q, a shortfall. It is conceivable that the entrepreneurs' Q draw may be so low that they cannot fully repay the owner. In effect, entrepreneurs may fully or partially default either because of their own incompetence or nature's perversity.[13]

This last point has, perhaps, not been adequately appreciated in new Keynesian models that do make use of risk (exogenous uncertainty). For one thing, new Keynesian models usually focus the spotlight on their asymmetric information features, bringing in exogenous uncertainty for analytical or conceptual convenience.[14] For another, new Keynesian formal models have typically been built using one-period frameworks. Whereas static frameworks

---

13. Allowing for the possibility of default in our formal model would add considerably to its complexity without generating qualitatively new insight into the problem at hand. We forego it for this reason.

14. It is, after all, a bit difficult to imagine a really convincing adverse-selection story in a world that lacks any exogenous uncertainty. But if an exogenous uncertainty device such as mean-preserving spread is introduced, one can posit the existence of "risk-loving" agents or exploit the interaction between a distribution of returns and limited liability in the case of a bad draw.

may be necessitated by the intricacy of information-based interactions within these models, the failure to consider the dynamic movement from ex ante to ex post to ex ante puts to one side the independent and potentially corrosive effects of exogenous uncertainty within these models.

5.2 Moral Hazard plus Risk

We now add risk of the same type to the moral-hazard environment of section 4.2. In that scenario, output varied with entrepreneurial effort, and the owner wanted entrepreneurs to work harder than they would have autonomously. So the owner put a monitoring system in place to coerce the extra effort from entrepreneurs. This pivotal feature of that moral-hazard scenario remains in place. What is different is that any given entrepreneurial effort level will not now yield a given Q with certainty. Instead, Q is subject to a stochastic shock and may equal either $\bar{Q}$ or $\underline{Q}$.

This mixed case of endogenous uncertainty and risk puts principals and agents in a similar position to that of the mixed case just considered, so the treatment of this case is brief.

Entrepreneurs' maximand is no longer the deterministic function $Q(K^e, eH^e(K^e))$, but the anticipated value of Q given some (e, K^e): $\hat{Q}(K^e, eH^e(K^e)) = \alpha\bar{Q}(K^e, eH^e(K^e)) + (1 - \alpha)\underline{Q}(K^e, eH^e(K^e))$. It is readily shown that entrepreneurs' first-order condition over K^e given $e(m) > e^*$ is essentially a combination of conditions (4) and (8):

$$\bar{Q}_1 - \alpha(\bar{Q}_1 - \underline{Q}_1) - Q_2 \, eH^e_{K^e} + \lambda_2\big(H^e_{K^e}\,(e(m) - e^*)\big) =$$

$$r\hat{P}^K + (U^s_2/U^s_1)\big(eH^e_{K^e} + \lambda_2(e(m) - e^*)\big) \tag{11}$$

where $\hat{P}^K = P^K(\hat{Q}(K^e, eH^e(K^e)))$.

The owner's course of action, in turn, remains unchanged except for one particular. The owner's first-order conditions remain (6) and (7), but in these equations P^K must be interpreted differently. Under moral hazard and risk, P^K is replaced by $\hat{P}^K$ (as just defined) in the owner's decision problem.

As in section 4.2, financial structure affects economic outcomes in that costly monitoring of borrower behavior occurs. There is one important difference from section 5.1: here, *both* owner and entrepreneurs should be able to insure themselves against risk. The argument for the owner remains the same: the owner faces no systemic risk. But entrepreneurs here do not have the type-revelation problem that made insurance impossible in scenario 5.1; so they are insurable too.

6 Keynesian Uncertainty and Financial Structure

In this section, we move out of the well-behaved world of subjective uncertainty and into the world of chapter 12 of Keynes's *General Theory*.[15] Our emphasis, in this section, is on the analytical and behavioral consequences of Keynesian uncertainty as opposed to risk.

In a world of risk, agents can take comfort in knowing that their fates are in the hands of stochastic processes with sufficiently regular properties as to be comprehended using statistical tools. Not so in the world of Keynesian uncertainty. Shackle, Davidson, and others, following Keynes's lead, argue that decision makers in any economic tableau will be faced with at least some "momentous decisions" (in Shackle's phrase). These are decisions wherein a significant amount of time will pass between choice and outcome; the circumstances surrounding the project in question are nonrepeatable; it is costly or impossible to reverse course once the decision is made, and the outcome is crucial to the agent's well-being.

To understand that decisions like these pervade economic life is not to somehow enter an invisible realm wherein secret truths are revealed to initiates. It is, rather, a matter of learning how to appreciate the deep consequences of some of the everyday assumptions that are made about how economies work. The model developed here has an everyday character; indeed, it was specified with that aim in mind. So where are the latent traces of Keynesian uncertainty in this model?

Four characteristics of risk were set out in section 3; given these characteristics, probabilistic risk adequately describes the exogenous-uncertainty version of our model. One way of grasping Keynesian uncertainty is to see it as what results when each of these four characteristics of risk is violated. Here we reverse each of the characteristics of this list, considering in each case the implications for behavior in the model of section 3.

1. The trajectory of any economic variable cannot be described as having a deterministic "trend," with "stochastic variation" around that trend understood on the basis of a stable probability distribution.

What is there in section 3 that agents do not know? They know they will receive $\bar{Q}$ or $\underline{Q}$ from nature, and their chances of either are governed by α. They simply do not know which draw they will get. But then they know a great deal, enough that the situation quickly becomes certainty equivalent and

15. This conception was developed by Keynes (1936; 1937) and Knight (1964), and has been explored at length in post-Keynesian writing, especially that of Shackle (1974), Davidson (1978, 1991), and Vickers (1987).

insurable. In contrasting risk with Keynesian uncertainty, G. L. S. Shackle wrote that *"actuarial risk . . . is a form of knowledge, but uncertainty . . . is another name for ignorance"* (1952, 115–116). What if these agents were instead truly ignorant about the magnitude of Q? Suppose substantial time passed between the ex ante decisions made at each period's initiation and the ex post realizations at period's end; suppose agents understand the passage through each period as a unique, nonrepeatable event. It would then be impossible to chop any realization into a "trend" and "stochastic variation" component with any confidence that one was capturing anything more than one's own hypothesis about the next event.

Further, implanting Keynesian uncertainty about Q into the model has the effect of unraveling or reducing the decisional consequences of the other conventions of the equilibrium world within this model. If the range of Q cannot be accurately gauged, and Q obeys the law of no stochastic process, then well-behaved continuous utility functions either cannot be constructed or become merely secondary to the agent's problems at hand. Outcomes are evidently not auctioneered (precoordinated). There is no residual technology, no safe harbor for the "risk averse." How then do agents proceed?

2. No agent is handed any costless information that provides sure-fire insight into the state of affairs in the economy.

How do agents operate in an environment of Keynesian uncertainty— that is, how do they form expectations? They cannot rely simply on price signals or market processes. Prices cannot by definition encompass all pertinent information needed to properly rank alternatives. Commitments requiring time to unfold, such as investment in Q, necessarily involve leaps into the unknown by irreducibly ignorant agents. This is not to suggest that agents will take their ignorance lying down. Suggestive historical information will be collected and analyzed, methods of extrapolating and predicting will be developed, and institutional mechanisms for synthesizing insights will be established. Agents develop ex ante anticipations, even knowing these have no scientific status or reliable properties, and compare these with ex post outcomes.

The confidence placed in any such method of uncertainty reduction depends on the size of ex ante/ex post gaps in recent experience. In stable periods, agents may construct subjective probabilities as they would in a merely risky world. In turbulent times, a method such as "potential surprise" may be substituted, in which attention centers on a smaller set of outcomes that arrest attention (Vickers 1987, chapter 12). In a yet more turbulent world, expectations about future outcomes may collapse onto points, instead of ranges, and may become more wishlike or willful than scientific. In this case, the stop/go decision may rest almost purely on unconstrained animal spirits (Davidson 1991). Agents may shift endogenously among these methods of making decisions. As outcome turbulence increases, agents may place less trust in the past as a guide to the future; they may also change their degree of risk aversion and become more wary of irreversible commitments. The definition of "rational behavior" itself becomes contextually contingent.

Because knowledge about events important to agents is socially constructed, and because no disciplining metric is available to tell agents which pieces of knowledge are "correct," and which "incorrect," the Harsanyi doctrine is routinely violated. To say that all agents do not know the same things is not the same as saying that all agents have identical knowledge about the things they do not know. The latter statement follows from the former only if assumptions are made about knowledge that are inadmissible in a Keynesian uncertain environment.

3. Agents cannot be precisely certain to what extent their own actions and to what extent "shocks" are responsible for the outcomes they experience.

A defining characteristic of the model of risk in section 3 is that agents can clearly distinguish the consequences of nature's actions from their own. But when there is no way to get "objective" knowledge about "nature's actions," the ability to discriminate between the consequences of shocks and of behaviors erodes.

Any knowledge constructed here about future events is necessarily self-referential and circular. One draws out those lessons from experience that one understands how to draw out, but not other lessons. What will happen at any future moment depends on what agents do, and also on what agents believe agents will do. But then a Heisenberg uncertainty principle exists at the root of the search for useful predictive knowledge.

One important implication of this circularity is that the distinction between exogenous and endogenous uncertainty fades. The principals and agents in section 3 understood their own capabilities, and the capabilities of their technologies, independent of the shocks to which they might be exposed. But suppose this is not so. Then agents could not know whether they had succeeded because they were good or because they were lucky.

4. It is impossible to preclude the possibility of systemic risk, because the economy has no parameters.

Thus far, we have shown that some of the crucial assumptions required for games of incomplete information are violated. Kreps observes (1990,

466–467) that some crucial shared assumptions underlie games of incomplete information. Among these are the ideas that there is a single, consistent "base model" in the minds of all the players, and that players agree on the prior distribution of initial states. These assumptions create a decisional context in which the model "closes" at a certain point.

But by replacing the features of risk with those of Keynesian uncertainty, we have cast the players in this "game" (in Gordon's phrase) adrift from the shore. What looms largest is not the equilibrium reached at any given point in time but the problem of getting from one moment to the next when so little is known. Actions are driven not just by the search for the trade winds but by the fear of the sudden, unpredictable storm.

In a risky world, agents can be partially or fully insured against the consequences of bad draws. A Keynesian uncertain world, on the contrary, anticipates continual feedback among ex post realizations, ex ante anticipations, expectations, and actions. Because the economy's stochastic variation obeys no parameters, agents' exposure in their momentous decisions cannot be insured. Such uninsurable decisions are inherently irreversible, and regret is a constant presence in agents' calculations.

6.1 Risk, Keynesian Uncertainty and Financial Structure

Our four anticharacteristics, taken together, considerably transform the way we think about the exogenous uncertainty discussed in section 3. This economy has no parameters and thus no given natural arc of movement through time and space. Any apparent stability in outcomes is due to a complex of historical forces. Agents' knowledge, especially knowledge pertinent to momentous decisions, is constructed, not given. The idea of "efficient" prices disappears: prices are what they are because of a particular set of perceptions, judgments, and decisions; and these all may change.

This post-Keynesian context has several important implications for financial structure. First, credit rationing may arise from the consequences of Keynesian uncertainty *alone*. To see this, note that attitudes about appropriate behavior depend both on views of the likely outcomes of uncertain processes and on views about the consequences of erring. But these assessments could both differ between the owner and the entrepreneur borrower, because no objective or subjective standard for the stochastic truth exists.

In the model of section 3, suppose the owner's attitude toward the entrepreneur's likelihood of success becomes more pessimistic (a high Q, $\bar{Q}$, is seen as less likely) while the entrepreneur's own attitude does not. Then the owner assigns a lower value to α, the entrepreneur a higher one. This expectational divergence could arise because of the entrepreneur's inherent commitment to her own well-being; it could arise from divergent readings of prior experience; from different methods for constructing α, and so on. In any event, owners, because they perceive α differently, will regard the entrepreneurs' "warranted" loan demand as being less, for any given r, than will entrepreneurs; owners' award of credit to the firm will thus be regarded by entrepreneurs as a rationing of credit in that it is less than entrepreneurs' own loan demand. There is no ready way of undoing this rationing, because it arises from different agents' views of a complex, changing whole.

There is a second implication of Keynesian uncertainty for why financial structure matters: the increased possibility of cumulative disequilibria due to ex ante/ex post tension. In an environment of Keynesian uncertainty, expectational shifts and the behavioral shifts that result can have cumulative effects in markets and on other agents. All agents are subject to feedback effects from other agents' expectational or behavioral shifts. Having external financial links among principals and agents in such an environment intensifies the likely magnitude of the shocks to expectations and to behavior of any given shift. Agents who have made irreversible commitments may become insolvent and may have to make dramatic adjustments in the future after experiencing an ex post shock.

7. Asymmetric Information plus Keynesian Uncertainty

In section 5, risk was added to the asymmetric information scenarios of section 4 with little apparent effect. In the moral-hazard scenario, both principals' and agents' leisure/consumption choices were shifted somewhat. But though risk was costly, it was readily borne: there was no systemic risk, and idiosyncratic risks were insurable. In the adverse-selection scenario, the main effect of a risky Q was to shift both owner and entrepreneurs on their utility surfaces. Here, the owner could insure against the risk itself, whereas entrepreneurs could not. This uninsurability opens up the possibility of stock/flow imbalances for entrepreneurs, including bankruptcy with a sufficiently bad draw. But this consequence is not acknowledged. This is hardly surprising, given that none of the other deviations from risk are allowed into the model. There is uninsurable risk, but it remains merely risk nonetheless.

But the idea that exogenous uncertainty has benign implications in an endogenous uncertainty setting is not borne out when it takes the form of Keynesian uncertainty. Under Keynesian uncertainty stochastic outcomes are nonparametric, stock/flow imbalances may be large and persistent, and agents' methods of assessing the outcomes of stochastic processes are historically contingent.

Taking any of these aspects seriously throws the adequacy of asymmetric information scenarios of financial structure into doubt. If, for example, the entrepreneurial quality variable, μ, is nonparametric, the suggested method for characterizing ex ante equilibrium, and hence for characterizing firm and bank behavior, falls apart. At minimum, this scenario would require more structure: one would have to specify how estimates of future variables were constructed in the absence of a parametric basis for so doing. This is the problem that Crotty's essay (in this volume) addresses.

Removing the assumption that the stochastic variables in section 5 center around their equilibrium values would have a similarly profound affect. In particular, it would suggest that any equilibrium found by the economy was purely temporary, since the entire historical context of the economy was—and thus economic outcomes themselves were—continually evolving. Attention could not be so narrowly focused on how exogenous shocks disturbed prior equilibria (as, for example, in Bernanke's 1983 paper, which limits its attention to how financial relations transmit the effects of a shock).

These asymmetric information scenarios would also be profoundly affected by allowing for feedback effects from ex post outcomes on ex ante decision making. Owner and/or entrepreneurs may react to bad draws by reassessing their attitude toward risk taking, leading to further feedback effects on other agents. And if there are no parameters underlying stochastic outcomes, agents may have diverse assessments of these evolving situations, and hence of their own best behavioral responses to this uncertainty. The notion that a representative agent (or firm) constitutes an adequate microfoundation for an aggregate analysis implicitly depends on the assumption that all agents will be much the same. But if they are not, then the assumption that any one's actions are independent of overall market conditions could err; in fact, the market could move against this agent.

In sum, if Keynesian uncertainty and not risk accompanies asymmetric-information scenarios, their sufficiency as microfoundations for aggregate analyses is doubtful. The notion of a (single) representative agent as a micro-foundational device becomes problematic, as does the idea that aggregate outcomes center on equilibrium values that are occasionally disturbed by exogenous shocks; and the agent's method of assessing stochastic outcomes would have to be considered explicitly. The asymmetric information aspect of frameworks encompassing Keynesian uncertainty can be retained, but only subject to a drastic reinterpretation of asymmetric information "parameters."

8. Conclusion

This paper began with Fazzari's challenge to the post-Keynesian notion of financial instability. Fazzari's core question is this: Is asymmetric information a sufficient basis for a Keynesian framework in which financial structure matters? His answer is yes. The two approaches are compatible, but not independent: the asymmetric information underlying new Keynesian analyses is necessary and sufficient to generate a role for financial structure. In drawing this conclusion, Fazzari discounted the importance of exogenous uncertainty for financial structure. Similarly, Bernanke has asserted that Minsky's financial instability—realized stock/flow disturbances—is relatively unimportant because it requires the assumption that agents are irrational.

The analysis in this paper has suggested that Fazzari and Bernanke reached these conclusions because they equated exogenous uncertainty with risk. It is true that when risk alone is added to a model of symmetric information, financial structure does not "matter." It is true that financial structure "matters"—because it can lead to credit rationing in equilibrium or costly monitoring—in models characterized by endogenous uncertainty and no exogenous uncertainty.

But if we think of exogenous uncertainty as involving Keynesian uncertainty, not risk, then Fazzari's and Bernanke's conclusions do not hold. For one thing, credit can be rationed in Keynesian uncertain contexts without any asymmetric information. For another, financial structure matters in the sense of worsening the prospect of stock/flow imbalances—that is, of making more likely the endogenous buildup and overextension of debt. Stock/flow imbalances are ruled out when risk but not Keynesian uncertainty exists: "too much credit" cannot build up when the volume of credit determined by creditors and debtors is always optimal because both can insure against adverse draws. But when insurance contracts cannot be written, as under Keynesian uncertainty, credit can be overextended despite agents' best efforts to be "rational." It is also true that the meaning of "rationality" itself is unclear in a Keynesian uncertain environment.

Fazzari and Bernanke have misinterpreted these points in their dismissals of the post-Keynesian perspective as a behavioral theory, again, because they see exogenous uncertainty as entailing only risk, not something more. That there is something more in the nature of uncertainty is understood by many economists who are playing Gordon's game. The question is whether that something more can be appropriated conceptually. Kreps writes,

> If the economic environment is as continuously complex as chess, then we would seem to have wasted a lot of time studying equilibrium techniques. But (of course) the implicit assertion is that economic situations are not in all respects so complex that equilibrium analysis is irrelevant. Pieces of the economic environment, parts of the greater 'game' each economic actor plays, are amenable to the form of analysis we have used. The problem comes in applying the forms of analysis we have used for larger chunks of the game each actor faces; especially chunks that involve large stretches of time and much uncertainty. (773)

This brings us to the compatibility of these two approaches. We have seen that risk is not only consistent with new Keynesian asymmetric information, but may even make this framework more behaviorally plausible. But Keynesian uncertainty is incompatible with at least some interpretations of asymmetric information models. Keynesian uncertainty suggests a world without parameters, in which agent behavior is extremely sensitive to outcomes. A representative-firm model cannot serve as an adequate microfoundation for aggregate outcomes in such a setting.

This is not to argue that asymmetric information is unimportant. One may gain important insights into credit markets by considering how principals overcome asymmetric information gaps even when those markets are surrounded by Keynesian uncertainty. The observed outcomes in at least some credit markets surely reflect, among other things, the extent of information asymmetry, the level of monitoring technology, and even the social structures that link debtors and creditors (as Varian (1990) argues). All these are elements taken up directly in new Keynesian models.

What is required to make Keynesian uncertainty and asymmetric information compatible is an appropriate reinterpretation of the "parameters" of asymmetric information frameworks, and a willingness to explore basic questions about microfoundational behavior at a deeper level than heretofore. Just as they emphasize different types of uncertainty, the post- and new Keynesian approaches to financial structure emphasize different aspects of credit relations. Both types of uncertainty are clearly present in the world: so Keynesian analyses of financial structure should encompass the entire spectrum of uncertainty, from asymmetric information to Keynesian uncertainty.

REFERENCES

Arrow, Kenneth. 1986. "Agency and the Market," in *Handbook of Mathematical Economics, Vol. III*, ed. Kenneth Arrow and M.D. Intriligator. Amsterdam: North-Holland, 1183–1195.
Bernanke, Ben. 1983. "Nonmonetary Effects of Financial Crises in the Propagation of the Great Depression," *American Economic Review* 73 (June).
Crotty, James. 1990. "Owner-Manager Conflict and Financial Theories of Investment: A Critical Evaluation of Keynes, Minsky, and Tobin," *Journal of Post Keynesian Economics*.
Davidson, Paul. 1978. *Money in the Real World*. New York: Macmillan.
Davidson, Paul. 1991. "Is Probability Theory Relevant for Uncertainty? A Post Keynesian Perspective," *Journal of Economic Perspectives* 5(1): 129–144.
Debreu, Gerard. 1959. *Theory of Value*. New York: Wiley.
Dymski, Gary, and Robert Pollin. 1992. "Hyman Minsky as Hedgehog: The Power of the Wall Street Paradigm" in *Financial Conditions and Macroeconomic Performance*, ed. Steven Fazzari and Dmitri Papadimitriou. Armonk, NY: M.E. Sharpe, 27–62.

Fazzari, Steven. 1992. "Keynesian Theories of Investment: Neo-, Post-, and New," in *Financial Conditions and Macroeconomic Performance*. Edited by Steven Fazzari and Dmitri Papadimitriou. M.E. Sharpe (Armonk, NY): 121–132.

Gertler, Mark. 1988. "Financial Structure and Aggregate Activity," *Journal of Money, Credit, and Banking* 20(3): 559–588.

Gordon, Robert J. 1990. "What is New-Keynesian Economics?" (1990), *Journal of Economic Literature*. 28:3, 1115–1171.

Keynes, John Maynard. 1936. *A General Theory of Employment, Interest, and Prices*. London: Macmillan.

Keynes, John Maynard. 1937. "The General Theory of Employment," *Quarterly Journal of Economics* 51: 209–223.

Knight, Frank. 1964. *Risk, Uncertainty, and Profit*. Augustus Kelley: New York.

Kreps, David. 1990. *A Course in Microeconomic Theory*. Princeton: Princeton University Press.

Mankiw, N. Gregory, 1990. "A Quick Refresher Course in Macroeconomics," *Journal of Economic Literature*. 28(4): 1645–1660.

Minsky, Hyman. 1975. *John Maynard Keynes*. New York: Columbia University Press.

Minsky, Hyman. 1986. *Stabilizing an Unstable Economy*. New Haven: Yale University Press.

Radner, Roy. 1968. "Competitive Equilibrium under Uncertainty," *Econometrica* 36: 31–58. Reprinted in *Uncertainty in Economics*, ed. Peter Diamond and Michael Rothschild. New York: Academic Press: 1978.

Rasmusen, Eric. 1989. *Games and Information*. Basil Blackwell: London.

Rothschild, Michael and Joseph Stiglitz. 1976 "Equilibrium in Competitive Insurance Markets: An Essay on the Economics of Imperfect Information," *Quarterly Journal of Economics* 90: 629–50.

Shackle, G. L. S. 1952. *Expectation in Economics*. Cambridge: Cambridge University Press.

Shackle, G. L. S. 1974. *Keynesian Kaleidics*. Edinburgh: Edinburgh University Press.

Stiglitz, Joseph E. 1987. "The Causes and Consequences of the Dependence of Quality upon Price," *Journal of Economic Literature*. 25(1): 1–48.

Varian, Hal R. 1990. "Monitoring Agents with Other Agents," *Journal of Institutional and Theoretical Economics*. March, 146:1, 153–174.

Vickers, Douglas. 1987. *Money Capital in the Theory of the Firm*. Cambridge: Cambridge University Press.

CHAPTER 5

Are Keynesian Uncertainty and Macrotheory Compatible? Conventional Decision Making, Institutional Structures, and Conditional Stability in Keynesian Macromodels

*James Crotty**

The theory of capital investment is the cornerstone of the theory of macro-economic dynamics, and the question of whether or not the agents involved in the investment decision have the information needed to make individually and collectively optimal choices is central to capital accumulation theory. New Classical and neoclassical theory assume that they do. Keynesian and Post Keynesian theory assume that they do not. The outcome of many significant debates in macrotheory depends on which theory is correct about this.

In section 1 of this essay I argue that the Keynesians are right about the information question and that once Keynes's views are accepted, neoclassical theory has little to tell us about how to theorize agent choice. We are then confronted with the question: Are a coherent theory of agent choice and a coherent theory of the macroeconomy possible in the seemingly chaotic world of Keynesian uncertainty? And, if they are, how do we construct these theories? Alternatively, was Lucas correct when he pronounced that "in cases of uncertainty, economic reasoning will be of no value" (1981, p. 224)? Is it true that Keynesian uncertainty is "analytically nihilistic . . . [creating an] all-embracing subjectivism" (Coddington 1983, p. 61)?

The main thesis of this paper is that economists can indeed construct coherent theories of agent choice and macrodynamics in a Keynesian world as long as they are willing to add new research methods to their analytical tool kit. Section 2 shows why decision making under uncertainty exhibits what I call "conditional stability," a situation in which behavioral equations will be relatively stable under conditions that hold most of the time. Section 3 then briefly discusses the centrality of institutions to the creation of conditional

*I would like to thank Gary Dymski, Bob Pollin and Douglas Vickers for helpful comments on an earlier draft of this paper.

macroeconomic coherence; however, these sections also argue that both the micro- and macrofoundations of coherence are contradictory in that they create the potential for outbursts of instability even as they help stabilize the economy. Section 4 reiterates the conclusions of the paper.

1. Keynes Versus the New Classicists and Neoclassicists on the Theory of Agent Choice

I first examine New Classical and neoclassical theories of agent choice, especially as they relate to macrotheory. The presumed macrotheoretical objective of these theories is to show how decentralized agent choice generates stable market-clearing macroeconomic equilibrium. We argue that in order to accomplish this, the theories must first assume a predetermined equilibrium to serve as the anchor or center of gravity for agent expectations. That is, they must assume their conclusion in order to prove it.

The first task is to clarify the domain of the Keynesian-Classical debate. Keynesians do not argue that the mainstream approach to choice is universally inappropriate. Some decisions, such as what clothes to buy or what food to eat, are repetitive, made over and over again in similar circumstances. Still other decisions may be unique and important, but reversible; if a choice turns out to have been a poor one, the agent can undo it quickly and without major loss. The debate is not about such decisions. Rather, it is about the correct way to theorize decisions that Shackle has designated "crucial" or "momentous".[1] Crucial decisions are unique or nonrepeatable (in part because they significantly alter the conditions under which they were taken), central to the agent's economic well-being, and reversible only at substantial cost.

The most important crucial decisions in macrotheory are the demand for major capital goods and the portfolio selection decision of financial institutions and wealthy individuals. On both sides of the capital investment decision we have agents who must put a present value on various long-lived assets that are subject to large potential capital losses. To evaluate an investment project, one must estimate the expected profit flows over its lifetime; to rationally compose a portfolio requires estimates of long-term financial asset prices over the agent's planning horizon.[2] The key question confronting the theory of agent choice is: What do the agents know about the future and how do they come to know it?

There are two mainstream approaches to the expectations question: the

---

1. See Shackle 1955 (p. 25), 1972 (p. 384), and 1983–84 (pp. 246–47) for a discussion of crucial decisions.

2. Although long-term financial assets are liquid, their value can undergo substantial decline within a short period of time. Thus, a decision to hold liquid long-term financial assets may not prove to be costlessly reversible.

subjective approach to probability of Savage, Ramsey, or Friedman and the objective approach of Muth, Lucas, or Prescott.[3] Neoclassical theory adopts the former, and New Classical theory the latter. Both assume that agents can compose a list of all possible future economic states—a list *known* to be complete—can assign numerical probabilities to all such states, and therefore can associate a probability distribution of expected returns with every possible choice available to them. Most important, both make the heroic assumption that the agent is absolutely certain that these probability distributions are *knowledge*—the truth, the whole truth, and nothing but the truth about future economic states and the future consequences of current choice.

The main distinction between the subjectivist and objectivist approach is that whereas the latter asserts that expectations are in fact correct or conform to the objective model, the former makes no such claim. "For the subjectivist, in fact, probabilistic knowledge does not necessarily correspond to anything in external reality" (Lawson 1988, p. 41), whereas the objectivist assumes that agents know "the true probability distributions governing the future state of [the markets they deal in] and the present and future states of all others" (Lucas 1981, p. 158). It turns out, however, that for the central question before us this constitutes a distinction without a difference.

Consider the subjectivist agent. There are only two ways that rational agents could logically arrive at the conclusion that they know for certain the true probability distributions of future economic states. First, agents could make a sufficient number of observations from an outcome-generating mechanism (or model) they know with certainty has not changed over the period of observation and will not change over the relevant future. The agents here need not know the particular structure of the model. Second, agents could know with certainty the complete structure and function of the mechanism that will generate all future outcomes, in which case they do not need historical observations to predict future states correctly.

In the absence of both of these conditions, it is *irrational* for agents to believe that their subjective probability distributions are knowledge rather than mere hunch or guesswork. But if either condition does hold, there is no distinction between the subjectivist and objectivist approach: subjective and objective realities are identical in both cases. Thus, either the subjectivist neoclassical theory of rational agent choice implicitly assumes agent irrationality or it is indistinguishable from the objectivist, New Classical theory of agent choice. Note that the charge that neoclassical choice theory posits an irrational agent cannot be deflected by an appeal to positivism or instrumentalism: this charge is based on the logical incompatibility of its assumptions—

---

3. See Lawson 1988 or Davidson 1991 for a discussion of the subjectivist-objectivist distinction.

that subjective and objective distributions have no necessary relation, and that the agent believes that the subjective distribution is knowledge—and not on the lack of realism of the assumption set.[4]

Both classical theories of agent choice use the probability calculus, a statistical theory developed for repetitive and mechanistic games of chance such as roulette or dice. The statistical properties of the probability distributions used in these theories are based on the assumption of at least potentially infinitely repeatable experiments in an unchanged structure.[5] As Davidson has stressed, classical expectations formation theory is applicable only to "ergodic" stochastic processes: "an ergodic stochastic process simply means that averages calculated from past observations can not be persistently different from the time average of future outcomes" (1991, p. 132). In ergodic processes, "economic relationships among variables are timeless (ahistoric) and immutable" (1987, p. 148).

The structure of ergodic stochastic games of chance is unaffected by any particular pattern of observations it generates: a run of sevens will not change the odds at a dice table. Similarly, an ergodic stochastic economic model cannot be affected by the particular choices of the agents who inhabit it; it cannot exhibit *hysteresis* or *path dependency*: the model and its outcomes—the future states of the world—must be independent of agent choice (so that agent choice is not, in any meaningful sense, free). For if future states of the economy were dependent on the pattern of current and future agent choice, if, in Shackle's words, choice was "originative," then every agent would have to know the present and future choices of every other agent (including the process used by each agent to adjust expectations in the light of realized results) in order to know the future. But there is no way, even in principle, that agents could gain knowledge of this kind. Indeed, the impossibility of gaining such knowledge is the foundation of the neoclassical rejection of central planning.

Thus, the neoclassical theory of agent choice is restricted to a world in which agents' decisions do not "create" the future. The axioms of New Classi-

---

4. There is a related problem with subjectivist theory. If subjective probability distributions are not anchored in a pregiven objective equilibrium state, then what can possibly give them stability across time? Conversely, if the subjective probability distributions of orthodox theory were dynamically unstable, then the neoclassical investment function would be unstable as well. In this case, the economy's future time path would itself be unstable because it would depend on unstable subjective probability distributions. Since there is no neoclassical theory of the "laws" governing unstable subjective probabilities, the future would be unknowable. Thus, the core assumption that there exists a predetermined equilibrium path that is independent of agent ignorance and therefore of agent choice is the sine qua non of neoclassical and New Classical investment theory.

5. As Katzner noted, "without the opportunity of at least hypothetical replication, the notion of probability simply does not make sense" (1987, p. 66).

cal and neoclassical expected utility theory hold if and only if the future equilibrium path of the economy and the prices associated with it are pregiven, if they are independent of agent choice, agent forecasting error, and out-of-equilibrium dynamics. That is, these classical and methodologically individualistic theories must assume what they are supposed to prove, by positing a stable market-clearing equilibrium path *prior* to constructing a theory of agent choice. Failure to do so would leave agents with nothing solid to anchor their expectations.[6]

Consider, for example, the auctioneered Walrasian general equilibrium model, the only complete neoclassical model of the *process* through which equilibrium is reached. In this model the equilibrium position is assumed to be independent of the process by which agents move from disequilibrium to equilibrium in logical time. It is thus independent of the "errors" that create the excess supplies and demands of disequilibrium. Indeed, the reason why the model *must* prohibit out-of-equilibrium trading is that every such "false" trade would generate a redistribution of wealth that would alter its equilibrium position and would create income-constrained demand and supply functions that could destroy the stability properties of the model. As Clower (1965) and Leijonhufvud (1968) stressed, with false trading, equilibrium would become a moving target whose location at any point in time would depend on the inherently unpredictable particularities of out-of-equilibrium dynamics. The model would thus be path dependent. The prohibition of false trades and the use of logical time make equilibrium a predetermined center of gravity to which the system is inevitably drawn.

Rational expectations macrotheories are similarly constructed. All of them provide the agent with a stable, correct and predetermined anchor for expectations formation. In some variants, such as the seminal work of John Muth (1961), it is simply asserted that agents know with certainty the true model of the economy. Given this assumption, rational agents will make decisions that are consistent with and reproduce the model. The vexing question of how agents come to know the full properties of a complex system of

---

6. To understand New Classical thinking about this crucial issue, consider Lucas's response to the following question: If people know the true distribution of future outcomes, why are autocorrelated mistakes such a common occurrence?

If you were studying the demand for umbrellas as an economist, you'd get rainfall data by cities, and you wouldn't hesitate for two seconds to assume that everyone living in London knows how much it rains there. That would be assumption number one. And no one would argue with you either. [But] in macroeconomics, people argue about things like that. (In Klamer 1983, p. 43)

What Lucas clearly has in mind is a model in which the distribution of outcomes (like the distribution of rainfall in London) is pregiven and independent of agent decisions (about whether or not to carry umbrellas) and agent errors. Future equilibrium states exist prior to and independent of the agent choice process that is supposed to generate them.

stochastic equations, each of which is subject to exogenous shocks, is not discussed.

In other rational expectations models agents may begin with some degree of ignorance; they then have to learn the true properties of the model. However, the observed outcomes are generated by the true equilibrium system of stochastic equations: the information provided to agents is untainted by their own ignorance. The model keeps generating unbiased information about the means and variances of the true distributions that agents can use to learn the model by, for example, Bayesian learning processes or through the use of time series regressions in which initial serial correlation is eventually incorporated in the forecasting equations.[7]

Yet other variants permit agents to be temporarily confused about, for example, the extent to which observed price changes are permanent or transitory.[8] It thus takes time to learn the complete truth about equilibrium; in the meantime, the economy *can* generate outcomes that are not consistent with its full-information, long-term equilibrium properties. However, since these models also assume that the new long term equilibrium position is unaffected by these temporary deviations from it, agents will eventually learn the truth about the future.

Thus, the quintessential character of New Classical models is not generated solely by the assumption that agents use information rationally, but rather requires the implicit assumption that the future is pregiven and independent of agent choice. Where outcomes *do* reflect agent choice, even if agents use all available information rationally, the New Classical results do not hold. Rational expectations are perfectly consistent with multiple equilibria.[9] They are also—and simultaneously—consistent with unstable equilibria. In a world in which agents cannot know a priori which of all possible stochastic equilibrium models is generating current outcomes but, rather, must try to learn the model through a rational interrogation of the data, instability is quite likely. Basing expectations on "false" data will generate "false" outcomes in an ongoing process that could move the system increasingly further from the initial full-

---

7. "The rational expectations approach is most often applied to models for which the actual outcomes are independent of agents' expectations. . . . In these cases, expectations may be pushed toward rational expectations equilibria by rational learning processes. Assuming that the . . . process is stationary and has well-behaved statistical properties, learning models could be imagined in which agents eventually correctly predict the distributions of variables" (Fazzari 1985, p. 72).

8. See, for example, the discussion in Lucas 1981 (pp. 224–31) or in Sheffrin 1983.

9. See, for example, Fazzari 1985, Bryant 1991, Woodford 1991 or the seminal article on "sunspot" equilibria by Cass and Shell 1983. Sen put the problem nicely. "The sunspot theorists have shown that not only are the existence of sunspot equilibria possible in New Classical models, there is also the possibility of a multiplicity of such equilibria. Therefore, the number of possible dynamic evolutions of a market economy may well be infinite" (1990, p. 565).

information equilibrium.[10] As Fazzari argued, when expectations affect outcomes,

> there are two related problems with the convergence to rational expectations equilibria. First, since agents learn and realized outcomes depend on expectations the uncertain process being forecast cannot possibly be stationary. Learning leads to changing expectations and changes in expectations cause changes in the underlying process. . . . [T]his kind of learning may never reach a self-sustaining state at all. . . . Secondly, suppose a rational expectations equilibrium exists. If the system is away from [it], any agent's expectation formation process must consider the expectations of other agents, since the actual outcome will depend on others' expectations. Hence, it is possible that even an agent who knows the properties of the [equilibrium] would forecast results different from the [equilibrium]. (1985, p. 73)

Finally, when current choice is allowed to influence future states of the world, as it does in the world in which we live, rational use of information is also consistent with a path-dependent macrodynamic process to which the term equilibrium does not properly apply at all. As Keynes once said: "In a world ruled by uncertainty, with an uncertain future linked to an actual present, a final position of equilibrium, such as one deals with in static economics, does not properly exist" (1979, p. 222). Or, as he put it less formally: "Equilibrium is blither" (in Shackle 1972, p. 233).

Keynes's own conception of uncertainty has been described and analyzed in detail by Shackle (1955, 1972), Vickers (1994), Davidson (1991), and many others. Its central thesis is that the future is *unknowable in principle*. Keynes theorized human decision making in a nonergodic, ever-changing economic and social environment. The economic outcomes we observe over time, he argued, are generated by an ever-changing system of agents, agent preferences, expectations, and economic, political, and social institutions, a system of "originative" choice in which future states of the world are in part created by the current agent choice process itself. "What is imagined for a coming period must, in an ultimate sense, help to shape what will, *ex post*, emerge as the ultimate facts of that period" (Shackle 1972, p. 440). Thus, each observation is drawn from a unique generating mechanism whose structure depends on current and future agent choice as well as the future pattern of institutional change, both of which are inherently unpredictable. There can be no pregiven

---

10. "The source of difficulty is that, in models with expectations, there is an aspect of simultaneity in the sense that beliefs affect outcomes and outcomes affect beliefs" (Bullard 1991, p. 57).

center of gravity to anchor the expectations of Keynesian agents; they can never have complete knowledge of the future.

Keynes's clearest treatment of uncertainty appears in the 1937 QJE article. I quote from it at length.

> [In classical theory,] at any given time facts and expectations were assumed to be given in a definite and calculable form; and risks, of which, tho admitted, not much notice was taken, were supposed to be capable of an exact actuarial computation. *The calculus of probability, tho mention of it was kept in the background, was supposed to be capable of reducing uncertainty to the same calculable status as that of certainty itself.* . . .
>
> Actually, however, we have, as a rule, only the vaguest idea of any but the most direct consequences of our acts. . . . Now of all human activities which are affected by this . . . preoccupation [with the remoter consequences of our acts], it happens that one of the most important is economic in character, namely, Wealth. The whole object of the accumulation of Wealth is to produce results . . . at a comparatively distant, and sometimes at an *indefinitely* distant, date. Thus the fact that our knowledge of the future is fluctuating, vague and uncertain, renders Wealth a peculiarly unsuitable subject for the methods of the classical economic theory. . . .
>
> By "uncertain" knowledge, let me explain, I do not mean merely to distinguish what is known for certain from what is only probable. The game of roulette is not subject, in this sense, to uncertainty: nor is the prospect of a victory bond being drawn. . . . Even the weather is only moderately uncertain. The sense in which I am using the term is that in which the prospect of a European war is uncertain, or the price of copper and the rate of interest twenty years hence, or the obsolescence of a new invention, or the position of private wealth-owners in the social system in 1970. About these matters there is no scientific basis on which to form any calculable probability whatever. *We simply do not know.* (1937, pp. 212–14, italics added)

There are at least two ways to formally distinguish Keynes's idea that the future is unknowable in principle from the neoclassical idea that the future is stochastic-stable and that agents know, or act as if they know, this distribution with absolute certainty. First, as Keynes, Shackle, Vickers, and others have stressed, it is logically impossible for agents to assign numerical probabilities to the potentially infinite number of imaginable future states.[11] Even Savage

---

11. See, for example, the discussion in Shackle 1972 (pp. 151, 365, and 400) and Carvalho 1988. Keynes himself observed that in the classical model of agent choice "one arrives presum-

acknowledged that, taken literally, the assumption that agents are able to consider all possible future economic states "is utterly ridiculous" (1954, p. 16). Worse yet, many possible future events are not even imaginable in the present moment: such events obviously cannot be assigned a probability. Shackle created a conceptual category to contain the unimaginable and unimagined events not evaluated by the agent—the "residual hypothesis."[12] Given the existence of the residual hypothesis, the sum of probabilities of evaluated outcomes must fall short of one by a margin of unknowable magnitude, and the neoclassical model is fatally flawed.

Alternatively, we could—for the sake of argument—think of firms and portfolio selectors as somehow forcing themselves to assign expected future returns to all the assets under evaluation even though they are conscious of the fact that their knowledge of the future is inherently incomplete and unreliable. The key point is that such subjective probability distributions would not be knowledge, and—most important—any rational agent would know they were not knowledge. Shackle correctly observed that "subjective probability . . . has no claim to be knowledge" (in Carvalho 1988, p. 71). And Hicks insisted that in the nonergodic real world, people "do not know what is going to happen and know that they do not know what is going to happen. As in history!" (in Davidson 1987, p. 149). Rational agents would *always* be conscious of their lack of complete knowledge of the future.

Therefore, even given the unrealistic assumption of the existence of these distributions, there is a crucial piece of information about agent decision making that would be missing from any subjectivist theory—the extent to

---

ably at the estimation of some system of arranging alternative decisions in order of preference, some of which will provide a norm by being numerical. But that still leaves millions of cases over which one cannot even arrange a preference" (1979, p. 289).

Bausor stated the problem rather elegantly:

Sample spaces must contain *all* possible future outcomes, including the "true" outcome, and this inclusivity must be *known*. No possibility can be neglected, overlooked or unimagined. States of the world, however, are not ontologically existential. Through effort and skill, they must be conjured up from the imagination, and imagination is always vulnerable to fallibility. People constantly experience previously unimagined phenomena, and the potential for surprise remains ubiquitous. Since sets of imagined possible outcomes cannot be known to be complete, no standard for measuring the relative strength of beliefs exists, and distributing weights so that their sum equals one–the construction of a probability measure—becomes invalid and meaningless. (1989–90, pp. 205–06)

12. "If [a business man] seeks to make up a list of the specific distinct things which can happen . . . as a sequel to any one move of his own, he will in the end run out of time for its compiling, will realize that there is no end to such a task, and will be driven to finish off his list with a residual hypothesis, an acknowledgement that any one of the things he has listed can happen, and also any number of other things unthought of and incapable of being envisaged before the deadline of decision has come; a pandora's box of possibilities beyond the reach of formulation" (Shackle 1972, p. 22).

which the agents believe in the *meaningfulness* of their forecasts or, in Keynes's words, the "weight of belief" or "the degree of rational belief" the agents assign to these probabilities. When knowledge of the future is subjective and imperfect, as it always is, the expectations of rational agents can never be fully and adequately represented solely by probability distributions because such distributions fail to incorporate the agents' own understanding of the degree of incompleteness of their knowledge. These functions neglect the agents' "confidence" in the meaningfulness of the forecasts—"how highly we rate the likelihood of our best forecast turning out to be quite wrong" (Keynes 1936, p. 148).

Keynes stressed the centrality of agents' consciousness of their ignorance: the state of confidence plays a crucial role in his theory of the investment decision. "The state of confidence [in the ability to make meaningful forecasts] is relevant because it is one of the major factors determining [investment]" (1936, p. 149). The central role of confidence in the investment decision-making process has disappeared from mainstream Keynesian models and cannot exist by assumption in New Classical and neoclassical models.

It is important to distinguish "optimism" and the neoclassical concept of "risk" from Keynes's degree of "confidence." Optimism means that the expected value of the subjective probability distribution of the expected return on an asset is high or attractive. Risk refers to the variance of the distribution or the degree of dispersion about the mean. Confidence is a measure of the extent to which agents believe that their best forecast or most preferred probability distribution reflects the "truth" about the future or conforms to the "objective" process that will generate future outcomes. Since a firm conviction concerning the future requires time to develop and take root in the consciousness of the agent, confidence should be closely related—though not identical—to the degree of *rootedness* of the forecast or its relative stability across time.[13]

Suppose, for example, that management's best guess about market conditions ten years from now is fluid or flighty over time. Suppose that the best guess shifts substantially from week to week or month to month. Suppose that the future looks so unpredictable that management wouldn't bet a nickel that its best guess was "true." If the best forecast about the future is flighty and unrooted across time, if it has no dynamic stability, then management must not have confidence in its ability to forecast the future.

Clearly, changes in the degree of confidence will shift the investment function even if our hypothetical subjective probability distribution is held

---

13. It should be noted that stability of the expectations function may be a necessary but not a sufficient condition for the development of a high degree of confidence. It is possible to have a relatively stable best forecast in which one does not have much confidence. The more likely case, however, is that confidence is eroded by frequent unexpected change in the relevant information available to the agent.

constant. An attractive subjective probability distribution in which management has no confidence will not provide a sufficient incentive to induce the firm to accumulate risky, illiquid physical capital. Keynes tells us that "if we expect large changes but are very uncertain as to what precise form these changes will take, then our *confidence* [in our ability to forecast] will be quite weak" (1936, p. 148). When confidence is weak, the incentive to invest in physical capital or to hold long-term financial assets is blunted.

The main point is this. In Keynes's model, the future time path of the economy depends on the decisions taken by agents conscious of their ignorance. They cannot obtain information about the future in which they have complete confidence because there is no predetermined future that is independent of the blind groping of ignorant agents. There is no roulette wheel. Keynes thus breaks the logical chain found in neoclassical or New Classical models linking agents (with given endowments and preferences) through the hard data represented by market prices and true probabilistic knowledge of the future to *determinate* (and often "correct," "rational," and optimal) decisions and outcomes. Keynes's markets do not provide his agents with sufficient information to predetermine their decisions. Agents must create or, as Shackle put it, must imagine a substantial part of the information used to make decisions. They must also decide on the degree of confidence they have in the information thus created. Clearly, agent choice under such conditions is a nondetermistic and originative process.

Thus, in a world of uncertainty there is an *empty space* in the logical chain linking agent characteristics and hard data to agent decisions. New Classical or neoclassical theories of choice are impotent in this environment because they define "rationality" as the optimization of a known objective function given complete and correct knowledge of the effects on outcomes of all possible rival courses of action. When the information required to logically connect decision to outcome is inadequate and undependable, New Classical and neoclassical theories have nothing—literally—to say about how agents choose. "Uncertainty recognized confronts rational economic man with the insoluble Humian puzzle, what do we do when we do not know the consequences of what we do? In the frame of rational economic man, the problem has no answer" (Fitzgibbons 1988 p. 83).

The main conclusion of this section is that the neoclassical theory of rational choice is not only irrational, in a Keynesian world it is also a methodological dead end. The obvious theoretical question, then, is where do we go from here? Is a world of true uncertainty inherently chaotic and untheorizable, as so many neoclassical economists presume?[14] Or, rather, is it possible

---

14. Woodford observed that "there is doubtless a fear that free use of the hypothesis of expectational instability makes things too easy. Any event, it might be argued, can be 'explained' after the fact by positing an arbitrary shift in expectations" (1991, p. 77).

to construct a theory of the logic and process of a nondeterminist Keynesian economy? If so, what methodology is appropriate and what properties would the theory possess?

Any attempt to answer these questions must confront the following dilemma. In a world of uncertainty the inherently unpredictable decisions of agents with genuine freedom of choice make future economic states nondeterministic. From the purely microeconomic perspective of the "isolated" agent, then, the path of the economy through time is extremely open ended, bounded only by the limits of technical knowledge, the natural environment, and the individual imagination. Yet history demonstrates that capitalist economies move through time with a substantial degree of order and continuity that is disrupted only on occasion by bursts of disorderly and discontinuous change. Thus, history shows agent choice to be, to a significant degree, bounded, constrained and coordinated—not entirely chaotic and unpredictable—much of the time.

The challenge to macrotheory, then, is to incorporate and reflect this dialectical tension between the nondeterminism inherent in individual choice under true uncertainty and the imperfect but significant order and continuity imposed on agent choice by the economic and social institutions and the decision-making "conventions" within which agents evolve and decide. As Fernando Carvalho wrote in one of the few insightful discussions of this tension: "There is a conflict between the order of the [economic] mechanism and the imagination of the solitary person which must be resolved" (1983–84, p. 269).

Much of macrotheory suffers from the failure to treat this dialectical relation in a balanced way. New Classical and neoclassical theory insist on determinism and nonoriginative, unfree agent choice. Shackle, on the other hand, though he recognizes the bounds placed on choice by "natural laws" and mentions on occasion the significance of conventions in the theory of agent choice, places inordinate and unbalanced stress on the limitlessness of imaginative decision making.[15] He has little to say about the institutions that determine which individuals will play what roles in our class-structured, hierarchical society, that mold agent attitudes and preferences, and that help create conditionally stable consensus forecasts and conventional wisdom out of the potentially unstable and infinitely disparate visions of the future held by managers and financial investors. "Shackle's approach . . . overemphasizes the freedom of the agent and underestimates the influence of conditions other than his own imagination. In this context, orderliness becomes an external necessity or constraint, something that cannot be explained *within* Shackle's theory" (Carvalho 1983–84, p. 270).

---

15. Of course, not all Post Keynesian work is vulnerable to this criticism.

Indeed, Shackle has little to say about the *macrostructure* and properties of the economic system, about how and why the system-as-an-organic-whole moves from relative order and smooth reproduction to disorder and crisis and back again. Rather, his most inspired work focuses on decision making by the isolated agent, a microeconomic question. His "potential surprise" function, for example, is a nondistributional expectations function that underpins a theory of agent choice at a point in time. He also has little to say—and may indeed believe that there is nothing that can be said—about the macrodynamic properties of an institutionally structured system of such agents. The one-sidedness of Shacklean theories of uncertainty may be one reason why "Keynes's (and Post Keynesian) economics is frequently accused of being nihilistic" (Carvalho 1988, p. 78).

The main thesis of this essay is that a macrotheory that acknowledges the centrality of uncertainty need not be nihilistic provided that it incorporates the sources of conditional stability built into the capitalist system.[16] We identify, at the most abstract level, two such sources, both stressed by Keynes: "conventional" expectations and confidence formation; and the institutional structure of the economy (and the society). The integrated effects of these two dimensions of economic life generate both the conditional stability and the periods of disorder that characterize the economic record.

It must be emphasized that the balance between order and disorder as well as the endogeneity or exogeneity of the sources of instability and crisis in the model will depend crucially on the character of the structural theory adopted, on whether it exhibits neoclassical, Keynesian, Kaleckian, or Marxian tendencies. In order to maintain our focus on the central methodological issues of the essay rather than on differences between conflicting structural theories we will attempt to keep the argument primarily in the spirit of Keynes's work, except as noted in the text.

In the section to follow we examine in some detail the contribution to conditional stability made by the theory of conventional expectations and confidence formation. Section 3 then briefly discusses the dialectical relation between institutional structures and economic order.

2. Human Agency and Conventional Decision Making

To help us understand the uniqueness of Keynes's treatment of agent choice, we will entertain the following thought experiment. Consider how a rational neoclassical agent inserted into the unfamiliar world of Keynesian uncertainty might deal with the choice problem. A neoclassical agent has well-defined

---

16. This thesis is also explored in an interesting paper by Lawson (1985), whose general line of argument is similar in spirit to the one made in this essay.

objectives but, in this case, would know that the available data base is inadequate to its task. Let us assume, however, that agents are familiar with the broad contours of economic history, that agents know that the economy exhibits a reasonable degree of coherence most of the time, interrupted on occasion by economic crises or financial panics.

Under these conditions, agents might well decide that some form of adaptive or extrapolative expectations function would generate predictions that were quite serviceable on average; however, they would also be aware that expectations thus formed would, from time to time, be disastrously mistaken. For those decisions that Shackle has termed crucial, the fact that agents would never know at what point catastrophe might strike would be especially chilling. As rational agents, they could never put the potential for a catastrophic crucial decision out of mind.

Thus, neoclassical agents might never develop sufficient *confidence* in the meaningfulness or truth content of extrapolative expectations to justify a positive decision in a crucial choice. They might be perpetually prevented from undertaking significant risky investment by a chronic case of liquidity preference: the economy could sink into a state of permanent stagnation. But this would represent a contradiction because we started with the realistic assumption that the economy is characterized by a history of fairly orderly motion (including relatively orderly cyclical patterns) punctuated with occasional bouts of instability (including abrupt and discontinuous cycle downturns).

Keynes himself engaged in precisely this thought experiment in *The General Theory* and came to the same conclusion. Keep in mind that the "spontaneous optimism" and "animal spirits" referred to in the following quote cannot characterize neoclassical agents.

> A large proportion of our positive activities depend on spontaneous optimism rather than on a mathematical expectation. . . . Most, probably, of our decisions to do something positive, the full consequences of which will be drawn out over many days to come, can only be taken as the result of animal spirits—of a spontaneous urge to action rather than inaction, and not as the outcome of a weighted average of quantitative benefits multiplied by quantitative probabilities. . . . If animal spirits are dimmed and the spontaneous optimism falters, leaving us to depend on nothing but a mathematical expectation, enterprise will fade and die. (1936, pp. 161–62)

Clearly, then, a Keynesian theory of decision making under uncertainty must have a theory of agency consistent with its unique premises; it cannot be constructed with displaced neoclassical agents. Neither the ontology nor the epistemology of neoclassical choice theory will do.

In chapter 12 of *The General Theory* Keynes posed the central problem of the theory of agent choice. Firms and wealth holders *must* make investment and portfolio selection decisions; they cannot avoid them. "We do not know what the future holds. Nevertheless, as living and moving beings, we are forced to act" (Keynes 1973b, p. 124). These decisions will profoundly influence their future economic and social status; wrong decisions in "crucial" circumstances will destroy managerial careers or eliminate wealth holders from their rentier positions. Agents, therefore, care deeply about the quality of their decisions; however, the information they need to assure safe, effective or optimal decisions is in principle unknowable.

With Keynes, we have to ask two basic questions. First, what effect would confrontation with decision-making dilemmas of this kind have on the constitution of agents? Second, what kind of decision-making process would such agents follow? An answer to the first question is required before we can address the second one. Keynes assumed that *agents are socially and endogenously-constituted human beings*, not autonomously constituted, lifeless Walrasian calculating machines. As he put it, "man himself is in great measure a creature of circumstances and changes with them" (in Rotheim 1989–90, p. 321).[17] The theory of agent choice, therefore, must reflect both the social constitution of the agent (which is contingent on, and changes with, the institutions, values, and practices specific to time and place) as well as the psychological complexity of the human-being-in-society.

Humans are distinguished from Walrasian atoms in this theory in two ways. First, the relation between agent and social environment is dialectical and interactive. Although individuals' values, preferences, modes of understanding, and so forth are socially constructed, through individual and collective action people transform their decision-making environment over time by, among other things, creating new institutions and adopting new practices designed to reduce the harmful effects of uncertainty.[18]

Second, because they are fully human, agents have a deep psychological need to create the illusion of order and continuity even where these things may

---

17. As Hayek argued, people's "whole nature and character is determined through their existence in society" (1948, p. 6). Discussing Keynes's methodology, Rotheim noted that the "nature of the individual as well as her perception of herself are functions of and change with her interactions with other individuals . . . The individual's very nature is molded by the social context in which she exists and in which she attempts to make decisions" (Rotheim 1989–90, pp. 322–33).

18. Lawson (1985) refers to Keynes's approach to the agent-structure problem as "societal interactionism."

not exist. "Part of the explanation which we are seeking is to be found in psychological phenomena" (Keynes 1971, p. 322). Both attributes of Keynesian agents, we shall see, help generate and sustain stability. We first examine Keynes's view of the effect on choice of the psychological need to reduce our perception of uncertainty. (The role of institutions in reducing uncertainty is considered in the next section.)

Keynes argues that even though "we simply do not know" the information that we must have to make safe decisions, we have a human need "to behave in a manner which saves our faces as rational, economic men" (1937, p. 214), a manner that allows us the comfort of the illusion of safety and rationality. People want to believe that they are in the same position in which economists place neoclassical agents, with all the information required to make optimal choices, even though they know at some subconscious or barely conscious level that it is not so. Keynes tells us that we have a psychological need to calm our anxieties, to remove the constant stress created by forced decision making under inadequate information, a need that is neither irrational nor socially or economically dysfunctional. We have, psychologists instruct us, a powerful need to reduce our "cognitive dissonance." We have good reason, in other words, to try to "overlook this awkward fact" that the reproduction of our economic and social status requires a knowledge of things that, in fact, "we simply do not know." In Keynes's words: "Peace and comfort of mind require that we should hide from ourselves how little we foresee" (1973b, p. 124). Though little has been written about this psychological propensity of the agent, it is an essential cornerstone of Keynes's theory.

Paradoxically, New Classical and neoclassical theories of agent choice are themselves a reflection of this deep-seated human need to impose knowledge, order, and controllability—rationality—on our environment even where it is patently clear that these characteristics are simply not there. Although no economist would claim to know someone who believes that he or she has certain and complete knowledge of the future, in their theoretical work most economists hold with ferocity to the assumption that everyone believes they have such knowledge precisely because it creates the comforting vision of a world of rationality, a world subject to conscious human control. As Shackle wryly observed: "Better a contradiction in terms than acknowledge a chink, let alone a gaping rent, in the armour of rationality" (1972, p. 115).

To help us accomplish this calming of our nerves, Keynes argues, we collectively develop a "conventional" process of expectations and confidence formation. Keynes's concept of conventional decision making is a sine qua non of Keynesian macrotheory. It is also one of Keynes's most important and most radical theoretical innovations.

The dictionary definition of conventional as "arising from custom and tradition" captures Keynes's meaning to some degree. In place of the complete information appropriate to the fairy-tale world of neoclassical agent choice, Keynes substitutes an expectations formation and decision-making process based on custom, habit, tradition, instinct, and other socially constituted practices that make sense only in a model of human agency in an environment of genuine uncertainty.[19]

Keynes's most extensive discussion of conventional decision-making appears in his 1937 *QJE* article. We quote from it at length because it highlights a number of crucial assumptions of his theory of agent choice. We save our faces as rational economic men, he argues, in the following ways.

(1) We assume that the present is a much more serviceable guide to the future than a candid examination of past experience would show it to have been hitherto. In other words we largely ignore the prospect of future changes about the actual character of which we know nothing.

(2) We assume that the *existing* state of opinion as expressed in prices and the character of existing output is based on a *correct* summing up of future prospects, so that we can accept it as such unless and until something new and relevant comes into the picture.

(3) Knowing that our own individual judgment is worthless, we endeavor to fall back on the judgment of the rest of the world which is perhaps better informed. That is, we endeavor to conform with the behavior of the majority or the average. The psychology of a society of individuals each of whom is endeavoring to copy the others leads to what we may strictly term a *conventional* judgment. (1937, pp. 214–15)

There are six propositions concerning a conventional theory of expectations and confidence formation that I wish to entertain here.

1. The conventions to which Keynes refers serve a dual purpose. The first is obvious: conventional expectations formation creates or imagines the previously missing data needed to link rival choices to expected outcomes. Conventions, Keynes tells us, are a "substitute for knowledge" (1973, p. 124).

Much more important, however, conventions calm our nerves and save our faces because they create *confidence* that expectations thus formed have a

---

19. In a recent study of decision making in financial markets, Zeckhauser, Patel, and Hendricks (1991) show that investors, "for whom rationality by itself provides little guidance as to what [choices] are appropriate" (p. 6), follow simple rules and heuristics (such as "barn-door closing," "regret avoidance," "status quo bias," and "herd behavior") that are excellent examples of the kind of behavioral conventions we have in mind.

degree of meaningfulness or validity or truth-content sufficient to sustain an investment decision of great moment for the agent.[20] This creation of confidence in the meaningfulness of forecasts or in the "scientific" character of the "conventional wisdom" is absolutely essential to both the growth potential and the conditional stability of the Keynesian model. Of course, the reason why an agent can sensibly attribute a quasi-objective or quasi-scientific character to conventional expectations is that conventions are socially constituted and socially and externally sanctioned. They are not mere idiosyncratic figments of the individual's imagination. For example, when the collective wisdom of "Wall Street" (as reflected in the views of the business and financial press, investor newsletters, television's market analysts, and so forth) is near unanimous in predicting a buoyant stock market, it is not unreasonable for an individual investor to conclude that this expectation has a solid foundation. After all, the institutions and individuals who constitute "Wall Street" are professionals and insiders, knowledgeable students of the market whose expertise in these matters is richly rewarded. To assume that this collection of experts is as ignorant of the future as the individual investor is to question the rationality of our economic and social institutions.

The willingness of Keynesian agents to believe that their expectations are firmly founded distinguishes them from neoclassical-agents-in-a-Keynesian-world and permits them to overcome the propensity toward perpetual liquidity preference that Keynes associated with the "nothing but a mathematical expectation" methodology of mainstream theories of agent choice. Conventions prevent agents from being perpetually confused and perhaps even psychologically immobilized by their comprehension of the extreme precariousness of their economic status. In the end, it is the propensity of agents to believe in the solidity and validity of the conventional forecast and not some innate or genetically transmitted "spontaneous urge to action" that defeats the forces of ignorance and prevents perpetual stagnation or perpetual chaos in a Keynesian world.[21]

Given the centrality of the psychological dimensions of confidence formation to Keynes's theory, it is surprising that the Post Keynesian literature

20. Samuels stresses the social and psychological underpinnings of the concept of confidence as it is used here. He comments on "the role of [convention] as psychic balm, to assuage the anxiety consequent to our living in a world of radical indeterminacy (uncertainty)" and observes that the "notion of 'confident' is essentially psychological and involves intersubjectivity and therefore both the internal psychological needs and/or drives of the individual and the sociology of the individual's relevant group, as well as questions of the nature and degree of commitment and consensus" (1991, p. 511).

21. Winslow complains that Keynes "does not explain why consciousness of fundamental uncertainty produces incapacitating anxiety or why and how use of the conventions eliminates this consciousness." He goes on to suggest that an "explanation can be found . . . in psychoanalysis" (1989, p. 1180).

has devoted so little effort to fleshing out its character and properties. Post Keynesians often write as if casual references to "animal spirits" and the simplest treatment of the term *convention* exhausts the Keynesian theory of expectations and confidence formation. This superficial treatment of confidence formation is one excuse given by neoclassicists for not taking Keynes's views on uncertainty more seriously.

For example, Davidson recently observed that "whenever decision makers recognize that they face nonergodic conditions and are therefore ignorant regarding the future, . . . they can sensibly adopt "haven't a clue" behavior one time and "damn the torpedoes" behavior at another, even if this implies that they make arbitrary and inconsistent choices when exposed to the same stimulus over time" (1991, p. 136). In a similar vein Shackle said that Keynes "had, essentially, only one thing to say about expectation: that it eludes reduction to clear and stable principles and laws, and is law unto itself" (1972, p. 180), and that he "gave no hint of a procedure of thought or judgement by which the place of knowledge could be filled" (1983–84, p. 246). And Fitzgibbons referred to the "radical irrationality" of the Keynesian investor, noting that "it is the psychology of *utter irrationality* that causes the volatility of investment behavior" (1988, pp. 80 and 82, italics added). The argument presented here, in contrast, is that Keynes sketched at least the outline of a coherent theory of conventional decision making that has more than "one thing to say" and cannot be adequately characterized by simple phrases such as "animal spirits" or "utter irrationality."

2. A stable set of conventions provides one of the two major sources of conditional stability in a Keynesian model.[22] (A stable set of institutions is the other.) The following quotation about conventional expectations from *The General Theory* helps clarify this point:

> The facts of the existing situation enter, in a sense disproportionately, into the formation of our long-term expectations; our usual practice being to take the existing situation and to project it into the future, modified only to the extent that we have more of less definite reasons for expecting a change. (1936, p. 148)

As long as conventions such as these maintain the allegiance of the majority of agents, they will help provide continuity and predictability to economic life. To assume that the existing state of affairs will continue indefinitely and to project the existing situation into the future is to adopt extrapola-

---

22. Heiner goes so far as to argue that consciousness of true uncertainty is the main source of stability in the economy. "Genuine uncertainty, far from being unanalyzable or irrelevant to understanding behavior, is the very source of the empirical regularity we have sought to explain by excluding uncertainty" (1983, p. 570).

tion as a mode of forecasting. Conventions thus help generate an illusion of continuity that can contribute to the creation of stability when conditions are right. Convention-based extrapolative forecasts help produce order and continuity where chaos might have been.

Extrapolative forecasts certainly can not guarantee perpetual stability; Minsky's theory of financial instability, for example, posits extrapolative expectations that at times become unstable. They are *consistent* with periods of stability, however, because they are not chaotic or discontinuous and can, under certain conditions and for certain periods, generate a series of non-increasing forecast errors. Under such conditions, expectations themselves will not initiate chaos (though they can transmit unstable behavior originating in other sectors or aspects of the model). They thus help make possible those periods of continuity that Keynes called "normal times" and that Joan Robinson referred to as periods of "tranquility." In tranquil periods confidence develops in the conventional view that there will be a great deal of continuity between the future and the relevant past. Under this convention, forecasts may, for a time, take on the character of self-fulfilling prophesies that reinforce confidence in the conventions that sustain extrapolative expectations.[23] For example, in a Kaleckian model the belief that investment will be profitable will stimulate investment, which in turn may stimulate profits. Conversely, extrapolative expectation formation in a deep depression will lead to investment decisions that will reproduce the depression.

Modified extrapolative forecasts can take highly complex forms and they can accommodate "specific reasons to expect a change" (such as the likely electoral victory of one political party or another) without necessarily undermining confidence in the conventions that sustain them. As long as the underlying conventions are maintained, the standard practice of modeling expectations through adaptation and extrapolation from truncated time series will be consistent with Keynes's theory of agent choice. Of course, in a Keynesian world the theorist has to model confidence as well as expectations. Confidence might be modeled using some variant of the following assumption. The degree of confidence in the meaningfulness of a forecast is a positive function of the time that has elapsed since the last major forecast error and of the time that has elapsed since the last "crisis of confidence" occurred. A crisis of confidence will take place when a majority of agents lose faith in the conventions that sustain the expectations-generating process.

Thus, in spite of the radical nature of Keynes's theory of the human agent, a Keynesian model of periods of tranquility can be constructed using

---

23. There "is frequently an insistence [in the expectations literature] upon the extent to which a change in expectations, once begun, produces effects that confirm and strengthen that very belief. . . . Changes in belief become important in generating fluctuations in circumstances in which they tend to be *self-fulfilling*" (Woodford 1991, p. 77).

traditional approaches to expectations formation (excluding, of course, strong versions of the "rational expectations" model). Economists are quite comfortable with models of agent choice conditioned on exogenous preferences; they should be just as comfortable with models of expectation and confidence formation conditioned upon a given set of conventions.

Far from being irrational, then, in a world of true uncertainty conventional decision making turns out to be both individually and socially functional. It is the neoclassical theory of rational choice that is both unrealistic and socially irrational.

3. In the absence of stable conventions (or, more accurately, the allegiance of most agents to a set of such conventions) the expectations-generating process is unstable. Since the process of expectations and confidence formation does not depend solely on hard data and immutable, pregiven economic structures but also depends on the "flimsy foundation" of social conventions and cognitive-dissonance-reducing psychological practices, it is, as Keynes observed, "fragile" and "subject to sudden and violent changes" (1937, p. 215). From time to time events take place that will make it impossible to sustain the convention that the future will look like the present extrapolated. For example, consider the convention that the business community as a collective has a solid understanding of likely future economic developments. Although this particular convention clearly contributes to investor confidence under ordinary circumstance, it is also fragile. On those occasions when the consensus forecast turns out to be disastrously mistaken, the irreducible ignorance of the collective wisdom will be made painfully manifest to all agents, the convention will collapse, and the confidence in the ability to forecast the future that is built on that convention will shatter.

Once confidence in the meaningfulness of the forecasting process is destroyed, irreducible objective uncertainty forces its way into the consciousness of agents, breaking down the conventional barriers they have constructed to conceal it. These are times of crisis and instability, points where the overheated boom cracks or the moderate expansion turns into an overheated boom, times when the conventional belief that the future can be accurately projected from the data describing the past—the main anchor of expectations formation—is destroyed. The fragility of social conventions and practices makes the behavioral equations that determine the marginal efficiency of capital and the cost of financial capital subject to "sudden and violent changes" as well. In Keynes's words:

A conventional valuation which is established as the outcome of the mass psychology of a large number of ignorant individuals is liable to change violently as the result of a sudden fluctuation of opinion due to factors which do not really make much difference to the prospective yield; since there will be no strong roots of conviction to hold it steady. In *abnormal times* in particular, when the hypothesis of an indefinite continuance of the existing state of affairs is less plausible than usual even though there are no express grounds to anticipate a definite change, the market will be subject to waves of optimistic and pessimistic sentiment, which are unreasoning *and yet in a sense legitimate where no solid basis exists for a reasonable calculation.* (1936, p. 154, italics added)[24]

If we expect large changes but are very uncertain as to what precise form these changes will take, then our confidence will be weak. (1936, p. 148)

The first quote reiterates the thesis that the problem of unstable or flighty expectations is rooted not in the psychoses of irrational investors but rather in the fundamental structure of the economy: in a world of uncertainty, "no solid basis exists for a reasonable calculation." The second suggests that a collapse of confidence is itself a sufficient condition for stagnant investment demand even in the unlikely event that the mean expectation is optimistic. Together they imply that there are two different regimes or states of expectation and confidence formation.

Within a given set of conventions it is possible to achieve stability of expectations and confidence formation and a relatively continuous and smooth melding of the present into expectations of the future. However, such stability cannot be eternal. At some point there will be a serious disjuncture between expectations and outcomes that will create a breakdown or rupture of the conventions themselves. Expectations will then be subject to flights of fear and fancy, to the unstable, unpredictable patterns that Shackle called "kaleidoscopic." The shattering of conventional belief will trigger an *ex post* identifiable though *ex ante* unpredictable series of shifts not only in expectations but in the form of the expectations-generating function itself, as well as in agent confidence in the whole process.

---

24. Keynes lays similar stress on the potential instability of all conventionally-grounded behavioral equations in his *QJE* article.

Now a practical theory of the future based on these [conventions] has certain marked characteristics. In particular, being based on so flimsy a foundation, it is subject to sudden and violent changes. The practice of calmness and immobility, of certainty and security, suddenly breaks down. New fears and hopes will, without warning, take charge of human conduct. The forces of disillusion may suddenly impose a new conventional basis of valuation. All these pretty, polite techniques, made for a well-panelled Board Room and a nicely regulated market, are liable to collapse. At all times the vague panic fears and equally vague and unreasoned hopes are not really lulled, and lie but a little way below the surface.

. . . I accuse the classical economic theory of being itself one of these pretty, polite techniques which tries to deal with the present by abstracting from the fact that we know very little about the future. (1937 pp. 214–15)

The concept of a rupture in the conventions that guide expectations and confidence formation is a central component of Keynes's theory of "the crisis—the fact that the substitution of a downward for an upward tendency takes place suddenly and violently" (1936, p. 314). For Keynes, it is the key to the construction of a convincing theoretical explanation of the economic crises and financial panics that have always plagued unregulated capitalism, of those discrete, sharp, "sudden and violent changes" in the pace and direction of economic and financial activity that are inexplicable in orthodox theory (1936, p. 315).

4. The relation between conventional decision making and stability is dialectical and contradictory. Some macrotheories, it is true, tend to blame expectational disappointment on sporadic exogenous shocks or unforeseeable changes in economic institutions or in the political regime. However, the hypothesis that profound expectational disappointment is an endogenous phenomena is compelling. Minsky and Keynes (in chapter 22 of the *General Theory*, for example) focus on the *endogeneity* of financial investor expectation and confidence formation. At some point in most cyclical and secular expansions, they argue, investor expectations outrun the ability of the real sector to generate profit and interest flows; the inevitable clash of run-away investor optimism with the limited ability of the real sector to generate property income can shatter investor allegiance to the conventions of expectation formation. Marxists, on the other hand, locate the cause of profoundly disappointed expectations in endogenous developments in both sectors; the downward pressure on profitability—the "profit squeeze"—that accompanies the end of expansions *and* buoyant investor expectations are jointly responsible for the shattering of conventional belief.[25]

In both Marxian and Keynesian-Minskian theories an expansion of extended vigor will, at some point, generate expectations whose disappointment is inevitable, as well as degrees of financial leverage that make disappointed expectations a likely trigger of financial crises and general instability. In models with realistic endogenous expectations formation, then, allegiance to the conventions of expectation and confidence formation cannot be maintained indefinitely: conventional decision making can never sustain more than *conditional* stability (or what Lawson (1985) refers to as "contingent laws"). Periods of coherence will occasionally be disrupted by bouts of disorder–"as in history."[26]

---

25. See Crotty 1985 for a discussion of the interaction of the real and financial sectors in Marxian theories of instability.

26. The thesis that the inherent unknowability of the future generates irregular cycles of optimism, confusion, and pessimism is of ancient lineage. For example, writing in the late seventeenth century the philosopher Spinoza observed that because men are

> often kept fluctuating pitiably between hope and fear by the uncertainty of fortune's greedily coveted favours, they are consequently . . . very prone to credulity. The human

5. Keynes's process of expectations and confidence formation is irreducibly social and interactive rather than individualistic and isolated. Expectations are not, as a rule, determined by isolated individuals performing complex autoregressions on their personal computers. Rather, every agent needs to divine where other agents think the market is headed. In chapter 12 of *The General Theory* Keynes argues that the situation facing investors in real and in financial capital is similar to that confronted by people who bet on horse races or who try to pick winners in beauty contests. The main task of every agent is to predict the expectations and future actions of other agents.

Indeed, chapter 12 contains one of the earliest "noise trading" or speculative bubble models, a fact noted by Robert Piron (1991) in a recent issue of the *Journal of Economic Perspectives*.[27] The main difference between modern noise-trading theories and Keynes's theory of speculative markets is that Keynes's model does not require the assumption that there exists a subset of irrational investors who refuse to base their expectations on the knowable "fundamentals" all the rational agents use.[28] In a world of true uncertainty there is no immutable, pregiven set of knowable distributions over all future states. The future depends on our expectations of it and the actions we take in the light of these expectations; Keynes's agents know this and therefore quite rationally form their own expectations by trying to guess the expectations of others in an endlessly iterative process.

Moreover, each agent also looks directly to the average or aggregate expectations of the collectivity of agents—to *conventional wisdom*—for guidance and treats group opinion as if it were, by some miracle, untainted by

---

mind is being swayed this way or that in times of doubt, especially when hope and fear are struggling for mastery. . . . No one can have lived in the world without observing that most people when in prosperity are . . . over-brimming with wisdom . . . whereas in adversity they do not know which way to turn. . . . No plan is too futile, too obscure or too fatuous for their adoption: the most frivolous causes will raise them to hope, or plunge them into despair. (1951, p. 3)

Spinoza then notes that "this is a general fact I suppose everyone knows" (1951, p.3). Apparently it took economists several hundred years to forget what everyone once knew. (Karen Graubart brought Spinoza's observations to my attention.)

27. In the *Treatise on Money* Keynes observed that "it may profit the wisest to anticipate mob psychology rather that the real trend of events, and to ape unreason proleptically," and that "it will be to the advantage of better-informed professionals to act in the same way [as the mob]— a short time ahead" (1971, pp. 323 and 324).

28. The standard noise-trading models also contain the following logical contradiction. The existence of pregiven fundamentals is assumed, but the model shows that financial asset prices can remain far from their equilibrium values for years or even for decades. This being the case, the returns on future real assets would have to stray far from their assumed fundamental or equilibrium values for years or even decades. Thus, these pregiven "fundamentals" have no practical meaning, and there is no reason to label some investors rational and others irrational.

the irreducible ignorance of the individuals who compose the group.[29] In sum, individual choice is constructed through complex patterns of social dynamics; as Keynes argued, "the whole is not equal to the sum of its parts" (1973a, p. 262) and macrotheory is more than the aggregation of isolated, autonomous, individual decision makers. In his words, economic theory must be "organic" rather than "atomic."[30]

6. Expectation and confidence formation are institutionally specific and historically contingent processes. Section 3 will argue that complex economic, political, and social structures socialize agents (helping form their attitudes and preferences), influence the allocation of differentially socialized agents to distinct economic roles, and, most important, set boundaries on expected outcomes. But even if we confine ourselves to the issues specific to this section, we will reach the same conclusion: both market and nonmarket institutions are central to expectations and confidence formation and, for this reason alone, agent behavior is institutionally and historically contingent. For example, the institutions and processes that make a corporate capitalist class or a business "community" out of individual capitalists—such as business magazines and trade journals, businessmen's clubs and social organizations, upper-class schools, industry trade associations, political parties, television, and the like—in concert with the institutitions and practices that constitute "the market" itself, influence individual decision making by molding expectations and creating the cultural and ideological climate that nurtures business optimism, confidence, and a positive attitude toward risk taking.

As I have argued elsewhere, (Crotty 1990), Keynes's macrotheory is based on an institutionalist methodology. His theory of agent choice is, therefore, totally incompatible with methodological individualism. Both Keynes's agents and their decision-making processes are socially constituted, changing and evolving whenever there are significant alterations in economic and social institutions, class structures and the social conventions of expectations formation.

To conclude this general discussion of conventional decision making we call attention to two of its implications. First, the assumption of true uncertainty does not imply that chaos must replace order in economic theory or that

29. This is not to deny that since conventional wisdom or the consensus forecast does influence the future direction of economic activity, it indeed provides useful (though limited and incomplete) information to individual agents. For example, sensible short term financial market speculation requires a sense of how the rentier class sees the future. However, the economic future is not solely determined by the hopes and expectations of agents; if that were true, both booms and depressions would be perpetual.

30. Brown-Collier and Bausor (1988) discuss Keynes's important distinction between atomic and organic processes and models. See also Davis 1989, Rotheim 1989–90, and Winslow 1989.

a coherent macrotheory is impossible. A world of uncertainty is characterized by conditional order and conditional stability much of the time. As Keynes once reminded Joan Robinson: "You must not confuse instability with uncertainty" (1973b, p. 137).

Second, the acknowledgment that agents do not possess complete and certain knowledge of the future makes neoclassical methodology an inadequate foundation for the theory of agent choice; the reconstruction of macrotheory requires a methodology appropriate to the study of conventional decision making. As Keynes warned in *The General Theory,* the analysis of uncertainty and conventional decision making is "on a different level of abstraction" than traditional economic theory; "There is not much to be said *a priori,*" or by deduction from first principles, about expectations and confidence formation, and they are not, therefore, amenable to neoclassical methods (1936, p. 149).

Keynes's theory of conventional decision making, on the other hand, though it does not provide a precise and universally applicable answer to the question of how agents make crucial decisions, does suggest a *method* for seeking the answer. Keynes suggested that "our conclusions [should] mainly depend on the actual observation of markets and business psychology" (1936, p. 149). This is sage advice. We cannot identify a realistic set of core axioms and postulates describing agent behavior using abstract analysis alone. Keynes in effect advised economists to add the "mundane" research methods normally associated with other social sciences to their analytical tool kit, methods such as: (1) experiments to learn more about the psychology of individual and group decision making;[31] (2) an examination of sources such as the business press to find out what investors actually think about future prospects at any point in time; (3) concrete studies of the decision-making processes of indus-

---

31. See, for example, Machina's (1987) survey article on the various and sundry problems with the neoclassical theory of choice under uncertainty that have been exposed by experimental studies. Astoundingly, most of the flaws in rational choice theory referred to in this article have occurred in experiments in which agents are confronted with simple mechanistic, ergodic games of chance where "subjects have been presented with explicit (i.e. 'objective') probabilities as part of their decision problem." In addition, "when individuals are asked to formulate probabilities they do not do it correctly" (p. 147). Finally, "evidence . . . suggests that when individuals making decisions under uncertainty are not explicitly asked to form subjective probabilities, they might not do it (or even act as if doing it) at all" (p. 147). How much greater, then, must be the inadequacy of neoclassical choice theory in circumstances in which objective probability distributions linking choice to outcomes simply do not exist?

See also the critique of neoclassical choice theory in Grether and Plott 1979 and in Tversky, Slovic and Kahneman 1990. According to Grether and Plott, experimental data "suggests that no optimization principles of any sort lie behind the simplest of human choices and the uniformity in human choice behavior which lie behind market behavior may result from principles which are of a completely different sort from those generally accepted" (p. 623). For Keynes, these different principles are those that underlie conventional expectation and confidence formation.

trial corporations and financial institutions; and (4) carefully constructed surveys of the state of mind of market participants. Recent survey research by Robert Shiller (1989) and Allan Blinder (1991) and the Donaldson and Lorsch (1983) study of decision making in large industrial corporations are good examples of the kinds of research methods Keynes had in mind.[32]

As noted, once we have established a realistic set of assumptions about agent behavior and an adequate specification of agent objective functions and perceived constraints through such research methods, there is an important role to be played (during conditionally stable periods) by traditional mathematical methods of representation of expectations formation. Such methods may even be of some help in modeling confidence; however, such formal exercises by themselves can only take us so far. Expectations and confidence formation are complex, institutionally contingent, and nondeterministic psychological and social processes that can never be fully or permanently captured by any *fixed* mathematical formula. The only way theorists can be sure that they have adequately represented the sense of the future prevalent in any particular time and place is to follow Keynes's advice and study the actual decision-making heuristics, social practices, and expectational conventions used by entrepreneurs, managers, rentiers, and workers in each concrete institutional setting.

Our conclusion about research methodology can be stated succinctly. Keynes's stress on the humanity of the agent suggests the use of observational and experimental methods for the study of the psychology of individual and group decision-making, and his work on conventional expectations formation calls for the legitimation of institutional, sociological, psychological, historical and survey research methodology as complements to the traditional deductive logic of economic theory. The profession's instrumentalist faith that the realism of our basic assumption set is irrelevant because econometric tests of derived hypotheses will sort truth out for us is more of a tribal superstition than a scientific methodology.[33] Increased reliance on the research methods

---

32. This call for broadening economists' set of research tools is hardly original. Lawson has argued for devoting "more resources into learning about the institutional behaviours, norms, conventions—or, more generally, rule systems—that are produced and reproduced by people in the various spheres of activity" (1985, p. 925). Shiller suggested that "we must base further modelling efforts on observation and human behavior and on the popular models that inform that behavior" (1989, p. 435). As distinguished an economist as Robert Solow, in a forceful rejection of instrumentalism and the use of unrealistic assumptions, stated that "we have no choice but to take seriously our own direct observations of the way economic institutions work. There will, of course, be arguments about the *modus operandi* of different institutions, but there is no reason why they should not be intelligible, orderly, fact-bound arguments" (1988, p. 311). Unfortunately, the profession has yet take such advice seriously.

33. For a discussion of the inherent inadequacy of instrumental methodologies in the social sciences, see Breed 1991 or McCloskey 1985.

used in psychology, history and sociology—the "weaker" social sciences—
can help us construct more realistic theory.

3. The Institutional Foundation of Conditional Stability

To explain the seemingly paradoxical coexistence of uncertainty and conditional stability requires the integration of a theory of conventional decision
making with an understanding of the institutional structure of the economy
and the ways in which it bounds and constrains agent choice. The orderly
reproduction of any society requires that the individuals who compose that
society accept the legitimacy of its basic institutions and that they internalize
to a significant degree the motivations and values associated with them and
respond to the rewards and sanctions inherent in them. Contrary to a fundamental tenet of methodological individualism, individuals do not enter society
armed with some "objective" or "autonomous" set of preferences, values and
motivations with which to assess and possibly to redesign the social structures
they confront. Rather, they are infused through a complex process of socialization with values and motivations that reinforce and reproduce society's
core institutions.

Sensible social theory must try to acknowledge and integrate the insights
of both individualist and structuralist methodology. To be sure, social structures can be changed by groups of individuals. And Keynesians insist that
individuals do have significant freedom of choice; they do not always make
choices consistent with the orderly reproduction of society. But institutions
also socialize individuals, and hierarchical societies do differentially socialize
distinct classes of individuals and assign them to qualitatively different economic and social roles. In addition, institutional structures constrain agent
choice and set bounds on expected economic outcomes.[34] Moreover, institutions are economic agents themselves. Institutional decision making requires
a theory of choice of its own, one that incorporates the effects of particular
organizational structures, strategies, and conventions. Marx's famous dictum
that "men make history, but they do not make it precisely as they choose" is
methodologically on the right track.

Institutional structures, therefore, exert a powerful and often a contro)-
ling influence on individual agent choice. As Carvalho noted:

> Institutions transcend individuals. They enforce constraints on actions
> and events because they orient, constrain and direct the behavior of

---

34. The treatment of semiautonomous institutional structures presented here, in which
institutions mold and constrain agent choice, is obviously in conflict with "rationalist" neoclassical theories in which autonomous agents can choose the set of institutional structures that
maximizes economic efficiency.

individuals. . . . Their existence implies the presence of a social fabric, a mechanism within which individuals perform their functions. (1983–84, p. 271)

For this reason, both microtheory and macrotheory must be institutionally specific and historically contingent.

In a well-functioning economy, relatively stable or inert institutional structures help create order and conditional stability. Indeed, many institutions have as their explicit purpose the reduction of uncertainty and/or the insulation of particular agents from its deleterious effects.[35] Here we can do no more than list several important institutional sources of order as examples of the general phenomenon.

1. *Money and forward contracts.* As discussed in Davidson 1987, 1991 and Kregal 1980, money (or relatively riskless, short-term financial assets) provides an insurance policy—a safe haven—in periods of unusual uncertainty. The ability to postpone risky or irreversible commitments by holding money helps calm nerves, stabilize expectations, and prevent panic. And forward contracts obviously can "limit the outcomes of an otherwise uncertain future" (Davidson 1987, p. 149).

2. *Institutions and practices that regulate competition.* Through cooperative interfirm relations such as oligopolistic structures, trade associations, mergers, enterprise-bank groupings, and so forth, firms have historically attempted to limit the damage done by anarchistic competition. Competition, someone once said, is a struggle to determine the identity of the monopolist. Cooperative arrangements raise average profits and make the future more predictable and controllable. Cooperative relations make it possible for firms to plan the rate of obsolescence of the capital stock and adopt long-term strategies for technical change, price setting, labor relations, R&D, and capital accumulation.

3. *The institutionalization of decision making.* Many important economic decisions have been institutionalized and therefore made more stable in the modern economy. Some institutional decisions are made

---

35. This proposition is consistent with a neoclassical interpretation of the role and function of institutions in economic life. For example, North argues that "throughout history, institutions have been devised by human beings to create order and reduce uncertainty in exchange" (1991, p. 97). In this neoclassical interpretation, however, institutions are merely instruments through which autonomously constituted, rational agents achieve utility maximization. They do not help socialize or constitute agents, and they always assist, never impede, the attainment of efficient economic outcomes. It is a one-sided, rather than a balanced or dialectical, vision of the relation between people and their institutional environment.

through the use of heuristics fixed by law, formal policy, or deeply rooted bureaucratic routine. Even decisions not completely legislated or routinized are often filtered through bureaucratic organizational structures and strategies possessing considerable inertia.[36] Moreover, institutions often have longer planning horizons and more stable objectives than do individual agents.[37] Take the national saving rate as an example. Business saving represents the lion's share of national savings; it consists of depreciation, which is controlled by tax laws, and retained profits, which are in part determined by a stable payout heuristic. Even the bulk of private saving is done through private pension plans and Social Security. As a result of this institutionalization, national savings rates are relatively stable over time (though quite variable across countries because of the diversity of institutional structures).

4. *Government regulation of the macroeconomy.* As events in the 1920s and 1930s demonstrated, in the absence of effective government regulation modern capitalism is neither economically nor politically viable. The success of the Keynesian state in the quarter century following World War II in using macropolicy and lender-of-last-resort powers to set effective lower limits on growth and upper limits on inflation and unemployment provided a solid foundation for long-term expectations formation, helping create both investor optimism *and* confidence in the belief that the future was, in broad outline, predictable.

5. *The Bretton Woods system and international order.* The existence throughout much of the postwar period of a stable and orderly system regulating international trade, investment, and finance was a necessary condition for the impressive growth and stability of the era. The partial deconstruction of that system in the early 1970s was a major contributor to the subsequent outbreak of economic instability in the capitalist world.

The key point is that institutions such as these can be successful in helping to control and reduce uncertainty much of the time. By setting appar-

---

36. See Crotty 1991 for an analysis of the effect of corporate organizational structures and strategies on the stability properties of the investment function.

37. Hargreaves Heap makes this argument as follows. Hierarchical firms can be expected to have longer time horizons than [individuals or] individualist organizations. Hierarchies offer a kind of long-term contract. They have internal labor markets where progress becomes routinized. So, the long-term prospects of the individual member are bound up with the long-term health of the organization. What matters is the long-term success of the organization, since this guarantees the individual's security. Hence, if individuals in an organization are concerned with security, their attention will be focused on the long-term horizon. (1986–87, p. 275)

ent bounds on likely future outcomes, they help contain and repress the chaos seemingly inherent in free agent choice. They thus help make it possible to construct a coherent theory of the laws and tendencies of a macroeconomy characterized by true uncertainty.

Unfortunately, the institutional foundation of conditional stability and the institutional specificity of the behavioral equations of macrotheory have been seriously neglected by most theoretical traditions (in part because their conceptualization requires that most difficult of all theoretical feats—the integration of individualist and structuralist methodologies).[38] But such neglect is profoundly debilitating because the combination of the institutional structuring of agent choice and the conventions of decision making is the key to solving the paradox of conditional order and stability in a world of apparently limitless individualistic choice.

It must be stressed that many of the institutions that underpin continuity in so-called normal times also contribute to the potential for severe instability in crisis periods, and some make the outbreak of crises more likely. Consider several of our examples. First, money and other liquid assets are essential to the smooth functioning of a capitalist economy yet, as both Marx and Keynes pointed out, it is the ability of agents to "flee" from commodities and risky financial assets to money in times of fear and uncertainty that makes aggregate demand failures and financial panics possible and Say's Law inoperable.

Second, forward money contracts can create what I have elsewhere (1985) called "contractual rigidity" in the economy. As agents precommit through contractual obligations ever larger percentages of their expected cash flows, the economy becomes, to use Minsky's phrase, "financially fragile." At some point in the growth process, then, contracts no longer reduce uncertainty; rather, they exacerbate it.

Third, by insulating firms from competitive pressure, oligopolistic relations permit above average profits and the development of bloated bureaucracies, outdated technologies, and excessively risk-averse strategies. The longer that cooperative interfirm relations are successfully maintained, the greater the incentive for some firm to undermine them by seeking a larger share of the market. Just as anarchic competition motivates cooperative relations, oligopoly eventually breeds aggressive and unpredictable competition.

Fourth, successful government regulation of the economy in the postwar era brought with it a now widely recognized moral hazard problem. The

---

38. Both institutionalists and Marxists have long been concerned with the institutional contingency of economic theory. Two notable neo-Marxian efforts to conceptualize the relation between concrete institutional structures and conditional stability are the "social structure of accumulation" approach of Bowles, Gordon, and Weisskopf and the French "Regulation" school associated with Aglietta, Boyer, and Lipietz. See Kotz 1990 for an explanation of these theories and a comparison between them.

prevention of depression and significant financial panic over many decades created a widely held perception that there was no serious downside risk in financial speculation. This perception in turn caused an ever-increasing tolerance for leverage that has left both industrial and financial industries in precarious financial position and has made it extremely difficult if not impossible for most governments to use macropolicy aggressively.[39]

Finally, the story of the endogenous developments that led to the collapse of the Bretton Woods system is an oft-told tale. See, for example, the treatment in Block 1977.

Thus, as was the case with the relation between conventional decision making and stability, the relation between institutional structures and order and continuity is dialectical: institutions can never create more than conditional stability. As noted, most of the stabilizing institutions and practices I discussed embody serious contradictions. They tend to create new obstacles to stability even as they eliminate old ones; they transform the effects of uncertainty and shift them across time rather than permanently eliminate them. A macrotheory based on the integration of institutional structures and conventional expectation and confidence formation should explain not only why, even in the face of uncertainty, capitalism is relatively orderly most of the time, it must also explain why it suffers periodic crises and malfunctions. The contradictory and dialectical role played by conventional decision making and uncertainty-reducing institutions makes the pursuit of permanently effective state control of the capitalist economy thorough traditional macropolicy perpetually elusive.

4. Conclusion

The future *is* unknowable; we exist in an environment of true uncertainty. In such an environment, neoclassical theory fundamentally misspecifies agent choice. Fortunately, the price of recognition of the existence and centrality of fundamental uncertainty is not theoretical chaos as neoclassicists would have us believe. The concept of the socially constructed human agent and conventional decision making in concert with an understanding of the institutional foundations of conditional stability create a world with nondeterminist or contingent laws and tendencies, a world that can indeed be appropriated through theory. However, a theory adequate to its task must be institutionally contingent and never lose sight of the dialectical relation between uncertainty and the structures and practices we have created to try to remove its sting.

---

39. See Crotty 1989 for an analysis of the rise and fall of the Keynesian regulatory regime in the post World War II period.

REFERENCES

Bausor, R. (1989–90), "The Contributions to Economics of Douglas Vickers," *Journal of Post Keynesian Economics*, vol. 12, pp. 203–213.

Blinder, A. (1991), "Why are Prices Sticky? Preliminary Results from an Interview Study," *American Economic Review*, vol. 81, pp. 89–96.

Block, F. (1977), *The Origins of International Economic Disorder*, Berkeley: University of California Press.

Breed, Clive. (1991), "Philosophy of Science and Contemporary Economics: An Overview," *Journal of Post Keynesian Economics*, vol. 13, pp. 459–494.

Brown-Collier, E., and Bausor, R. (1988), "The Epistemological Foundation of *The General Theory*," *Scottish Journal of Political Economy*, vol. 35, pp. 227–241.

Bryant, J. (1991), "A Simple Rational-Expectations Keynes-Type Model," in Mankiw, N. G. and D. Romer (eds.) *New Keynesian Economics: Volume II*, pp. 25–30, Cambridge, Mass.: MIT Press.

Bullard, J. (1991), "Learning, Rational Expectations and Policy: A Summary," Federal Reserve Bank of Saint Louis, *Review*, Jan/Feb., pp. 50–60.

Carvalho, F. (1983–84), "On the Concept of Time in Shacklean and Shraffian Economics," *Journal of Post Keynesian Economics*, vol. 6, pp. 265–280.

Carvalho, F. (1988), "Keynes on Probability, Uncertainty, and Decision Making," *Journal of Post Keynesian Economics*, vol. 11, pp. 66–81.

Cass, D., and Shell, K. (1983), "Do Sunspots Matter?," *Journal of Political Economy*, vol. 91, pp. 193–227.

Clower, R. (1965), "The Keynesian Counter-Revolution," in Hahn, F. and F. Brechling (eds.) *The Theory of Interest Rates*, pp. 103–125, London: Macmillan Press.

Coddington, A. (1983), *Keynesian Economics: The Search for First Principles*, Winchester, Mass.: Allen and Unwin.

Crotty, J. (1985), "The Centrality of Money, Credit and Financial Intermediation in Marx's Crisis Theory," in Resnick, S. and R. Wolff (eds.) *Rethinking Marxism*, pp. 45–82, New York: Autonomedia.

Crotty, J. (1989), "The Limits of Keynesian Macropolicy in the Age of the Global Marketplace," in MacEwan, A. and W. Tabb (eds.) *Instability and Change in the World Economy*, pp. 82–100, New York: Monthly Review Press.

Crotty, J. (1990), "Keynes on the Stages of Development of the Capitalist Economy: The Institutionalist Foundation of Keynes's Methodology," *Journal of Economic Issues*, vol. 24, pp. 761–780.

Crotty, J. (1993), "Rethinking Marxian Investment Theory: Keynes-Minsky Instability, Competitive Regime Shifts, and Coerced Investment," *Review of Radical Political Economics*, vol. 25, pp. 1–26.

Davidson, P. (1987), "Sensible Expectations and the Long-Run Non-Neutrality of Money," *Journal of Post Keynesian Economics*, vol. 10, pp. 146–153.

Davidson, P. (1991), "Is Probability Theory Relevant for Uncertainty? A Post Keynesian Perspective," *Journal of Economic Perspectives*, vol. 5, pp. 129–144.

Davis, J. (1989), "Keynes on Atomism and Organicism," *Economic Journal*, vol. 99, pp. 1159–1172.

Donaldson, G., and Lorsch, J. (1983), *Decision-Making at the Top: The Shaping of Strategic Decision*, New York: Basic Books.

Fazzari, S. (1985), "Keynes, Harrod and the Rational Expectations Revolution," *Journal of Post Keynesian Economics*, vol. 8, pp. 66–80.

Fitzgibbons, A. (1988), *Keynes's Vision: A New Political Economy*, New York: Oxford University Press.

Grether, D., and Plott, C. (1979), "The Economic Theory of Choice and the Preference Reversal Phenomenon," *American Economic Review*, vol. 69, pp. 623–638.

Hargreaves Heap, S. (1986–87), "Risk and Culture: A Missing Link in the Post Keynesian Tradition," *Journal of Post Keynesian Economics*, vol. 9, pp. 267–278.

Hayek, F. (1948), *Individualism and Economic Order*, Chicago: University of Chicago Press.

Heiner, R. (1983), "The Origin of Predictable Behavior," *American Economic Review*, vol. 83, pp. 560–595.

Katzner, D. (1987), "More on the Distinction between Potential Confirmation and Probability," *Journal of Post Keynesian Economics*, vol. 10, pp. 65–83.

Keynes, J. M. (1936), *The General Theory of Employment, Interest and Money*, Cambridge: Cambridge University Press (1972).

Keynes, J. M. (1937), "The General Theory of Employment," *Quarterly Journal of Economics*, vol. 51, pp. 209–233.

Keynes, J. M. (1971), *The Collected Writings of John Maynard Keynes. Volume 6. A Treatise on Money: The Applied Theory of Money*, London: The Macmillan Press.

Keynes, J. M. (1973a) *The Collected Writings of John Maynard Keynes. Volume 10. A Treatise on Probability*, London: The Macmillan Press.

Keynes, J. M. (1973b), *The Collected Writings of John Maynard Keynes. Volume 14. The General Theory and After: Part II*, London: The Macmillan Press.

Keynes, J. M. (1979), *The Collected Writings of John Maynard Keynes. Volume 29. The General Theory and After: A Supplement*, London: The Macmillan Press.

Klamer, A. (1983), *Conversations With Economists*, Totowa, N. J.: Rowman and Allanhead.

Kotz, D. (1990), "A Comparative Analysis of the Regulation Theory and the Social Structure of Accumulation Theory," *Science and Society*, vol. 54, pp. 5–28.

Kregal, J. (1980), "Markets and Institutions as Features of a Capitalist Production System," *Journal of Post Keynesian Economics*, vol. 3, pp. 21–31.

Lawson, T. (1985), "Uncertainty and Economic Analysis," *Economic Journal*, vol. 95, pp. 909–927.

Lawson, T. (1988), "Probability and Uncertainty in Economic Analysis," *Journal of Post Keynesian Economics*, vol. 11, pp. 38–65.

Leijonhufvud, A. (1968), *On Keynesian Economics and the Economics of Keynes*, New York: Oxford University Press.

Lucas, R. (1981), *Studies in Business-Cycle Theory*, Cambridge, Mass.: MIT Press.

McCloskey, D. (1985), *The Rhetoric of Economics*, Madison: University of Wisconsin Press.

Machina, M. (1987), "Choice Under Uncertainty: Problems Solved and Unsolved," *Journal of Economic Perspectives*, vol. 1, pp. 121–154.

Muth, J. (1961), "Rational Expectations and the Theory of Price Movements," *Econometrica*, vol. 29, pp. 315–335.

North, D. (1991), "Institutions," *Journal of Economic Perspectives*, vol. 5, pp. 97–112.

Piron, R. (1991), "Keynes as a Noise Trader," *Journal of Economic Perspectives*, vol. 5, pp. 215–218.

Rotheim, R. (1989–90), "Organicism and the Role of the Individual in Keynes' Thought," *Journal of Post Keynesian Economics*, vol. 12, pp. 316–326.

Samuels, W. (1991), " 'Truth' and Discourse in the Social Construction of Economic Reality: An Essay on the Relation of Knowledge to Socioeconomic Policy," *Journal of Post Keynesian Economics*, vol. 13, pp. 511–524.

Savage, L. (1954), *The Foundation of Statistics*, New York: Wiley.

Sen, K. (1990), "The Sunspot Theorists and Keynes," *Journal of Post Keynesian Economics*, vol. 12, pp. 564–571.

Shackle, G. L. S. (1955), *Uncertainty in Economics*, Cambridge: Cambridge University Press.

Shackle, G. L. S. (1972), *Epistemics and Economics*, Cambridge: Cambridge University Press.

Shackle. G. L. S. (1983–84), "The Romantic Mountain and the Classic Lake: Alan Coddington's *Keynesian Economics*," *Journal of Post Keynesian Economics*, vol. 6, pp. 241–251.

Sheffrin, S. (1983), *Rational Expectations*, Cambridge: Cambridge University Press.

Shiller, R. (1989), *Market Volatility*, Cambridge, Mass.: MIT Press.

Solow, R. (1988), "Growth Theory and After," *American Economic Review*, vol. 78, pp. 307–317.

Spinoza, B. (1951), *A Theologico-Political Treatise and A Political Treatise*, New York: Dover Publications.

Tversky, A., Slovic, P., and Kahneman, D. (1990), "The Causes of Preference Reversal," *American Economic Review*, vol. 80, pp. 204–217.

Vickers, D. (1994), *Economics and the Antagonism of Time*, Ann Arbor: University of Michigan Press (forthcoming).

Winslow, E. G. (1989), "Organic Interdependence, Uncertainty and Economic Analysis," *Economic Journal*, vol. 99, pp. 1173–1182.

Woodford, M. (1991), 'Self-Fulfilling Expectations and Fluctuations in Aggregate Demand," in Mankiw, N. G. and D. Romer (eds.) *New Keynesian Economics: Volume II*, pp. 77–110, Cambridge, Mass.: MIT Press.

Zeckhauser, R., Patel, J., and Hendricks, D. (1991), "Nonrational Actors and Financial Market Behavior," National Bureau of Economic Research, Working Paper No. 3731.

Part II
Empirical Papers in
International Economics

CHAPTER 6

Minskian Fragility in the International Financial System

H. Peter Gray and Jean M. Gray*

"In the light of the evidence of the 1960s and early 1970s it is clear that in the semi-open system that rules among the advanced capitalist economies, the significance of financial disturbances and instability is if anything greater than if each of these economies were treated in isolation." (Minsky 1975, pp. x–xi)

As the lead quotation from Minsky suggests, the probability of financial instability will be increased if national financial systems of given degrees of fragility are not isolated from each other. Put another way, the self-seeking goals of the major actors in the advanced capitalist nations in competition with each other are likely to seek gains without fully countenancing the effects of their conduct for the robustness of the global economy. Shocks originating abroad are capable of having a negative impact on the financial sector of a home economy either directly through financial linkages or indirectly through the goods sector.[1] In addition to shocks or disturbances that have their origin in foreign economies, it is quite possible for the actual linkages between pairs of national financial markets to prove to be sources of disturbance and fragility. This paper examines the extant international financial system in a Minskian framework and finds that the danger of financial instability is substantially enhanced by greater integration of global financial markets. The added fragility deriving from increased international integration of financial markets could be reduced by the existence of a strong hegemon[2] or by a regime of

*The authors were students of Hyman P. Minsky at Berkeley. They are grateful to the editors of this book for valuable comments on an early draft.

1. Gray and Gray (1981) argue that the preoccupation of economists with allocative efficiency leads them and the governments that they advise to neglect the possibility of interaction between efficiency in production and the stability of the system (stability efficiency). This is true a fortiori in decisions made by private, profit-seeking units.

2. It is worth noting that the largest major global collapse took place in the absence of a strong hegemon when the Bank of England was forced to renounce its ability to play its prewar role.

institutional agreements that limit the scope for self-aggravating crisis in international financial markets.[3]

Section 1 very briefly recapitulates the essence of Minsky's thesis as a basis for its extension to the current international setting and develops the equivalence between the role of the central bank in a closed economy and the hegemon in the international economy. Section 2 assesses the recent development of fragility in the existing international financial system. Section 3 examines the stability- enhancing measures[4] already either taken or broached by the authorities to reduce the fragility of the international financial system. Section 4 briefly examines the policy measures that need, in the light of our analysis, prompt consideration.

1. Minksy's Framework for the International Financial System

Any analysis of Minsky's framework must revolve around two different aspects of fragility:

1. The first aspect is the extant state of the financial system; that is any chronic tendency on the part of the financial and/or the nonfinancial sectors in the economy to degenerate into greater fragility, and the probability that turbulence will generate adverse exogenous events to strike that system. These factors determine the natural tendency for a system to become increasingly fragile.
2. The second avenue of analysis concerns the ability of the authorities to counter the natural tendency toward fragility by robustness-enhancing policy measures including activist central bank intervention and regulatory oversight of firms in the financial sector. Once the analysis is transposed from a closed to an international economy, the role of the national central bank is allotted to a lender of last resort to the international financial system, that is from the central bank to the international hegemon (or substitute regime).

Reduced to its simplest terms, Minsky's theory of inherent financial

---

3. Thus a regime of institutional arrangements can, in theory, substitute for a hegemon, but necessarily a "committee-type hegemon" suffers from the possible lack of concerted action and a slow reaction time. The existing regime—its strengths and vulnerability—is the subject of section 3 below.

4. Policy measures to enhance stability efficiency (to reduce actual or potential fragility) can be divided into (preventive) regulatory measures and associated institutional changes (such as the first Basel Accord) and countermeasures or "insurance-type arrangements" (including strengthening lender-of-last-resort capability) that permit governments to counter disturbances when they arise in order to prevent a financial crisis.

instability relies on a basic tendency for nonfinancial corporations and deposit intermediaries and other financial corporations, encouraged by recent stability and driven to secure enough profits to validate their financial commitments, to increase their financial leverage.[5] This tendency toward ever-higher financial leverage (with its ever-greater vulnerability to shock) decreases the ability of a corporation to withstand a major adverse shock or serious recession. The actions within the nonfinancial and the financial sectors reinforce each other in the sense that as nonfinancial firms become more highly leveraged, the expected value of their commitments is effectively reduced (risk is enhanced). These commitments constitute a major component of the portfolios of assets of financial firms. The increase in the leverage of nonfinancial firms increases their cost of debt and commits still more of the cash flow. Thus the system as a whole is tending to grow more vulnerable with the passage of time. (This is the mechanism by which an advanced capitalist system seeks productive efficiency while disregarding the implications for the stability efficiency of the system.) In practice, additional leverage is encouraged by continued absence of crisis. Corporate executives in both sectors obey the availability and threshold heuristics developed by cognitive psychologists: the longer the period without crisis, the lower the subjective probability attached to crisis, and, when that probability has reached some low number, the possibility is dropped from the personal calculus and the absence of crisis is assumed as a certainty.[6] Minsky's theory has seismological overtones in that it allows for the steady buildup of stress, for the possibility of major misadventure if the stress is not released (earthquakes), and for reductions of the accumulated stress by minor malfunctions (tremors). This tendency toward ever-greater fragility can be interrupted by periods of retrenchment and reevaluation in which the authorities have rescued the system from serious recession and in which new sets of regulations are introduced to keep up with an evolving system.[7]

The stability-enhancing measures imposed on the economic system by the authorities would include normal Keynesian contracyclical policies (Min-

---

5. This summary draws on Minsky 1986b. Unfortunately this extension of Minsky's closed-economy analysis was not published in an easily available outlet.

6. These heuristics are discussed in Guttentag and Herring 1986. For original discussion see Tversky and Kahneman 1982 and Simon 1978. Statistical theory argues that an event with one hundred possible triggers, each with an independent probability of occurence of one in a hundred, is a mathematically certain event. Even allowing for the difficulties of determining independence, the implications of the heuristics for the viability of a complex system are dangerous.

7. "What stability and orderly growth we observe is at least as much due to interventions and regulations that constrain and affect market processes as it is to the characteristics of the market processes. This can be formalized by interpreting interventions and regulations which abort a dynamic process that would yield a disaster as imposing new initial conditions. This way of looking at the economy makes history the result of piecing together constrained runs of dynamic processes which if left alone would have produced chaotic behavior" (Minsky, 1986b).

sky 1989) as well as activist central bank initiatives in the realms of regulation and oversight.[8] Whether executives in financial and nonfinancial corporations adjust their subjective evaluations of the probability of crisis during a period of retrenchment is not clear. The lesson would have to be very severe before the heuristics were renounced, and the psychological element in Minsky's thesis would seem to have little chance of reversal (correction) prior to major crisis and financial instability.

We assert that the national financial markets of the industrialized (OECD) countries can now be considered fully integrated so that a single global financial market exists, which will not be partitioned except in the wake of crisis.[9] This integration can be attributed to the technological innovations in communication and datahandling and to the development of new financial instruments and markets that give the appearance of providing hedge facilities for investors.[10] Our approach is to examine four ways in which the integration of national markets has increased the possibility of financial crisis:

1. Integration of national markets may have increased the fragility of a national financial system;
2. Shocks are more likely to occur in an integrated international system than in a national system;
3. Fragility in the international financial system becomes more probable if governments do not understand the interaction between national imbalances of payments and potential disruptive shock;
4. The international arena will, in the absence of a strong hegemon,

---

8. The possibility that new technologies require substantial structural change in the financial sector that will involve the elimination of a substantial number of financial firms is not confronted either by orthodoxy or the Minskian hypothesis. Such a possibility is likely to reinforce the increased fragility of the financial sector that is at the heart of the Minsky hypothesis. Capitalist financial firms will strive to survive so that competitors, and not themselves will be eliminated in the "shakedown": the collective losses inflicted on the industry are, in this way, spread across all its members. Only when the requisite number of firms has been eliminated will the industry begin to make collective profits again. As a result, all firms in the industry experience losses, and their capital adequacy is reduced. This is an essential feature of financial capitalism. It affects all industries but has particularly important implications for financial firms where capital adequacy is an important safeguard against contagion.

9. It is possible that enlightened policy analysts might decide that some barriers must be placed between pairs of national markets: Tobin's (1978) proposal for a transactions tax on international capital flows is a good example of a proposal of a stability-enhancing measure for the international linkages.

10. Many of the new instruments and means of covering exposure are likely to hold only for limited ranges of movement in the price of the hedged asset because the assets of the person supplying the hedge position are finite and exhaustible. Moreover, such hedge markets would not be renewed in a time of financial crisis, and any unit with a hedged position might well choose to eliminate the original position and carry the hedge as a speculative position so that exposed funds could be withdrawn, thus reinforcing the crisis.

make stability-enhancing measures more difficult to effect (a lack of international cooperation may weaken the ability to create and to put into action fragility-reducing measures).

One point should be made explicit here. Minsky's major thesis is built on the twin, mutually reinforcing aspects of behavior in the financial and nonfinancial sectors. This paper addresses the question of the effect of internationalization of financial activity. Any increase in the international activities of nonfinancial firms is assumed to result in greater capacity for attempted movement of funds out of a currency perceived to be potentially weak, by loss-avoiding firms. The nonfinancial sectors are expected to work within national systems in the way that Minsky suggests and to make no direct beneficial contribution to international financial stability efficiency.

2. Stability Efficiency of the International Financial System

To frame the Minskian hypothesis in an international setting is to ask whether the recent internationalization of financial markets has played a significant role in making the global financial system more fragile. (There is a second question to be addressed in section 4: Is the relationship a progressive one; that is, does greater international integration imply a natural tendency toward international fragility in the same way that, in the absence of deliberate counteracting macroeconomic and prudential policy measures, national economies tend naturally toward greater fragility?) The first question has three (inevitably interdependent) aspects: (1) the effect of greater integration on national fragility, (2) the fragility of the international linkages (foreign exchange markets) among national financial markets; and (3) the potentially large fragility-enhancing role of balance-of-payments policy errors by governments.

2.1 The Effect of Greater Integration on National Fragility

The internationalization of the financial system (a growing ratio of assets and liabilities of financial firms being owned by and accepted from agents whose functional currency is different from the currency of denomination)[11] will be

---

11. A functional currency is the currency in which the entity's financial calculations are made and in which financial results are reported and assessed. The functional currency will usually be the currency of the home nation in which the head office is located and in which the majority of shareholders are resident. There are severe problems of balance-sheet consolidation and accurate measurement of net worth for firms that have operations in many countries (Gray and Miranti 1990).

likely to increase the fragility of a national system directly and possibly to increase the likelihood of contagion within an individual system (as well as among systems). [12]

The implications of international financial involvement of national financial firms for the fragility of a domestic system depend in part on the wisdom (understanding of risks involved) of executives of financial corporations and in part on the turbulence (frequency of shocks) prevailing in the world. [13] Financial firms in major national capital markets in industrialized nations have always conducted cross-border financial transactions; that is, they have made loans to and accepted liabilities from foreign residents. Frequently foreign loans have gone sour and brought down the issuing institution, creating a financial crisis; the first event of this kind was the loan by the three major Florentine banks to Edward III of England. [14] In addition to the possibility of deliberate default, it is simply harder to assess (and to keep track of) the creditworthiness of foreign borrowers than domestic ones; the desirability of foreign loans relies on their higher profit margin and the presumed ability to diversify the assets in order to reduce average risk exposure. Repayments of both sovereign and corporate foreign loans are subject to the availability in the borrower's nation of hard (convertible) currency [15] as well as to the debtors' having adequate amounts of local currency. In times of global recession, the ability of such borrowers to obtain hard currency is often frustrated by protective commercial policies and the lack of demand in countries that are "internationally solvent." [16] The effect of a loan default on the lending institution's capital depends on the relative size of the loan and the lender's capital; a weakened institution is less able to act as a buffer or resistance in the chain of contagion of financial stress within a national system. Even allowing for the

---

12. Eichengreen and Portes (1987) put special emphasis on the role of linkages among "markets" (debt defaults, foreign exchanges, and the banking system) in creating financial crisis. They neglect (or accept as inevitable) the question of contagion within the markets as well as the Minskian thrust that there will be a general tendency on the part of all markets to weaken together: similarly, their analysis does not confront the possibility of interdependence between the fragility of the markets and the lack of robustness of the linkages. In context, the role of the authorities is to quarantine a weakness within a market and to prevent its spread (p. 18); in this way a crisis is kept on a relatively small scale.

13. These implications are also quite sensitive to the existence or nonexistence of a hegemon, which is, in reality, a shock absorber of major proportions (Gray 1991).

14. This was literally "sovereign debt"! It was also based on a war, which is unlikely to be a cash-generating investment. Ehrenberg (1963, p. 50) reports that suspension of payments on the part of the three major banks brought down most of the other Florentine banks.

15. Guttentag and Herring (1986, pp. 5–6) refer to this problem as "transfer shock."

16. For example, recall the performance of France and the United States between the wars when these countries, blessed with large amounts of international liquidity, were running current surpluses and drawing funds to them rather than aiding, officially, the financial systems under pressure. Minsky (1986b) calls this condition "fiscal independence."

greater difficulties in assessing creditor risk, the major problem in default on international loans in recent years seems to have been lenders' naiveté on macroeconomic or balance-of-payments risk.

If cross-border lending inevitably carries a higher risk of default, there would seem to be a prima facie argument that greater fragility is associated with an internationally integrated financial system. It would also be possible to argue that the likelihood of severe defaults on sovereign and commercial debt by foreign borrowers grows with the fragility of the international financial system as lenders become less willing to refinance foreign debt and debtors are less willing to pay the premiums charged by their creditors. In other words, internationalization of financial markets strengthens the Minskian thesis by introducing another mutually-reinforcing strand of interaction.

This idea that internationalization reinforces the Minskian hypothesis draws additional evidential support from the way in which the Third World debt crisis was fostered: tranquility had seemed to reign and, since the loans were being serviced, ostensibly favorable results had prevailed in the decade prior to the collapse of the Latin American debt in 1982.[17] Guenther (1981) reported that Citibank's loss rate on foreign loans was less than on domestic loans between 1971 and 1980.[18] Recent apparent successes had made for greater indulgence in exposure to foreign risks. Major U.S. banks have been made much weaker by the losses sustained on their Latin American exposure. The interaction here is self-evident: as banks have weaker capital positions, the temptation to withdraw funds (deposits) from these banks in a period of turbulence will grow, increasing the possibility that a major bank will need bail out support by its central bank. This will reduce the confidence of non-resident depositors in all banks and will spread fragility and contagion within the financial system.[19]

In a national market, Minsky's analysis revolves around the steadily increasing financial leverage of nonfinancial and financial national firms and the possibility of contagion among them magnifying a shock into a crisis and, ultimately, a collapse. In an international version, there are additional chains of contagion and sources of fragility. Minksy's hypothesis gains strength by

---

17. It is interesting to note that the international banking community had regarded the 1970s as a period of financial tranquility despite the huge shift in the pattern of the international flow of funds brought about by the 1974 and 1979 oil-price shocks. On the validity of the assumption that loans to Latin America were sound, see Dymski and Pastor 1991.

18. This does not excuse U.S. bankers from their failure to analyze some of the additional risks that could be brought about by international turbulence and balance-of-payments constraints in the borrowers' country.

19. The effective insurance of all (domestic and foreign) liabilities of Continental Illinois was an example of the need for intervention when a major bank collapsed. Fragility in the system was contained but at a considerable cost both in terms of money and in terms of the failure of the authorities to take steps to reduce the systemic fragility.

adding another strand of interaction and another layer of vulnerability. Because the existing foreign loans can reinforce any innate tendency toward fragility, the internationally integrated financial system is potentially more exposed to shock. The weakest national system can now serve as the source of the disturbance, which launches its own crisis, and the effects can be spread out through the global system, endangering the systems in other countries. Thus the fragility of a national system is no longer, in an internationally integrated system, exposed only to disturbances and mistakes that arise within its own economy but must also have the strength to ward off any disturbances that have their origin in foreign but connected financial systems.[20] Clearly, the relative size of the systems is important here: a collapse of the financial market in Ruritania will not cause major global repercussions (unless the country has been the recipient of huge amounts of loans sourced from private institutions), but a collapse of the (already weak) U.S. financial system has a different order of magnitude.

2.2 The Fragility of Linkages among National Markets

The possibility that fragility will be enhanced by the linkages among national markets derives from the two possibilities that foreign exchange markets will be sources of instability (fragility in a linkage) and that exogneous shocks will generate stress and possible instability in those international-linkage markets. The root problem may currently be that the world has internationally integrated *global* financial markets based on assets and liabilities denominated in *national* currencies. This state of affairs presents no problems provided that change comes slowly and at a measured pace within the ability of the global economy and the international financial system to adjust and adapt without creating unstable conditions, that is, without exceeding the capacity of the system to adjust to change. Change which meets these conditions will only occur in a tranquil world in which national governments follow sensible policies that neither create shocks nor allow any natural (Minskian) tendency to fragility to go unhindered.

The possibility that shocks are more likely to occur in an internationally integrated system than in a national one must revolve around the susceptibility of foreign exchange markets to perturbations (their fragility) and the fact that these markets serve as linkages among national economies. There are two possible sources of disturbances within the economic system: (1) the likelihood of instability in the foreign exchange markets is greater when the national financial markets are integrated and there are larger amounts of funds

20. Such disturbances could lead to defaults on international loans, weakening of nonfinancial firms with assets in the country experiencing crisis, or sudden large international movements of currencies.

that can be moved internationally at short notice at the instigation of fact, fear, or rumor; and (2) the existence of foreign-owned deposits will enhance the fragility of a national banking system and will instigate flight from a national currency.[21] These two aspects of fragility are obverse sides of the same coin.

A flight from a currency will establish its own contagion within the national system as funds are withdrawn from financial assets and erode their value. What matters is the range over which the rate of exchange is unstable and whether or not such an event could bring about a collapse of values and, in this way, a full debt deflation. Clearly, this possibility depends on the institutional arrangements already agreed to by the coterie of lenders of last resort and by their willingness and ability to fulfill the commitments. If the problem is a run on a national currency in foreign-exchange markets, international co-operation will be necessary to dampen the fluctuations and prearrangement will be necessary if the flight is to be countered quickly enough not to have caused widespread bankruptcies.

A major change in foreign exchange rates, even if it does not precipitate a cumulative deflation of the prices of financial assets, can exert substantial strain on the nonfinancial economy and through that on the health and strength of financial firms. Neoclassical (mainstream) economics has never paid sufficient attention to the mechanics of adjustment to changes in relative prices or in patterns of demand, and, in its assumption of an attainable equilibrium, has implicitly assumed a Marshallian world of small disturbances with sustainable adjustment. But the collapse of an industry and its firms because of a change in market conditions puts great strain on local economies and, where something approaching a unit banking system exists, on the local banks. A major change in the composition of demand, the level of total demand held constant, requires substantial expansions in some industries and decreases in capacity in others. This process causes severe losses of value in the declining sectors and in the level of employment and the value of industry-specific or immobile nonfinancial assets in regions in which the declining sectors are concentrated. To be sure, there are booming sectors, but the transfer of resources from the declining to the rising sectors may not occur smoothly if the input requirements differ.

When the source of a violent movement of funds among currencies derives from a departure of the nominal rate of exchange from its sustainable or underlying rate by virtue of international capital flows, the change in exchange rates may be said to be endogenous. When a major wave of international capital flows and a shift in exchange rates are triggered by some non-

---

21. Because nonresidents are likely to have other currencies as their functional currency, they may be more prone to withdraw funds from a currency in a defensive, risk-avoidance posture than residents, who would flee the currency in search of a speculative gain. Clearly, once a run on the currency is established, both kinds of motivations apply equally.

economic phenomenon, such as war or assassination, the results are likely to prove quite similar. Such noneconomic phenomena spread their effects much further in a world of integrated financial markets and, if they adversely affect an already fragile system, they could trigger a financial crisis.[22]

2.3. Balance-of-Payments Policy Errors

One feature of the international financial system in recent years—since the global integration of financial markets beginning with the rapid growth of the eurocurrency markets in 1974—is the passive acquiescence of governments and central banks toward the limits of exposure of their economies to international debt. This problem is another example of neglect of stability-efficiency considerations and has two dimensions: net worth and liquid liabilities.

The net worth dimension has been partly recognized in the past by registered concern by economists with the burden of the foreign debt of developing countries when measured in terms of total (or discretionary) export revenues (Avramovic 1964). When an economic unit borrows money abroad, it has to pass the credit standards of the lender with respect to its ability to service the debt. If the foreign financial institutions impose appropriate lending standards, then there will be no major default on the outstanding debt short of some unforseeable economic cataclysm. Such loans must be viewed from two perspectives: The first perspective concerns the ability of the borrower to service or repay the loan in its own currency, that is, will the use to which the loan is put engender a rate of return that will validate the loan?[23] The second perspective refers to the ability of the borrower's economy to generate enough hard currency to service or repay the loan. The bases for the two assessments are quite different: the first concerns project-level financing, and the second is macroeconomic. It would seem that international bankers have of late concerned themselves predominantly with the first assessment and in the case of sovereign (government) debt have relied on the recent historic record of repayment of sovereign debt (Guttentag and Herring 1986). The macroeconomic dimension seems to have escaped the lenders' attention entirely, which suggests that lenders have become involved in international lending without adequate analysis of the additional (macroeconomic) risks involved. Clearly, any serious neglect of the macroeconomic dimension can lead to huge losses on loans and drastic weakening of capital adequacy on the

---

22. One should not overlook the possibility that a shock can be either fragility enhancing or stability enhancing but logic suggests that shocks will be biased toward adversity in a fragile system. Similarly, not every financial crisis leads to a debt deflation or to a depression (Gray 1990).

23. This question is, of course, fundamental to Minksy's vision of a capitalist economy.

part of lenders. The effect of the Latin American debt problem on the capital adequacy of the U.S. money market banks is incontrovertible.[24] The liquidity aspect of international debt is an obvious component of the burden of debt service by virtue of its repayment implications. The effect on the interest cost of rollover provisions (an issue of substantial importance in the Latin default) should also be seen as a liquidity phenomenon since it can affect the burden of a given amount of debt in the short run.

The possibility of financial crisis in the 1990s is likely to revolve around the weakness of the U.S. financial system. Here the international dimension is a critical component. Table 1 shows the easily encashable claims on the U.S. financial system held by nonresidents—the liquidity dimension. A substantial portion of these claims is directly attributable to the cumulative and huge current-account deficits of the United States since 1982 (see table 2)—the net worth dimension. The current deficits are, in turn, responsive to the unwarranted strength of the U.S. dollar from 1982 to 1985, which must be attributed to the higher real interest rates.[25] Despite the U.S. dollar's continued role as the major currency in international finance as both a transactions currency and a reserve currency (*faute de mieux*), the U.S. dollar is at risk of becoming a soft currency. Some perception of this possibility by private holders of dollar-denominated assets and some other functional currency could trigger a flight from the dollar with all of its potential for crisis. Such a state of affairs would involve a major change in the structure of the global and the constituent national economies and would burden the international financial system with severe problems of transition.

It would seem self-evident that permissible balance-of-payments imbalances and cumulative negative international net worths have their limits.[26] Only the United States could have financed a period of such profligacy, and it could only have done so in a world in which an absence of default was taken as a given. The way in which the cumulative current deficits were financed is even more unusual in that (as Table 1 shows) the bulk of the indebtedness has been financed by private nonresidents acquiring claims on private assets (pre-

---

24. There is no need here for a detailed analysis of this source of fragility, but even the excellent analysis of Guttentag and Herring underestimates the effect of intergenerational change on the capacity of lenders to neglect potential risks. Bankers who lived through the 1930s were more conservative because they had scar tissue to remind them of the possibility of default on foreign loans. Training of loan officers in line with the Minskian hypotheses might have made them more sensitive to the possibility of overexposure to certain nations and to the assumption of independence among borrowers' risk where macroeconomic interdependence existed.

25. For an explanation of the failure of the (relative) weakening of the dollar in 1986 to restore the competitiveness of U.S. industry and to eradicate the current deficit, see Milberg and Gray 1992.

26. Howard (1989) supplies an estimate of the limiting factor for the United States.

TABLE 1. Outstanding Financial Assets of Non-Americans in U.S. Financial Markets (End-of-Year Data in Billions of U.S. Dollars)

	1982	1983	1984	1985	1986	1987	1988	1989	1990
Officials' Assets	189.2	194.5	199.7	202.5	241.2	283.1	322.0	337.3	371.1
Private Assets	374.3	455.3	533.8	679.9	883.6	994.8	1,141.9	1,336.7	1,341.4
U.S. Treasury Securities	25.8	33.9	62.1	88.0	96.1	82.6	100.9	134.5	130.7
Other Bonds	16.7	17.5	32.4	82.3	140.1	166.1	191.3	223.9	240.7
Stocks	76.3	96.4	96.1	125.6	168.9	175.6	201.0	260.6	231.2
Liabilities of Nonbank Concerns	27.5	26.9	31.0	29.5	26.9	29.8	35.0	40.6	45.4
Liabilities of Banks	228.0	280.6	312.2	354.5	451.6	540.7	613.7	677.1	693.4

Source: *Survey of Current Business* (June 1992, p. 49).

TABLE 2. U.S. International Net Worth
(With Direct Investments at Current Cost)[a]
($ Billions at End of Year)

	1983	1984	1985	1986	1987	1988	1989ᵖ	1990ᵖ	Total or Net Change (1983–90)
INW (End of Prior Year)	+364.0	+285.0	+164.0	+64.3	−74.1	−135.0	−306.0	−439.7	−803.7
Current Account Balance	−40.1	−99.0	−122.3	−145.4	−160.2	−126.2	−106.3	−92.1	−891.6
Total Adjustments[b]	−50.3	−49.5	+2.6	−8.8	+106.0	−35.6	−45.8	+56.1	−25.3
Statistical Discrepancy[c]	+11.4	+27.5	+20.0	+15.8	−6.7	−9.2	+18.4	+63.5	+140.7
INW at End of Year	+285.0	+164.0	+64.3	−74.1	−135.0	−306.0	−439.7	−412.2	−697.2
Memorandum: INW at end of year									
At Historical Cost	+89.0	−2.2	−117.2	−273.7	−378.1	−531.1	−663.7	−526.6	−615.6
At Market Value	+224.1	+111.0	+64.5	+14.6	−42.2	−150.6	−267.7	−360.6	−584.7

Source: *Survey of Current Business* (June 1991), pp. 44–45; Landefeld and Lawson 1991 and Scholl 1991.
[a] Gold is valued at year-end market price (see note 7). INW at historical cost and market valuations are given in the memorandum. For detail, see sources.
[b] This number includes value changes of both real and financial assets as well as net capital flows.
[c] When positive, the "statistical discrepancy" shows "unexplained credits." Clearly, incomplete data tend to reduce the reduction in INW.
ᵖ Preliminary.

dominantly U.S. financial intermediaries). This feature combined with the weakness of some major U.S. financial institutions makes the system ever more prone to crisis.

3. Enhancing Stability Efficiency in the System

In a Minskian world, financial market stability is as dependent on interventions and regulations as on market efficiency.[27] For the most part, the central bankers and bank supervsory agents of the industrial world would agree. Over the past two decades they have become increasingly aware of the need to coordinate oversight activities in potentially fragile, globally integrated financial markets. This section addresses the difficulties inherent in identifying and defining the variables to be controlled, in reaching consensus on the nature of the regulatory oversight, and in applying the agreed-on rules evenhandedly in a multicountry environment. We will review the relative strengths and weaknesses of the existing oversight arrangements and identify some potential sources of instability that lie beyond the reach of the present safety net.

The existing international supervisory framework relies on the cooperation of the Group of Ten central banks operating under the aegis of the Bank for International Settlements.[28] Prior to 1975, consultation among the member and cooperating central banks was, at best, infrequent and uncoordinated. Then two events with the potential for generating global financial crises, the Herstatt and Franklin National Bank failures in 1974, prompted recognition of the need for greater coordination in monitoring the safety and soundness of banks operating across national boundaries. The first step was the establishment of the Committee on Banking Regulations and Supervisory Practices.[29] The committee's first achievement was development of the Basle "Concordat," which spelled out the division of responsibilities among national authorities for the supervision of banks operating internationally. With agreement reached on the Concordat in 1975 and on a number of refinements in 1983, the committee put forth a number of recommendations to improve the quality and the quantity of data on international banking and to promote greater convergence of bank regulatory standards across countries. The culmination of these

---

27. "Observations from history indicate that the management of financial markets cannot be left to market forces. Interventions, which reflect knowledge of how market processes can make things worse and which adjust as markets evolve, can make things better". (Minsky, 1986b).

28. The Group of Ten consists of twelve countries: Belgium, Canada, France, Germany, Italy, Japan, Luxembourg, the Netherlands, Sweden, Switzerland, the United Kingdom, and the United States.

29. The committee is better known as the Cooke committee–after its long-time chairman, Peter Cooke of the Bank of England–or simply as the Basle committee.

efforts was an agreement in 1987 to establish common risk-based capital standards.

The committee's recommendations have evolved as a supervisory response to the perceived threats to bank safety and soundness that accompanied the emergence of a rapidly growing, increasingly competitive, innovative, and unregulated international banking system. The first agreement, the Concordat, established the guiding principle that no foreign banking establishment should escape supervision deemed to be adequate by both host- and parent-country regulators. Oversight for foreign branches is the responsibility of the parent-bank regulator, foreign-owned subsidiaries are jointly monitored by host- and parent-country authorities, and every international bank is to be monitored on the basis of its consolidated, worldwide activities (Bryant 1987).

The second agreement, to establish common risk-based capital standards, reflected growing regulatory concern about two major structural changes taking place in the international banking system: the rapid growth of off-balance sheet business and the growing discrepancies in capital requirements among nations with active international banking sectors. The twin objectives of the agreement are to strengthen bank capital in countries where the core of the international banking system is located and to equalize the impact of supervision on the competitive positions of banks in those countries (Lamfalussy 1988). Off-balance-sheet activities, such as issuing standby letters of credit, intermediating interest rate swaps, and writing futures contracts on a broad array of financial instruments, create contingent claims on banks' resources. Although these activities are an integral part of normal commercial banking, the contingent claims are neither assets nor liabilities in the accounting sense. As a result, they were not subject to the costs of maintaining regulatory capital adequacy ratios based on traditional balance sheet components. As increased competition in globally integrated markets narrowed banks' profit margins, and as corporate borrowers abandoned bank intermediation in favor of direct debt, off-balance sheet activities became an increasingly attractive business option: one of unknown risks, but free of regulatory costs.

Minimizing regulatory costs became particularly important to multinational banks operating in a globally competitive environment in which the rapid growth in assets in the 1970s was followed by the need to write down the book values of Third World loans in the 1980s. Capital-to-asset ratios had been reduced to very low levels, increasing the probability that even relatively minor shocks could lead to the insolvency of large banks, bringing with it concomitant risks of worldwide contagion. Unfortunately, regulatory efforts to raise capital standards in one country put that country's banks at a competitive disadvantage vis-à-vis foreign banks both at home and abroad, thereby creating incentives for banks to switch business to geographic locations with relatively low regulatory costs—leading to what Bryant (1987) called "a competition in laxity" on the part of would-be host countries.

The risk-based capital Agreement addresses both of these issues. Capital requirements are based on the presumed relative riskiness of each type of bank asset, and convergence factors are used to translate off-balance-sheet items to their asset-equivalent risk categories. Reasonably uniform definitions of the various components that qualify either wholly or partially for inclusion in the capital base have been agreed upon.[30] For twelve countries with twelve different banking, regulatory, and accounting systems to have reached consensus on capital standards is a remarkable achievement. The agreement strengthens stability-enhancing oversight, reduces incentives to shop for low-cost regulatory locations, and establishes a common approach to safety and solvency issues.

Despite these very positive contributions, supervisory convergence alone cannot provide fundamental robustness to an already fragile system. First, the risk-based capital agreement may be faulted on several points; second, the current mandate of the Basle Committee is too narrowly defined; and third, at least one systemwide problem, disaster myopia, may not be amenable to regulatory oversight as that is traditionally practiced.

3.1 Risk Based Capital

The agreement establishes a basic 8 percent capital-to-assets book-value requirement for all banks. Regulatory compliance is determined by applying a common set of risk-adjustment ratios to various asset categories. One problem is that risk-adjusted capital requirements derived from traditional accounting book values do not necessarily provide an effective early warning system against individual bank failures. Neither do they necessarily equalize regulatory capital costs across either banks or countries, and they can distort the allocation of bank funds. Finally, the agreement does not consider the issues of transfer (country) risk or interest rate risk: two important contributors to financial instability.

Common required book-value capital ratios do protect the institutions that serve as deposit guarantors in that high ratios provide a greater cushion against insolvency and allow more erosion of asset values before public funds need to be used to pay off creditors. On the other hand, they have little or no

---

30. There is some flexibility that allows for national discretion in the treatment of intangibles and banks' equity holdings in other banks as part of the Tier 2 supplementary capital components. See Hall (1989) for details of the agreement and Bardos (1987/88) for discussion of issues giving rise to the definitions agreed upon.

impact on the probability that individual banks may become insolvent. Bank failures are typically the result of fraud, bad management, or overconcentration in asset markets subject to unanticipated shocks. In the case of fraud or incompetent management, any capital ratio of less than 100 percent puts shareholders and deposit guarantors at risk. In the absence of shocks, well-managed banks can carry very low book-value capital ratios without adding to system risks. Better measures of insolvency or capital risks would be provided by using market-value or market-to-book-value capital ratios for large publicly traded banks active in international financial markets. High market-value ratios reflect analysts' and investors' perceptions of balanced, low-risk portfolios. Although analysts' judgments may be as subject to disaster myopia as those of bankers and regulators, their interpretations of readily available data on bank operations can be quickly transmitted into changed market values.

The agreed-upon capital requirements do not guarantee common regulatory costs of capital across countries. Although common definitions of "core" (equity) and "supplementary" capital components have been established, national authorities still have discretion in interpreting and applying the standards. To the degree to which some are more lenient in applying the standards to banks in their jurisdictions, the playing field will remain slanted toward financial centers with lower regulatory costs.[31] More important, common book-value requirements do not imply common regulatory costs of capital. The true costs of compliance are bank specific and are determined by the cost of capital to that bank in the marketplace. These costs are determined by market risk/return perceptions and the degree to which funds can be sourced in noncompetitive, low-cost markets. The agreement will not alter these fundamental market-based relationships.

The risk weights attached to each asset category, and the conversion factors attached to off-balance-sheet items, provide simple, albeit arbitrary, distinctions among the credit risks inherent in different types of lending. As such, they give regulators objective measures that can be easily applied by those to whom oversight responsibilities have been delegated. They also make possible peer group comparisons within, but not between, countries.[32] Insofar as the emphasis on asset categories directs the attention of both regulators and bankers to the importance of risk-balanced portfolios, the weighting system can contribute to stability within and among the agreement countries. On the other hand, asset quality and portfolio effects are at least as important as asset type and neither has been considered in establishing the risk weights. Hall (1989) points out that the assignment of the risk weights will affect a bank's

---

31. See Gray and Walter (1991) for an indication of the hidden support that can be provided.

32. Distinctions in legal and fiscal systems as well as in accounting conventions, preclude intercountry comparisons (Hall 1989).

business strategy, pricing policy, and capital allocation. If the assigned weights do not accurately reflect true asset risks, an emphasis on capital ratios in the assessment process could lead to potentially serious distortions in business policy and resource allocation, with their concomitant impact on the real economy.[33] Moreover, for banks under pressure to raise capital ratios, efforts to cover the costs of the new requirements could lead to acquisition of higher yielding, riskier assets, and/or assets whose returns are more highly correlated. In either event, adverse swings in asset values would increase the probability of insolvency. The potential for contagion would depend on the number and size of banks adopting these kinds of defensive strategies.[34]

Despite these limitations, the risk-based capital standards agreement represents an important step forward in coordinating international regulatory management of bank credit and capital risks. The members of the Basle Committee were unable to reach any consensus, however, on the management of two other banking risks critically important in maintaining the stability of global financial markets: transfer risk (the risk that debtors may not be able to obtain the currency in which their loan and its debt service are denominated) and interest rate risk (the risk that unanticipated interest rate changes will adversely affect asset values and funding costs). Neither is treated explicitly in the agreement, though both are to be taken up by the committee at some future time. For now, claims on foreign governments are simply assigned to the standard (100 percent) risk-weight category[35] and national authorities are given carte blanche in determing what, if any, risk weights are to be assigned to significant maturity mismatches.[36]

3.2 Committee Mandate

The mandate of the Basle committee is quite narrowly defined. It is only to take up issues related to bank supervision and regulation. Indeed, some

---

33. The Basle committee is aware of these shortcomings and stresses that there is no substitute for qualitative assessment.

34. Hall (1989) cites Lomax (1987) to point out that higher capital requirements mitigate against writing down the values of poorly performing assets. Note that the need to meet higher capital requirements calls for greater profits to provide internal sources of funding: this is very close to the emphasis that Minsky (1986b) puts on the need for profits. The additional capital can be thought of as *mandated investment*, and there is a stability-efficiency argument for treating this as an expense for tax purposes.

35. Another anomaly will be created if the European Community decides to treat all claims on member governments and banks similarly to those on domestic counterparts. A claim by a U.S. bank on the German government would then carry a higher capital-risk weight than would the same claim held by a French bank (Bardos 1987/88).

36. Although numerous opportunities exist to hedge maturity mismatches in both domestic and foreign currencies, few hedges are perfect and most will hold only when price fluctuations occur within some expected range (see note 8).

governments have claimed that the committee has no authority even to consider the international aspects of lender-of-last-resort responsibilities or monetary control issues.[37] Further, although it should, logically, be within the scope of committee consideration, no common ground has yet been found for developing recommendations for greater international supervision of securities markets.

Bank regulation and supervision are concerned with the avoidance of conditions leading to insolvency in individual banks when these conditions are caused by excessive credit risks or incompetent management. The importance of the oversight function for the smooth and uninterrupted operation of banking systems cannot be minimized, either domestically or internationally. But neither can it be separated from the lender-of-last-resort function. Insolvency avoidance, or even full deposit guarantees in the event of a large bank failure, makes up only one side of the stability-efficiency equation. Supervision and regulation do not provide liquidity to a system faced with an event that has the potential for destructive contagion effects. Such events may be triggered by a major bank failure, the inability of a major commercial enterprise to refinance short-term debt obligations, disarray in stock, commodities, futures and derivative securities markets,[38] or disruption to payments and clearing systems (Brimmer 1989, Moser 1990, Saunders 1988). Some of the underlying claims in these markets are subject to various degrees of domestic supervision, others are purely supernational. All are traded and cleared globally. All have the potential for contagion effects in the absence of multilaterally coordinated lender-of-last-resort facilities.[39]

Over the last fifteen years, shocks—such as the Third World debt crisis, the failure of Continental Bank, and the global stock market crash of 1987—have been deflected with minimum disruption to the system by the provision of central bank liquidity and deposit guarantees. The assumption can be made

---

37. The Concordat "sets out guidelines covering the responsibilities of the different supervisory authorities for the ongoing supervision of banks where those banks operate in more than one national jurisdiction. It is not, and never was intended to be, an agreement about responsibilities for the provision of lender-of-last-resort facilities to the international banking system, and there should not necessarily be considered to be any automatic link between acceptance of responsibility for ongoing supervision and the assumption of a lender of last resort role." (Bank of England, "Developments in Cooperation among Banking Supervisory Authorities," p. 240; cited in Bryant 1987, p. 148).

38. Derivative securities are created by pooling a large number of smaller loans and repackaging them for sale as a new security. Commonly called "securitization," examples include issues of Ginnie Maes and collateralized mortgage obligations.

39. Minsky points out that the internationalization of trading in derivative (synthetic) securities could be disruptive in that declines in the market value of the collateral create contingent claims on bank assets: claims that are senior to those of depositors. He suggests that securitization may be the market's answer to a world in which more recognized sources of fragility have been contained (1986b).

that central banks, in their own national interest, would continue to intervene to provide the necessary liquidity within their own jurisdictions, but there is no guarantee that their actions would be coordinated, that all would be willing participants, or that efforts to stem runs against a currency or a country's institutions could be sustained without multilateral policy coordination. As Kindleberger has argued, international public goods in the form of crisis management or last-resort lending may not be provided if there is no hegemon (leadership regime) both willing and able to do what is needed.[40] In the international financial markets of the 1990s, the absence of a hegemon with the necessary resources and authority makes international coordination of lender-of-last-resort responsibilities particularly important. The more fragile the system, the more important lender-of-last-resort cooperation among the Group of Ten countries becomes. Minsky (1986b) suggests that a crisis that verges on disaster may be necessary before serious efforts are made to define the responsibilities of the key cental banks to the international financial community.

Agreement on the provision of international liquidity is particularly important given the low probability of achieving regulatory convergence in securities markets in the near future, even though the Basle committee recognizes that this is an important next step. Not only are securities markets global, but the advent of securitization, as well as the erosion of restrictions on underwriting, has blurred the distinctions between commercial and investment banking in those countries, most particularly Japan and the United States, where legal constraints and separate regulatory jurisdictions enforce separation. Thus, convergence among domestic regulatory regimes becomes the necessary precursor to greater supervisory integration at the international level. On the other hand, the achievement of greater convergence in the regulation of securities activities will in no way diminish the need for coordination of lender-of-last-resort facilities. After all, shocks to securities markets take their toll through the liquidity pressures imposed on the banking system.

3.3 Disaster Myopia

Finally, there is at least one major risk that has systemic implications for the stability of the international financial system and that does not appear to be amenable to regulatory oversight as it is currently conceived. This is the risk of disaster myopia: a systematic tendency to underestimate the probability of a shock to the system, especially when the event giving rise to the shock occurs

---

40. Kindleberger (1986) provides a number of examples in which there was an inadequate supply of stability-enhancing international public goods.

only infrequently. In competitive banking markets, the need to maintain required returns can lead to a systemwide concentration of assets in those segments of the economy that appear to be the most prosperous and the fastest growing, and/or to excessive reliance on sources of funds that may prove renewable only at very high cost.[41] In the absence of recent adverse experience, disaster-myopic bankers, investors, analysts, *and* regulators are unlikely to anticipate problems until it is too late to retrench.[42] The problem is not so much one of identifying problems at individual banks as it is the emergence of system wide instability. Randall (1990) suggests that market analysis and regulatory oversight may be able to identify a bank in trouble in a sea of tranquility, but they are much less likely to perceive problems developing simultaneously in a number of large banks with similar asset concentrations unless onset of a period of fragility is already evident. The potential for disaster myopia provides the ultimate argument for integrating international lender-of-last-resort responsibilities.

4. Implications

The preceding sections have argued that the Minskian hypothesis of inherent fragility applies to the extant international financial system as well as to individual national systems. With the growing interdependence of national money and capital markets (with financial instruments denominated in national currencies), the fragility has increased substantially over recent years. How much of this increase is due to technological innovation and how much to ever-increasing leverage and a concomitant insouciance about crisis by international financial firms and governments is not clear. Certainly, technological innovation, which is not a key component in Minsky's hypothesis, has played a large part but the other aspects of Minsky's thinking are clear contributors to the existing fragility of the international financial system.[43] Large reliance on offshore sources of liabilities is analogous to a funding problem in the sense that the source of funds may dry up very quickly. Foreign loans to nonindustrialized nations have become less popular since the debacle of Latin American and other Third World debt, but the willingness to extend credit to

---

41. Guttentag and Herring (1986) identify five types of shocks that may affect the solvency of financial institutions: credit shocks, funding shocks, interest rate shocks, transfer shocks, and foreign exchange shocks. The latter two are specific to international banking activities, but in an internationally integrated system, all five have international implications.

42. The time dimension is vital here. Even given perfect cooperation, the regulatory and lender-of-last-resort functions may be too slow starting to prevent crisis and collapse. Devotees of Alice will recall the problem of Humpty-Dumpty and all the king's horses and all the king's men.

43. On a personal note, Minsky recently told the authors that he regards his 1957 *QJE* article on the interrelationship between new process technologies and the cost of funds as the best paper he has ever written.

erstwhile members of the eastern bloc may prove more tempting than wise. Disaster myopia has been present in real estate loans in many parts of the United States. Certainly, the need for banks to generate profits in order to meet their capital requirements has contributed to the banks' willingness to incur off-balance-sheet liabilities and to seek apparent profits at every opportunity.

There are two major, related sources of the current fragility of the international financial system and two tasks to be confronted. The first source to consider is the profligacy of the United States and the vulnerability to collapse of private financial firms in that country in the face of a flight from dollar-denominated assets (see table 1). This condition is the aftermath of a hegemon that could not stand the strain. Unfortunately, there has been no explicit recognition of the need for the international financial system to confront the absence of a hegemon and to find a substitute. The Basle committee has achieved miracles of international negotiation in terms of establishing supervisory regulations for international banks, but it has made no progress in terms of providing a lender of last resort. This is a crucial aspect of any financial system but central banks, however willing to act, can only create and lend their own national currency. Thus nothing exists to confront a major crisis in the foreign exchange markets caused by a flight from a major currency, presumably the U.S. dollar. The United States does not have reserves adequate to inspire confidence, let alone to fund a run on the dollar. The nation suffering the rash of withdrawals from its currency cannot act as lender of last resort; the central banks of the currencies being sought must be prepared to support the falling currency by buying it in the foreign exchange markets. Close cooperation among central banks will, in the event of such a run, be vital, and clearly the debtor nation (the United States) must obtain public long-term liabilities in foreign currencies. It is vital that the agreements (the infrastructure) for such cooperation be firmly in place before the event occurs because speed will be of the essence. If price instability in foreign exchange markets is to be avoided and some natural floor left unplumbed, countermeasures will come too late if central bankers have to worry about the minutiae of their own domestic, legal responsibilities at the same time that there is an urgent need for massive extensions of credit to the U.S. Treasury.[44] Nor does this allow for the possibility of irresponsible politicians making domestic hay out of the embarrassment of the United States. Erstwhile hegemons have often left scar tissue in other nations (Kindleberger 1986).

The second source is the fundamental stability-inefficiency that follows from the existence of integrated global financial markets without a global currency. This is the stuff nightmares are made on: it opens the door to

---

44. It should not be supposed that the crisis will leave the real economies of the creditor nations untouched and that the only sufferer will be the United States.

massive movements of liquid funds from one national currency to another. Moreover, at present, most of the funds invested are traded in highly efficient markets so that they can be withdrawn at very short notice indeed. The existing system might be tenable if the funds were essentially illiquid so that owners of financial instruments were effectively locked into the currency of denomination for four weeks or so prior to withdrawal or, more probably, if the funds were owned by national treasuries and central banks (that is, public not private debt) ready to supply international public goods rather than by private entities seeking to maximize their own wealth. The question of the net benefits derived from the existence of uninhibited international financial integration is whether the gain in allocative efficiency that derives from highly integrated financial markets is worth its cost in stability efficiency foregone (Gray and Gray 1981). It is a reasonable question whether perfect freedom of financial capital movements is consistent with a stable international financial system given the lack of a hegemon or a workable substitute arrangement (even in the absence of the existing imbalance in international net worths).[45] One thing is clear; it is far too late now to think in terms of imposing conditions on capital movements because the slightest hint of such a measure would trigger the crisis the measure was trying to avoid.

The two tasks to be confronted are, by now, self-evident. The first task is to make the existing system survive without crisis pending the completion of the second task: the development of and agreement to a replacement system that does not have the inherent weaknesses of the existing bastard child of Bretton Woods. Had the monetary authorities of the major nations had the Minskian hypothesis as one dimension of their consciousness, the world would have gone less deeply into the hole of fragility both within the United States and internationally. Nothing here would have prevented the profligacy of the U.S. domestic and international deficits, but the dangers would have been more apparent and the severity of the two tasks much less severe.

I also suggest that global financial stability makes it necessary to define the domain of responsibility of the key central banks as lenders of last resort to the international financial community. (Minsky, 1986b)

REFERENCES

Avramovic, Dragoslav (1964), *Economic Growth and External Debt*, Baltimore: Johns Hopkins Press.

---

45. The freedom of private international capital movements should be limited by the strength of the regime or hegemonic system. The weaker the hegemon, the greater the need for limits on capital controls. Contrariwise, if the technology precludes controls over private international capital movements, then the need for a strong hegemonic system is paramount.

Bardos, Jeffrey (1987/88), "The Risk-based Capital Agreement: A Further Step towards Policy Convergence," *Federal Reserve Bank of New York Quarterly Review* vol. 12, pp. 26–34.

Brimmer, Andrew F. (1989), "Distinguished Lecture on Economics in Government: Central Banking and Systemic Risks in Capital Markets", *Journal of Economic Perspectives* vol. 3, pp. 3–16.

Bryant, Ralph C. (1987), *International Financial Intermediation*, Washington, D.C.: The Brookings Institution.

Dymski, Gary A. and Manuel Pastor, Jr. (1991), "Bank Lending, Misleading Signals and the Latin American Debt Crisis," *The International Trade Journal* vol. 6, pp. 151–192.

Ehrenberg, R. (1963), *Capital and Finance in the Age of the Renaissance: A Study of the Fuggers and their Connections*, New York: Augustus M. Kelly, p. 50.

Eichengreen, Barry and Richard Portes (1987), "The Anatomy of Financial Crises," in Portes and Alexander Swoboda (eds.), *Threats to Inter-national Financial Stability*, Cambridge: Cambridge University Press.

Gray, H. Peter (1990), "A Model of Depression," *Banca Nazionale del Lavoro Quarterly Review*, pp. 269–288;

Gray, H. Peter (1991), "Why Does a Hegemonic System Work Better?" paper presented at the Eastern Economic Association Annual Meetings, Pittsburgh.

Gray, H. Peter and Paul J. Miranti (1990), "International Financial Statement Translation: The Problem of Real and Monetary Disturbances," *International Journal of Accounting* vol. 23, pp. 19–31.

Gray, H. Peter and Ingo Walter (1991), "The Integration of the EC Markets for Financial Services and the U.S. Banking and Insurance Industries" in George Yannopoulos (ed.), *Europe and America, 1992*, Manchester: Manchester University Press.

Gray, Jean M. and H. Peter Gray (1981), "The Multinational Bank: A Financial MNC?" *Journal of Banking and Finance* vol. 5, pp. 33–64.

Guenther, Jack D. (1981), "Is a Global Debt Crisis Looming? 'No' says a Citibank Senior V. P.," *ABA Banking Journal*, pp. 49–50 and 105.

Guttentag, Jack M. and Richard J. Herring (1986), "Disaster Myopia in International Banking," *Essays in International Finance* no. 164, Princeton: International Finance Section of Princeton University.

Hall, M. J. B. (1989), "The BIS Capital Adequacy 'Rules': A Critique," *Banca Nazionale Del Lavoro Quarterly Review*, pp. 207–227.

Howard, David H. (1989), "The Implications of the U.S. Current Account Deficit," *The Journal of Economic Perspectives* vol. 3, pp. 153–166.

Kane, Edward J. (1990), "Incentive Conflict in the Risk-Based Capital Agreement," *Federal Reserve Bank of Chicago Economic Perspectives*, pp. 33–36.

Kindleberger, C. P. (1986), "International Public Goods without Inter-national Government," *American Economic Review* vol. 76, pp. 1–11.

Lamfalussy, A. (1988), "Globalization of Financial Markets: International Supervisory and Regulatory Issues," *Financial Market Volatility*, Kansas City: Federal Reserve Bank of Kansas City, pp. 133–140.

Milberg, William S. and H. Peter Gray (1992), "International Competitiveness and Policy in Dynamic Industries," *Banca Nazionale del Lavoro Quarterly Review*, pp. 59–80.

Minsky, Hyman P. (1957), "Central Banking and Money Market Changes", *Quarterly Journal of Economics* vol. LXXI, pp. 171–187.

Minsky, Hyman P. (1985), *John Maynard Keynes*, New York: Columbia University Press.

Minsky, Hyman P. (1986a), *Stabilizing an Unstable Economy*, New Haven, Conn.: Yale University Press.

Minsky, Hyman P. (1986b), "The Global Consequences of Financial Deregulation," *The Marcus Wallenberg Papers on International Finance*, Washington, D.C.: International Law Institute and School of Foreign Service, Georgetown University.

Minsky, Hyman P. (1989), "The Macroeconomic Safety Net: Does It Need to Be Improved?" in H. Peter Gray (ed.), *The Modern International Environment*, Greenwich, Conn.: JAI Press, pp. 17–28.

Moser, James T. (1990), "Circuit Breakers," Federal Reserve Bank of Chicago *Economic Perspectives*, pp. 2–13.

Randall, Richard E. (1990), "The Need to Protect Depositors of Large Banks and the Implications for Bank Power and Ownership," *New England Economic Review*, pp. 63–75.

Saunders, Anthony (1988), "The Eurocurrency Interbank Market: Potential for International Crises," Federal Reserve Bank of Philadelphia *Business Review*, pp. 17–26.

Scholl, Russell B. (1990), "International Investment Position: Component Detail for 1989," *Survey of Current Business*, pp. 54–65.

Simon, Herbert A. (1978), "Rationality as Process and as Product of Thought," *American Economic Review* vol. 68, pp. 1–16.

Tobin, James (1978), "A Proposal for International Monetary Reform," *Eastern Economic Journal* vol. 4, pp. 153–159.

Tversky, Amos and Daniel Kahneman (1982), "Judgement under Uncertainty: Heuristics and Biases," in Daniel Kahneman, Paul Slovic, and Amos Tversky (eds.), *Judgment under Uncertainty: Heuristics and Biases*, New York: Cambridge University Press, pp. 3–22.

CHAPTER 7

Debt Crisis Adjustment in Latin America: Have the Hardships Been Necessary?

David Felix

Economics is a branch of moral philosophy struggling to become a science.

—Joan Robinson

Humankind cannot stand much reality.

—T.S. Eliot

The thesis of this paper is that the hardships of the heavily indebted Latin American economies have been needlessly augmented since 1982 by moral lapses and failures of policy analysis. The moral lapses relate to burden-sharing inequities imposed by the creditors when the debt crisis first exploded, and to the shameful avoidance by both debtors and creditors of an early solution to the crisis more consistent with capitalist rules of the game, at least in their normative versions, than that actually pursued. The policy failures refer to ill-timed policy advice and pressures on the debtors emanating from official Washington and the Washington-based international financial institutions (hereinafter IFIs), namely the IMF, the World Bank, and the Inter-American Development Bank. The policies, shaped by neoclassical notions of macro-dynamics, were ill-suited for handling Minsky-type macrodynamic instabilities that had been further worsened by the burden-sharing inequities. The policies needlessly intensified inflation, production decline, physical and human decapitalization and income inequality in most of the debtor economies.

To develop the case I proceed as follows. Section 1 summarizes the evolving debt crisis as of mid-1992. Section 2 outlines relevant differences between the Minskian and neoclassical macrodynamic perspectives. Section 3 details the initial burden-sharing inequities and the remedy not taken. Section 4 analyzes why the Washingtonian restructuring policies tended to backfire and speculates on whether the recent shift from restructuring by "getting prices right" to stabilizing by "getting prices wrong" is more viable.

1. A Mid-1992 Assessment of the State of the Debt Crisis

For the creditor governments, notably the United States, Latin America's debt crisis is now downgraded from serious danger to minor irritant. Major progress has been made toward the two primary goals motivating the crisis containment strategy of the creditor countries: preventing open Latin American defaults from triggering an international banking crisis, and keeping the economic and political burden of debt servicing from triggering leftist political upheavals in the debtor countries. The strategy went through tribulations and permutations during the 1980s.[1] But by the early 1990s the nominal value of Latin American debt held by foreign commercial banks had dropped markedly; conservative regimes oriented to "market friendly" policies, to use the World Bank's slippery jargon, now pervade the region; and, in any event, with the collapse of the Soviet Union the leftist threat has lost much of its geopolitical importance to the creditor governments.

Table 1 shows that most of the decline of commercial loan exposure occurred after 1987. Previously, the relative share of Latin American debt held by private lenders, almost all commercial banks, had only fallen modestly—from 73 percent in 1982 to 65 percent in 1987, or to 67 percent when interest arrears are included—while its dollar value had risen 22 percent. From 1987 to 1991, however, these claims including arrears declined 24 percent, while their share of total Latin American debt dropped to little more than half.

The turnaround reflected a reversal of bank strategy. Until 1987 the banks had refused to give partial debt writeoffs, but had contributed, albeit reluctantly, to the "concerted" packets of official and bank loans by which the official lenders cajoled debtor governments into maintaining full debt service and adopting IMF-approved restructuring policies.[2] By 1987, the banks, having considerably expanded their non–Latin American portfolios, felt robust

---

1. See Felix 1990.

2. The bank reluctance is captured succinctly by the label "involuntary loans" applied initially to the bank loans by the IFI debt crisis publications. Subsequently, IFI wordsmiths shifted to the more chummy term "concerted loans." The reluctance took two forms. Less-exposed members of the lending syndicates supplying the pre-crisis bank loans had to be strong-armed by syndicate leaders and creditor central banks to participate in the initial "concerted loan" packets. Strong-arming notwithstanding, more and more of these banks dumped their Latin American paper on the market at discounted prices, terminating their syndicate memberships and further participation in "concerted lending." The over-exposed banks, whose loan quotas were being pushed up by the defections, bargained down the the overall bank shares in the negotiations of concerted lending, with IFI lending taking up the slack. See Devlin 1989, chapters 5 and 6, for a detailed description and analysis of the concerted lending negotiations, and the cajoling tactics used on the debtor governments by the creditor governments and the IFIs.

TABLE 1.   Size and Distribution of the External Debt of Latin America and its Major Debtor Countries, 1982, 1987, 1991

	Argentina	Brazil	Chile	Mexico	Peru	Venezuela	L. America
1982							
Total Debt (US$ Millions)	43634	91922	17314	86111	12285	32045	333210
% Govt. Guaranteed	36.4	55.9	30.3	60.2	61.9	38.5	53.7
% Private Lenders	62.0	79.6	75.3	62.9	55.3	55.4	73.1
1987							
Total Debt (US$ Millions)	56813	123931	21239	107882	18058	36519	442481
% Govt. Guaranteed	89.8	77.2	80.0	81.5	81.8	69.1	80.6
% Private Lenders	77.7	54.2	67.3	81.7	48.8	86.6	65.2
% Comm. Bank Loans	71.0	83.8	92.4	87.2	64.7	89.6	82.4
% Other[a]	29.0	16.2	7.6	12.8	35.3	10.4	17.6
Interest Arrears (US$ Millions)	351	3430	0.0	0.0	1904	0.0	8074
1991							
Total Debt[b] (US$ Millions)	56273	116803	19313	97823	19888	35998	429174
% Govt. Guaranteed	92.5	71.3	58.9	85.3	70.8	84.3	78.3
% Private Lenders	54.5	48.5	25.8	52.6	30.5	68.4	46.0
% Comm. Bank Loans	56.8	82.9	88.4	12.2	64.9	4.1	48.4
% Other	43.2	17.1	11.6	87.8	35.1	95.9	51.6
Interest Arrears[b] (US$ Millions)	7544	10607	0.0	0.0	4067	0.0	27258

Source: The World Bank, *World Debt Tables*, various years.
[a] Includes exit bonds, supplier credit, dollar collateralized paper etc. No breakdown given in source for 1982.
[b] Interest arrears and all Peruvian data are for 1990.

enough to resist official pressures for new "concerted" loans and became amenable to exchanging partial writeoffs for more secure collateralizing of the remaining claims. By 1991 about half the reduced claims were externally collateralized under various negotiated arrangements. These make up the bulk of the "other" category in Table 1. The dramatic drop in 1991 of commercial bank loans and the rise of "other" claims on Mexico and Venezuela are primarily due to the completion of Brady Plan workouts, in which old loans were partly written down and rolled over into new paper collateralized with U.S. Treasury bonds, which the debtor governments acquired with the help of official, mostly IFI, loans. Comparable Brady workouts are now in process for Argentina and Brazil, presaging further reductions of total bank claims and increases of "other" claims and official loans.

Latin American defaults are therefore receding fast as threats to the solvency of the banking system of the United States or other major creditor countries. And banks that had overlent to Latin America are, according to bank analysts, emerging with only moderate net losses (Lipin 1992). If their balance sheets again look shaky, it's because they used the time bought them by the concerted lending and other default-deflecting strategems of the creditor governments and IFIs to diversify excessively into high-flying real estate and leveraged buyout financing that has now soured.

On the other hand, for only a few of the Latin American debtors is the travail stemming from the debt crisis palpably moderating. Debt servicing has been less a constraint on economic recovery in the past couple of years for most Latin American debtor countries, but some of the contributing factors appear transient. Moreoever, major physical and human capital losses and damage to the social and political fabric of the debtor countries from the severe and inequitable distribution of the adjustment burden over the past decade now compete with debt service as prime obstacles to sustained economic recovery.

We turn first to debt servicing. Table 1 shows that in current dollars the region's overall foreign debt, including interest arrears, was almost constant during the years 1987–1991, though the country variance increased. The debt of all six countries in the table rose during the years 1982–1987, but the upward trend persisted after 1987 for only three of the countries. Deflated by the U.S. rate of inflation, the region's dollar debt in 1991 was 6 percent lower than in 1982 and 14 percent lower than in 1987, with all but one (Peru) of the six countries sharing in the improvement. But when deflated by the drop of the terms of trade during the 1980s, which averaged 25 percent for the region, the real foreign debt burden of the region in 1991 was above that of 1982, and barely below that of 1987. However, deviations from the regional average qualify that conclusion; for example, Chile's terms of trade fell much less and Argentina's and Mexico's considerably more than the regional average (CEPAL 1991, cuadro 24).

The debt-service ratios in Table 2 generally show a declining trend since 1982, though with exceptions and mid-decade retrogressions; for example, Argentinian and Peruvian ratios worsen between 1982 and 1991 and Brazilian ratios worsen after 1987. Falling dollar interest rates, reinforced in varying degree by export growth, mainly account for the ratio declines, with length-

TABLE 2. Latin American Debt Ratios, 1978–91

	Debt/ Exports[1]	Debt Service/ Exports[1,2]		Interest/ Exports[1]		Average Years Maturity
Argentina						
1978	1.26	0.27		0.06		9.1
1982	4.47	0.54		0.37		9.0
1987	6.95	0.74	(0.78)	0.48	(0.52)	11.0
1991	4.29	0.45	(1.02)	0.25	(0.82)	16.0
Brazil						
1978	2.45	0.31		0.07		10.0
1982	3.95	0.81		0.49		11.4
1987	4.30	0.42	(0.54)	0.26	(0.38)	13.1
1991	3.20	0.27	(0.56)	0.15	(0.44)	12.3
Chile						
1978	1.99	0.41		0.10		8.1
1982	3.36	0.71		0.46		9.2
1987	3.31	0.37		0.26		14.4
1991	1.77	0.27		0.18		14.5
Mexico						
1978	2.25	0.55		0.16		8.3
1982	3.11	0.57		0.40		7.4
1987	3.64	0.40		0.28		12.3
1991	2.22	0.30		0.18		10.0
Peru						
1978	2.24	0.31		0.13		10.7
1982	2.94	0.55		0.26		10.3
1987	4.87	0.12	(0.64)	0.07	(0.59)	15.2
1991	4.37	0.03	(0.95)	0.03	(0.92)	14.7
Venezuela						
1978	0.68	0.07		0.04		9.8
1982	1.60	0.29		0.17		9.3
1987	2.69	0.38		0.21		8.3
1991	1.88	0.23		0.15		10.0
Latin America						
1978	1.35	0.26		0.09		10.2
1982	2.70	0.48		0.15		10.0
1987	3.70	0.38	(0.40)	0.24	(0.26)	13.4
1991	2.68	0.25	(0.32)	0.13	(0.20)	14.2

Source: World Bank, *World Debt Tables*, various years.

[1] Exports include services.

[2] Numbers in parenthesis include arrears on interest payments.

ened maturity and debt-equity swaps also contributing for some of the countries. Yet if we take 1978 as the last "normal" year before Latin American debt and its interest bill took off, the ratios of all save Chile and Mexico will have to fall much further to regain "normality."

Will it happen? Probably not. Future Brady writeoffs and debt-equity swaps related to sales of state assets will be working against the tide. The predominance of fixed interest claims in the current debt, brought about by the growth of IFI lending and commercial bank loan conversions, has lessened the sensitivity of debt service to interest rate declines. Prolonging the recession currently afflicting the industrialized countries, on which the further decline of dollar interest rates appears to depend, would flatten exports, as would also the renewed reliance of many debtor governments on overvaluing the exchange rate to dampen inflation.

The mixed debt-service prospects nothwithstanding, foreign exchange constraints on growth have recently loosened for most of the debtor countries, including even Argentina and Peru. Widening current account deficits are being financed by arrears on interest payments, portfolio capital inflows including returning flight capital, the sale of state assets, an increased pace of IFI lending, and, for some Andean countries, clandestine drug exports. These inflows have been financing rapidly rising imports and have helped sustain exchange rate overvaluation. Thus should the inflows—much of it nervous speculative money and one-time proceeds from privatizations—cease expanding, devaluation-inflation spiraling would again intensify, and the foreign exchange constraint on economic growth would again bind.

Table 3 highlights a prime domestic obstacle to sustained economic recovery. The stocks of physical capital of five of the six countries in the table shrank and aged during the 1980s, in Chile during the 1970s as well, the 1980s deterioration being greatest in Argentina and Venezuela. The two capital/labor ratios measure different aspects of the decapitalization. Declining K_e/L traces mainly the decay and technological obsolescing of the industrial structure, whereas falling K/L reflects also the decay of the physical infrastructure.

The physical decapitalization can be expected to have a double-edged impact on economic growth, creating investment possibilities but thwarting their implementation. The latter is likely to dominate, since an increased incidence of bottlenecks should retard exporting and raise the import intensity of investment. Investment pickups are likely to bump fatally against the foreign exchange constraint, unless more debt relief and/or official lending come to the rescue, or private foreign capital is again willing to finance widening current account deficits on the scale that brought on the 1980s debt crisis. Neither seems likely in the next few years. Generous official lending for Latin American debt relief is a political non starter, while memories in international financial markets of the lending excesses of the late 1970s will take some years more to fade away.

Human capital loss, like the concept itself, is more difficult to quantify directly, as is its adverse feedback on the balance of payments and output growth, especially in a region ridden by underemployment and brain draining. Employment and labor income data imply serious losses. Thus between 1980 and 1987 average real income of wage-salary earners fell 15 percent in the Latin American formal private sector and 30 percent in the public sector, while combined employment in the two sectors rose a bare 3 percent. Concurrently, the economically active in the urban informal sector rose 55 percent while their average real income fell 42 percent (PREALC 1990A, 1990B). Even in Chile, hyped by IFI publicists as the success model for the other debtors, the average real wage of the formal sector in 1989 was 5.5 percent below that of 1982 and 8 percent below that of 1970, while average real income of the informal sector in 1989 was 30 percent below that of 1982 (Mújica and Larranaga 1992, cuadros 2.3, 2.4).

Poverty line estimates also suggest deterioration: families earning below that line rose to 37 percent of all Latin American families in the 1980s, reversing a drop from 40 percent to 35 percent in the 1970s (CEPAL 1992, cuadro I-6). By this measure, Chile shows up worse than the regional average. In 1970, 17 percent of all Chilean families and 20 percent of the population were below the poverty line; by 1987 it was 38 percent of all families and 44 percent of the population. The proportions below the more exiguous Indi-

TABLE 3. Growth of Net Stock of Non-Residential Fixed Capital Relative to the Labor Force, 1951–89

	Ke/L	K/L	Ke/L	K/L	Ke/L	K/L
			(Percent Change per Decade)			
	Argentina		*Brazil*		*Chile*	
1951–60	43.9	30.7	56.4	137.1	70.8	20.3
1961–70	81.6	42.2	26.0	57.9	28.0	33.6
1971–80	47.8	46.0	114.1	108.3	−3.3	−1.1
1981–89	−34.3	−18.6	−30.8	−2.9	−2.2	−11.4
	Colombia		*Mexico*		*Venezuela*	
1951–60	73.2	6.8	58.1	48.7	185.7	130.0
1961–70	1.8	8.2	216.2	26.2	−26.3	−6.0
1971–80	65.0	27.1	60.1	28.3	67.5	38.8
1981–89	4.2	7.5	−18.8	−5.2	−25.1	−19.5

Source: Computed from data series in Hofman 1991.
Definitions: Ke = the net stock of machinery and equipment,
  K = Ke plus the net stock of non-residential structures,
  L = the economically active population.

gency line also rose sharply: from 7 percent of families and 10 percent of the population in 1970 to 14 percent and and 17 percent respectively in 1987.[3]

Other regional indicators are more mixed. Infant mortality continued to decline substantially during the 1980s, but life expectancy at age one leveled off. Illiteracy continued to decline, but so did the quality of public education. Specialists on these matters foresee the adverse effects of the reduced real public outlays on health, education and other social programs registering more strongly in social statistics of the coming years (CEPAL 1992, capítulo 1). No doubt this will impede economic growth, but one suspects that for the next few years human capital deterioration will remain largely a slack variable, subordinated to physical, financial (including foreign exchange), and political obstacles.[4]

The political obstacles relate to social tensions generated by the increased income concentration that accompanied the deepened poverty. Prior to the "lost decade" of the 1980s, income concentration rose secularly but not monotonically, since profits and rents tended to rise more than labor income during expansionary periods, and to fall more during depressions. The 1980s broke with this procyclical pattern, income distribution becoming more polarized during that depressed decade. The polarization—strongest in urban incomes, with the wage and salaried workers, the most politicized of the popular classes, taking the hardest hit (CEPAL 1992, cuadro I-5; Mújica and Larranaga 1992, cuadro 2.7)—has explosive potential. Foreign capital appears well aware of this, as witness its quick exodus from Venezuela in response to an aborted populist military coup in February 1992.[5]

2. Perspectives on the Debt Crisis: Neoclassical versus Minskian Macrodynamics

Theoretical perspectives define reality. Central to neoclassical macrodynamics, which has been guiding creditor analysis of Latin America's debt crisis, is an axiomatic belief that competitive market processes, given time, are fully error correcting at the macro- as well as micro-level. Macroeconomic instabilities in capitalist economies are transitory deviations from their "natu-

---

3. See CEPAL 1990, p. 5 and cuadros 12 and 13. Incomes below the Poverty line are insufficient to purchase a consumption basket that includes food adequate to meet FAO minimum daily requirements for calories and proteins plus shelter, clothing, and other household essentials meeting other minimum standards. Incomes below the Indigency line fall short of what's needed merely to acquire the food component of the above bundle. Income includes in-kind as well as cash income.

4. World Bank researchers have found marginal rates of return from years of education to have dropped significantly in the 1980s in their LDC samples, which are apparently heavily weighted with debtor countries. Reported in Fanelli, Frenkel, and Taylor 1992.

5. Stoga 1992. The coup leaders have become popular heroes in Caracas.

ral" growth paths along which all factor markets are in equilibrium. The deviations are set off by shocks originating outside the market processes and are compounded by lags in the corrective responses of markets. The lags get extended and the natural rate lowered when markets are ridden with private monopoly elements and government regulations and controls, since these hamper the correction by distorting the price signals guiding output and investment decisions of private agents. Hence where such distortions are widespread, deregulating and liberating markets of monopoly elements should be an essential component of macroeconomic stabilizing policies.

Since the error-correcting power of free competitive markets works for all manner of shocks, differences in initial conditions do not require qualitatively different policy approaches, but merely call for adjusting the timing and sequencing of elements in the universal policy set. The distinctions of structure and culture between less-developed countries (LDCs) and developed countries (DCs) that had been central to postwar development theorizing, including under the rubric of market imperfections and failures most neoclassical development theorizing, fade from view. The fading is not because the distinctions no longer exist, but because, in the current neoclassical macrodynamic view, LDCs can finesse underdevelopment by transforming themselves into small, open, purely competitive economies, letting the untrammeled inflow and outflow of goods, capital, and enterprise compensate for production, managerial, entrepreneurial, technological and financial shortfalls and excesses (Balassa et al. 1986).

In Minskian macrodynamics, on the other hand, natural steady state growth paths do not exist for capitalist economies because the financial dynamics inherent in the capital accumulation process may diverge from, as well as converge toward, equilibrium. In making future commitments wealth-accumulating agents are prone to choose fallible path dependency and follow-the-leader strategies, since markets cannot provide the set of future prices needed to transform the uncertainties surrounding private investing, lending, and borrowing decisions into securely calculable risks.[6]

Minsky's microeconomics are also at odds with the neoclassical perspective. Oligopoly is not merely typical of modern capitalism, but it is unavoidably so because economies of scale and scope are so widespread that marginal costs remain below average costs over the normal output range in the majority of markets. Price fixing, market sharing, collusive technology agreements and other manifestations of market power are, however, also "thwarting mechanisms" in Minsky's terminology; they reduce borrowing and lending risks and

---

6. My summary of Minsky's perspective relies heavily on Minsky 1975 and 1986 and on Ferri and Minsky 1992. Minsky, of course, freely acknowledges his intellectual debt to Keynes and Kalecki, and to a lesser extent, to Marx, Schumpeter and Irving Fisher.

prolong tranquility in financial markets by stabilizing cash flows. Monopoly power has its social uses in Minsky's perspective.

Financial tranquility, however, also reduces risk perceptions, which induces more venturesome investment, lending, asset pricing, and debt leveraging. The economy moves toward greater financial fragility, that is, to a condition that overstrains the capacity of the private thwarting mechanisms to handle exogenous shocks and endogenous bubbles. Capital accumulation dynamics thus threaten intermittently to bring on systemwide financial crises accompanied by downward spiraling asset prices, investment rates, output and employment. To contain these requires extra-market, i.e., governmental, thwarting mechanisms, such as lender-of-last-resort actions by the central bank, fiscal interventions, and regulatory and legislative modifications of market institutions and permissible behavior. Minsky acknowledges that intercessions can also be ineffective or counterproductive, but not that such failures gainsay his basic contention that destabilizing dynamics of private markets rather than poorly designed interventions are the *causae primae* of the recurrent crises.

Successful governmental intervention also comes with a kicker. In recreating favorable but somewhat altered conditions for a resurgence of private capital accumulation, agents are also induced to innovate around the new restrictions, gradually eroding their effectiveness as thwarting mechanisms and requiring policy revisions. But, unlike the Lucas-Sargent neoclassical thesis that such market reactions render interventionist policies impotent to affect long-term growth (Lucas 1975, Sargent and Wallace 1975), for Minsky, governments and markets are engaged in interactive games, with trends in real time of output, employment, and other social desiderata depending crucially on how skillfully the government plays the game.

The two perspectives also diverge as regards property rights. In neoclassical macrodynamics the security of property rights and contract enforcement are crucial stabilizers and "policy surprises" destabilizers of markets. In Minsky's perspective, on the other hand, intermittent policy surprises and alterations of property rights and contracts are essential for stability. His "Anti-Laissez-Faire theorem" asserts:

"In a world where the internal dynamics imply instability, a semblance of stability can be achieved or sustained by introducing conventions, constraints and interventions into the environment. The conventions imply that variables take on values other than those which market forces would have generated; the constraints and interventions impose new initial conditions or affect parameters so that individual and market behavior change." (Ferri and Minsky 1991, pp. 20–21)

The two perspectives are, however, equally ambiguous about political power. In urging LDCs to transform into small open competitive economies, the neoclassical perspective, with its antipathy to market power, may be implying either that international markets for goods, capital, and technology approximate purely competitive markets with powerless price-taking agents, or that powerless LDCs have little choice but to subordinate themselves to omnipotent international capital.[7] This ambiguity between textbook economics and *real politik* is present also in the Minsky perspective, which leaves unexplored the question, what prevents firms from using their market power to gain political power and rig the thwarting policies in their favor? Kindleberger's economic hegemon requirement for stabilizing the world market system, which internationalizes the Minskian perspective, merely internationalizes the *cui bono* question (Kindleberger and Laffargue 1982).

3. Initial Burden Sharing Inequities

3.1 Ex Post Guarantees of Private Foreign Debts

When the debt crisis exploded, the international *cui bono* question was answered quickly and brutally. The banks, about three-fifths of whose Latin American loans were strictly private contracts carrying no government guarantee, were freed from having to do workouts with their distressed private borrowers by the Latin American governments, who under creditor pressure agreed to give *ex post* guarantees that private bank loans would be serviced. Neoclassical sanctity of contract gave way to a Minsky-type property right alteration.

For all Latin America, government-guaranteed bank loans rose from 40 percent in 1982 to 85 percent in 1987, with *ex post* guarantees adding around $44 billion or 25 percent to the 1982 public foreign debt of the region.[8]

---

7. IFI papers and publications wobble around this basic issue. Some working papers emphasize the dangers to LDCs of liberalizing the capital account or adopting other facets of the market liberalization strategy, with imperfectly competitive international markets and LDC institutional weaknesses at the core of the critiques. These heterodoxies are ignored or enter as mere asides in official IFI publications such as the World Development Reports of the World Bank. On the other hand, working papers advising LDCs that, international market power inequities of capital markets nothwithstanding, they have little recourse but to open up, get more prominence in official IFI publications. Mathieson and Rójas-Suárez 1992, an IFI working paper recently highlighted by the IMF *International Financial Survey*, is illustrative. It urges LDCs to liberate their capital markets, using *faute de mieux* "realism" rather than optimality arguments.

8. These figures were estimated from table 1, which shows that 53.7 percent of the region's debt in 1982 was publicly guaranteed, about half being official loans to government entities. Dividing the other half, or 27 percent, by total private lending, which was 73 percent of the total

debt service to debt

Servicing that added public debt increased the financial as well as the fiscal burden, most heavily when the public sector, as in Argentina, was a negligible exporter, so that the central government had to purchase its foreign exchange. Argentina was further hard hit because its *ex post* guarantees, as table 1 shows, were disproportionately large. Although this was also true of Chile and Venezuela, the fiscal-financial blow was cushioned there, as government firms were the dominant exporters.

concerted loans

The creditors had, in effect, forced an adverse tradeoff on the debtors: concerted lending in return for the *ex post* guarantees. Concerted lending provided short-term debt-service relief but added in the longer term to the fiscal, financial, and debt-service overloads. The burden of saving the banks could have been shared more fairly. Even if, under the crisis conditions prevailing in the debtor countries, workouts with their private debtors might have pushed the more fragile banks into open insolvency, the creditor countries had infinitely more resources than the debtor countries to bail them out. Forcing an *ex post* change of contract terms in order to shift part of the burden to the debtors was a power play that violated both capitalistic moralizing about the inviolability of contracts and social norms of fairness.

There were some unavailing complaints from debtor governments. To Chile's Chicago Boys, then in charge of economic policy, making private foreign borrowing a purely private affair had been a much-publicized feature of their free-market strategy. IMF support for that policy also seemed rock solid, as when the Director of the Western Hemisphere Division of the IMF pronounced to a Chilean Central Bank seminar in 1980:

> "In the case of the private sector, I would argue that the difference between domestic and foreign debt is not significant—barring governmental interference with the transfer of service payments or other clearly inappropriate public policies—if it exists at all. The exchange risks associated with foreign borrowing are presumably taken into account as are the other risks associated with borrowing, whether it be from domestic or foreign sources. More generally, private firms can be expected to be careful in assessing the net return to be derived from borrowing funds as compared with the net cost since their survival as an enterprise is at stake."[9]

---

debt, yields 37 percent as the share of private lending with an *ex ante* public guarantee. Allowing for the small portion that was nonbank, such as multinational intracorporate loans, raises the share of bank loans with *ex ante* public guarantees to around 40 percent. A similar calculation for 1987 shows that around 85 percent of bank loans had become publicly guaranteed. Around $40 billion represented "involuntary" new loans which were guaranteed *ex ante*, leaving around $44 billion as *ex post* guaranteed bank loans.

But when the banks in 1982 demanded the *ex post* guarantees as *quid pro quo* for rescheduling Chile's debt, the IMF offered no public objection and privately urged acceptance of the bank demands (Devlin 1989, p. 219). Saving the banks on their terms apparently took precedence for the IMF over doctrinal consistency.[10] Neither have the *ex post* guarantees been incorporated explicitly in most subsequent debt crisis analyses. Even critics of Washingtonian restructuring policies generally start from the premise that the entire debt had been incurred *ab initio* by governments.

3.2 Domestic Financial Bailouts

The resistance of many debtor governments was no doubt weakened because they were already enmeshed in bailing out their banks and firms from severe domestic financial crises. The crises were deepest in Southern Cone countries that had adopted expansive market liberalization strategies in the 1970s. Argentina's banking system began crumbling in 1980 under mounting bad loans and excessive dollar liabilities. Chile's and Uruguay's followed suit in 1981. With the exchange rate under pressure, the central banks, as part of the crisis containment effort, had set up subsidized exchange rate facilities for domestic banks and firms to service their foreign obligations. Brazil and Mexico, with less severe domestic financial turbulence, did the same. In that context, *ex post* guarantees to foreign banks appeared less shocking.

What was shocking was the cost to the fisc and to the rest of the society of the damage control. Argentina's overall fiscal deficit shot up from 6.5 percent of GDP in 1978–79 to 15.1 percent in 1981–82, with two-thirds due to interest payments on sharply increased domestic and foreign debt obligations and another one-sixth to falling tax receipts. Concurrently, the quasi-fiscal deficit of the central bank, negligible in 1979, reached 5 percent of GDP on a cash and 3.5 percent on an accrual basis in 1982.[11] This represented the dual cost of refinancing business liabilities at a highly negative real interest rate and recapitalizing insolvent banks. As the latter involved putting a cap on deposit interest, using the same negative real interest rate, depositors took a

---

9. The statement is from a paper by E. Walter Robichek, then Western Hemisphere Director, which was published in Banco Central de Chile, *Estudios Monetarios VII* (Santiago, Chile, December, 1981), cited in Díaz-Alejandro 1985, p. 9.

10. According to Harberger (1986), "The major international banks seem to have acted in concert, leaving the Chilean government with no serious alternative but to assume the position of reluctant guarantor. There can be little doubt that if each foreign creditor and each Chilean debtor bank had been left to work out its financial affairs under applicable laws, a fair share of the foreign debt of the failed or failing Chilean banks would have been written off, and Chile's debt service problems would consequently have been less."

11. Computed from appendix tables in Chisari et al. 1992.

major hit. Estimates of wealth losses to time and savings depositors range from 8.3 percent to 8.9 percent, and to demand depositors 4.4 percent, of GDP, while the immediate subsidy to private sector balance sheets from these financial operations is estimated at from 10.8 percent to 13.4 percent of GDP. (Baliño 1991, table 18). Income losses were also substantial: the government's wage bill dropped 2.3 percent of GDP while real wages nationally fell 20 percent between 1980 and 1982 (Chisari et al. 1992, cuadros 1 and A3).

The wealth transfers were part of a premeditated Fisher-Minsky-type debt deflation.[12] The architect of the 1982 financial bailouts asserted that negative real rates were needed for a limited time to erode the value of existing bank loans and deposits, since "there is a manifest disproportion between the magnitude of enterprise and household liabilities, both in pesos and in dollars, and in the liabilities of the public sector itself, in relation to the value of real assets, especially productive assets."[13] Chile and Uruguay had comparable wealth transfers and income redistributions, Chile's amounting to over a third of GDP in 1982–1988 (Fanelli, Frenkel and Taylor 1992, pp. 25, 35–36). I have found no formal estimates of Uruguay's wealth transfers, but since the 1980s saw rounds of official refinancing of private debt on successively easier terms followed by reneging by most firms and banks on the reduced debt payments, the Uruguayan wealth transfers must surely have approached Chilean proportions (Pérez-Campanero and Leone 1991, pp. 318–335). Less extensive private-sector rescues also occurred in the early 1980s in the other major debtor countries (Massad and Zahler 1988).

3.2 Capital Flight: A Neoclassical-Minskian Debt Crisis Solution Not Taken

Capital flight, which increased in almost all the debtor countries, worsened fiscal-financial burdens and distributional inequities. Capital flight primarily involves outflows of liquid assets, owned in Latin America almost entirely by the top decile of households, according to survey data. The increased outflow meant, therefore, that the affluent stratum containing the direct beneficiaries

12. Irving Fisher coined the term "debt deflation" to describe the effort by overborrowed firms concurrently to ease their debt servicing stress by cutting back investment and selling off assets to reduce debt. The aggregate effect, Fisher pointed out, was periodically to transform recessions into "great depressions," like that of 1929–33. A quantity theory devotee, Fisher contended that the "thwarting" remedy was monetary expansion to hold up commodity and asset prices and hold down the real interest rate (Fisher 1933). To Minsky, who puts financial instability and debt deflation in a Keynesian framework, Fisher was defective on theory and too simplistic on remedy (Minsky 1975).

13. Quoted in Baliño 1991, pp. 94–95. The architect, Domingo Cavallo, was then President of the Central Bank and now, as Minister of Finance, is the architect of Argentina's current exchange-rate-freezing stabilization program, el Plan Cavallo.

of the financial bailouts was concurrently draining scarce foreign exchange and grossly underdeclaring its foreign income, thus placing more of the augmented fiscal-financial burden on the poorer deciles.[14]

The sizeable private foreign assets, however, could have enabled the debtor countries to engineer a partial, and for some of them a complete, extrication from the debt crisis by mobilizing their private foreign assets to liquidate their foreign debt, or, alternatively, mobilizing the income from these assets to service the debt. For Argentina, Mexico, and Venezuela, each of which had a stock of private foreign assets about equal to its foreign debt, complete extrication was possible.[15]

Mobilizing foreign assets centers on their compulsory registration and exchange for domestic government bonds, the mobilized assets being then formally escrowed as collateral against the public foreign debt.[16] Mobilizing the income from these assets instead involves tightening taxation of the income from foreign assets. Such Minsky-type policy interventions have ample historic precedents in 20th-century capitalism. Britain in the two world wars and France in World War I required nationals to register their foreign securities with the treasury, which could sell them outright or use them as collateral against U.S. loans, the original owners being compensated in domestic currency bonds. More relevant perhaps was the peacetime Marshall Plan effort of European governments to mobilize and repatriate clandestine European flight capital. The efforts were backed in the congressional act authorizing the Marshall Plan, which included a clause requiring any government receiving Marshall aid to "locate and identify and put into appropriate use" the foreign assets of its citizens (Helleiner 1992, p. 17).

That clause was a compromise between U.S. bankers objecting to interference with their lucrative activities as purveyors and repositors of flight capital, whose interests were defended by the U.S. Treasury, and the interventionist views of radical proto-Minskians such as Henry Cabot Lodge, Marriner Eccles, and Herbert Hoover. Lodge asserted, "In a lot of these countries it is a well-known fact that there is a small, bloated, selfish class of people whose assets have been spread all over the place and that is a very bad thing for the morale of these countries and it is a bad thing for the morale over here" (Helleiner 1992, p. 10).

He wanted U.S. authorities to search out and turn over the assets of the recreant owners to their governments, a position supported in U.S. Senate

---

14. The 1980s balance of payments of the debtor countries with reported capital flight shows no comparable increase of interest and dividend inflows.

15. The estimates are for 1985, and include reinvested earnings not repatriated. Felix and Caskey 1990, table 1.7.

16. For an elaboration with emphasis on creditor government help to the debtor governments in identifying foreign assets, see Felix 1985.

testimony by Eccles, the chairman of the Federal Reserve, and Hoover. Eccles asserted that "the question was whether this Government was going to protect the private rights of foreign citizens as against the efforts of their governments to survive," while Hoover observed, "If there is a protest that taking over these privately held resources is a hardship on the owners, it may be pointed out that the alternative is a far greater hardship for the American taxpayer" (Helleiner 1992, pp. 10,15).

Less crisis driven has been the spread of international agreements for the exchange of information on the laundering and squirreling of assets related to drugs and tax evasion. These now require the banks of fifteen signatory countries (including Switzerland!) to report to the respective monetary authorities the true owners of large foreign deposits and the identity of all participants in large international banking transactions (Helleiner 1992, pp. 30–31).

The theoretical rationale for such intervention is, moreover, *echt* neoclassical. In conventional national income and growth accounting, which is based on neoclassical value theory, as well as in normative neoclassical trade models used to extol the welfare gains from free trade, foreign assets and liabilities of all national agents are combined to make up the net patrimony of each country, and income from foreign assets, repatriated or not, is part of national income. National wealth and income are employed as aggregate welfare indices in neoclassical macroeconomic policy analysis, because social mechanisms—markets, taxes and subsidies—are assumed to integrate individual costs and benefits of each country effectively into these aggregates. But this was clearly not true of Argentina, Mexico and Venezuela—zero net debtors, yet severely depressed by massive debt overhangs. Their integrating mechanisms had sufficed only to socialize the private sector's foreign liabilities and domestic insolvencies, not its foreign assets. Thus as the debt crises persisted in the debtor countries, doctrinal consistency, reinforced by historic precedents, should have turned the attention of the debtor and creditor governments to measures for utilizing the private foreign assets to lift the debt burden.

Of course, that didn't happen. Mexico's Lopez Portillo regime made noises about going after *los sacadólares* (dollar looters) but this was criticized as mere "financial populism" by the successor regime, whose attitude became the prevailing government stance in Latin America. In contrast to the European governments of the Marshall Plan era, who had pressured Washington for help in forcing flight capital back home, Latin American governments made no such requests.

They had no reason, of course, to believe that such requests would be honored by Washington. In contrast to its Marshall Plan predecessors, the Reagan Administration enthusiastically backed the free capital mobility position of the U.S. banks, who were benefiting handsomely as conduits and repositories of Latin American flight capital and were cavalierly contravening the laws of the debtor countries in the process.[17] The U.S. backing was tangible as well as rhetorical. In 1984 it abolished the witholding tax on interest income paid to non-resident owners of U.S. securities, and in 1985 the U.S. Treasury began for the first time to issue "bearer bonds" to facilitate clandestine ownership. Helleiner contends that Washington's worries over the rapidly expanding U.S. balance of payments deficit primarily motivated these actions; Latin American flight capital was needed to help fund the deficits (Helleiner 1992). Yet a further explanation is needed to account for why the U.S. was simultaneously promoting the shipment of "concerted" loans to the debtor governments. Since stupidity seems too facile an explanation for such contradictory behavior, one turns to possible *real politik* motives. Encouraging capital flight while rewarding compliant debtor governments with dollops of concerted lending strengthened U.S. political and economic hegemony over the region, and at moderate financial cost, since non-U.S. creditor governments and banks supplied the bulk of the concerted loans, directly and through their participating quotas in the IFIs. Forcing back flight capital to enable the debtors to regain balance of payments and macroeconomic stability with their own resources would give erstwhile debtor governments more autonomy in dealing with *el Coloso del Norte*, which from a U.S. hegemonic perspective might make it a less appealing alternative.

The debtors, independently or in concert, could have tried forcing Washington's hand with a carrot-stick approach. They could have proposed a comprehensive asset-registering or tax-collecting effort, which would require creditor help in fingering asset ownership. To sharpen creditor interest, the proposal could have been accompanied by a unilateral suspension of debt service until agreement was reached. This would have been a "conciliatory default," in the terminology of Kaletsky's monograph, which contends that historic precedents and legal tradition show the risk of retaliation to be minor for payment suspensions without debt repudiation (Kaletsky 1985). In 1984–85, the threat of even a single large Latin American debtor suspending pay-

---

17. For details see Díaz-Alejandro 1984, Henry 1985, and Lissakers 1991. Especially notorious was back-to-back lending in Argentina. CITIBANK and other major U.S. banks holding large dollar deposits of Argentine firms encouraged the firms to borrow against the deposits. The firms then declared the loans and received dollars from the Argentine Central Bank at highly subsidized rates for servicing the loans. Since interest on the dollar deposits covered most of the servicing, the firms profited lavishly by reselling most of the dollars in the parallel market and by including the interest on the loans as a tax-deductible expense. The U.S. banks in turn received a lucrative markup over their CD deposit rate for the risk-free collateralized loans. The U.S. banks rebuffed the Argentine government's request for information on these loans as an outrageous request that they violate their sacred commitment to client confidentiality. Information from my interview, April 1, 1991, with Dr. Bernardo Grinspun, treasury minister of the Alfonsín government, December 1983 to Feb. 1985, who issued the formal request.

ment might have sufficed to catch Washington's attention—possibly even its cooperation, since U.S. exports and balance of payments would have benefited from the early recovery of the debtor economies. But retaliation from irate, politically powerful owners of the foreign assets was probably of greater concern to Latin American governments than was fear of Washington's reaction. In any event, none attempted the strategy.

By 1985, however, Washington's *real politik* and the banks' bottom-line concerns were diverging over the Baker Plan, which called for substantial new concerted bank loans. Resisting the call, the banks for the first time began pointing up capital flight, contending it was unfair to have them send more money south only to have it return north as flight capital. At the annual meeting of the IMF Board of Governors, Walter Wriston, who as head of Citicorp had led the 1970s rush into Latin American lending, now argued that the debtors owned sufficient flight capital to solve their debt problems on their own (Helleiner 1992, p. 26). Needless to say, the banks did not propose asset mobilization; they merely refused any more loans, absent "sound" Latino monetary-fiscal policies.

The IFIs also played down capital flight in their initial debt crisis assessments. But in 1985 came a semiauthoritative article by two senior IFI economists attempting to demonstrate that capital flight was a rational response of wealth holders to expropriation risks from their governments.[18] This strange article begins with an all-encompassing definition of expropriation risk as "overvaluation of the exchange rate, high and variable inflation rates, general financial instability and so forth . . . including any differences between the foreign and home countries in formal taxation, possibilities of confiscation, destruction of private property, changes in political and economic regimes and so on" (Khan and Ul Haque, p. 618). It then wends its way to the tautological conclusion that capital flight would cease if governments would stop doing all those things that cause it to happen. The analysis, however, gets lost en route, the government oscillating at different phases of the argument between being Count Dracula and Good Fairy to private wealthholders: frightening wealth into fleeing, but giving subliminal assurances to the wealth owners and foreign banks that they would be bailed out were they to overdo their borrowing and lending.[19] Blaming the government and absolving private market behav-

---

18. Khan and Ul Haque 1985. Khan in 1985 was chief of the Macroeconomic Division of the Development Research Department of the World Bank. The authors express gratitude to big-gun IMF economists such as Jacob Frenkel and Willem Buiter, as well as to Robert Lucas "for extremely helpful comments." The article has been favorably referenced in many subsequent IFI articles and reports, such as Mathieson and Rójas-Suárez 1992, which takes a similar policy position. See, however, qualifying comments in note 7.

19. The formal analysis compounds confusion by working from a one-person, one-good model that combines private consumers, investors, and the government as well as traded and nontraded goods, and whose behavioral inconsistencies requires an Oliver Sacks to disentangle.

ior had become an IFI maxim, as we will see in the next section on restructuring the debtor economies.

4. The Contradictory Role of Relative Prices in IFI Restructuring Strategies

The initial IFI restructuring approach was textbook neoclassical, centering on "getting prices right." At the aggregate level, this means exchange rate devaluation to raise domestic prices of traded goods relative to nontraded goods, plus tight monetary-fiscal policies to keep reactive price rises of nontraded goods from eroding away the initial real devaluation effect. At the microlevel the approach would progressively abolish quantity controls and subsidies and would allow the relative prices of individual goods and services, as well as key economywide prices such as the exchange rate and the interest rate, to become strictly market determined.

Timing and sequencing remain unsettled. Comparative static textbook models are no help, and there is meager consensus on the lessons to be drawn from past liberalization efforts. Different political conditions have also caused timing and sequencing to vary between IFI-sanctioned restructuring programs. There are, however, fixed points in the IFI get-prices-right approach. Devaluing the real exchange rate is top priority, but manipulating quantity controls and subsidies to attain it is unacceptable. Direct controls are anti-market, hence an early lifting of exchange and import controls and interest rates is high priority, whereas tariffs and subsidies are viewed as market friendly, hence their removal can be stretched out.

Wages are a delicate matter. Nominal wage increases have to be held below the devaluation-induced price increases of traded goods so as not to erode profit margin improvements in that priority sector. Nor should they overtake the lesser price rises of nontraded goods and set off wage-price spiraling that would reverse intersectoral relative prices. Since wage goods straddle the two sectors, getting prices right requires, initially at least, a drop of real wages. This initial tilt toward income concentration is reinforced by import liberalization, which repeals the characteristic anti-luxury good bias of quantity controls and tariffs, thereby lowering the prices of previously restricted luxury imports relative to previously subsidized wage goods imports.

The aggregating, we are told, is needed to analyze "the more difficult case of simultaneous external borrowing and foreign and domestic investment, without any distinction being made between the government and private individuals" (p. 607). The case, however, also has little to do with the circumstances of Latin American capital flight, in which most of the aforementioned activities occurred sequentially. Private borrowing and foreign investment had largely ceased when capital flight took off, upon which the governments expanded their short-term borrowing and reduced their public investment in an effort to offset the foreign exchange outflow.

4.1 The Flawed General Case for the Feasibility of "Getting Prices Right" Restructuring

Why did the IFIs believe that this restructuring approach with its built-in inequities was appropriate or even feasible for economies already wracked with macroeconomic disorders and the gross inequities of the financial bailouts and capital flight? Apparently both doctrinal and ideological factors persuaded them that market liberalization was globally feasible; differences of initial conditions might require modifying details but not the essentials. The alternative Minsky-type perspective that major differences of circumstance could require major qualitative differences of stabilization strategies is a heresy that has only recently been appearing in World Bank discussion papers and has not yet infiltrated the more official publications.[20]

The doctrinal factor was a growing IFI attachment to new classical macroeconomics, an extreme version of neoclassical macrodynamics, which after the 1960s had been displacing the eclectic Keynesian-neoclassical synthesis as mainstream macroeconomics in the United States and Britain. The synthesis believed that market forces eventually converged on the natural growth rate, but also that interventionist policies could facilitate the converging. The new classicism rejected such interventionism as at best ineffective and more often counterproductive. When "the government is the problem not the solution" became White House ideology after 1980, IFI convergence toward new classicism accelerated; Washington, after all, holds controlling seats on the IFI boards.

Finding explanations for the embarrassing blow-ups of the Southern Cone liberalization efforts of the 1970s that were consistent with IFI policy certitude became an obsession among IFI economists and their confreres in academia. The shared premise was that "policy inconsistencies were the main reason for the eventual failure," destabilizing market behavior that would otherwise have been safely equilibrating.[21] But converting the premise into a valid conclusion merely produced a mélange of analytic inconsistencies.

The analyses focused on three disequilibrating features of private behavior in the liberalizing Southern Cone countries that ought not to happen, according to the small open economy model. Arbitraging in liberated domestic and foreign financial markets should, according to the model, have brought domestic interest rates adjusted for the dollar exchange rate to parity with

---

20. Recent heretical examples are Cho and Khatkate 1989 and Pereira and Sundararajan 1990. Orthodoxy still holds forth in official and semiofficial IFI publications such as Roe and Popiel 1990 and the World Bank's annual World Development Reports.

21. The quotation is from the summary by the editors of the World Bank symposium papers on liberalization with stabilization in the Southern Cone of Latin America. See Corbo and de Melo 1985, p. 864. The premise is offered, of course, as a researched conclusion.

U.S. interest rates. Instead, annual bank real lending rates in Chile averaged 77 percent with the CPI as deflator and 51 percent with the capital goods index as deflator, during the years 1975–1982 (Velasco 1991, tables 14 and 15), while comparable premia over U.S. dollar rates persisted in Argentina and Uruguay (Baliño 1991, table 6; Pérez-Campanero and Leone 1991, appendix tables 11 and 12). High real interest rates should discourage borrowing and promote savings, according to the model. Instead, private borrowing rose dramatically—from 30 percent to 76 percent of GDP in Chile and from 20 percent to 78 percent of GDP in Uruguay between 1975 and 1982 (Velasco 1991, table 9; Pérez-Campanero and Leone 1991, appendix table 9)—while private savings rates declined.

The increasingly overvalued exchange rates, which all three countries experienced in the two to three years prior to their financial crises, seemed *prima facie* to be the smoking gun. All three countries had then been devaluing according to preannounced schedules, popularly dubbed *tablitas cambiarias*, that diminished the successive devaluations toward zero, in the expectation that this would squeeze out inflationary markups on traded goods and reduce inflation to "international" rates, that is, to low single digits. But in each case inflation declined less than expected, causing a progressive decline of the real price of foreign exchange that was flagrantly at odds with the expanding balance of payments deficits. Anticipating a breakdown of the *tablitas* and more massive devaluation, rational lenders would surely add large exchange risk premia to their lending rates.

On second glance, however, the *tablitas* proved a damp squib. They accounted neither for the persistently large interest premia under the previous policy of keeping the devaluations in step with inflation, nor for the contradictory expectations between lenders and borrowers about exchange risk during Uruguay's *tablita* period. On the eve of the *tablita* breakdown Uruguayan banks were minimizing open dollar positions, offering rates on dollar loans that were substantially lower than the exchange adjusted rates on peso loans, whereas their clients were shifting more to dollar loans. Above all, IFI analysts were restrained by the strong neoclassical credentials of the *tablita* approach; many IFI economists had initially welcomed it as a promising way to lower inflationary expectations and markup premia.[22] The analysts therefore targeted accompanying policies rather than the *tablitas* as such for the runaway overvaluation.

At this point analytic inconsistencies took over. It was not possible to identify either fatal policy flaws common to the three countries or "sound" policy alternatives that had been overlooked by all three. Fiscal deficits,

---

22. The initial model rationalizing the *tablita* tactic had all the key small open economy assumptions: perfectly substitutable assets, the law of one price, etc. See Rodriguez 1982 and Fernandez 1985 for the formal modeling.

allegedly Argentina's fatal flaw, were absent during the *tablita* years in Chile and Uruguay. A companion flaw, Argentina's failure to complete the tariff reduction program before all controls were lifted on external capital movements, was also not relevant for Chile, which had fully completed its tariff reductions before lifting capital controls. Excessively rising real wages, due to backward wage indexing as the *tablita* was slowing inflation, was allegedly Chile's fatal flaw. The real wage increase—10 percent per annum during Chile's three *tablita* years—did exceed the GDP real growth rate of 7 percent, but that merely brought real wages in 1981 to 97 percent of their 1970 level, a feeble candidate for fatal flaw. Moreover, Argentina and Uruguay had rising real GDP and no increase of real wages during their *tablita* years, yet blew up.[23]

Moral hazard explanations of the excessive lending and borrowing were also offered; for example, that deposit insurance encouraged banks to take greater risks. But that "flaw" was factually irrelevant. Of the three countries, only Argentina had government-backed deposit insurance, and it provided merely 80 percent coverage on peso deposits above the equivalent of 5,000 U.S. dollars. Argentina raised its coverage and Chile introduced deposit insurance *after* the bank crises hit, in order to allay bank runs. Implicit "too big to fail" assurances were alleged to have encouraged overleveraging in Chile, but the "evidence" used to back the allegation was sardonic observations by hostile critics of the free market strategy that the repeated public warnings by cabinet-level Chicago Boys to the private sector not to expect government bailouts were mere blowing in the wind (Arellano 1983; Díaz-Alejandro 1985). These critics were making a political economy point that the Chicago Boys had underestimated the political clout of Chilean business, not the neoclassical point that ill-advised government signaling had thrown the behavior of private agents off track. That Uruguayan business could get the government to wipe out most of its bank debt in the 1980s by deliberately stopping payment generalizes the point. The regimes implementing the liberalization policies were, after all, tight-knit military-business alliances.

As the vapidity of the efforts became more patent, the obsession subsided. IFI economists now observe self-critically that "while it was recognized that the financial crisis in these countries emanated from wrong and inconsistent macro policies, the reverse question whether financial sector disequilibrium following financial reform also adversely affected the macroeconomic outcome is rarely asked" (Cho and Khatkate 1989, p. 97). Ronald McKinnon, in the 1970s an influential academic advocate of financial liberalization, is now having second thoughts about the strength and universality of

---

23. The discussion summarizes the articles and main references in Corbo and de Melo 1985.

the case (McKinnon 1991). Official IFI publications still put the blame for any and all financial instability firmly on macroeconomic mismanagement, but such reductionism is now itself reduced to a tautological inference nurtured by ideology, rather than a validated conclusion.

4.2 Getting-Prices-Right Restructuring in the 1980s

The degree of responsibility of the getting-prices-right programs for the mixed but mainly disappointing outcomes summarized in Section 1 is difficult to pin down decisively. The programs were suspended and renegotiated frequently in many of the debtor countries, which allows defenders to blame lack of political will for the disappointing results. But this is too facile. The governments usually backslid because implementing the programs was dangerously worsening politically destabilizing variables such as inflation, unemployment, and bankruptcy. Moroever, debtor countries that stuck it out over the programs' typical timeframe—about three years—found no pot of gold at the end, only another concerted loan package, conditional on their making another IMF-programmed effort. At the least the IFI programmers badly underestimated the timeframe for restructuring. My contention goes beyond this. The mixed outcomes reflected differences in initial conditions. In very few debtor countries would the economic structures and political parameters permit solving their severe fiscal-monetary disarray crises while also liberalizing their markets. In most, the getting-prices-right approach merely worsened the disarray.

One relevant structural difference was between countries like Chile, Mexico, and Venezuela, in which state-owned mineral firms produced half or more of the nation's exports, and countries like Argentina and Brazil, whose exports were privately generated. The treasuries of the first group obtained foreign exchange averaging in the 1980s around 8 percent of GDP directly from the state exporters (CEPAL 1992, cuadro IV-6); in the second group, foreign exchange for debt servicing had to be purchased or taxed away from private exporters. Devaluation increased fiscal revenues from the sale of surplus foreign exchange in the first group; it only increased fiscal expenditure in the second group.

Differences of industrial structure were also relevant. The industrial sectors of most large Latin American countries had developed since World War II under highly protectionist import substituting industrialization (ISI) policies. The market-liberalizing efforts of the Southern Cone countries notwithstanding, ISI policies were still in place in most of the industrializing Latin American countries when the debt crisis broke. Mired in economic depression and monetary-fiscal disorder, these countries were forced by the getting-prices-right strategy to undertake a wrenching industrial restructuring.

Only Chile, the one Southern Cone country that had largely completed such industrial restructuring before the debt crisis, was free from that task. Its experience in the 1970s, however, indicates the extent of the changes required by market liberalization. The ISI subsector shrank mainly through liquidation and vertical disintegration; firms in consumer durables, clothing, and capital goods that survived did so by increasing their import dependence and transforming themselves primarily into assembly, finishing, and marketing firms. Conversely, natural resource processing industries grew and deepened their vertical integration. Yet even though the restructuring took place under favorable external borrowing conditions, the net effect was a decline of industrial employment and value added, the industrial share of total employment falling 22 percent between 1974 and 1981, while the urban unemployment rate, which had averaged 6 percent in the 1960s, hovered above 15 percent in the 1970s (Meller 1992, section 6).

Why impose this burden on economies already reeling from falling output and employment, capital flight, scarce foreign exchange, and overburdened fiscs? Because, according to getting-prices-right backers, the plight of these countries was in large part the culmination of decades of distortion of their economies by import substituting industrialization (ISI), making industrial restructuring central to the restructuring of the economy. World Bank and other IFI publications, to strengthen the case for industrial restructuring, went, however, beyond the facts to denigrate the mixed record of accomplishments and failures of ISI. Growth accounting estimates for the six countries of table 3 show that the residual—which the World Bank uses frequently as a measure of allocative efficiency—was strongly positive for all six during the years 1950–1973, the heyday of ISI. All the residuals fell during the period 1973–1980, the years of foreign debt splurging, but they fell relatively less in Brazil, Colombia, and Mexico, where the ISI strategy still held full sway, than in Argentina and Chile, which were liberalizing their structures.[24] In any event, industrial restructuring might have been better advanced by using the ISI sector of the debt-constrained economy to finance the expansion of industrial exporting. This cash-cow alternative would sustain production in the ISI sector rather than squeeze it, while redirecting the investible surplus by appropriate taxes and subsidies to finance export-oriented investment. Such an alternative reduced the cost and duration of Korea's 1980s debt crisis. It might have done the same in Latin America had the IFIs encouraged rather than discouraged the adoption of the requisite capital controls, taxes, and subsidies.

The ability of the debtor governments to engineer real wage cuts without setting off explosive wage-price spirals depended on political parameters that also favored Chile, with its brutal dictatorship, and Mexico, with its one-party democracy and government-controlled unions. For the debtor countries that

---

24. Unpublished estimates by Andres Hofman of CEPAL, reported in Felix 1992, table 2.

were edging back to political democracy, dampening wage-price spirals while cutting real wages further was bound to be more difficult if not impossible.

Finally, ideological and geopolitical factors favored Chile and Mexico over the other debtors. Chile's ratio of IFI loans to debt during the years 1983–1986 was 2.5 times greater than the regional average (Felix and Caskey 1990, table 1.8). That helped to ease the fiscal-financial costs of the Chilean bailout and to sustain government investment during those critical years. Washington's extra assistance to Mexico's debt management and market liberalization efforts needs no elaboration.

When few of these favorable conditions were present, the clash between market liberalizing and macroeconomic stabilizing produced explosive wage-price-devaluation spiraling, increasing fiscal deficits, along with sharply declining public and private investment that thwarted the industrial restructuring. Staying within the monetary limits set by the IMF agreements required governments to finance deficits by open market sales of treasury bills. With capital flight as the alternative, the financial markets would take only very short maturity-high interest bills. The high interest rates drew private capital away from physical and toward financial investing, while also driving up the fiscal cost of debt servicing. To hold down interest rates, the harried authorities would turn to central bank financing of the deficit, which would accelerate monetary expansion beyond the IMF limits, leading to suspension of the agreement and the concerted loans. It would also intensify inflation, exchange depreciation, and domestic capital flight; that is, the dollarizing of financial savings by smallholders.[25] Dollarization eroded the effectiveness of the inflation tax, raising the spectre of hyperinflation.

By the mid-1980s some debtor countries were attempting partial to complete wage-price freezes, with the IMF grudgingly acquiescing in most of them. The freezes broke up in Argentina, Brazil, and Peru, in large part because the deficit financing was increasingly at odds with frozen interest and exchange rates. Mexico, with its government-controlled unions, has had more lasting success. Peru, and later Argentina and Brazil, also suspended part of its foreign debt service to ease the fiscal burden and foreign exchange shortage when the banks withdrew from concerted lending. The getting-prices-right restructuring strategy was disintegrating.

4.3 The Shift to a Getting-Prices-Wrong Approach

In reaction, getting-prices-wrong has recently been displacing getting-prices-right. Lagging the exchange rate behind inflation is once again a key instru-

---

25. Morley and Fishlow 1987 is a formal modeling of these dynamics, highlighting the incompatibility between IMF monetary and fiscal deficit targets in overindebted countries. The model's specifications seem especially tailored to mid-1980s Brazil.

ment for slowing inflation. This time there are no *tablitas*, merely the sense that since slowing inflation by lagging the nominal wage rate or interest rate has worked poorly, the nominal exchange rate is the only anchor left. The result has been slower inflation but increasing exchange rate overvaluation and current account deficits in most of the debtor countries.

The renewed dependence on overvaluation by depressing the relative prices of traded goods contradicts a central tenet of the market-liberalizing approach. Privatizing public utilities and other nontraded public assets, which has also been going on apace, is reinforcing the perverse relative price trend. Earlier the governments had tended to lag prices of public services, which decapitalized the public firms, but slowed the rise of nontraded goods prices. Exploiting their liberated market power, the new owners have been imposing above-average price increases to recapitalize the firms and extract profits.

At the IFIs a peculiar schizophrenia has set in. Their recent case studies and think pieces emphasize that crucial to the success of market liberalization strategies is an initial real exchange rate devaluation, which must be prolonged until the structural adjustments are firmly in place and the trade flows are equilibrated (Papageorgiou, Michaely, and Choksi 1991, volume 1; Corbo and Fisher 1990). Concurrently, the contradictory exchange anchoring strategies are being rewarded with increased IFI loans and official accolades. Motivating the official enthusiasm seem to be the commitments of the debtor governments to privatize and to liberate capital markets, which are given precedence at the highest IFI levels over getting prices right. Thus Argentina's Cavallo Plan, whose centerpiece is a legislated permanent freeze of the dollar exchange rate, has attracted extensive IFI loans, a Brady debt writedown, and a generous Paris Club rollover of bilateral official debt. These, plus front-end money from privatization, have allowed Argentina to maintain its fixed exchange rate thus far despite the persistence of two-digit inflation and a rapidly expanding current account deficit. Portfolio capital inflows drawn to short-term financial opportunities that remain attractive only if the exchange rate remains stable also support that stability, giving Argentina a financial version of the Dutch Disease. The pickup of physical investment, however, has been meager, and chiefly in nontraded goods: in privatized utilities and commercial and residential construction. Gratified, Lewis Preston, the president of the World Bank, praised the Cavallo Plan in a recent Argentine visit and announced that the World Bank "has supported and will continue to support this great effort" (Latin American Regional Reports–Southern Cone, July 1992). Economic logic may be with the IFI analysts, but ideology is with Mr. Preston.

5. A Brief Summary

The pain and travail inflicted on the Latin American countries and most of their citizenry by the debt crisis and its aftermath were in good part avoidable.

A Minsky-type perspective on the macroeconomic dynamics of capitalist economies could have shaped a more effective set of stabilization and restructuring policies than those actually chosen. That, however, is not a sufficient condition, since the flaws were not merely intellectual. Domestic and international political power asymmetries were also critical in shaping the policies and in unfairly allocating adjustment burdens between the bank creditors and the debtor countries, and within the latter, between the rich and the poor. To fulfill Keynes's vision of economists contributing like good dentists to society's well-being, economists will need to enlighten themselves and their fellow citizens better on the power dimensions of policy making.

REFERENCES

Arellano, José P. 1983. "De la Liberación a la Intervención: El Mercado de Capitales en Chile," *Colección Estudios CIEPLAN*, No.11 (Santiago de Chile, Diciembre).

Balassa, Bela, Gerardo M. Bueno, Pedro-Pablo Kuczynski, and Mario H. Simonsen 1986. *Toward Renewed Growth in Latin America* (Washington, D.C.: Institute for International Economics).

Baliño, Tomas J.T. 1991. "The Argentine Banking Crisis of 1980" in Sundararajan and Baliño 1991.

CEPAL (Comisión Económica para América Latina y el Caribe) 1990. "Una Estimación de la Magnitud de la Pobreza en Chile" (Santiago de Chile: Naciones Unidas, 19 de Octubre).

CEPAL 1991. *Estudio Económico de América Latina y el Caribe 1990* (Santiago de Chile: Naciones Unidas, Diciembre).

CEPAL 1992. *Equidad y Transformación Productiva: Un Enfoque Integrado* (Santiago: Naciones Unidas, Enero).

Chisari, Omar, José Fanelli, Roberto Frenkel, and Guillermo Rozenwurcel 1992. "Ahorro Público y Recuperación del Crecimiento en la Argentina", Banco Interamericano de Desarrollo, Documento de Trabajo 110.

Cho, Yoon-Je, and Deena Khatkate 1989. "Lessons of Financial Liberalization in Asia: A Comparative Study," World Bank Discussion Paper No.50 (Washington, D.C., April).

Corbo, Vittorio and Jaime de Melo eds. 1985. "Liberalization with Stabilization in the Southern Cone of Latin America," *World Development* special issue, vol.13 no.8 (August).

Corbo, Vittorio and Stanley Fisher 1990. "Adjustment Programs and Bank Support: Rationale and Main Results," World Bank paper (November).

Devlin, Robert 1989. *Debt and Crisis in Latin America: the Supply Side of the Story* (Princeton: Princeton University Press).

Díaz-Alejandro, Carlos 1984. "Latin American Debt: I Don't Think We Are in Kansas Anymore," *Brookings Papers on Economic Activity*, no. 2.

Díaz-Alejandro, Carlos 1985. "Goodby Financial Repression, Hello Financial Crash," *Journal of Development Economics* vol. 19.

Fanelli, José M., Roberto Frenkel, and Lance Taylor 1992. "The World Development Report 1991: A Critical Assessment" (February).

Felix, David 1983. "Income Distribution and the Quality of Life in Latin America: Patterns, Trends and Policy Implications," *Latin American Research Review* vol. 18, no. 2.

Felix, David 1985. "How to Resolve Latin America's Debt Crisis," *Challenge* (November/December).

Felix, David 1990. "Latin America's Debt Crisis," *World Policy Journal* (Fall).

Felix, David 1992. "Reflections on Privatizing and Rolling Back the Latin American State," *CEPAL Review* (Santiago, Chile, April).

Felix, David, and John P. Caskey 1990. "The Road to Default: An Assessment of Debt Crisis Management in Latin America," in David Felix ed. *Debt and Transfiguration? Prospects for Latin America's Economic Revival* (Armonk, N.Y.: M.E. Sharpe Inc.).

Fernandez, Roque B. 1985. "The Expectations Management Approach to Stabilization in Argentina during 1976–82" in Corbo and de Melo 1985.

Ferri, Piero, and Hyman P. Minsky 1992. "Market Processes and Thwarting Mechanisms," Jerome Levy Economics Institute Working Paper No.64.

Fisher, Irving 1933. "The Debt-Deflation Theory of Great Depressions," *Econometrica* vol. 1, no. 4 (October).

Harberger, Arnold 1986. "Observations on the Chilean Economy," *Economic Development and Cultural Change* vol. 33 no. 1.

Helleiner, Eric 1992. "Capital Flight and the Receiving Country: Contrasting US Policy in the Marshall Plan and the 1980s Debt Crisis." Paper presented at the Annual Meeting of the Canadian Political Science Association, May 31–June 2.

Henry, James 1985. "Where the Money Went," *The New Republic*, April 14.

Hofman, Andres A. 1991. "The Role of Capital in Latin America: A Comparative Perspective on Six Countries for 1950–1989," Working Paper no. 4 (United Nations Economic Commission for Latin America and the Caribbean, December).

Kaletsky, Anatol 1985. *The Costs of Default*, New York, 20th Century Fund.

Khan, Mohsin S. and Nadeem Ul Haque 1985. "Foreign Borrowing and Capital Flight: A Formal Analysis," *IMF Staff Papers* vol. 32, no. 4.

Kindleberger, Charles P., and Jean-Pierre Laffargue eds. 1982. *Financial Crises: Theory, History and Policy* (Cambridge: Cambridge University Press).

Lipin, Steven 1992. "Banks Escape the Latin American Debt Crisis with Little Damage: Losses in the Region Look Tiny Next to Real Estate Collapse, Analysts Say," *The Wall Street Journal* (July 21).

Lissakers, Karin 1991. *Banks, Borrowers and the Establishment: A Revisionist Account of the International Debt Crisis* (New York: Basic Books).

Lucas, Robert E. Jr. 1975. "An Equilibrium Model of the Business Cycle," *Journal of Political Economy* vol. 83, no. 6 (December).

McKinnon, Ronald L. 1991. "Financial Liberalization and Economic Development: A Reassessment of Interest Rate Policies in Asia and Latin America," *Oxford Review of Economic Policy* vol. 5, no. 4.

Massad, Carlos, and Roberto Zahler eds. 1988. *Deuda Interna y Estabilidad Financiera*, 2 vols. (Buenos Aires: Grupo Editor Latinoamericano).

Mathieson, Donald J., and Liliana Rójas-Suárez 1992. "Liberalization of the Capital Account: Experiences and Issues," IMF Working Paper WP/92/46.

Meller, Patricio 1992. "La Apertura Chilena: Enseñanzas de Política," Banco Interamericano de Desarrollo Documento de Trabajo 109 (Marzo).

Minsky, Hyman 1975. *John Maynard Keynes* (New York: Columbia University Press).

Minsky, Hyman P. 1986. *Stabilizing the Unstable Economy* (New Haven: Yale University Press).

Morley, Samuel A., and Albert Fishlow 1989. "Deficits, Debt and Destabilization," *The Journal of Development Economics*, vol. 27.

Mújica, Patricio, y Osvaldo Larranaga, 1992. "Políticas Sociales y Distribución del Ingreso en Chile," Documento de Trabajo 106, Banco Interamericano de Desarrollo (Washington, D.C., Marzo).

Papageorgiou, Demitris, Michael Michaely, and Armeane M. Choksi 1991. *Liberalizing World Trade*, 7 vols. (Published for the World Bank by Basil Blackwell, London).

Pereira Leite, Sergio, and V. Sundararajan 1990. "Issues in Interest Rate Management and Liberalization," IMF Working Paper WP/90/12.

Pérez-Campanero, Juan, and Alfredo M. Leone 1991. "Liberalization and Financial Crisis in Uruguay, 1974–87," in Sundararajan and Baliño 1991.

PREALC (Programa Regional de Empleo para América Latina y el Caribe) 1990A. "Employment and Equity: The Challenge of the 1990s," Working Paper no. 354 (Santiago, Chile, October).

PREALC 1990B. *"Informal Sector as in PREALC,"* Working Paper no. 349 (Santiago, Chile, August).

Rodriguez, Carlos A. 1982. "The Plan of the 20th of December," *World Development*.

Roe, Alan, and Paul A. Popiel 1990. "The Restructuring of Financial Systems in Latin America," The World Bank, EDI Policy Seminar Report no. 25 (Washington, D.C., March).

Sargent, Thomas J., and Neil Wallace 1975. "Rational Expectations, the Optimal Monetary Instrument and the Optimal Money Supply Rule," *Journal of Political Economy* vol. 83, no. 2 (April).

Stoga, Alan 1992. "Doubting the Inevitable: Venezuela's Coup has Shaken Global Confidence," *The International Economy* (May/June).

Sundararajan, V., and Tomas J.T. Baliño eds. 1991. *Banking Crises: Cases and Issues* (Washington, D.C.: International Monetary Fund).

Velasco, Andres 1991. "Liberalization, Crisis, Intervention: The Chilean Financial System, 1975–85," in Sundararajan and Baliño 1991, table 9.

Part III
Empirical Papers
on Advanced Economies

CHAPTER 8

Financial Fragility and the Great Depression: New Evidence on Credit Growth in the 1920s

*Dorene Isenberg**

Hyman Minsky has shown how the interaction between financial and production decision making introduces an inherently destabilizing dynamic into the market economy. His financial fragility hypothesis (FFH) links the firm's financial decision making to a financial cycle that may initiate or exacerbate the business cycle. But though Minsky has explored at length the relevance of the FFH to economic fluctuations in the post–World War II United States, he has written little about whether the FFH can explain aspects of the prewar period.[1] This paper begins the process of bridging this gap by investigating financial conditions in the U.S. economy during the 1920s. It finds evidence of financial fragility at the firm level and suggests that this provided a foundation for the ensuing Great Depression.

This investigation of the contribution of financial fragility to the Great Depression is laid out in six sections. The first section presents a brief description of Minsky's financial fragility hypothesis and an outline of an FFH explanation of the Great Depression. The second section reviews salient financial and nonfinancial explanations of the Great Depression and then juxtaposes them with the FFH. The third section reports on empirical studies from the Depression period that shed light on economic activity, and especially financial conditions of the 1920s. The fourth section explains the methodology used herein; in particular, it explains why a disaggregate approach to understanding financial fragility is warranted. The fifth section then presents disaggregated, firm-level evidence that demonstrates that financial fragility

*Special thanks are due to the editors of this volume, who have provided guidance and thoughtful comments; to Fred Curtis who provided transitions and collegial support; to Fred Pastore, who was diligent and attentive in his research assistance; and to the Dean's Council of the College of Liberal Arts, Drew University, for their research funding.

1. Some of the empirical analyses that have drawn upon the insights of the FFH to describe the post–World War II economic activity include Minsky 1982a, 1986, Niggle 1989, Pollin 1983, and Wolfson 1986. Kindleberger (1978) presents FFH in an international and historical framework.

was indeed rising in key industries in the 1920s, thus laying the groundwork for the Great Depression. The sixth section concludes.

1. Financial Fragility and the Great Depression

Minsky's financial fragility hypothesis (FFH) is microeconomically founded on the financial decision-making behavior of a representative firm.[2] This firm's behavior is determined to some extent by structural forces within its industry and its market, and by the state of the macroeconomy. The firm's expectations are another crucial determinant, especially because the firm must bound the uncertainty associated with investment projects and the firm's perceptions of the strength and duration of a business cycle expansion or contraction.

The FFH asserts that the firm's behavior depends not just on these factors but also on its financial structure, that is, how it finances its investment expenditures. Investment projects that are internally financed add only their own inherent uncertainty to the firm's balance sheet. But external finance exposes the firm to additional risk: it adds borrower's risk and lender's risk, thus creating more uncertainty than when financing is generated internally.[3] In Minsky's FFH, firms' financial structures fall into three types: hedge, speculative, and Ponzi. Each successive category indicates a more highly leveraged, and thus a riskier, financial position than the previous one. At any point in time, all there types of firms exist, so aggregate financial vulnerability depends on the comparative weight of each in the economy.

The crux of the FFH is the assertion that normal economic behaviors by firms endogenously produce a financially fragile economy. The shift from what Minsky terms a "robust" to a "fragile" financial structure derives from the interplay of industry-specific factors, macroeconomic conditions, and the firm's expectations and financial structure.

It is useful to contrast the separate effects of industry-specific and macroeconomic (economy-wide) variables on firms' behaviors. In a period of sustained boom or stagnation, the firm will base its behavior largely on conditions within its industry and its markets. When market conditions change, however, the firm will look more to macroeconomic indicators, which are perceived to be more reliable indicators of future conditions than firm-specific indicators. The shift in the basis of firm judgment from industry- and firm-specific condi-

---

2. The following description of financial fragility has been crafted to explain the particular components that are especially salient to this paper. For a more comprehensive explanation see Minsky 1975, 1982b, and 1986 and other papers in this volume.

3. Minsky's conception of borrower's risk incorporates two aspects, uncertainty and financial exposure due to debt finance (1975: 106–113). Uncertainty emerges because of the possibility that the expected yield may not be realized. Financial exposure is dependent on the levels of debt finance relative to liquid financial assets. Minsky argues that this risk can be reduced, but not eliminated, through portfolio diversification.

tions to macroeconomic factors, and back again, creates a uniformity in firms expectations and behavior that, in turn, stimulates a uniformity in aggregate economic activity. This encourages herd movements toward expansion or contraction based on broadly synchronized changes in expectations, which in turn shift the direction of economic activity.

So cyclical economic activity is driven by firms' investment/financing decisions. In the expansion phase of the business cycle, firms have the confidence to borrow and lenders the assurance to lend; both strongly share the expectation that the expansion will continue. The emphasis on investment opportunity and the tendency to downplay financial risks leads to increased reliance as the expansion continues upon external finance, resulting in high debt/equity and interest/income ratios.

With the rising incidence of debt on the firms' balance sheets and a swing in expectations regarding the expansion's continuation, the expansion moves toward its end. After the business cycle peaks, Minsky notes that the process described by Fisher (1933) causes the contraction to be deeper and longer than one without debt buildup. Fixed debt-payment commitments increase in real terms as price levels fall. A cumulative process of defaults, bankruptcies, and reductions in output institutes a negative psychology in which expectations for a continued decline dominate. The contraction ensues and deepens.

Using the FFH framework, an analytical construction of the phases of the Great Depression can be forged: the expansion phase of debt buildup, the 1920s; the peak of the expansion and the stock market's crash; and the contraction phase of debt deflation, the 1930s. During the expansion, the initial phase of debt build up should be found in the industrial sector. In this fast growth period, firms would invest in themselves and increasingly tap debt sources of funds, and the debt ratios would rise. Initially, the debt/equity ratio, especially the long term debt/equity component, and the interest/income ratio should rise. Then, as the expansion extends, the short-term debt ratios, the quick, current, short-term debt/equity, and short-term debt/long-term debt ratios should rise. Other sectors may also increasingly have used debt; however, their debt usage is a response to, not an initiation of, the expansion. Their activities are ancillary in the FFH. It is the sum of this sectoral behavior in the expansion, however, that produces financial fragility.

1.1 Minsky on the Great Depression

Although Minsky has not analyzed the depression years extensively, he argues that this period was brought on by the speculative financial activity in the 1920s.[4] In one of his only empirical references, Minsky (1982a: 11) presents

---

4. Minsky has made numerous allusions to the period prior to the Great Depression as being financially fragile. In *Can "It" Happen Again?* and *Stabilizing an Unstable Economy*, there

a table of changing debt/income ratios in the 1920s. Using Goldsmith's (1956) data, Minsky measured a rise in the debt/income ratios of households and corporations between 1922 and 1929. Households' leverage rose from 0.38 to 0.62, and nonfinancial corporations' leverage rose from 5.70 to 6.08. The average annual rates of growth for these ratios were 7.2 percent and 0.9 percent, respectively.

So debt and leveraging grew in the 1920s, but only household debt increased significantly. This pattern of debt growth is problematic. In a FFH scenario, 1920s industrial, not household, debt ratios should experience a major rise. The FFH emphasizes the causal role of investment as the engine of growth. Debt financing of investment is the core of the model, so industrial leverage ratios, including both short-and long-term debt, should rise in an expanding economy.

Although household debt is an element in the FFH, it holds a residual position. As the economy expands, households' incomes and expenditures increase. These increases promote greater debt usage, so leverage ratios rise. This increase in debt usage adds to the overall financial fragility of the economic system since more sectors have higher debt ratios. When the downturn arrives, the debt-deflation process will also envelop households; however, their economic role in the FFH is one of respondent, not initiator. Households spread the credit-income-expenditure nexus from one sector to another, but do not initiate the growth/contraction process.

In sum, Minsky argues that the FFH explains the GD; however, the small amount of data he has put forward suggests that the FFH is not relevant to the GD.[5] The remainder of this paper shows, to the contrary, that the FFH is very useful for understanding the causes of the Great Depression, but it does so by shifting the emphasis from the volume of debt financing per se in the industrial sector to the entire web of credit relations.

2. Competing Views on the Great Depression

Most accounts of the Great Depression, in stark contrast to the FFH, ignore financial factors and focus on the disruptions in real factors. This section explores the explanations of Peter Temin (1976; 1991) and Michael Bernstein (1987), whose very different accounts of the Great Depression both emphasize

---

are references to the debt-deflation process as the mechanism that made the depression great. In both of these volumes, Minsky implies that the 1920s were an era of debt buildup. There are two tables (1982a: 11] that present statistics from Goldsmith showing that liabilities-income ratios grew between 1922 and 1929. This, however, is the extent of his investigation.

    5. Kindleberger (1978) used some of the major speculative manias between 1720 and 1975 to emphasize the insights of the financial fragility hypothesis. He provides no in depth analysis of any speculative period, however; the stock market frenzy of 1929 is cited as a speculative period, but the period that preceded it is not investigated.

real factors. This section also reviews three financial-side explanations–those of Milton Friedman and Anna Schwartz (1963), Frederic Mishkin (1978), and Ben Bernanke (1983). These three accounts differ significantly not only from each other but also from Minsky's FFH. This section briefly reviews each view and contrasts it with the FFH.

2.1 Peter Temin

Temin proposes that the Great Depression can be viewed as having two phases, initiation and propagation. Its initiating shock was caused by a drop in autonomous consumption: the crash of the American stock market reduced wealth and in turn caused a reduction in consumption. This financial disruption with its real sector impacts occurred during a period of deflationary monetary and fiscal policies that exacerbated and prolonged the impact of the consumption decline. Indeed, Temin's propagation mechanism is the fiscal and monetary policy required once the United States and Europe had decided to remain on the gold standard.

Temin views "the crash" as the event that set the ball rolling, but without the restrictive policies required to stay on the gold standard, the Depression would not have transpired. The restrictive monetary policies led to deflation, which initially–via real balance effects–would counteract the policy. In the longer run, Temin blames the formation of nonrational deflationary price expectations, which then dominated and exacerbated the effects of the initial decline in consumption.

Temin's argument is historically provocative, but the deflationary environment that he posits can not be found in the United States during the mid- to late 1920s. His own set of price indices shows little or no aggregate price changes between 1924 and 1929 (1976: 6). The fear of the mid- to late twenties was inflation, not deflation. The Federal Reserve's monetary policy became restrictive only in 1928. In contrast to Minsky, Temin integrates the activities of the financial and real sectors at the macroeconomic level, he incorporates international dimensions, and he makes no connection between the macroeconomic sphere and firms or industries. Although his current analysis of the Depression incorporates some financial elements, there is no effective role for debt in his macroeconomic framework.

2.2 Michael Bernstein

Bernstein presents an innovative analysis of the Great Depression that focuses on the real sector: the timing of innovations and technological changes and their relative importance in the nation's production bundle. His focus is thus the long period; the short period plays a secondary role.

Bernstein argues that though many innovations were introduced in the

1920s, by 1929 their growth potentials were exhausted. This exhaustion meant not only that growth fostered by investment expenditures would slow but that demand generated by these expenditures would also subside. These products and processes had come to the end of their life cycles, so new products and processes were needed if economic growth was to continue.

But a resurgence of innovations was forestalled. In the short term, Bernstein notes the capital markets were in disarray after 1929. This meant that finance for investment projects was harder to arrange, so many worthwhile projects were aborted. Another short-term factor was the shifts in consumer demand due to new products in the 1920s. In the longer run, these shifts in demand led to qualitative and quantitative changes in investment and produced long-term structural changes in production, in the demand for labor, and in capital intensity. But the innovations brought to market in the 1930s did not generate adequate production and demand. More immediately, the decline in demand for and investment in products and processes introduced in the 1920s was not counterbalanced by spending in new areas, so, the economic structure of the 1920s effectively degenerated without a replacement.[6]

Bernstein categorizes financial market disarray as incidental, but in the FFH, this is the fundamental reason for the depth and duration of the contraction. It is financial market disarray that prevents inventions from being converted into investments, thus explaining the overall downturn in economic activity. This disarray also increases uncertainty and thus exacerbates the declines in investment. Without investment, product innovations that might spur growth by producing new wants in consumers and process innovations that might reduce production costs are not implemented. Short- period disruptions lie at the heart of the problem in the FFH.

2.3 Milton Friedman and Anna Schwartz

In contrast to these analyses, Friedman and Schwartz adopt a financial approach to the Great Depression, however, their monetarist explanation differs as markedly from the FFH as the real sector analyses do. Although the monetarists are concerned with activity in the financial sector, their analysis reduces to an explanation based on the activity of one financial variable, the

---

6. Josef Steindl (1952) utilizes a model of stagnation to explain the GD. Like Bernstein, he emphasizes the downturn in capital accumulation; however, he shows that the decline in investment began in 1900, as did profit rates. The 1920s with their turn toward equity finance allowed outside saving to be transformed into equity capital. Debt ratios fell, and for a short period, this compensated for the fall in internal accumulation. This change in finance, however, could not hold off the process of stagnation indefinitely. Since profit rates did not rise along with the number of shares, the inadequate rate of capital accumulation finally dominated and the economy stagnated.

money supply. They argue that the Federal Reserve's tight monetary policy was responsible for the downturn and that the duration and depth of the contraction was due to the continued shrinkage in the money supply as banks failed.

Whereas changes in the composition of the money supply and its size figure heavily in F&S's account, the financial structure of the nonfinancial sector does not. F&S concede that loans extended at the end of the 1920s may have been of lesser quality than their counterparts in the early 1920s, however, they argue that the money supply effect caused the decline in output, which in turn was responsible for these loans falling into default. They also assert that the factors leading to the money supply reduction could have been altered had the Federal Reserve responded quickly and properly (1963:244–249 and 353–357). Since it did not, it bears the responsibility for the Great Depression.[7]

2.4 Frederic Mishkin

Frederic Mishkin (1978) extends the F&S account of the Great Depression in a Keynesian direction. His premise is that the decline in consumer durable expenditures was accentuated by the Keynesian multiplier-accelerator process; this produced the major decline in aggregate demand, thus explaining the depth and duration of the Great Depression. Mishkin proceeds by linking consumer durable expenditures to two financial variables, debt and financial assets.[8]

Mishkin's notion that the decline in consumer durable expenditures was due to a financial propagation mechanism corresponds loosely with Minsky's perspective. Their analyses diverge because Mishkin assumes, as do Friedman & Schwartz, that the Federal Reserve's 1928 tight monetary policy was the initiating shock. Instead of emphasizing debt's buildup on the balance

---

7. Karl Brunner (1981) finds Friedman and Schwartz's explanation to be inadequate. In *The Great Depression Revisited* he invites many economists to explain the GD, but after serious consideration he finds difficulties with each solution. In his closing essay, Brunner constructs a model using an AD-AS framework. Financial markets do affect output markets on the AD side, and on the AS side, his labor market is afflicted with Friedmanian imperfect information. In his construction, a decrease in the money supply produces a leftward shift of both the IS and LM curves, so that both output and interest rates decline in the short run. These changes are incorrectly interpreted due to imperfect information, so the AS reacts in the short run also, which exacerbates the downturn. Brunner's model remains faithful to the monetarist approach while updating and expanding it.

8. Econometrically, he establishes debt's negative and financial assets's positive relationship to consumer durable expenditures; however, his econometric simulation is only capable of accounting for the declines in consumer durables expenditures in 1930. His model fails to account for consumer activity in the period 1931–1933.

sheets of firms with its negative impact on investment expenditures, Mishkin relies on the decline in the money supply to induce the price deflation and stock market crash that reduce consumers's net financial worth.

2.5 Ben Bernanke

Finally, Ben Bernanke (1983) has proposed a financial analysis of the GD that is based on an asymmetric information model. The propagation effects instigated by informational asymmetry in the credit market explain the depth and duration of the GD. Informational asymmetry in a period of financial market disarray made it harder for banks to distinguish between good and bad borrowers. Such disorder produced higher lending risks that translated into a higher cost of intermediation; as a result, fewer loans were extended. This credit constriction forced a decline in investment and consumption expenditures and hence in the level of economic activity. Dynamic price effects from the rising interest rates resulted in spiraling declines in output, Fisher's debt-deflation process.

The FFH acknowledges that costs of intermediation and risk associated with it may rise during a financial crisis, but the motivating force behind this change is alterations in firms' expectations. As explained in section 1, firms form similar expectations of the future that cause them to act as do Keynes's "herds." Thus a long expansion like that in the 1920s produces actions that Minksy calls "euphoric" because both risks and costs are perceived as very low. The debt-deflation process of a contraction initiates actions based on perceptions of high risks and costs. Costs and risks change not on the basis of information being more or less asymmetrical but because of changes in the expectations about the future.[9]

3. Prior Studies on Debt in the 1920s

Whereas the previous section detailed some of the more popular and interesting theoretical analyses of the Great Depression, this section details several empirical studies that summarize 1920s economic activity and debt usage in financial and non-financial sectors. Before showing that the FFH provides a better explanation of the actual economic activities of the 1920s, an economic overview is necessary.

These studies on debt usage indicate that several characteristics account for variations in the use of debt by different firms, industries, and sectors: these characteristics are firm size, industry, and inclusion in a growing or

---

9. See Dymski in this volume on the relationship between expectation, information asymmetry, and Keynesian uncertainty.

declining sector. In the summaries of the studies that follow, these characteristics have been isolated so that their unique role in the debt accumulation process becomes apparent.

3.1 The Industriales

A financial overview of the 1920s requires information on the growth of debt, interest payments, income, and wealth. Further, to provide insight on the applicability of the FFH, the overview must look at leverage ratios and types of external finance undertaken. Raymond Goldsmith (1956) estimates a debt-to-asset ratio of the nonfinancial private sector at 0.30 in 1922 and 0.31 in 1929. Robert Taggart's (1986) update of Goldsmith resulted in a 0.28 debt-to-asset value in 1922 and a 0.28 value in 1929.[10] Evans Clark's (1933) study of debt use showed that industrial debts rose by 111 percent between 1922 and 1929, but manufacturing output also increased by 78 percent, so leverage increased only slightly in the intervening eight years.

In an extensive analysis of corporate finance, Hickman (1953) detailed the annual net changes of total corporate bond offerings between 1900 and 1950. His study, though focused on bond financing, also includes data on other forms of finance. From 1900 to 1940 the trend was negative for net corporate offerings; the only major deviation from this trend was the period 1918–1927 (1953: 61). This was the period in which the industriales experienced their only substantive expansionary activity. Table 1 displays financing data. In 1920 and 1921 there were major increases in net debt offerings. After 1921, although there was still a positive increase in net offerings, the rate of change was negative through 1925. Then in 1927 and 1928 there was another major net increase in offerings. The only net decrease of outstandings was in 1929. This resulted in a cumulative net change in industrial corporate bonds outstanding at par value between 1922 and 1929 of $1.8 billion.

These data indicate that there was a shifting expansion in industrial sector use of external finance. The fluctuations in bond finance ran counter to the business cycles of that period. In general, for the fifty-year time span of his study, Hickman found that net expansions in bonds outstanding rose during the business cycle recession and that net retirements rose in the expansion phase. The net increases and decreases in outstandings moved counter-cyclically. In the 1920s, however, the pattern was not maintained. As the data in Table 1 imply, this alteration in behavior could, in part, be due to the use of other forms of finance. Hickman (1953: 133) notes that in the 1920s retained

---

10. Goldsmith used historical cost data for asset valuation and book value for debt. Taggart measured assets at replacement cost and debt at market value. Although different valuation methods may produce different debt and asset values, a standardized valuation method has not been adopted for financial reporting.

TABLE 1. Sources of Finance (figures in millions of current dollars)

	Net Bond Offerings[1]	New Funds from Debt Securities[2]	Internal Finance[2]	New Shares[2]	New Short-Term Debt[2]
1920	507.5				
1921	591.9	224	−179	126.7	−645.6
1922	383.0	60	200	159.9	−110.1
1923	243.4	297	347	265.8	124.0
1924	134.8	35	332	60.6	−99.4
1925	186.6	42	546	115.2	148.3
1926	545.1	188	506	196.1	6.2
1927	642.3	148	245	−34.7	−220.6
1928	78.2	83	532	107.1	159.8
1929	−405.7	564	599	957.0	11.9

[1] These data are taken from Hickman 1953 (table A-2).
[2] These data are taken from Koch 1943 (pp. 102–107).

earnings were an important source of finance.[11] Equity finance also became important by the end of the decade. As Koch's (1943) and Hickman's figures show, net bond offerings declined and both internal finance and new shares rose after 1927.

In addition to the cyclical variability, the NBER studies of Koch (1943) and Merwin (1942) found that firm size was a crucial determinant of debt issue and access. Large manufacturing firms utilized long-term debt as a source of new funds to a much greater degree than small manufacturing firms. Small firms relied on short-term debt, usually in the form of bank debt and accounts payable (trade credit).

These studies do not dwell on the barriers that small firms faced in the debt markets, but their results suggest unequal access existed. The asset thresholds used to categorize the firms were very low, so the impact of unequal access was heightened. Koch's study utilized 111 large firms from 15 industries. The study covered the years 1920–1939. He defined large firms as having total assets valued at $10 million or more. Merwin's study, covering 1926–1936, drew on approximately 1,000 small firms from 5 different industries. His definition of a small firm required the firm to have assets that were valued at less than $250,000.

Koch found that large firms had very different levels of long-term debt; in particular, those in fast-growing industries accrued more long-term debt than those in slow-growing industries. These fast-growing large firms relied primarily on their internal finance for new funds, but external funds were a

11. Since Hickman's study investigates bond financing, he relies on Dobrovolsky (1951) for his information on the use of retained earnings. Merwin (1942) also emphasized the importance of retained earnings for operating capital and investment finance.

necessary complement to internal funds. Koch's results indicate that debt was an important source of finance, and long-term debt was especially important for firms of this type.[12] His study found that, in the 1920s, large firms decreased their reliance on short-term debt and used stocks and bonds instead.

Koch also noted that large firms tended to move out of debt finance at the end of the 1920s. This behavior may be explained not only by the cheap equity finance in the late 1920s but also by the bond-rating companies' perceptions that even large firms were in riskier financial positions. Hickman (1958) noted that the percentage of newly offered industrial bonds of investment grade declined as the decade advanced. In the period 1920–1923, 79 percent of the new bonds were investment grade. In 1924–1927, quality was maintained, as 77 percent were rated investment grade. By 1928–1931, there had been a change in perception, as only 66 percent received the investment-grade rating. This deterioration was also noted in the grade on outstanding bonds. In 1920, 86 percent of the outstanding industrial bonds were investment grade. By 1928, this number had been reduced to 75 percent. Such changes indicated an increase in perceived financial exposure by the end of the 1920s.

Merwin's study showed that even in the expansion of the late 1920s, very small firms relied primarily upon retained earnings to finance expansion. In the period 1927–1929, 75 percent of their finance for land and plant expansion was internal, supplemented with short- and long-term debt. According to Merwin long- and short-term debt accounted for 10 percent and 6 percent of finance, respectively. Equity finance was a minor source of funds for the small firm, 4 percent (1942: 85). This financing pattern shows that small firms faced a dilemma: if they financed their expansion internally, they faced slow growth when the flow of retained earnings lagged behind desired investment levels; but if they used short-term debt to augment internal funds and expand more rapidly, they developed financially fragile balance sheets.

These two studies accentuate the role of firm size and industry growth rates in determining firms' financial structure. The large firm had access to all major forms of finance: long- and short-term debt, retained earnings, and shares. The small firm did not; it relied on internal finance and short-term debt. Overall, the large firm decreased it short-term debt usage while the small firm increased its usage. Further, the large firm in a rapidly expanding industry accrued more long-term debt than the large firm in a slowly expanding industry.

In general, these studies' evidence on debt accumulation by industrial sector firms in the 1920s does not conform with the FFH. Although external

---

12. Hickman pointed out that an interesting deviation from this use of long-term debt to finance expansion was found in the automobile industry. Isenberg (1989) determined that this behavior was also common to the large firms in the consumer durables sector in the 1920s.

finance was important to firms' operations, the use of debt did not result in rising leverage ratios between 1922 and 1929. Neither did the expected trade-off between long- and short-term debt emerge.

As the next section will detail, the extensive use of equity finance in the late 1920s appeared only to reduce risk. The common method for purchasing equity was credit. The call loan had a 10 percent margin requirement, which made it the most popular method of finance. These financial arrangements meant that equity finance, instead of producing greater financial stability, spread debt use into the consumer and financial sectors.

3.2 Financial, Real Estate, and Public Utility Sectors

Debt usage trends in the financial, real estate, and public utility sectors conformed more closely to the FFH. A study by Evans Clark (1933) showed that the outstanding values of debt in financial and real estate sectors between 1921 and 1929 had nominal increases of 208 percent and 193 percent, respectively. The bonded debt and mortgages of financial institutions stood at $6.7 billion in 1921–1922 and had increased to $19.8 billion in 1929. Urban mortgage debt stood at $9.0 billion in 1921 and at $27.6 billion in 1929. Together these two classes of debt composed 40 percent of the total outstanding long term debt in 1929. In contrast to these increases, nominal national income was estimated as having increased only 63 percent during this time period.

The credit extended by the weekly-reporting commercial banks provides a good indication of the normal activities of financial intermediaries between 1922 and 1929.[13] Table 2 partially shows the changing composition of these banks' balance sheets. Total loans grew by 152 percent during this period, and short-term loans on securities grew even faster, 198 percent; this loan category, which included call loans, represented 35 percent of outstanding loans in 1922 and 45 percent in 1929. Further, loans for securities accounted for a growing share of banks' earning assets: in 1922, 25 percent of banks' total loans and investments consisted of loans for securities; by 1929, this share had risen to 34 percent. This balance-sheet shift increased risk: assets' term to maturity declined, and collateral took the form of market-valued securities.

Apart from loans, investments constitute the other category of banks' earning assets. Although the statistics on the banks' investments are available only after 1924, the information provided in Table 2 suggests increased bal-

---

13. These are all members of the Federal Reserve System. On average they hold about 70 percent of the loans and investments of all member banks. In general, the reporting banks are located in large cities, where banks respond quickly to the effects of short-term money market activities. These banks' activities are not necessarily reflective of smaller country banks, whose response time is usually much slower (Board of Governors, Federal Reserve System 1946: 127).

TABLE 2. Financial Institutions

	Securities Loans as % Total Loans	Securities Loans as % Loans & Investments	Investments in Corporate Securities as % Total Investments
1922	35	25	
1923	35	25	
1924	36	26	
1925	39	28	40
1926	40	29	41
1927	42	30	42
1928	44	32	41
1929	45	34	

Source: Board of Governors of the Federal Reserve System 1946, table 22, p. 79, and table 48, pp. 135–142.

ance sheet risk owing to the rising proportion of securities, both debt and equity. In the four reporting years, corporate securities accounted for at least 40 percent of total investments. Since banks by their nature are highly leveraged, the purchase of these securities was accomplished only by the issuance of more debt claims.

Although commercial banks were the primary source of securities loans, the New York Stock Exchange, was also important in the debt-equity nexus. Banks would make loans to the Stock Exchange members, who would then finance their own and their clients' purchases of shares. The debt exposure of the members and banks financing equity positions increased dramatically: loans outstanding grew from $3.1 billion in 1926 to $8.5 billion in 1929 (New York Stock Exchange, 1932: 123–124).[14] The magnitude of this increasing debt exposure was obscured, however, because the tremendous growth in equity prices kept the ratio of outstanding brokers' loans to the market value of stocks listed on the exchange low. At year's end 1926 and 1927, this value was 8.4 percent. By the end of 1928 it had grown to 9.7 percent; in October 1929, it peaked at 9.8 percent. So debt both increased the volume of equity purchases and linked the balance sheets of institutions in the financial sector.

The household sector, too, increasingly used debt to finance equity holdings. Although not every household purchased stock, debt-financed stock purchases were largely responsible for increasing consumers' liabilities on securities from $4.5 billion in 1922 to $11.6 billion in 1929 (Goldsmith, 1955: vol. 3, p. 66). These purchases explain the rise in the debt/equity ratio

14. Although the brokerage houses on the New York Stock Exchange were the major conduit for securities sales, there were investment banking houses and brokerage houses on other exchanges that also intermediated funds for investment. The figures for their brokers' loans are not included here, because they made little or no difference in the total loan figures (Board of Governors, Federal Reserve System 1946: table 139, p. 494).

from 0.09 in 1922 to 0.13 in 1929, as well as increase in the debt/income ratio from 0.37 to 0.62 over these same years.

Hickman's 1953 study analyzes public utilities' debt use.[15] In 1923, a trend-breaking expansion in debt began that continued without pause until its 1927 peak. After 1927, the expansion slowed, but retirements did not exceed new issues until 1933. The cumulative net increase in outstanding public utility bonds from 1922 to 1929 was $4.0 billion, almost 2.2 times as great as the increase in industriales. Although debt grew at a rapid pace, so did the value of output. In 1919, the electric light and power companies accounted for 0.48 percent of the national income, and by 1929, the figure had climbed to 1.6 percent (Soule 1947: 182).

Towering over other debt categories in terms of level and rate of growth during the 1920s was nonfarm mortgage debt. Leonard Kuvin's (1936) National Industrial Conference Board's (NICB) study showed that household mortgages grew almost as rapidly as public utility debt and that they accounted for 46 percent of the total outstanding private long-term debt in 1929.[16] Mortgage debt was the largest component in total private long-term debt. The level of outstanding nonfarm mortgage debt stood at $14.8 billion in 1922 and increased to $32.6 billion in 1929. Using the data of the NICB study, the increase in mortgage debt was almost as large in 1929 as the combined outstanding values of public utility and industrial debt, $19.7 billion.[17]

On the asset side of the ledger, the total value of nonfarm real estate rose from $108.9 billion in 1922 to $197.4 billion in 1929, and concomitantly, the industrial debt-to-asset ratio increased from 13.5 percent to 16.5 percent. Although this increase does not indicate an overleveraged financial position, it is an increase in the risk level. The market value of real estate was strongly influenced by the speculative activities of the period.

In contrast to the industrial sector, debt in the financial, real estate, and public utilities sectors was steadily and positively related to growth. These sectors outstripped the industrial sector in debt use. Nonetheless, this accrual of debt involved increasing risk because the assets securing these debts were less secure than in the industrial sector.

In sum, this overview of 1920s financial behavior indicates that the

---

15. In Clark's study, financial debt includes the debt of the railroad and public utility holding companies. Therefore, in his analysis, the change in public utility debt from 1922 to 1929 is much smaller than Hickman's. Clark recorded the 1929 value of outstanding bonds as being equal to 76 percent of the 1922 value of outstandings.

16. Until the early 1900s the railroads had been the dominating debtor in the U.S. economy. According to the National Industrial Conference Boards's study, the level of outstanding non-farm mortgages surpassed the value of outstanding railroad bonds in 1918.

17. The value of industrial debt stood at $7,206 million, whereas public utilities debt was $12,473 million. The NICB data differ from the Hickman estimates by consistent and relatively insignificant amounts. (Hickman 1953: 414–421).

industrial sector, which Minsky suggests should be at the center of financial fragility, increased its debt usage, but it was not the principal user of debt. It also underscores the differences in credit usage that are associated with size and sector. The financial, real estate, and public utilities sectors overwhelmed the industrial sector both in debt added during the 1920s and in total debt outstanding. Although this evidence does not support the FFH, the next two sections show that a different disaggregated story lurks beneath the surface of these aggregate data trends.

4. Using Disaggregated Data to Examine Financial Fragility

The evidence of the two previous sections suggests that aggregate analysis is inappropriate for capturing shifts in debt and in financial fragility. Trends are very different for different segments of the economic whole. Only a disaggregated sectoral analysis can capture the external financing patterns in sufficient richness to avoid fallacies of composition. In using disaggregation to understand the fabric of macroscopic phenomena, this paper clearly owes a methodological debt to the NBER studies on debt use in the 1920s and Bernstein's study of the Great Depression.

At the macroeconomic level, economic growth is captured by one statistic, the growth rate of real GNP. Not all economic sectors grow at this rate, however; some sectors are typically declining. Disaggregation uncovers the disparity and interplay between the growing and declining industrial sectors. Since the engine-of-growth industries foster macroeconomic growth via their forward and backward linkages, they should be analyzed separately from the declining industries. These growth industries are by definition increasing their capital investment and their output levels. Their balance sheets thus should be characterized by growing assets and increasing debt ratios. The declining industries should suffer from the opposite problems: shrinking investment and output levels, and as a consequence declining asset values and debt ratios.[18]

In this study, industries are categorized as growing or declining based on their output growth in the 1920s. Industries with an average growth rate exceeding the average national manufacturer's growth rate for the period 1922–1929 are classified as growing, and those with growth rates less than the national average are declining.[19]

The FFH identifies the sphere of production as the locus of debt accu-

18. Although the need to finance investment expenditures in declining industries is reduced, these industries may continue to use debt to finance operating costs in an attempt to forestall their demise. Such behavior would produce rising leverage ratios, as both asset and debt values would rise.

19. Bernstein's determination of innovative processes/products that emerged in the 1920s was used as an initial indicator of growing and declining industries.

mulation and instability, and utilizes a representative firm in portraying the financial fragility hypothesis.[20] A sample of sixty-one industrial firms that represented both growing and declining industries was chosen from Moody's *Manuals of Industriales*. The firms chosen represent nine different industries. Six were growing—paper, stone, brick and glass, chemicals, iron-steel, tobacco, and rubber—; and three were declining—lumber, food and textiles.[21] The statistics shown are averages for each industry—in effect, they depict a "representative" firm.

The previous section has argued that in addition to growth rate, firm size is also a key determinant of debt use and financial structure. Three size categories were delineated on the basis of asset size. Small firms had total assets of under $10 million in 1922; thirty firms in the sample were small. Medium firms had total assets in the range from $10 million up to $40 million; twenty firms were classified as medium. Large firms total assets were greater than $40 million; there were eleven large firms. Categorizing the sample firms by size on the basis of the growth/decline category gives the following results: the "growing industry" category consists of fourteen small firms, fourteen medium firms, and nine large firms; the "contracting" category has sixteen small firms, six medium firms, and two large firms.[22] For each combined size/growth category, a statistically average firm was constructed from the data. The average firm's activity was charted for the 1920s.

Analysis then proceeds by evaluating trends in the financial variables that indicate financial vulnerability—especially changes in expenditures, in types of finance, and in the values of financial ratios. Some financial ratios are charted over time: total debt to net worth (DT/NW), short-term debt to net worth (ST/NW), long-term debt to net worth (LT/NW), long-term debt to short-term debt (LT/ST), current ratio (CURR), and quick ratio (QUIK). Trends in these leverage indicators determine whether there is a buildup in debt. In particular, the annual change in these variables is used to indicate

20. The use of a representative firm suffers from many of the same problems that were discussed in regard to the macroeconomic level of aggregation. The average or representative firm fails to acknowledge the unequal use of credit, which is based on firm size differences; the varying operational strategies of management; industry and sector-dependent factors; the age of a firm; and its borrowing track record. Although there is no available data on many of these factors, this study utilizes growth, size, and industry variables.

21. Steindl (1952) categorizes the industrial sector as either competitive or oligopolistic. The industries he categorized as competitive are this study's declining industries. The oligopolistic industries are this study's growth industries. This convergence indicates that industrial structure may be an important factor in determining growth.

22. Merwin's study on the finance of the small firm used very small firms. The small and medium firms in this study fall to the other end of the spectrum; they are very large. This skewness derives from the data source, *Moody's Manual of Industriales*. All firms rated by Moody's Investment Services must have publicly traded securities. This precludes very small firms from the data set.

behavioral shifts. Tracking these changes provides a view of the coordination of expenditures and finance. Changes in debt and expenditure levels were also tracked. The expenditures include plant and equipment (PE) and current assets (CURASS). The finance variables include changes in total debt (DT), in short-term debt (ST), in long- term debt (LT), and in number of outstanding common shares (COM).[23] Each variable is constructed on an annual basis for each of the categories analyzed.

According to the FFH, industrial debt ratios should rise between 1922 and 1929. As the economic expansion moves out of its initial stages, debt should increase, both absolutely and relative to net worth. As the expansion moves into its later stages, the firm should increase its short-term debt relative to long-term debt. At the peak of the expansion, the absolute value of total debt and the ratio, debt to net worth, should have increased compared to their initial levels. Since there were very minor cyclical downturns in 1924 and 1927, a growth pause or actual decline in the ratios at these points would be understandable.

As Minsky (1982b) has noted, not every firm must move into a more fragile financial position for financial fragility to emerge in the aggregate. There will always be a mixture of hedge, speculative and Ponzi financiers. Thus we focus attention on whether the average leverage ratios rose between 1922 and 1929. Since this study is confined to balance-sheet data, the debt-equity ratio is our only insolvency ratio, and CURR and QUIK are the only liquidity ratios that could be constructed.

5. Debt Accumulation by the Industrial Sector in the 1920s, Reconsidered

The data on finances, expenditures, and financial ratios for the "average" firms, which are shown in the appendix, are consistent with a FFH explanation of the Great Depression.[24] This support, however, is not unequivocal. On average for the whole sample, the total debt-equity ratios did not experience an extended and continuous rise, and as was expected, the behavior of the debt ratios for the disaggregated categories varied. The large- and medium-sized firms, and to a lesser extent the growth firm, experienced continuously rising debt ratios throughout most of the period. The large firm was the major source of debt use, but the medium firm was not far behind it. Since the large and medium firms had the largest representation in the growth firm, the rising total debt-equity ratio of the average growth firm is logical. The debt ratios of

---

23. Income statements were only reported sporadically by these firms in this time period. For consistency in the data set, the balance sheet was used as the primary data source. Therefore, the flow concepts were constructed from changes in stocks.

24. The data are found in the appendix.

the small and declining firms experienced declines throughout most of the period.

Another important finding was the shift out of debt into equity at the end of the 1920s. This behavior indicates the pivotal role the Wall Street frenzy played in the financing process. After 1927, equity, not short-term debt, became the cheapest source of external finance. It also shifted the debt buildup from the industrial sector to equity's final purchasers, who commonly used debt finance. The declining firm experienced a secular decline in DT/NW between 1922 and 1929. Initially, the average declining firm had a higher percentage of its net worth absorbed by debt than did the average growth firm. By 1925, however, this position had been reversed, as the growth firm incurred more debt while the declining firm extinguished its debt. The rise in the growth firm's DT/NW ratio continued until 1926, when it began a stair-step decline. The final DT/NW level was 0.23; this is lower than its 1922 value, 0.28.

The behavior of the total debt ratio is explained by its components, long-term debt and short-term debt. For the average declining firm, the secular behavior of DT/NW results from the secular decline in the ST/NW and LT/NW ratios. The data indicate that declining firms in mature industries did not take a precarious position through an extreme or even strategic use of leverage. Although the ST/NW ratio accounted for at least 50 percent of the DT/NW ratio, total debt usage was very low. If this same pattern had prevailed and there had been heavier debt usage, then financial vulnerability would have emerged as a problem for the declining firm. The pattern that did emerge, however, showed a small increase in the use of long-term debt early in the decade and then a switch to short-term debt after 1926. The growth in stock market speculation after 1927 meant that management switched into equity finance and away from debt. The overall impact of these financial decisions was a decline in debt usage, which caused the average declining firm to end the decade with a DT/NW value smaller than in 1922.

The behavior of the growth firm's DT/NW ratio is not as easily decomposed. Although it, too, experienced a secular decline in its ST/NW ratio, there was a major movement away from trend in 1925 and then a slight deviation in 1927. Overall, however, the ST/NW ratio induced the DT/NW ratio to fall. Conversely, the LT/NW ratio rose throughout most of the decade. The peak value of the ratio was reached in 1926 and was maintained through 1928. In 1929, the ratio fell to 0.14, which left it marginally higher than its initial value. Thus the peak that DT/NW reached in 1925 and 1926 was due to the increased use of both short- and long-term debt. Its decline, thereafter, was primarily due to the fall in short-term debt usage, but the fall in long-term debt usage and the rise in net worth were also important.

This disaggregation of the sample into growth and declining firms shows

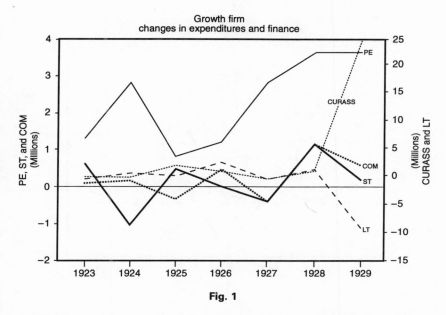

Fig. 1

the difference in behaviors of the debt ratios for these two types of firms. Through the decomposition it is ascertained that not all sectors are equally responsible for debt's buildup in an expansion. The responsible sectors depend on the structure of the economy and its changes. The average firm in the sample experienced very little debt buildup and a peak of that in 1925, whereas the growth firm continued its larger debt run-up until 1926 and the declining firm had major debt reductions after 1924. The growth firm accounted for a larger proportion of economic activity than the decliners, so their debt burden carried a larger economic impact.

Although shifts in the debt-equity ratio signal the changing debt burden on the economy, the composition and uses of debt are also important in uncovering the links between financial and real activity. Figures 1 and 2 show the changing patterns of expenditures and finance for the growth and declining firms. A secular increase in plant and equipment expenditures (PE) for the average growth firm started directly after the 1920–1921 recession, peaked in 1924, reignited in 1926, and continued until 1929. Changes in expenditures on current assets (CURASS) ran counter to those in PE. Initially, the firm's expenditures were funded with a combination of short- and long-term debt. Then, in an alternating sequence, short- and long-term debt was issued. This pattern was maintained until 1927, when equity finance supplanted debt.

Figure 1 shows the important role equity played in financing the expansion. The first major sale of new shares took place in 1926 and was followed

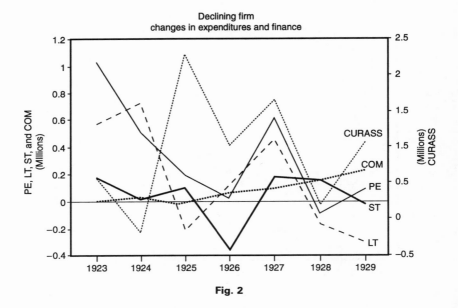

Fig. 2

by larger sales in 1928 and 1929. The funds from these sales of stock were used to finance PE and CURASS expenditures, as well as to retire long-term debt. It was this move into equity in the final years of the decade that caused the leverage ratios to decline.

Figure 2 bears out empirically the idea that the declining firm should not have had a run-up in debt or capital expenditures. The changes in PE expenditures showed a secular decline, and the changes in CURASS oscillated throughout the period. Short-term debt changes usually fluctuated sympathetically with CURASS, but with a much smaller amplitude. Changes in long-term debt showed a secular decline that was interrupted with minor fluctuations away from trend. Like the growth firm, the declining firm also moved into equity finance after 1927, which, along with its move out of debt, accounted for its declining DT/NW ratios.

Both Figures 1 and 2 show that at the end of the decade there was a movement out of long-term debt and into equity. The reason behind this shift was the declining cost of equity finance. Usually, the cost of equity finance to a firm is dividend payments; however, in the 1920s speculators were not interested in rising dividends. Stock market speculators were clamoring for more equity shares so they could realize a capital gain as the market's prices seemed to rise without pause. The rise in equity finance substituted for short- and long-term debt after 1928, driving both ST/NW and LT/NW down and driving up the value of owner's equity. Both of these effects served to reduce the DT/NW ratio of the growth and declining firms after 1926. The largest value that DT/NW reached was 0.31, which is a relatively low figure, and since the major source of debt finance was long-term debt, financial fragility was tempered.

Other indicators of the financial health of firms also pointed to their relative stability. Both the quick ratio (QUIK) and the current ratio (CURR) are liquidity indicators. The long- to short-term debt ratio (LT/ST) indicates the proportional relationship of these two types of debt on the firm's balance sheet. The liquidity ratios for the growth and declining industries are detailed in the appendix. The declining firm's initial current ratio was 4.6, and it rose to more than 11 by 1929. The floor value for a healthy firm is 2.00.[25] The quick ratio, a subset of the current ratio, was also within a healthy range, falling between 1.4 and 3.48. Both of the liquidity ratios showed a secular rise over the time period, indicating that the firms had reached more liquid positions by the end of the 1920s.

The long-term to short-term debt ratios (LT/ST) of the growth and declining firms exhibited very different behaviors over the seven years studied. Initially, LT/ST for the decliner was 0.8. It ended the decade with that same value. There were only minor changes during the intervening years. If this firm had a much higher DT/NW ratio, then it might have indicated potential trouble because of the heavy use of short-term debt.

Although the values of the growth firm's liquidity ratios were quite stable through time, the LT/ST ratio swung in a very wide arc. The current ratio had an initial value of 5.1 and finished the decade at 7.5. It fluctuated in the interim, but 5.1 was its lowest value. The quick ratio essentially followed the pattern of the current ratio, only at lower values. It never fell below 1.00; it peaked at 2.1 in 1924 and then settled into a mild fluctuation around 1.75, which is where it finished in 1929. The LT/ST ratio's initial value was 1.8 in 1922, and even with its roller coaster behavior it never fell below that. Major spikes were experienced in 1925 and 1927 that were attributable to declines in short-term debt and increases in long-term debt. At the end of the decade, long-term debt was twice as large as short-term. All of these ratios indicate the financial stability of the growth firm.

A simple comparison of the financial behavior of the size-categorized firms to that of the growth and declining firms is enough, in some cases, to confirm that size is an important variable in the discussion of financial instability. Although there are twice as many small and medium firms as large ones

---

25. Ray Foulke, the chief economist at Dun and Bradstreet, cites this as the "rule of thumb" safe value. He notes that in the early 1900s the acceptable range for the current ratio was between 2.5 and 1. Prior to his textbook's publication, the accepted healthy value for the current ratio was 2 (1945: 173–201). More recent sources, Robert Morris Associates (1977) and Dun and Bradstreet (1978), still use this value.

in the growth category, a comparison of the large firms' behavior to the growth firms' indicates their similarities. The dramatic swings in the behavior of outstanding shares and the sustained rise in LT/NW were primarily due to the large firms' actions. As desirable borrowers, they had easy access to the capital markets given their longevity, track record, activities in national product markets, and market power.

Just as the small number of large firms had an impact on the LT/NW ratio, the large number of small and medium firms affected the growth firms' ST/NW ratio. The small and medium firms had a heavy dependence on short-term debt, which became even heavier in 1925. This is also the only year in which the ST/NW ratio rose for the growth firm. Again, the prominence of short-term debt on the balance-sheets of the small and medium firms is a result of their inadequate track records, positions in more competitive markets, and participation only in regional markets. Although determining which of these effects—growth phase or size—dominates is not the focus of this study, establishing their importance and role in producing a financially fragile economy is.

5.1 Discussion

The empirical analysis shows the industriales moving away from debt use in the final phase of the 1920s expansion. This appears to counter the FFH explanation of the Great Depression; however, the movement out of debt is complemented by a move into equity. The debt buildup continues, but it shifts from the industriales to the financial and household balance-sheets, where the liabilities from the debt-financed equity emerge. The relationship between external finance and financial fragility surfaces only in the reinterpreted FFH. In the rest of this section, the findings from this study are analyzed in a modified FFH framework and contrasted to the other views on the GD.

The disaggregation into expanding and contracting industries showed the divergence in the effects of the macroeconomic expansion on these industries. As expected, the average declining firm did not rely heavily on external finance in the expansionary 1920s. In contrast, the average growth firm experienced a strong expansion in investment and current assets expenditures, and an increased reliance upon external finance, both debt and equity. Its increased use, however, did not produce financial instability as measured by financial ratio thresholds. The liquidity and leverage ratios rose prior to 1928 but remained in very healthy ranges.

One reason for this behavior can be traced to the historical period. Part of the roar in the "Roaring Twenties" came from the bulls on the stock market. The public's clamoring for more stocks with which to speculate meant a cheap form of finance for business. The new common stock issues were used to retire long-term debt, to finance current assets, and to reduce debt/equity ratios.

This seeming move to stability for the industrial sector is, however, a mask; for purchasers of debt and equity securities commonly financed these securities on margin. Such practices meant that the debt burden was not reduced but merely shifted on to other sectors. Increased borrowing for debt and equity securities was one of the two major causes of the growth in consumer debt/income ratios. Also, the larger proportion of call loans on the balance-sheets and in the portfolios of banks and stock exchanges produced higher risk levels.

Although debt in the industrial sector fluctuated, in the financial, real estate, and public utilities sectors, it grew rapidly. Real estate debt, like financial sector debt, was not only held by financial and non-financial firms but was spread to consumers through mortgages. The equity and debt securities of the public utilities were also distributed to other sectors.

This web of credit finance intertwined the financial and nonfinancial sectors. Although the financial relationship among individual consumers is not strong or well-integrated, the same is not true of financial institutions and markets. They are wellintegrated, so that a disruption is easily communicated to other sectors in the economy. The implication of this integration is that a financial calamity in one area would not necessarily remain isolated. Once it emerged, the problem could spread throughout the financial sector and into the production sector. Since financial intermediaries hold the debt of the economy, a major disruption in any sector could be transmitted through the financial sector and produce an economic disruption.

6. Conclusion

This empirical analysis points to important economic phenomena that most of the explanations of the Great Depression fail to incorporate. The FFH explanation cites the move to a more financially fragile position in specific sectors, and the linkages of these sectors to the less fragile ones, as the basis for the GD. Temin emphasizes the stock market crash, with its destruction of wealth and the destructive domestic impacts of the monetary policy that supported the gold standard. He fails to consider, however, how these factors were important in rupturing the financial structure. This structural disruption is pivotal in explaining the depth and duration of the GD.

Bernstein presents a long-period, structural analysis of the GD that is motivated by a decline in introduction and dissemination of innovative products and processes. The FFH's short-period approach focuses on the economic consequences produced by disruptions in the financial sector. The primacy of the financial sector's credit associations to the rest of the economy resides in its ability to stifle or disrupt investment projects by restrictive lending. Inadequate access to finance for firms means that the economy's growth path, its structural development, will be inextricably altered.

While paralleling Minsky's analysis to a greater extent than the other analysts, Bernanke, like Mishkin, theoretically situates his analysis with the monetarists. Empirically, each of these studies regards the role of the financial sector and in particular, debt, as pivotal, so superficially they appear similar. At their theoretical foundations, however, they are incompatible. The motivations for incorporating the financial sector and the implications drawn from its data are fundamentally inconsistent. Empirically, the differences can be seen in the monetarists' emphasis on the debt-deflation process rather than the debt buildup. Although debt-deflation is usually a phenomenon of the contraction, in order for it to have the impact required for producing a Great Depression a large buildup of debt is necessary. Minsky draws upon Fisher's process of debt-deflation, but he changes the emphasis so that debt accumulation is the focal point. As the results from this study indicate, the potential for economic disruption begins long before the actual disruption occurs.

Given the evidence about the financial stress that the economy was experiencing by the end of the 1920s, it is clear that any explanation of the Great Depression that does not incorporate these events is neglecting a major component. Since the production side of the economy is not protected by firewalls from its financial side, a disruption beginning in one side can spread to the other. The debt-deflation theory of Fisher, as amended by Minsky, indicates that this connection between the financial and production sectors may cause a recession to be longer and deeper—a Great Depression.

APPENDIX

Data for the 61 firms in the study arranged by size and growth categories.

VARIABLE	1922	1923	1924	1925	1926	1927	1928	1929
DECLINING FIRM								
DT/NW	0.288	0.297	0.298	0.27	0.205	0.197	0.166	0.154
LT/NW	0.112	0.149	0.142	0.126	0.108	0.097	0.076	0.065
ST/NW	0.176	0.149	0.156	0.143	0.097	0.1	0.091	0.089
PE		1,057,432	527,811	180,271	15,160	608,667	(92,079)	76,600
CURASS		588,663	(147,886)	2,287,084	1,007,273	1,639,397	214,935	1,054,081
LT		550,162	731,545	(217,187)	126,694	469,122	(172,273)	(314,444)
ST		186,007	14,938	89,476	(357,514)	169,950	151,252	(33,844)
COM		3,331	27,915	(25,775)	52,733	89,906	140,797	223,374
CURR	4.564	6.897	7.316	6.083	8.215	8.561	9.503	11.698
QUIK	1.378	1.993	2.295	2.041	2.572	2.707	3.465	3.437
LT/ST	0.762	0.99	1.123	1.239	1.392	1.37	0.83	0.63
GROWTH FIRM								
DT/NW	0.28	0.274	0.278	0.313	0.313	0.289	0.288	0.227
LT/NW	0.132	0.131	0.158	0.17	0.196	0.192	0.192	0.139
ST/NW	0.148	0.143	0.12	0.144	0.117	0.097	0.096	0.088
PE		1,114,705	2,782,784	784,416	1,146,172	2,690,849	3,540,554	3,570,557
CURASS		385,662	(534,128)	1,761,227	777,328	(546,685)	839,707	24,549,217
LT		(209,879)	490,359	(133,151)	2,175,044	(421,454)	1,058,633	(10,991,054)
ST		733,099	(1,075,906)	434,499	(35,866)	(428,957)	1,071,555	127,846
COM		50,893	121,274	(373,761)	411,858	(431,720)	1,094,015	474,913
CURR	5.216	5.379	7.748	6.951	6.82	6.568	7.176	7.501
QUIK	1.135	1.069	2.159	1.712	1.756	1.759	1.664	1.697
LT/ST	1.772	1.83	2.921	7.034	2.548	8.302	2.438	2.373

(*continued*)

APPENDIX (Continued)

VARIABLE	1922	1923	1924	1925	1926	1927	1928	1929
AVERAGE FIRM VARIABLE								
DT/NW	0.286	0.286	0.285	0.297	0.275	0.256	0.243	0.205
LT/NW	0.127	0.141	0.153	0.153	0.167	0.158	0.149	0.114
ST/NW	0.16	0.145	0.132	0.144	0.108	0.098	0.095	0.091
PE		1,536,150	1,616,031	1,344,985	1,514,218	1,466,693	1,368,371	896,590
CURASS		651,807	(466,819)	1,912,540	866,341	270,367	577,609	5,442,819
LT		117,077	556,927	(170,637)	1,569,830	(131,823)	399,429	(6,422,961)
ST		443,306	(773,513)	(357,503)	(360,032)	(98,606)	752,287	325,839
COM		12,376	105,600	(220,186)	250,761	(273,652)	673,008	367,897
CURR	5.123	6.153	7.846	7.053	7.887	7.717	8.467	9.33
QUIK	1.249	1.457	2.22	1.895	2.129	2.165	2.384	2.371
LT/ST	1.352	1.482	2.251	4.622	2.13	5.462	1.786	1.685
LARGE FIRM								
DT/NW	0.341	0.317	0.319	0.299	0.38	0.352	0.404	0.301
LT/NW	0.207	0.203	0.246	0.225	0.313	0.283	0.312	0.225
ST/NW	0.134	0.114	0.073	0.074	0.066	0.068	0.092	0.075
PE		3,005,998	6,843,810	1,983,346	2,377,440	8,980,776	8,561,263	5,287,375
CURASS		122,361	(1,242,377)	2,326,075	330,638	969,250	(681,176)	23,103,641
LT		(501,710)	1,421,190	(1,436,500)	6,458,539	(1,680,936)	3,209,222	(36,388,262)
ST		2,384,019	(3,358,086)	(217,569)	647,545	(890,379)	3,713,489	(138,246)
COM		267,391	446,307	(830,479)	772,806	(986,734)	3,025,377	567,195
CURR	5.858	6.263	8.403	8.751	9.197	7.805	6.813	9.824
QUIK	1.437	1.577	1.97	1.948	1.948	1.678	1.365	2.082
LT/ST	2.081	2.188	3.636	3.208	4.859	3.93	3.197	4.22

MEDIUM FIRM

DT/NW	0.218	0.259	0.289	0.298	0.317	0.332	0.304	0.268
LT/NW	0.12	0.148	0.188	0.178	0.214	0.24	0.218	0.174
ST/NW	0.098	0.11	0.101	0.121	0.103	0.092	0.086	0.093
PE		1,515,438	1,907,505	(53,397)	1,045,877	426,419	1,756,535	2,568,164
CURASS		852,532	(605,809)	1,437,014	1,259,417	120,397	1,592,444	988,392
LT		423,016	983,790	90,615	884,358	518,777	69,139	(479,871)
ST		394,116	(321,777)	647,959	(372,537)	(199,538)	(26,771)	374,433
COM		64,206	(44,763)	(68,325)	140,573	(162,261)	257,141	323,443
CURR	5.274	5.565	7.897	6.968	6.318	6.08	6.995	6.375
QUIK	1.065	0.854	1.969	1.696	1.632	1.588	1.843	1.468
LT/ST	1.245	1.299	3.175	2.032	2.202	2.671	3.03	2.243

SMALL FIRM

DT/NW	0.252	0.229	0.232	0.266	0.173	0.138	0.103	0.081
LT/NW	0.096	0.107	0.092	0.109	0.069	0.05	0.028	0.017
ST/NW	0.209	0.18	0.18	0.185	0.13	0.114	0.101	0.09
PE		108,257	73,283	420,034	(143,240)	228,416	(76,600)	716,133
CURASS		333,361	82,345	2,190,943	803,678	201,616	380,412	1,735,116
LT		83,228	13,049	128,337	(173,793)	125,997	(54,977)	(144,913)
ST		(83,923)	130,816	255,266	(319,321)	66,411	98,821	(70,370)
COM		(10,690)	8,383	(5,238)	29,103	(12,205)	56,182	109,373
CURR	5.206	6.942	8.023	6.874	9.021	8.499	8.948	11.115
QUIK	1.271	1.809	2.492	1.909	2.461	2.721	3.234	3.205
LT/ST	1.202	1.38	1.05	7.136	0.993	8.152	0.303	0.26

REFERENCES

Bernanke, Ben (1983), "Non-Monetary Effects of the Financial Crisis in the Propagation of the Great Depression," *American Economic Review*, vol. 73, pp. 257–276.

Bernstein, Michael (1987), *The Great Depression*, Cambridge: Cambridge University Press.

Board of Governors of the Federal Reserve System (1946), *Banking and Monetary Statistics*, Washington, DC: Board of Governors of the Federal Reserve.

Brunner, Karl (ed.) (1981), *The Great Depression Revisited*, Hingham, MA: Kluwer.

Clark, Evans (ed.) (1933), *The Internal Debts of the United States*, New York: MacMillan Co.

Dobrovolsky, Sergei (1951), *Corporate Income Retention, 1915–1943*, New York: National Bureau of Economic Research.

Dun and Bradstreet, Inc. (1978), *Key Business Ratios, 1977*, New York: Dun & Bradstreet.

Eckstein, Otto, and Allen Sinai (1986), "The Mechanisms of the Business Cycle in the Postwar Era," in Robert J. Gordon (ed.) *The American Business Cycle*, Chicago: University of Chicago Press.

Fisher, Irving (1933), "The Debt-Deflation Theory of the Great Depression," *Econometrica*, vol. 1, pp. 337–357.

Foulke, Ray (1945), *Practical Financial Structure Analysis*, New York: McGraw Hill Book Co.

Friedman, M. J., and Schwartz, A. (1963), *A Monetary History of the United States 1867–1960*, Princeton: Princeton University Press.

Galbraith, John (1962), *The Great Crash 1929*, New York: Time Inc.

Goldsmith, Raymond (1956), *A Study of Saving in the United States*, vol. 1–3, Princeton: Princeton University Press.

Haberler, Gottfried (1963), *Prosperity and Depression*, New York:Atheneum.

Hickman, W. B. (1953), *The Volume of Corporate Bond Financing Since 1900*, Princeton: Princeton University Press.

Hickman, W. B. (1958), *Corporate Bond Quality and Investor Experience*, Princeton: Princeton University Press.

Isenberg, D.L. (1989), "The Financially Fragile Firm: Is There a Case for It in the 1920s?," *British Review of Economic Issues*, vol. 11, pp. 27–51.

Kindleberger, Charles (1975), *The World in Depression 1929–1939*, Berkeley: University of California Press.

Kindleberger, Charles (1978), *Manias, Panics and Crashes*, New York: Basic Books, Inc.

Koch, Albert (1943), *The Financing of Large Corporations, 1920–1939*, New York: National Bureau of Economic Research.

Kuvin, Leonard (1936), *Private Long-Term Debt and Interest in the United States*, New York: National Industrial Conference Board Inc.

Merwin, Charles (1942), *Financing Small Corporations*, New York: National Bureau of Economic Research.

Minsky, Hyman (1975), *John Maynard Keynes*, New York: Columbia University Press.

Minsky, Hyman (1982a), *Can "It" Happen Again?* Armonk, NY: M.E. Sharpe, Inc.

Minsky, Hyman (1982b), "The Financial-Instability Hypothesis: Capitalist Processes and the Behavior of the Economy," in C. Kindleberger, and Jean-Pierre Laffargue (ed.) *Financial Crises*, Cambridge: Cambridge University Press.

Minsky, Hyman (1986), *Stabilizing an Unstable Economy*, New Haven: Yale University Press.

Mishkin, Frederic (1978), "The Household Balance Sheet and the Great Depression," *Journal of Economic History*, December, pp. 918–937.

Moody, John, *Moody's Manual of Industriales*, vol. 1919–1930, New York: Moody.

New York Stock Exchange (1932), *New York Stock Exchange Year Book, 1930–1931*, New York: New York Stock Exchange.

Niggle, Christopher (1989), "The Cyclical Behavior of Corporate Financial Ratios and Minsky's Financial Instability Hypothesis," in W. Semmler (ed.) *Financial Dynamics and Business Cycles*, Armonk, NY: M.E. Sharpe, Inc.

Pollin, Robert (1986), "Alternative Perspectives on the Rise of Corporate Debt Dependency: The U.S. Post-War Experience," *Review of Radical Political Economics* 18(1–2): 235–65.

Robert Morris Associates (1977), *Annual Statement Studies, 1977*, Philadelphia: Robert Morris Associates.

Soule, George (1947), *Prosperity Decade from War to Depression 1917–1929*, Armonk, NY: M.E. Sharpe, Inc.

Steindl, Josef (1952), *Maturity and Stagnation in American Capitalism*, New York: Monthly Review Press.

Taggart, Robert (1986), "Secular Patterns in the Financing of U.S. Corporations," in B. Friedman (ed.) *Corporate Capital Structures in the U.S.*, Chicago: University of Chicago Press.

Temin, Peter (1976), *Did Monetary Forces Cause the Great Depression?* New York: W.W. Norton, Inc.

Temin, Peter (1991), *Lessons From the Great Depression*, Cambridge, MA: MIT Press.

Wolfson, Martin (1986), *Financial Crises*, Armonk, NY: M.E. Sharpe, Inc.

CHAPTER 9

A Political Economy Model of Comparative Central Banking

Gerald A. Epstein*

1. Introduction

Hyman Minsky has been an astute observer and analyst of central banking for many years. In fact, in 1957 he published his first professional paper on the subject (Minsky 1982). As usual, on this subject as on most others, Minsky poses a challenge to the standard ways of looking at things and an opening for a whole line of research previously thought closed. Long before it was fashionable, at least on this side of the Atlantic, during a period when the neoclassical IS-LM synthesis was in the ascendancy, Hyman Minsky was questioning whether the neoclassical synthesis view of monetary policy was much too sanguine: is it really the case, he asked, that monetary policy can adjust the money supply and interest rates to achieve full employment, as the IS-LM model implied? By shifting the LM curve, can monetary policy really stem an inflationary expansion, or thwart a developing recession?

Emphasizing the role of expectations and the endogeneity of money and credit, Minsky replied to this question in the negative. With regard to anti-recessionary policy, Minsky reminded economists of the problems of pushing on a string when borrowers' expectations are depressed. Analyzing booms, Minsky argued that thwarting an expansion would be difficult, if not impossi-

*This paper is part of a joint research project on Comparative Central Banking with Juliet Schor, who shared in the development of many of the ideas presented here. Thomas Weisskopf generously supplied some of the data used in this study. I would like to thank Bob Pollin for many helpful comments on the latest draft of this paper. Samuel Bowles, James Crotty, Peter Dorman, Mohan Rao, Juliet Schor and members of the University of Massachusetts Political Economy Seminar and two anonymous referees made very helpful comments on an earlier draft. Emily Kawano and Elizabeth Kruse provided excellent research assistance. Thanks also to the World Institute for Development Economic Research and the University of Massachusetts Economics Department for financial support. Part of this paper has been previously published as "Political Economy and Comparative Central Banking", *Review of Radical Political Economics*, 24(1)1–30, 1992. All errors and omissions are my own.

ble, because, as opposed to the synthesis assumption, the money supply is endogenously responsive to euphoric expectations. In response to restricted reserves, banks would develop financial innovations that would allow them to continue expanding credit without increased reserves. In order to restrict a boom, central banks may have to pursue extremely restrictive policy that, rather than restoring the economy to a noninflationary position of full employment, would push the economy way beyond into a recession.

Later, Minsky (1982, 1986) emphasized that central banks would not tend to pursue highly restrictive policy because such policies would drive many companies, both financial and nonfinancial, into bankruptcy. The central bank would have to pursue its lender-of-last resort function and bail out these institutions, thus undermining its restrictive policy.

Thus for Minsky, in contrast to the Neoclassical synthesis that suggests that the money supply is exogenous, the money supply is endogenous for two reasons: first, because of private banks' ability to endogenously create money; and second, because the central bank must fulfill its lender-of-last-resort function. This endogeneity, along with other aspects of the economy emphasized by Minsky will make it impossible, according to him, for the central bank to use monetary policy to maintain a noninflationary full employment equilibrium.

Minsky's work thus presents a double challenge to analysts of monetary policy: the first is to take seriously the potential endogeneity of money and credit which arises from financial market behavior. The second is to take seriously the endogeneity of monetary policy: central banks are not simply exogenous institutions that can be assumed to make any type of monetary policy the analyst desires; their behavior is created and restricted by the operation of the economy.

Minsky himself has pursued the first challenge to a much greater extent than he has pursued the second. Indeed, it is not clear that Minsky recognizes that his work poses this second challenge—the need to develop a theory of central bank behavior—as well. For the most part, Minsky has simply assumed that the lender-of-last-resort imperative was the overriding determinant of Federal Reserve monetary policy. This hypothesis, however, has been relatively undeveloped and untested in Minsky's own work. Certainly, in the case of the U.S. central bank, the Federal Reserve has pursued highly restrictive policy that has generated a large number of bankruptcies, most recently in 1981–1982. Moreover, in other countries, there have certainly been periods of highly restrictive policy; take for example the policies of the Bundesbank in the early 1990s.

Thus, there is a striking need for research to develop Minsky's basic insight that central bank policy is itself endogenous, both for the U.S. Federal Reserve and for other central banks. But it is important to develop this theory in the context of an analysis that includes Minsky's other point: that private financial institutions themselves endogenously create money and credit and thereby play an important role in helping to generate cycles of financial instability.

This need to develop an analysis of endogenous central bank policy may be especially important in the current period, since the political power of central banks is rising in the capitalist world. In the United States, where fiscal policy is crippled by budget stalemate, the Federal Reserve is generally seen as the premier macroeconomic agency. Across the Atlantic, the European Economic Community is planning to create a European central bank. While the outcome is still in doubt, many argue that the European Central Bank will be dominated by West Germany's Bundesbank, widely believed to be the most politically independent central bank in the world. To some extent, such a move would simply ratify the existing situation where members of the European Monetary System already follow the Bundesbank's lead. On both sides of the Atlantic, then, macroeconomic policy is increasingly made by independent and powerful central banks, insulated from control by elected governments.

Paradoxically, the *political* power of central banks is rising just as central banks' *economic* power is increasingly doubted. Economists from many traditions are taking Minsky's points seriously that money and credit are endogenous phenomena and that expectations are central to the operations of monetary policy. These economists cite dramatic changes in domestic and international financial markets that severely circumscribe central banks' abilities to affect the real economy. The factors most widely thought to limit the economic powers of central banks are two: international financial integration, which forces domestic financial conditions to match those abroad; and, huge, highly speculative financial markets, which overwhelm the operations of central banks.

To be sure, the nature of financial markets and international integration have altered the functioning of central banks. Yet most evidence suggests that central banks in large financial markets have retained their ability to alter conditions in domestic and world credit markets (see Epstein, 1993, for a review.) There is little doubt, however, that changes in the financial system, the role of endogenous money and credit, and the importance of expectations in financial markets are part of the central environment within which monetary policy is made, just as Minsky and others have suggested.

Yet, with all the attention paid to their operations by the business press, the financial markets appear to believe that these few central banks are powerful, which, in speculative financial markets, is virtually sufficient to make it so. Indeed, the new importance of internationally integrated speculative financial markets may have *increased* both the economic and political power of major central banks. As financial markets become more speculative, pressures for more independent central banks emerge. Central bank control over financial conditions depends more and more on their ability to affect market expectations, and less on their ability to affect the money supply. Independent banks are thus better able to conduct monetary policy with speculative markets because they are better able to impose policies unfettered by the uncertainties of the democratic process. Thus the common appearance of independent central banks and more speculative financial markets may not be an accident.

The expanded role of nondemocratic central banks seems certain to damage the liberal democratic structure of European and U.S. capitalism. What, in addition, will be the economic effects? Will increased central bank independence in the context of integrated international financial markets and financial deregulation be conducive or harmful to world economic growth? Will the constraints placed on international macroeconomic coordination by independent central banks lead to what Keynes referred to as a "deflationary bias" in the world economy and a period of restrictive macroeconomic policy? Or are there reasons to believe that these central banks will promote more expansionary policy?

These are important, if highly complex questions. Yet the major theories of the political economy of central banking are not much help in answering them. As I have suggested, Minsky's view that central banks will always be accommodating because of their lender-of-last-resort responsibilities—while pointing to the need for a theory of central banking—is itself undeveloped. Even less helpful are the two major mainstream views: the social welfare approach, which argues that central banks, like the state in general, make policy in the interests of society as a whole; and the bureaucratic approach, which argues that central banks make policy in their own narrow bureaucratic interests (for recent surveys, see Willet, 1988 and Mayer, 1990).

Radical critiques of these mainstream approaches are well founded: in a capitalist economy, capital—not society, or the state itself—is the dominant influence on state policy. Yet radical theories of the state disagree profoundly among themselves about the forms and limits of capitalist dominance (for recent surveys see Przeworski 1988 and Carnoy 1984.) Some radicals have argued that the central bank acts like the executive committee of the capitalist class, and makes policy in the interests of that class as a whole (Magdoff and Sweezy 1987). Others have argued that the central bank is rentier, making policy in the interests of the finance *fraction* of capital (Greider 1987). Still others have argued that the central bank, like the rest of the state, is structurally dependent on capital, because financial panic or capital strike can veto policies that capital opposes. The capitalist class does not need to control the state directly because its indirect control will suffice (Block 1977). Few radical political economists have suggested that noncapitalist groups have strongly influenced central bank policy, though some have spoken of a corporatist state where all major groups make policy jointly.

A major problem with these views is that they deny the multiplicity of state and economic structures that appear to characterize modern capitalism. Elements of each of these theories might apply at different times and places, but none of them is likely to be appropriate in all modern capitalist countries at all times.[1] My colleague Juliet Schor and I have thus tried to develop a theory of central banking that both incorporates the characteristic features of capitalism and allows for the multiplicity of capitalist practices in today's world.

In this spirit, we developed a "contested terrain" model of central banking.[2] This approach is based on two principles (Epstein and Schor 1988, 1990(b)).[3] First it views the state, and therefore the central bank, as a terrain of both class and intraclass struggle. And second, policy is constrained by structural factors, including the structure of capital and labor markets, the position of the domestic economy in the world economy, and the dynamics and contradictions of capital accumulation itself.

Unlike the view arguing that central bank policy is always made in the interests of capital as a whole, or the populist view, that it is always made in the interests of the banks, the contested terrain approach argues that central bank policy will depend on the relative power of finance, industry and labor. And, along with the structural dependence school, the contested terrain model recognizes the power of capital strike and financial panic, though it suggests that these factors will dominate policy only under particular conditions.

In this paper, I develop a macroeconomic model that derives analytically some of the central conclusions of the contested terrain theory of central banking. The model shows how four key factors—the structure of labor markets, the connections between finance and industry, the position of the economy in the world economy, and the relation of the central bank in the state apparatus—determine monetary policy.

One implication of the model is that different views of central banking will be appropriate in different institutional contexts. For example, where central banks are independent and connections between finance and industry are weak, as they are in the United States, the central bank will tend to be a rentier bank. It will thus pursue relatively restrictive policy, as the populist analysis suggests. Where connections between finance and industry are close,

---

1. For more specific criticisms of each of these theories on their own terms, see Przeworski 1988 and Epstein and Schor 1986.

2. See Edwards 1979 and Bowles and Gintis 1982 for the notion of a contested terrain view of politics.

3. See Hall 1984 for an early related view to which I am greatly indebted. Also see Kurzer 1987 and 1988 for very interesting related work.

and the central bank is independent, as in Germany, the central bank will attempt to make policy in the interests of the capitalist class as a whole and can be either restrictive or accommodating depending on, among other things, the power of labor. Where connections between industry and finance are strong, labor is cooperative, and the central bank is integrated into the state, central bank policy will be corporatist and more expansionary. Sweden fits this category. Where the economy is small and highly integrated into the international financial markets, central banks' will be structurally dependent, having to follow the policies of the internationally dominant central banks. Most of the central banks in the European Monetary System, for example, fit this category, after they dismantled their capital controls in 1992.

The paper concludes that future trends are not likely to encourage expansionary monetary policy. As speculative financial markets become more important and central banks become more independent, tight monetary policy is more likely and its effects on accumulation, employment, and growth become more severe. Moreover, as the international financial markets become more highly integrated, the transmission of this contractionary policy from one country to another will be more complete. Hence the increased power of the Bundesbank, the Federal Reserve and the Bank of Japan, in combination with international financial deregulation and international financial integration, is likely to impart a deflationary bias to the macrosystem.

Taking into account some of the central insights of Minsky's work, this paper concludes that in the United States a simple call for an integrated central bank that will make expansionary monetary policy to achieve full employment might not suffice when the economy is characterized by speculative financial markets. In a world of endogenous expectations and endogenous money, which characterize a world of speculative financial markets, a return to a Keynesian policy of expansion might be subject to euphoric expectations and would either set off a financial boom that central bank policy would have trouble controlling, or would be thwarted by financial speculation, domestically or internationally.

As a result, to sustain a policy of expansionary monetary policy which could avoid the current tendencies toward a deflationary bias, it might be necessary to restructure the financial markets themselves, to reduce the significance of speculation and create nonspeculative financial institutions. Hence, to enhance the likelihood that progressive monetary reform will work, reform of the central bank and reform of the private financial system should go hand in hand.

In the next section I present the basic macroeconomic model that shows the effect of economic expansion on profit shares and profit rates. In section 3, I indicate how the model of section 2 can be used to analyze the political economy of central bank policy. In section 4, I discuss the implications of

Minsky's work for the analysis of the previous sections. In section 5 I present econometric evidence that supports the model developed in sections 2 and 3. In section 6, I extend the model to the international sphere and discuss the effects of tripartite management on the economy. Section 7 presents conclusions.

2. The Model

To present the arguments just described, I develop a simple macroeconomic model[4] (Bowles and Boyer 1989, 1990; Marglin and Bhaduri 1990). The model possess two important Keynesian features. First, effective demand is an important determinant of output. Second, the distribution of income has a powerful effect on effective demand. The model also incorporates some important neo-Marxian features. Reductions in the "reserve army of labor" or increases in the cost of job loss can squeeze the profit rate (Schor and Bowles, 1987; Bowles and Boyer, 1989, 1990; Weisskopf 1988; Boddy and Crotty 1975; Glyn and Sutcliffe 1972). The distinctive feature of the model is that it analyzes the distributional relations and macroeconomic conflicts among three groups—industry, finance and labor.[5]

National income is distributed among the three groups: finance, industry, and workers.[6]

$$Y = R^I + R^F + w \tag{1}$$

and:

$$1 = \pi^I + \pi^F + W^L \tag{1'}$$

where

Y = national income

R^I = industrial profits

R^F = financial profits

---

4. This model draws heavily on the models of Marglin and Bhaduri (1990) and Bowles and Boyer (1989 and 1990). It differs from both in a number of ways. It incorporates a third class—finance—into the analysis that before incorporated only two—capital and labor. Second, my model analyzes the effects of interest rates on income distribution and the macroeconomy.

5. Tracy Mott (1989) has recently developed a three-"class" macroeconomic model. His differs from the one presented here in that it assumes that the markup is constant. The analysis of this paper focuses on both constant and variable markup behavior.

6. At this stage we abstract from the fiscal and international sectors.

w = wages

π^I = profit share of industry

π^F = profit share of finance

W^L = income share of labor.

The rate of profit in industry and finance depends on the profit share in each sector, the rate of capacity utilization, and the capital output ratio at full capacity.[7]

$$r^I = \pi^I \bar{a}_I^{-1} z = \frac{\text{industrial profits}}{\text{income}} \times \frac{\text{capacity output}}{\text{capital stock in industry}} \times \frac{\text{income}}{\text{capacity output}} \tag{2}$$

where:

r^I = rate of profit in industry

$\bar{a}_I^{-1}$ = capacity national output/capital ratio in industry

z = capacity utilization rate in the economy

$$r^F = \pi^F \bar{a}_F^{-1} z = \frac{\text{finance profits}}{\text{income}} \times \frac{\text{capacity output}}{\text{capital stock in finance}} \times \frac{\text{income}}{\text{capacity output}} \tag{3}$$

where:

r^F = rate of profit in finance

$\bar{a}_F^{-1}$ = capacity national output/capital in finance ratio

z = capacity utilization rate in the economy.

We assume that financial and industrial capitalists do all the saving and workers only consume. Furthermore, we assume that both groups of capitalists have the same marginal propensity to save.

---

7. The model implicitly assumes that the ratio of total capacity output to capital in each sector remains constant. This restriction can apply only because of the short-run nature of the model. In a long-run or dynamic model, this assumption would of course have to be relaxed.

Let

S = total savings

K^I = capital stock in industry.

Then the rate of saving as a percentage of the capital stock in industry is

$$S/K^I = (S^I/R^I)(R^I/K^I) + (S^F/R^F)(R^F/K^I). \tag{4}$$

If the savings rates are equal in the two groups, then the rate of savings relative to the capital stock in industry (g^s) is given by

$$g^s = s(\pi^I + \pi^F)\bar{a}_I^{-1} z \tag{5}$$

I assume that all investment takes place in the industrial sector. The idea here is that investment in the industrial sector is real investment (in the national income accounting sense) whereas in the financial sector, accumulation of capital takes the form of financial accumulation that is then lent to the industrial sector.[8]

The investment function in industry depends positively on the expected rate of profit in industry (r^{Ie}) and negatively on the real rate of interest (σ). The expected rate of profit in turn depends positively on the profit share in industry and the rate of capacity utilization.[9]

$$g^d = I/K^I = i(r^{Ie}(\pi^I, z), \sigma) \tag{6}$$

---

8. In a more general model, the savings could also be lent to the state or abroad. The assumption that finance does not engage in real investment is, obviously, a major simplification. For one thing, I must assume that the initial capital for finance must have fallen like manna from heaven. It would be easy, but messy, to introduce real financial investment into the model. The assumption, moreover, is not innocuous if investment is a positive function of financial profits as well as industrial profits. In that case, increased interest rates might raise financial investment as they lower industrial investment and, therefore, they will not reduce capacity utilization in the economy overall (though they might reduce it in the industrial sector). In this kind of model, conflicts between industry and finance might remain, though workers might not be as opposed to high interest rates since they could find employment in the (expanded) financial sector. A dynamic model incorporating these effects would explain the relative growth of the financial sector by the unusually high real interest rates of the last decade or so.

9. This follows the argument in Marglin and Bhaduri 1990. Other formulations are possible (see their discussion). Note that in this model interest rates can affect investment through direct effects on the cost-of-capital or indirectly through their effects on industry's profit share. Even if the cost-of-capital effect is minor, the other effect can still be important. If neither is important, higher interest rates can still reduce aggregate demand by shifting the distribution of income away from workers, who consume, and toward rentiers, who do not (see the mathematical appendix).

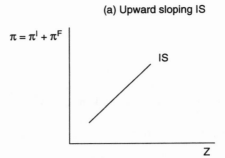

(a) Upward sloping IS

$\pi = \pi^I + \pi^F$

IS

Z

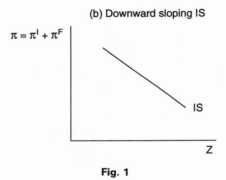

(b) Downward sloping IS

$\pi = \pi^I + \pi^F$

IS

Z

Fig. 1

In equilibrium, desired saving and investment equations (5) and (6) must be equal.

$$i(r^e(\pi^I, z), \sigma) = s(\pi^F + \pi^I)z\bar{a}_I^{-1} = s\pi z\bar{a}_I^{-1} \tag{7}$$
where $\pi = \pi^F + \pi^I$

Equation (7) is an IS curve. It represents combinations of profit shares and capacity utilization rates for which investment and saving are equal. In principal, the IS curve can be upward or downward sloping (see figures 1a and 1b). (See the mathematical appendix for the derivation of results.) In the downward-sloping case, reductions in the profit share (increases in the wage share) increase capacity utilization. Increased consumption demand resulting from increased wages is greater than the decline in investment induced by the reduced profit share. In the upward-sloping case, a reduction in the profit share reduces capacity utilization because the decline in investment resulting from a decrease in profits outweighs the increase in consumption spending.

Capital labor Finance industry	Effects of capacity utilization and interest rates on profit shares	
	Kaleckian	Neo-Marxian
Enterprise finance	$\pi_z^I \geq 0$ $\pi_\sigma^I = 0$ $\pi_z^F \geq 0$	$\pi_z^I < 0$ $\pi_\sigma^I = 0$ $\pi_z^F < 0$
Speculative finance	$\pi_z^I \geq 0$ $\pi_\sigma^I < 0$ $\pi_z^F \gtrless 0$	$\pi_z^I < 0$ $\pi_\sigma^I < 0$ $\pi_z^F \gtrless 0$

Fig. 2

As we shall see, the analysis of this paper is less affected by the slope of the IS curve than by the slope of the producers' equilibrium condition to which I now turn.

2.1 Producers' Equilibrium (PE)

The producers' equilibrium condition (PE) represents capitalists' pricing and production decisions. In particular, it represents markup behavior in product and credit markets. The profit share going to industrial and financial capital thus depends on markup behavior as a function of the level of capacity utilization and the real interest rate.

$$\pi^I = \pi^I(z, \sigma). \tag{8}$$

$$\pi^F = \pi^F(z, \sigma). \tag{9}$$

The nature of the relationships in equations (8) and (9) is crucial for the political economy of macroeconomic policy. The effect of capacity utilization and interest rates on the profit shares, or, in other words, the partial derivatives of the functions in equations (8) and (9), depend on the structure of labor, product and financial markets, and more broadly on finance-industry and capital-labor relations. Figure 2 describes the important possibilities.

If increased capacity utilization reduces competition, then firms might be able to increase their markups as capacity utilization rises. In this case, the profit share will rise as capacity utilization increases. Here, $\pi^i_z > 0$. I refer to this as the Kaleckian case because Kalecki often assumed that the profits stayed constant or even increased as capacity utilization increased.[10]

On the other hand, the profit share will fall if workers are able to shift the distribution of income in their favor as the "reserve army of labor" falls (Boddy and Crotty 1975; Bowles and Boyer, 1989,1990; Schor and Bowles 1987; Schor 1985; Weisskopf 1988; Bowles, Gordon and Weisskopf 1989). In this case, $\pi^i_z < 0$. I call this the neo-Marxian case because of the importance of the so-called full employment profit squeeze in the Marxian tradition.

Whether profit shares fall (the Neo-Marxian case) or not (the Kaleckian case) has important implications for the effects of economic expansion on the profit rates of industry, and therefore on the political economy of monetary policy.

The effects of interest rates on firms' profit shares depend on the structure of financial markets and the connections between finance and industry. In the *General Theory* Keynes referred to arms-length credit relations that are conducive to real investment as those which promote "enterprise"; by contrast, he referred to credit relations through speculative security markets as "speculation" (Crotty 1985).[11] Following his usage, I will refer to these two cases as enterprise finance and speculative finance. As a crude way to capture these relations in this model, I will assume that with enterprise finance changes in interest rates do not redistribute income between finance and industry since their interests are so closely tied together; however, if their relationship is distant, as in speculative finance then such changes *will* redistribute income between them. Hence, under enterprise finance $\pi'_\sigma = 0$ and under speculative finance $\pi'_\sigma < 0$.

These concepts contain much richer meanings, obviously, than those represented by these partial derivatives. The general idea I am trying to convey, however, is that where finance and industry have close relations, their fortunes are tied together positively, rather than competitively.[12]

---

10. Kalecki assumed that the markup might be slightly countercyclical, but that the share would be procyclical because of the existence of overhead labor. I thank an anonymous referee for this observation.

11. See also Zysman (1983), who refers to the distinction between credi- market-based financial systems and capital-market-based financial systems.

12. The effects of industry finance relations on profit shares and cost-of-capital are active areas of research. McCauley and Zimmer (1989) present a survey of this burgeoning literature. They indicate that in Germany and Japan, countries that are commonly believed to be characterized by what I have called enterprise finance, banks and industrial firms engage in risksharing that tends to produce a positive correlation in their profitability. Among the evidence they cite is the much lower level of bankruptcy of German and Japanese firms at high levels of real interest rates. This evidence provides some basis for modeling enterprise finance as a situation where changes in real interest rates do not redistribute income between finance and industry. See McCauley and Zimmer 1989 and the references therein.

With enterprise finance, where connections between finance and industry are very close, one would expect finance to share in industry's profits. In this case changes in capacity utilization would have the same effect on both profit shares. Where speculative finance prevails, there would be no such presumption. Indeed, in a particularly predatory financial environment, where finance prospers from hostile takeovers and the like, one might expect the relations between capacity utilization and profit shares to move in opposite directions. In general, there is no presumption of the effects in the case of speculative finance ($\pi^F_z \gtreqless 0$).

Evidence suggests that finance generally gains from higher interest rates (Federal Reserve Bank of New York 1986). An increase in real interest rates will increase finance's profit share ($\pi^F_\sigma > 0$).[13]

Table 1 presents the important possibilities. Capital-labor relations can be characterized as either Kaleckian, or neo-Marxian. Finance-industry relations can be characterized as either enterprise finance or speculative finance. In the enterprise finance case, relations between industry and finance are generally cooperative; whereas in the speculative finance case, they are more likely to be conflictual.

The workings of the model can be illustrated graphically.

One can add equations (8) and (9) to give the producers' equilibrium from finance and industry.

$$\pi = \pi^I + \pi^F = \pi(z, \sigma). \tag{10}$$

To simplify the presentation, assume the benchmark case where changes in capacity utilization have no effect on the financial profit share ($\pi^F_z = 0$). In that case, the slope of the PE line (equation (10)) depends only on the effect of capacity utilization on the industrial profit share.

Figures 3a and 3b present two cases. In the first, industrial capital's share increases as capacity utilization increases. In the second case, its share declines.

Figures 4a and 4b show the determination of the profit share and capacity utilization with the downward-sloping IS curve.[14] Assume that expansionary

---

13. This is certainly true for rentiers. Whether it is true for financial institutions depends on the institutional structure, as well as on the time frame of the analysis. In the case of the United States, for example, most studies show that increases in real interest raise the profits of banks in the long run (Federal Reserve Bank of New York 1986). This analysis abstracts from the issue of credit rationing. Where credit rationing is important, the relation between monetary policy and real interest rates will be muted. Moreover, the financial effects of monetary policy on investment will need to contain a term for the degree of rationing as well as for the real rate of interest. Nonetheless, changes in the real interest rate will continue to have the distributional effects assumed here.

14. These results are not materially affected by the slope of the IS curve, as long as the stability condition noted in the mathematical appendix is satisfied.

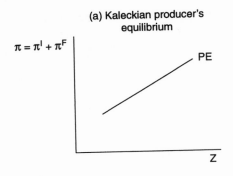

(a) Kaleckian producer's equilibrium

$\pi = \pi^I + \pi^F$

PE

Z

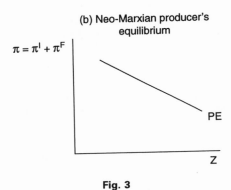

(b) Neo-Marxian producer's equilibrium

$\pi = \pi^I + \pi^F$

PE

Z

Fig. 3

fiscal policy shifts the IS curve outward. When the PE curve is upward sloping, expansionary policy will increase the industrial profit share. By assumption, the financial profit share remains constant. Where the PE curve is downward sloping figure (4b), however, such expansionary fiscal policy will reduce the industrial profit share. Thus the slope of the PE curve is crucial to the distributional effects of macroeconomic policy.

Until now I have focused on the relationship between profit shares and capacity utilization. However, *profit rates* are likely to be of greater importance in the determination of the political economy of monetary policy. As we saw in equations (2) and (3), however, profit rates are related to profit shares in a straightforward manner.

The profit rates in industry and finance are given by the following equations:

$$r^I = \pi^I(z,\sigma)\bar{a}_I^{-1}z \text{ industrial profit rate} \tag{11}$$

$$r^F = \pi^F(z,\sigma)\bar{a}_F^{-1}z \text{ financial profit rate} \tag{12}$$

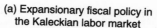

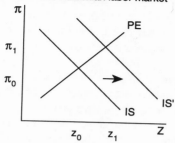

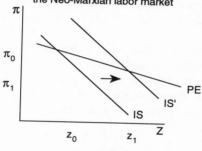

Fig. 4

Equations (11) and (12) represent sets of rectangular hyperbolas in $\pi-z$ space. They make clear that even if an industry's profit share declines, its profit rate can increase if capacity utilization rises. Only if the profit share declines at a more rapid rate than capacity utilization increases will increases in capacity utilization reduce the rate of profit.[15]

2.2 Monetary Policy

To complete the model, it is necessary to describe the determinants of the real interest rate, σ. One can think of six possible closures for the model: the classical, neoclassical, neo-Keynesian, Sraffian, Kaleckian/Minskian, and

15. In this analysis I have not made the distinction between static and dynamic gains and losses. Implicitly, the gains and losses to financial and industrial capitalists should be those they consider to hold for the medium run, the run within which they feel they can predict the results and after which they believe they can influence policy to make a change. I thank an anonymous referee for raising this point.

open economy.[16] Under the classical closure, the real interest rate is determined by the rate of profit.[17] With the neoclassical closure, it is determined by the marginal productivity of capital and the rate of time preference.[18] With the neo-Keynesian closure, the real rate is determined by the interaction of the monetary authority, the financial markets and the product markets. With the Kaleckian/Minskian closure, it is determined in the financial markets through animal spirits and assessment of risk by lenders and borrowers. With the Sraffian closure, the real interest rate is determined by the central bank. And with the open economy closure, it is determined by external real interest rates, expected rates of change of real exchange rates, and risk premia.[19]

A full discussion of the determinants of real interest rates is beyond the scope of this paper. As Marx stressed, these determinants are likely to depend heavily on the institutional context.[20] Evidence indicates that the major central banks can influence real rates of interest, at least in the short to medium run.[21] I adopt that assumption initially here.[22] In section 5 I will discuss the implications of adopting the Kaleckian/Minskian approach to real interest rate determination.

If monetary policy can alter the real rate of interest, then expansionary monetary policy will shift out the IS curve thereby increasing capacity utilization.[23] At the same time, changes in interest rates can alter the distribution of income between finance and industry. Figure 5 illustrates how monetary policy works in the model for the case of Kaleckian labor markets and specula-

---

16. For a discussion of these, see Panico 1987 and Dymski 1990.

17. Marx did not subscribe to this view, however. He argued that there was a great deal of independence between the rate of interest and the rate of profit. (see Panico 1987).

18. Nevertheless, as in Wicksell's, Keynes's and Fisher's models, monetary policy might have a temporary effect on the real rate of interest until the market interest rate has time to adjust to the natural rate.

19. Monetary policy may or may not play a role in this case. See the discussion in section 6.

20. Marx himself focused on the relative power of lenders and borrowers.

21. For a theoretical model in which monetary policy matters, see Dymski 1992. For evidence, see Radecki and Reinhart 1988 and the review in Epstein 1993.

22. I do not deny the influence of other important factors on real interest rates, particularly those factors emphasized in the Kaleckian/Minskian approach. There will be important contexts in which those may dominate the effects of central bank policy. Indeed, in a more complete model, I would endogenize the real interest rate and allow for the possibility that the central bank can affect it. In terms of figures 6a and 6b, a financial equilibrium line would be included in the space, with the possibility that the central bank could affect it. A full development of this model must await future research, however.

23. In this model, I will not distinguish between two ways in which real interest rates can change. First, nominal interest rates might change, holding inflation constant. Second, inflation might change, holding nominal interest rates constant. One would expect that at lower levels of capacity utilization, most of the real interest rate decline (for example) would be accounted for by decreases in nominal interest rates, and at higher levels, most would be accounted for by increases in inflation.

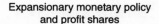

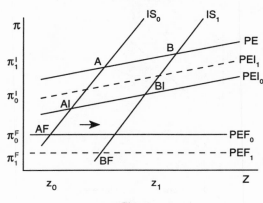

Fig. 5

tive finance. Here PEI refers to the producers' equilibrium line for industry and PEF refers to the producers' equilibrium condition for finance. In the case represented in figure 5, increases in capacity utilization are assumed to have no effect on financial profit shares ($\pi_z^F = 0$) and to increase the profit share of industry ($\pi_z^I > 0$). Changes in interest rates are assumed to shift the distribution of income between finance and industry ($\pi_\sigma^I = -\pi_\sigma^F$).

As figure 5 shows, a reduction of interest rates will shift out the IS curve. The reduction in interest rates will increase the profit share going to industry at every level of capacity utilization (PEI$_0$ to PEI$_1$) and will reduce the profit share going to finance (PEF$_0$ to PEF$_1$). Industry's profit share will increase from AI to BI, while finance's profit share will fall from AF to BF, as the economy's capacity utilization rate increases from Z$_0$ to Z$_1$.

The discussion of monetary policy represented in figure 4 can be simplified by deriving the producers' equilibrium conditions for finance and industry so that they include the effects of changing interest rates. In figure 5, the reduction of interest rates cause industry's producers' equilibrium curve (PEI) to shift up, reflecting an increase in industry's profit share at every level of capacity utilization. Its profit share thus increases from AI to BI as interest rates fall. Thus, under the conditions of figure 5, industry's producers' equilibrium line, which *includes* the effects of changing interest rates, holding all else constant, will have a steeper slope than the line that does not include those effects. In figure 6a, this line that includes the effects of changing interest rates is marked as the PEIσ line. Similarly, finance's producers' equilibrium line, which includes the effects of changing interest rates (PEFσ), will be more negative in slope, under these conditions (figure 6b).

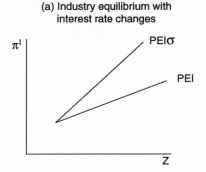

(a) Industry equilibrium with
interest rate changes

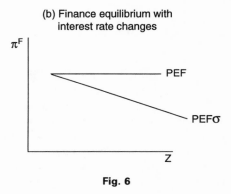

(b) Finance equilibrium with
interest rate changes

Fig. 6

Using this construction, we can see graphically the effects of monetary policy (holding all else constant) on profit rates in industry and finance. Figure 7a illustrates the case of Kaleckian ($\pi^I_z \geq 0$) labor markets and speculative finance ($\pi^I_\sigma < 0$). It is clear that under these conditions, industrial profit rates are maximized at full capacity utilization (z^{FE}). However, with neo-Marxian labor markets($\pi^I_z < 0$) and enterprise finance ($\pi^I_\sigma = 0$), in general industrial profit rates will be maximized at less than full capacity utilization (Figure 7b).

Figures 8a and 8b illustrate that under speculative finance, financial profit rates will be maximized at less than full capacity utilization whereas with Kaleckian labor markets and enterprise finance, finance's profit rates will be maximized at full capacity utilization.

These results can be derived analytically. Maximize (11) and (12) with respect to z, assuming that changes in monetary policy through their changes in the real interest rate (σ) are altering capacity utilization (z). (See the

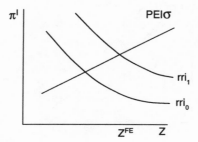

(a) Monetary policy and industrial
profit rates
Kaleckian labor markets and speculative finance

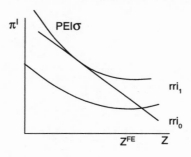

(b) Monetary policy and industrial
profit rates
Neo-marxian labor markets and enterprise finance

Fig. 7

mathematical appendix for more details.) Thus, by assumption, σ is a negative function of z, as reflected by the effects of lowering the real interest rate (σ) on the IS curve ($\sigma_z = d\sigma/dz < 0$). In (16) and (17) zI^* and zF^* are the optimal capacity utilization rates. Equations (14) and (15) can be solved for these optimal rates.[24] The first-order conditions are

$$\delta r^I/\delta z = \bar{a}_I^{-1} \left[\pi^I + z(\pi_z^I + \pi_\sigma^I \, \sigma_z)) \right] = 0 \tag{14}$$

$$\delta r^F/\delta z = \bar{a}_F^{-1} \left[\pi^F + z((\pi_z^F + \pi_\sigma^F \, \sigma_z)) \right] = 0, \tag{15}$$

24. For a similar construction, see Bowles, Gordon, and Weisskopf 1989.

**(a) Monetary policy and
financial profit rates**
speculative finance

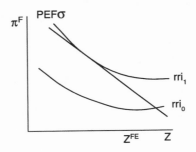

**(b) Monetary policy and financial
profit rates**
Kaleckian labor markets and enterprise finance

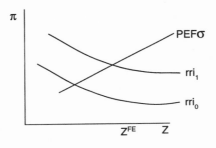

Fig. 8

or alternatively,

$$-\pi^I/z^{I*} = (\pi^I_z + \pi^I_\sigma\, \sigma_z) \tag{16}$$

$$-\pi^F/z^{F*} = (\pi^F_z + \pi^F_\sigma\, \sigma_z)]. \tag{17}$$

The left-hand sides of equations (16) and (17) are the slopes of the isoprofit lines. The right-hand sides are the slopes of the producer equilibrium lines, which include the effects of changing interest rates. Equations (16) and (17) are illustrated in figure 9.

If industrial capital's profit share declines with increases in capacity utilization as real interest rates fall, then equations (16) and (17) will hold

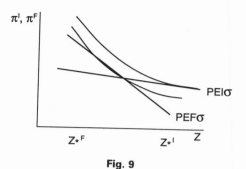

Optimal capacity utilization
for finance and industry

Fig. 9

with an interior solution. Industrial capital, like financial capital, will then oppose full employment. Finance and industry's profit rates will, in general, be maximized at different rates of capacity utilization (Figure 9).

Although their interest will generally differ, with enterprise finance, finance and industry's optimal capacity utilization rates will be closer together than under speculative finance. The reason is that changes in interest rates will no longer redistribute income between industry and finance and hence will not divide the two groups. As a result, changes in capacity utilization induced by changes in interest rates will have more similar effects on profit shares in industry and finance. In terms of the diagram, the slopes of the PE lines will become more similar, and hence their profit rates will be maximized at similar rates of capacity utilization (see the Mathematical Appendix). In short, they will be more likely to support similar macroeconomic policies (figure 10).

I have not yet spoken about the interest of workers. I take the simplest possible assumption, one that is analogous to the assumptions I have made about industrial and financial interests. I assume that workers want to maximize their wage bill W.[25]

$$W = (1 - \pi^I - \pi^F)za^1 \text{ wage bill} \tag{19}$$

normalizing K, the total capital stock, at 1.

The effects of capacity utilization associated with changes in real interest rates are given by

$$\delta W/\delta z = ((1 - \pi^I - \pi^F) - z(\pi_z^I + \pi_\sigma^I \sigma_z + \pi_z^F + \pi_\sigma^F$$

$$\sigma_z))\bar{a}^{-1}. \tag{20}$$

---

25. Marglin and Bhaduri (1990) make a similar assumption.

Forming a capitalist coalition

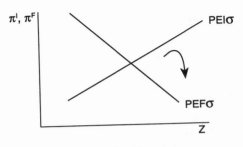

Fig. 10

If changes in interest rates redistribute income from industrial to financial capital, then $\pi_\sigma^I = -\pi_\sigma^F$ and (19) reduces to

$$\delta W/\delta z = ((1 - \pi^I - \pi^F) - z(\pi_z^I + \pi_z^F))\bar{a}^{-1}. \tag{21}$$

Workers have an interest in expansion as long as neither industrial capital nor financial capital can greatly increase their shares as expansion proceeds. If π_z^I and π_z^F are negative, then workers have a definite interest in expansion. In general, as long as the PEI or PFI curves are not highly upward sloping, workers optimal rate of capacity utilization will be greater than financial capital's and at least as great as industrial capital's.[26] (See the mathematical appendix for more details.)

$$z^{w*} \geq z^{I*} \geq z^{F*}. \tag{22}$$

Equation (22) holds except where the PE curve for industry is very steeply downward sloping. In that case, industrial capitalists prefer less expansionary policy than will finance. These results are summarized in figure 11.

This four-way categorization yields what I will refer to as the corporatist, Keynesian, and capitalist coalitions. I call the fourth possibility fractured capitalism for reasons that will soon be apparent.

In the corporatist case with a Kaleckian labor market and enterprise finance, all groups gain from economic expansion and full employment. In the Keynesian case, however, which is characterized by a Kaleckian labor market and speculative finance relations, labor and industry share a common

---

26. $\delta W/\delta z > 0$ if $\bar{a} > -\Sigma \pi wz$ where $\Sigma \pi wz = (z/\pi^w)\pi_z^w$, the elasticity of the wage share ($\pi^w = 1 - \pi^I - \pi^F$) with respect to capacity utilization. If workers' wage share goes up with capacity utilization, they have an interest in expansion.

Capital labor / Finance industry	Optimal monetary policy and class coalitions	
	Kaleckian	Neo-Marxian
Enterprise finance	CORPORATIST All support loose money.	CAPITALIST Industry and finance support tight money.
Speculative finance	KEYNESIAN Industry and labor support loose money. Finance supports tight money.	FRACTURED Labor supports loose money. Industry supports unemployment, *but* loose money. Finance supports tight money.

Fig. 11

interest in expansion against finance, which gains when interest rates rise, and which is hurt by economic expansion.[27]

With a neo-Marxian labor market and enterprise finance, finance and industry are united against full employment, since both are hurt by expansionary policy. I call this the capitalist case. Finally, with a neo-Marxian labor market and speculative finance relations, industrial capital opposes full employment policies because they squeeze profits, but neither does it support high interest rate policies which also harm industrial capital. Finance, on the other hand, supports high interest rates. I refer to this as fractured capitalism.[28]

Although classes and class fractions have desired policies, their policies will not be implemented unless they have political power vis-á-vis the state. Thus policy will be determined by a combination of the political structure of the economy and the political structure of the state.

---

27. I refer to this as the Keynesian case because Keynes himself more or less self-consciously tried to build such a coalition in his writings. He railed against finance more than once, his most famous, perhaps, being his call for the "euthanasia of the rentier," followed by his bitter attack against finance for its support of the British return to the gold standard in 1925. One could call this the populist case.

28. This description differs from the categorization in Marglin and Bhaduri (1990). They refer to conflictual versus cooperative capitalism and wage-led versus profit-led regimes. Their categorization concerns the shape of the IS curve whereas mine is most concerned with the shape of the PE curve. In that sense, my categorization has more in common with that of Bowles and Boyer 1989a, 1990). Mine differs from theirs, however, in the emphasis here on finance-industry relations.

3. The Political Economy of Monetary Policy

Macroeconomic policy making is subject to numerous influences, including the desires of the state institutions. As a rule, central banks are not passive servants, waiting for the dust to settle to get their marching orders from victorious classes. For example, there is ample evidence that the Federal Reserve attempts to mobilize constituencies to support its desired policy initiatives, which may reflect, among other things, its own conception of what is best for the economy.[29] Economic actors may not always mobilize to promote their own narrow economic interests. In addition, the capitalist economy is fraught with uncertainty and complex political and economic constraints. Hence, any attempt to model the policy making process inevitably requires heroic simplification. This is especially true when one attempts to formally model policy making, as I do in this paper. The archival and other research into the political economy of central bank policy I and my colleagues have completed, however, suggests that the simple model described below captures some crucial elements of central bank behavior (see, for example, Epstein and Ferguson 1984, 1991; Epstein and Schor 1989, forthcoming).

In this paper, I make the simplifying assumption that one can model central banks as if they maximize a weighted average of industrial and financial profit rates and labor's wage bill. The weights they place on these different groups depends on the relative political powers of these groups with respect to the central bank.

$$Max \ CB = \alpha(r^I) + \beta(r^F) + (1 - \alpha - \beta)W \qquad (23)$$

where:

r^I = industrial profit rate

r^F = financial profit rate

Maximizing (23) amounts to choosing a weighted combination of optimal capacity utilizations and therefore real interest rates.

$$z^*(\sigma^*) = \epsilon z_I^* + \tau z_F^* + (1 - \epsilon - \tau)z_W^*$$

Optimal Central Bank Policy   (24)

where the z^* are the optimal capacity utilization ratios for industry, finance and labor.

---

29. For evidence see Epstein and Schor's (forthcoming) discussion of the 1951 Treasury-Federal Reserve Accord.

The key issue is, what determines those weights? I have analyzed so far the structure of finance and industry relations, and labor capital relations. A third important determinant of central bank policy is the relation between the central bank and the state. Here I can distinguish between central banks that are independent of the state and those which are integrated into the state apparatus. Since our case studies give information about the likely implications of central bank independence, I will only briefly summarize them here.[30]

Independent central banks are little influenced by labor; however, their policies can be affected by industry and finance depending on the connections between the two capitalist fractions. Under enterprise finance, the independent central bank therefore is likely to take into account both the interests of industry and finance. With speculative finance, however, where industry and finance are divided, independent central banks tend to be dominated by the interests of finance.[31]

If the central bank is independent and the political connections between industry and finance are weak, then $\epsilon \approx 0$ and $\tau \approx 1$. If, on the other hand the central bank is independent and the connections are strong, then $0 \le \epsilon \le 1$, $0 \le \tau \le 1$, and $\epsilon + \tau \approx 1$. If central bank is integrated into the government, then $0 \le \epsilon \le 1$, $0 \le \tau \le 1$, and $\epsilon + \tau < 1$.

The contested terrain model of central banking argues that the structure of the state can make an important difference in the process of articulation between economic interest and state policy. Figure 12 presents the possibilities.[32] Here, each of the four possible cases have been divided in two, where the top triangle represents the case of the independent central bank and the bottom half represents the integrated central bank. For example, in the bottom left square, an independent central bank can turn a Keynesian policy into a finance-dominated one, yielding a macroeconomic policy that maximizes bank profits but hurts both labor and industry. Similarly, an independent central bank can transform a fractured capitalism into a monetary policy dominated by finance and again maintaining a macroeconomic policy of less than full employment. At the same time, an integrated central bank can yield a macroeconomic policy that does not follow capitalist interest (top right square—neo-Marxian labor market, enterprise finance.) The only place where the relation of the central bank to the state does not seem to matter is in the corporatist case.[33]

---

30. See Epstein-Schor (1990) and the references to our other papers cited there.

31. Another way to say this is that independent central banks tend to be dominated by finance, but that with enterprise finance, finance's interests are similar to industry's.

32. See Epstein and Schor 1988 for a related diagram.

33. Note that political parties and other aspects of the political structure of the state are only implicit in the model. The assumption I am making is that where central banks are not independent the political process has more effect on central bank policy. What policy the central bank takes in that situation will depend on the political powers of all the groups in parties and the state.

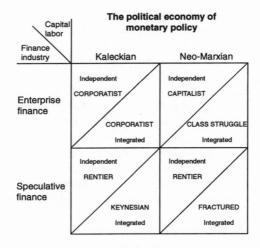

Fig. 12

The key point is that the institutional structure of the state can make a difference in the political economy of policy. Independent central banks can thwart a Keynesian coalition of labor and industry that supports expansionary policy; and it can veto expansionary policy that a labor led government might support.

By contrast, the structural dependence view is that the structure of the state, and central bank independence, is irrelevant to macroeconomic outcomes. Adherents of this position would argue that capital's control over finance and investment can veto undesired policies. Thus, for example, where enterprise finance and neo-Marxian labor markets prevail (top right box of Figure 12), industrial capital strike can veto any labor attempt to expand the economy beyond maximal industrial profit rate (z^{I*}); hence the independence or integration of the central bank makes no difference; the line dividing the square in figure 12 should be obliterated. With speculative finance and a Kaleckian labor market (bottom left row), the structural dependence school would make a similar argument. Financial panic would be sufficient to thwart any Keynesian coalition that tried to influence an integrated central bank. Once again, central bank independence makes no difference, according to the structural dependence view.

Minsky's work relates to these important issues raised by the structural dependence view. Some of Minsky's insights can be incorporated into the analysis developed in section 3 to help this analysis address important issues in contemporary comparative monetary policy.

4. Some Minskian Themes

Minsky's work emphasizes the limits placed on central banks by the dynamics of financial markets and the overall economy. In the framework of section 3 above, represented in figure 12, these constraints apply both to what I have called rentier central banks, which would like to pursue restrictive policies to raise financial profits, and Keynesian central banks, which would want to pursue more expansionary policy to achieve high levels of employment.

First, with regard to the rentier central banks, Minsky emphasizes that central banks are constrained from pursuing overly restrictive policy because such policy may lead to bankruptcies and threaten the stability of the overall system. As a result, central banks, in fulfilling their lender-of-last-resort responsibilities, would have to bail out many institutions, thereby undermining their restrictive policy.

This dilemma, which Minsky insightfuly refers to as being between a "rock and a hard place," becomes particularly difficult if firms have taken on a great deal of debt in the process of economic expansion. In that case, high interest rates or a recession is more likely to cause financial stress and to generate widespread problems of instability.

Historically, central banks have been warned about not letting a boom get out of hand, for precisely this reason. As a result, these Minskian insights about the tendency for speculative capitalist financial markets to generate runaway euphoria imply that rentier central banks must be more consistently restrictive than otherwise. They must ensure that optimistic expectations don't generate a boom that the central bank would then be unable to halt later on without dire consequences for the banks themselves. In short, Minskian insights reinforce the likely policy directions of rentier central banks.

Minsky's work, however, undermines the case for a viable Keynesian central bank structure. Where speculative markets, an integrated central bank, and Kaleckian labor markets prevail (figure 12, bottom left square), the analysis so far suggests that a Keynesian central bank would be able to pursue expansionary monetary policy to achieve high levels of employment. Minsky suggests that such an "equilibrium" is not viable in the long run. Euphoric expectations would tend to take over, driving the economy to a highly leveraged speculative boom which would move the economy beyond full employment equilibrium. In this case, even a Keynesian central bank would be placed between a rock and a hard place and would ultimately be forced to restrict credit in extreme fashion in order to break the boom, or would preside over an unstable expansion.

Moreover, Minsky's theory of interest rate determination complicates the argument that an integrated central bank can pursue a Keynesian monetary policy to maintain high employment. According to Minsky, interest rates are determined by lender's risk and borrower's risk, which in turn depend on expectations. Whether the central bank can lower interest rates will depend on how its policy affects perceptions of risk in the market. If an expansionary policy is seen to lower risk, then expectations will reinforce the low interest rate policy. If the expansionary policy is seen to increase risk to lenders or borrowers, however, then it will not succeed in lowering rates and may even raise them.

This analysis suggests that the political structure of the central bank—whether it is independent or integrated—may not make as much difference as I have suggested. Ultimately, the financial markets may call the tune to the central bankers, regardless of their formal political connections to the government.

To the extent that these Minskian concerns are important, they suggest that the chances of creating a policy structure for Keynesian monetary policy would require adjustment both in the political structure of the central bank and in the structure of the financial markets. For with enterprise finance, euphoric Minskian booms and counterproductive financial speculation may be less likely. Indeed, there is some evidence that countries with enterprise finance are less subject to Minskian problems of excessive leverage and speculation (see Jacobs 1984).

Theory, by itself, cannot settle these issues. The degree to which central bank-state and financial structures make a difference to monetary policy outcomes is, to some extent, an empirical issue. It is to that empirical evidence that we now turn.

5. Empirical Evidence

Macroeconomic policy making is, to be sure, a highly complex business. At the level of abstraction at which the model in this paper operates, one cannot hope to do justice to the vast array of factors that affect monetary policy. Still, the model provides a framework and hypotheses that can operate as a starting point for analyzing the political economy of central banking. To be useful, however, it must be applicable to concrete cases.

The model suggests that the four key structural factors—the connections between finance and industry, the relations between capital and labor, the degree of central bank independence and the position of the economy in the world economy—will strongly affect monetary policy. Since I will discuss the open economy aspects of the model in the next section, here I will focus on the other three factors.

To apply the model empirically, one must be able to identify these characteristics in particular countries. Moreover, the implicit assumption of the model is that these structural factors are sufficiently stable that they can be assumed to be important determinants of monetary policy over time.

Central bank independence, and the connections between finance and industry, are relatively stable, though they can change. For example, the Bank of Canada was relatively independent until 1967, when a political crisis brought it under the control of the government; by contrast, the Bank of Italy was integrated into the Italian government until 1980, at which time it was made significantly more independent (Epstein and Schor 1989). Yet these changes are infrequent.

The relationship between capacity utilization and profit shares seems to have changed more frequently in the postwar period. This is partly because this relationship is affected by product market competition as well as by the relationship between capital and labor. Thus, for example, changes in exchange rate regimes (Epstein, 1991) or anti-trust legislation, as well as capital-labor relations can alter these relations. Still, one can presume that these relations do not change every year, or even every five. ·

To apply the model it is necessary to develop estimates of the structural characteristics. In several related papers, we have described the institutional characteristics of a number of OECD countries (Epstein and Schor, 1986, 1988, 1990b) and have developed estimates, however imperfect, of the key structural determinants (Epstein and Schor, 1986, 1992). Table 1 presents some of these estimates.

TABLE 1.

Country	Central Bank Independence	Finance Industry Relations	Capital Labor Relations	Energy Imports (%)	GNP GAP (%)
Canada	1.000000	0.100000	0.000000	11.00000	1.100000
France	1.000000	0.720000	1.000000	33.00000	1.000000
Germany	3.000000	0.580000	1.000000	23.00000	3.000000
Italy	1.250000	0.320000	0.000000	41.00000	1.500000
Japan	1.000000	0.390000	1.000000	48.00000	2.500000
Sweden	1.000000	0.250000	0.000000	25.00000	1.700000
UK	1.500000	0.100000	0.000000	14.00000	2.200000
US	2.000000	0.080000	0.000000	36.00000	3.600000

Central Bank Independence: Epstein-Schor Index. From 0–3. 0 is completely integrated into the government; 3 is highly independent.

Source: Epstein and Schor, 1986;1988;1990b (b). Finance-Industry Relations: Bank share of non-financial corporate liabilities. Stocks, except for Canada, where flows are used; average over available data, 1970–1984. France: adjusted with national data. Capital labor relations: based on two-stage least squares regression of profit share in manufacturing against rate of capacity utilization, 1964–1980 for most countries; see data appendix. Dummy variable based on these coefficients: 0 for Kaleckian, where the coefficient was non-negative; 1 for neo-Marxian, where the coefficient was negative. Energy Imports: Energy Imports as a share of merchandise exports in 1981; Source: IBRD (1984), p. 233. See empirical appendix for more information.

The first variable is an index of central bank independence. We constructed this variable from information on statutory relations between the government and the central bank, as modified by institutional practice gleaned from the institutional literature. The index runs from 1 to 3, and the higher the number, the more independent the bank (See Epstein and Schor, 1986).[34]

The second variable represents finance-industry connections. It represents the average share of nonfinancial corporate liabilities held by banks. The higher the share, the greater the extent to which the financial system is characterized by enterprise finance. (See the data appendix for more information).

The data on central bank independence and finance industry relations are consistent with conventional wisdom about these relations. Germany and the United States have relatively independent central banks, whereas those in the other countries are less independent. Germany, France, Japan, and Italy have a large share of nonfinancial corporate liabilities held by banks, reflecting what I have been calling enterprise finance, whereas the United Kingdom, United States, and Canada do not, indicating they are characterized by speculative finance.

The information on the structure of labor-capital relations is much more difficult to come by. For one thing, capital-labor relations change over time. Second, relations between capital and labor are multi-dimensional. Labor may appear strong in some realms, (wage setting) and weak in others (control over technology decisions.) For the model of this paper, I need a relatively "narrow" measure of capital-labor relations, namely, the degree to which workers are able to capture a larger share of the national product as capacity utilization rises.

The "capital labor relations" measure presented in figure 4 is a dummy variable, 0 for Kaleckian and 1 for neo-Marxian. It is based on estimates of the producers' equilibrium relation for the manufacturing sector of these eight countries for 1970–1985.[35] (See the statistical appendix). To calculate the capital-labor measure, I regressed the profit share in manufacturing against the rate of capacity utilization and real interest rates. Since both the IS and the PE curves determine profit shares and capacity utilization, both the profit share and capacity utilization are endogenous variables. Hence, I used two-stage least squares to estimate the relation.

---

34. We modified statutory data with institutional information because the statutes might not reflect actual practice. The danger with modifying the index in that way, however, is that we might be using institutional information that reflects the dependent variable that we are trying to explain and would thereby generate the predicted results. When we used only unmodified statutory information (see Bade and Parkin, 1980), however, the coefficient on central bank independence reported in table 6 was even stronger. The significance of some of the other coefficients did change, however.

35. I am indebted to Thomas Weisskopf for giving me the data on the basis of which I calculated this measure.

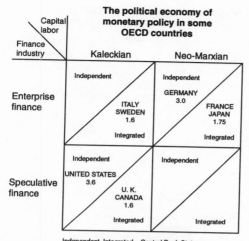

Fig. 13

If the coefficient on capacity utilization was statistically significant and negative, then the PE curve is downward sloping and the capital-labor relationship is neo-Marxian. In that case, the dummy variable is 1. If the coefficient was positive or 0, that would indicate that capital-labor relations are Kaleckian. In that case the dummy variable is 0.[36]

Using these measures, I have characterized eight major industrial countries in figure 13 for the period of the 1970s and early 1980s. Each box also presents the average GNP gaps, as calculated by the OECD, for the period 1970–1983.

According to the estimates of the structural variables, Sweden and Italy have corporatist central banks. Germany, on the other hand, has a capitalist central bank. France and Japan have class struggle central banks. Of course, since in Japan the working class is relatively unorganized, the capitalist class dominates. The United States has a rentier central bank, and the United Kingdom and Canada have Keynesian central banks. As figure 13 indicates, the GNP gaps were higher for countries with independent central banks and lower for countries with enterprise industry-finance relations (see figures 14a and 14b). The effects of labor markets on average gaps, however, are less clear from these data.

---

36. Note that I am implicitly assuming that the effect of capacity utilization on the financial profit share is zero. Lack of good, comparable data on financial profit share prevented me from estimating the PE line as a whole. In future research I will try to use one minus the wage share to estimate the line.

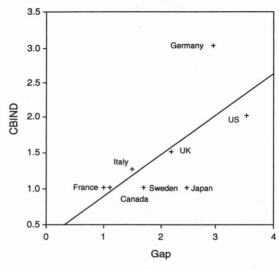

Central bank independence and GNP gaps
1970–1984

Fig. 14a

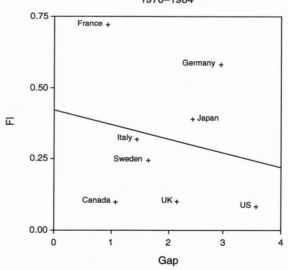

Finance-industry connections and GNP gaps
1970–1984

Fig. 14b

TABLE 2. Central Banking and GNP Gaps in Some OECD Countries
Dependent Variable: Average GNP Gap (1970–1983)

C	Central Bank Independence	Finance/Industry	Capital/Labor	Energy	$\bar{R}^2$
1.					
.42	1.0***	−3.7**	1.0*	.03**	.81
(.71)	(4.5)	(−2.9)	(1.6)	(2.40)	

T-Statistics in parentheses. ***: Significant at the 5% level; **Significant at the 10% level. *Significant at the 20% level. Data: See Table 4 and empirical appendix.

A simple cross-sectional regression analysis supports this interpretation of the data. The dependent variable is average GNP gap for the 1970–1983 period. The model predicts that countries with independent central banks, speculative finance-industry relations (that is, a *low* percentage of industry liabilities held by banks), and neo-Marxian labor relations would have higher GNP gaps, holding all else constant. We know from the experience of the 1970s that a significant factor affecting GNP gaps was also dependence on imported energy products, so I include a variable to capture that dependence. Table 2 presents the results.

The regression supports the results of the model. The higher the degree of central bank independence, the greater the GNP gap; however, the greater the degree of bank intermediation of industry—which I have referred to as enterprise finance—the lower the gap. And neo-Marxian labor markets tend to be associated with higher gaps, though less definitively. Of course, considering the small number of countries and the crudeness of the variables, these results are hardly definitive.[37]

Other variables were also tried, including the structural budget deficit, which in this regression was not significant. The most robust result, virtually invariant to specification, was the effect of degree of central bank independence. More independent central banks tend to be associated with higher GNP gaps. This result is supported by other work showing that more independent central banks are associated with lower inflation (Epstein and Schor 1986; Willet 1988), lower credit growth (Epstein and Schor 1986), and a lower propensity to put on capital controls (Epstein and Schor 1992).

I extended the sample to fourteen countries.[38] Lacking the capital-labor

---

37. One possible interpretation of the result on finance-industry relations is that these affect the gap independently of the political economy of monetary policy. Indeed, some authors argue that these relations affect the cost of capital independently of monetary policy (see, for example, McCauley and Zimmer 1989). Sorting out these effects is an important issue for future research.

38. The additional countries were Austria, Belgium, Denmark, Finland, the Netherlands, and Norway.

measure I constructed for the original eight countries, I used a measure of the degree to which workers'wages were indexed to inflation taken from Bruno and Sachs 1985.[39] The results (not shown) were less successful. Once again, more independent central banks were associated with higher gaps. Although the other variables had the expected sign, however, they were not significant at standard levels. This result may be due to the poor capital-labor variable. More likely, they reflect the inability of small countries in internationally integrated financial markets to pursue independent monetary policies. This latter view is supported by the fact that an index of capital controls was significantly associated with lower gaps in this sample (Epstein and Schor 1992).

Although they support my model, these results are nonetheless open to numerous objections. In addition to the small size of the sample and the crudeness of the measures, such cross-sectional regressions are subject to other possible criticisms. The variables might be a proxy for other variables. For example, the central bank measure might simply be a proxy for Germany, which is well known for its tight fisted macroeconomic policies. When Germany was dropped, however, central bank independence was still significant.

Another possible criticism is that there were structural changes during the time over which the variables were averaged. This possibility cannot be so easily dismissed. The regressions in which the slopes of the PE lines were estimated, for example, showed a high degree of instability over time. This problem is a general one, but perhaps it is particularly problematic for models that suggest the importance of structures in determining outcomes.

For these and other reasons, such regression results can only be suggestive, at best. They must be supported by other research, for example, by detailed case studies. For some of these, I direct the reader to some of our other work.

6. Open-Economy Macroeconomic Policy

The evidence of the previous section suggests that small countries have trouble making independent monetary policy in an open economy. Still, central banks whose financial markets are large in world terms will be able to strongly affect world financial conditions. Although they might not be able to establish interest rates independently of those of the rest of the world, they can influence domestic interest rates to the extent that they can influence world interest rates.[40]

In the 1950s and 1960s, the U.S. central bank had a great deal of power

---

39. I used their so-called labor responsiveness measure. See Bruno and Sachs 1985, p. 238.

40. This section is highly preliminary and speculative. The vast subject discussed here obviously requires separate treatment.

to influence world financial conditions. In the 1970s and 1980s, as the size and influence of financial markets denominated in nondollar currencies have expanded, the power of the U.S. Fed has surely fallen. Increasingly, the policies of the Bundesbank and Bank of Japan are important determinants of world financial conditions.

A full analysis of the international monetary policy of these major central banks is well beyond the scope of this paper—requiring, for example, an analysis of the interaction between monetary policy and exchange rate policy and therefore analyzing the strategic interactions among the three central banks. Still, the framework of the previous section can be helpful in identifying some important considerations, though the discussion must necessarily be sketchy and highly speculative.

To a first approximation, one can analyze the determination of world interest rates as being a weighted average of the optimal interest rates of the three major central banks.

$$\sigma^w = \alpha\sigma^{*US} + \beta\sigma^{*G} + \Gamma\sigma^{*J} \tag{25}$$

where

σ^w = world interest rate

α,β,Γ = weights on national rates in determining world rates.

$\sigma^{*}US,G,J$ = interest rates in United States, Germany, and Japan.

The simplest way to analyze the political economy of international monetary policy would be to identify the structural characteristics of the three main countries and infer their likely monetary policy from these, as I did in section 5 (see figure 13).

Such an approach would be misleading, however, because the existence of the open economy itself can critically affect the interests and constraints facing the relevant actors. These effects are likely to be quite complicated; but, I can speculate on some of the more important ones.

With highly mobile international investment, multinational industrial firms will increasingly face a world labor force since they can move their production locations around the globe (Bowles and Gintis 1986). Hence, their appropriate labor market is likely to be Kaleckian rather than neo-Marxian. Should labor in one country increase wages and squeeze profits, firms will shift production to another country where reserve pools of labor still exist.[41]

---

41. The incentive of firms to invest abroad will depend on the degree to which their governments can ensure that the host countries will not nationalize or, in less extreme cases,

As industry becomes more multinational in nature, it will support policies that promote world economic growth.

Finance, however, will be in a different situation. Financial deregulation and innovation is proceeding rapidly throughout the industrial world. Even in Germany and Japan, where, enterprise finance has dominated, connections between industry and finance appear to be weakening. It is likely, therefore, that even their financial systems are probably going to be joining the ranks of speculative finance. This trend toward speculative finance will be reinforced to the extent that the Japanese and German financial sectors and governments encourage the use of their currencies as international key currencies. National banks' comparative advantage in world financial markets become tied to the use of their key currencies which in turn depend on maintaining a stable value for those currencies (Epstein 1981). Hence finance becomes increasingly concerned with fighting domestic inflation and less concerned with maintaining world economic growth.

In short, multinational industry becomes increasingly global Keynesian,[42] and paradoxically, global finance becomes increasingly nationalistic and rentier. With the multinationalization of business, one is likely to witness an increasing split between industry and finance over monetary policy, unless of course the move toward financial motives begins to dominate industry itself (Wachtel 1987).[43]

The result is that the three major countries are likely to be characterized by Kaleckian labor markets, and speculative finance markets (see figure 15). In this case, the increasing dominance of independent central banks will be particularly damaging and conflictual. They will be particularly damaging because with speculative finance, tight monetary policy is more harmful to industry than under enterprise finance. It will be conflictual because industry will support more expansionary policy, but finance will support more contractionary policy. If history is any guide, independent central banks are more likely to carry out the wishes of finance than industry. World economic growth and employment will likely be the victim.

Notice that the configuration in figure 15 also contains the possibility of a

---

discriminate against foreign assets. Large and powerful countries are likely to be better positioned to prevent such treatment than smaller countries. Still, because of these problems of enforcement of property rights, international financial markets are not characterized by "perfect capital" mobility as implied by some neoclassical economists. Therefore, even as multinationalization proceeds apace, firms are unlikely ever to be able totally to ignore domestic labor. See the discussion of this point in Epstein and Gintis 1992.

42. This Keynesian orientation of multinational business is confined to loose monetary policy, not fiscal policy, since expansionary fiscal policy might require tax increases.

43. This view contrasts with the view in Epstein 1991, where it was argued that finance and industry will be increasingly united over tight monetary policy. The difference stems from the assumption in that paper that industry and finance were primarily domestically based rather than multinational.

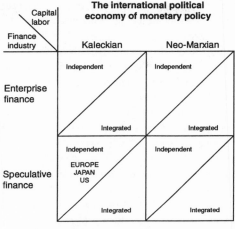

Fig. 15

new Keynesian coalition between labor and industry against finance in support of loose monetary policy. Hence this emerging configuration contains the possibility of internationally coordinated economic expansion that has become the major Keynesian solution to the current stagnation. Note that a minimum condition for such a policy to be successful is that the central banks must be integrated into the governments in order to reduce the influence of finance. Otherwise, finance can veto any attempts by the three major governments to coordinate expansionary policy. Only by reversing the trend toward more independent central banks will the much-heralded Keynesian reflation produced by international coordination of expansionary policy be possible.

7. Conclusion

I have suggested that reversing the trend toward more independent central banks must be an important component of an internationally coordinated Keynesian reflation, which many progressives have called for (see for example, Faux 1988 and Mead 1989). Will it suffice? It is here that the issue of structural dependence and many of the important issues raised by Hyman Minsky come back into their own. Where speculative financial markets have become so important domestically and internationally, can an internationally coordinated Keynesian coalition supported by integrated central banks really work? Or will speculative financial markets veto loose monetary policy, coordinated or not?

It is probably the case that the more economies are dominated by speculative financial markets and the more highly integrated are international capital markets the higher is the elasticity of financial and real investment with respect to changes in expected rates of return. As financial deregulation and international financial integration expand, it may become less possible for labor or industrial capital to influence central bank policy, and therefore we are less likely to see a Keynesian coalition emerge (Crotty 1993)[44]

By implication, in order to promote policies in the interest of labor, it may be necessary both to integrate the central banks into government and to reduce the scope and power of speculative markets. Neither policy by itself will suffice. Speculative markets with integrated central banks may be less and less able to sustain a Keynesian coalition. And enterprise finance with an independent bank will only serve the interests of capital. Reproduced on a world scale by a few powerful central banks, then, central bank independence and speculative markets are likely to be a deadly combination. The challenge is to promote financial market restructuring to reduce many of the problems identified by Hyman Minsky, while at the same time making central banks more accountable to the populations they are supposed to serve.

APPENDIX

The model of the paper is represented by the IS equation and the producer equilibrium conditions, given by equations (7), (8) and (9).

$$i(r^e(\pi^I, z), \sigma) = s(\pi^F + \pi^I)z\bar{a}_I^{-1} = s\pi z\bar{a}_I^{-1} \tag{7}$$

$$\pi^I = \pi^I(z, \sigma) \tag{8}$$

$$\pi^F = \pi^F(z, \sigma) \tag{9}$$

Totally differentiating equations 7, 8, and 9, one can derive the following system:

$$
\begin{bmatrix} i'_\pi - sza - 1 \\ 1 \\ 0 \end{bmatrix}
\begin{bmatrix} -sz\bar{a}_I^{-1} \\ 0 \\ 1 \end{bmatrix}
\begin{bmatrix} i_z s\pi\bar{a}_I^{1} \\ -\pi'_z \\ -\pi^F_Z \end{bmatrix}
\begin{bmatrix} d\pi^I \\ d\pi^F \\ dz \end{bmatrix}
=
\begin{bmatrix} -i_\sigma\, d\sigma \\ \pi'_\sigma\, d\sigma \\ \pi^F_\sigma\, d\sigma \end{bmatrix}
$$

44. Notice that the Keynesian coalition with multinational capital is likely to be a pyrrhic victory for labor unless controls over capital mobility are instituted, since industry's interest in it is based on its ability to locate production anywhere in the world to protect against the increased power of labor in one locale.

Let: $A = i'_\pi - sz\bar{a}^{-1}$
  $B = -sz\bar{a}^{-1}$
  $C = i_z - s\pi\bar{a}_I^{-1}$

$$Det = - (B(-\pi_z^F) - C) + A(\pi_z') \tag{1A}$$

The slope of the traditional IS curve is: $-C/A$.

The standard Keynesian stability assumption is that, $C < 0$, though as Marglin and Bhaduri (1990) point out, this is not necessary for stability in this type of model. As is typical, however, we will make the assumption, $C < 0$. In that case, the slope of the traditional IS curve in $\pi - z$ space depends on the sign of A. If $A > 0$, then the IS curve is downward sloping; if $A < 0$, the IS curve is upward sloping. In the IS curves described in the text, the implicit assumption is the $d\pi^I = d\pi$. Changes in π^F shift the IS curve.

The determinant will not necessarily be negative, but stability of the system will depend on the negativity of the determinant. The negativity of the determinant is roughly equivalent to the condition that the IS curve is steeper in absolute value than the PE curve. So we will analyze the model only for conditions where:

$$Det < 0. \tag{2A}$$

Comparative static results are the following:

$$dz/d\sigma = -[B\pi_\sigma^F + i_\sigma + A\pi_\sigma']/Det < 0 \tag{3A}$$

In general, increases in the real interest rate will lower capacity utilization. Notice that this is true even if changes in interest rate have no direct affect on investment ($i_\sigma = 0$) or indirect effect, as in the case of Enterprise Finance ($\pi_\sigma' = 0$). Under Enterprise Finance a higher finance profit share ($\pi_\sigma^F > 0$) will increase saving and reduce consumption without increasing investment.

The effect of changes in the interest rate on the profit share of finance will always be positive, as long as $\pi_z^F = 0$. In that case,

$$d\pi^F/d\sigma = [\pi_\sigma^F(A \pi_z' + C)]/Det > 0 \tag{4A}$$

which reduces to:

$$d\pi^F/d\sigma = \pi_\sigma^F \text{ as long as } \pi_z^F = 0. \tag{5A}$$

If, however, the share of profits going to finance changes with capacity utilization, holding real interest rates constant, then the relationships are more complex. In particular, if π_z^F is positive and sufficiently large, then increases in real interest rates can lower finance's profit share because they lower capacity utilization.

The effect of interest rate changes on industrial profit shares is:

$$d\pi^I/d\sigma = -[(i_\sigma\pi_z' + c\pi'_\sigma) + B(\pi_\sigma' \pi_z^F - \pi_z' \pi_\sigma^F)]/Det \tag{6A}$$

The sign of (6A) is indeterminant and depends on the structure of financial and labor markets.

Enterprise Finance/Kaleckian Labor: $\pi'_\sigma = 0; \pi'_z > 0.$

$$d\pi^I/d\sigma = [-\pi'_z(i_\sigma + B\pi^F_\sigma)]/Det < 0 \tag{7A}$$

Increases in the interest rate lower the industrial profit share.

Enterprise Finance/Marxian Labor: $\pi'_\sigma = 0; \pi'_z < 0.$

$$d\pi^I/d\sigma = \pi'_z(i_\sigma + B\pi^F_\sigma)/Det > 0 \tag{8A}$$

Increases in the interest rate raise the industrial profit share because they lower the rate of capacity utilization without shifting the distribution of income to finance from industry.

To analyze the effects of changes in the real interest rate (σ) on profit rates, totally differentiate equations (11) and (12):

$$r^I = \pi^I(z,\sigma)\bar{a}_I^{-1}z \qquad \text{industrial profits} \tag{11}$$

$$r^F = \pi^F(z,\sigma)\bar{a}_F^{-1}z \qquad \text{financial profits} \tag{12}$$

$$dr^I/d\sigma = \bar{a}_I^{-1}[(z\,\pi'_z + \pi^I)\,dz/d\sigma + z\pi'_\sigma] \tag{9A}$$

$$dr^F/d\sigma = \bar{a}_F^{-1}[(z\,\pi^F_z + \pi^F)\,dz/d\sigma + \pi^F_\sigma] \tag{10A}$$

To evaluate the monetary policy which will maximize the rates of profit in industry and finance one could set (9A) and (10A) to 0.

In terms of Figure 8 in the text, it's easier to interpret conditions (9A) and (10A) by finding the optimal rates of capacity utilization (z^{*F}, z^{*I}) achieved by altering real interest rates. Multiply (9A) and (10A) by $d\sigma/dz$ and set them to 0.

$$dr^I/dz = \bar{a}_I^{-1}[(z\,\pi'_z + \pi I) + z\pi'_\sigma\,d\sigma/dz] = 0 \tag{11A}$$

$$dr^F dz = \bar{a}_F^{-1}[(z\,\pi^F_z + \pi^F) + z\pi^F_\sigma\,d\sigma/dz] = 0 \tag{12A}$$

$$0 \le z \le 1; 0 \le \pi I \le 1 \tag{13A}$$

Enterprise Finance/Kaleckian Case: $\pi'_\sigma = 0; \pi'_z > 0.$

Industry

$$\pi'_z = -\pi^I/z \tag{14A}$$

The left hand side of the equation is the slope of the PEIσ line; the right hand side is the slope of industry's iso-profit line. Since the left hand side of (14A) is positive, there is no internal solution to (14A). Industrial profit rates will be maximized at the interest rates that generate full capacity utilization.

Finance

$$(\pi_z^F + \pi_\sigma^F \, d\sigma/dz) = -\pi^F/z \tag{15A}$$

The left hand side of equation (15A) is the slope of the PEFσ line and the right hand side is the slope of finance's iso-profit line. Since $\pi_\sigma^F > 0$ and $d\sigma/dz < 0$, the sign of the left hand side depends on π_z^F, the effect of capacity utilization on finance profit share, holding real interest rates constant. In the base line case where $\pi_z^F = 0$, then (15A) might have an interior solution, ie, financial profit rates will be maximized at a rate of capacity utilization less than one.

Enterprise/Neo-Marxian: $\pi_z^I < 0$; $\pi_\sigma^I = 0$.

Industry

$$\pi_z^I = -\pi^I/z \tag{16A}$$

Since $\pi_z^I < 0$, then industry's profit rate may be maximized at an interest rate that produces $z < 1$, as will finance's.

Speculative Finance/Kaleckian: $\pi_z^I > 0$; $\pi_\sigma^I < 0$.

Industry

$$\pi_z^I + \pi_\sigma^I \, d\sigma/dz = -\pi^I/z \tag{17A}$$

Since the left hand side is positive, again industry profit rates will be maximized at full employment.

Finance
$$(\pi_z^F + \pi_\sigma^F \, d\sigma/dz) = -\pi^F/z \tag{18A}$$
With speculative finance, $\pi_z^F \leq 0$, so finance's profit rate may be maximized at an interest rate which produces $z < 1$.

Speculative Finance/Neo-Marxian: $\pi_z^I < 0$; $\pi_\sigma^I < 0$.
Assume: $\pi_\sigma^I = -\pi_\sigma^F$, and $\pi_z^F = 0$.

Industry

$$\pi_z^I + \Omega = -\pi^I/z \tag{19A}$$

where: $\Omega = -(\pi_\sigma^I C)/(i_\sigma + i_\pi \pi_\sigma^I) > 0$

Industry's profit rates fall as capacity utilization rises due to the effect of the reduced reserve army of labor ($\pi'_z < 0$); on the other hand, its profit rate falls as interest rates increase ($\pi'_\sigma < 0$). Firms' profit rates will be maximized at a monetary policy induced $z < 1$ if the reserve army effect is greater than the interest rate effect. Otherwise their profit rates will be maximized at $z = 1$.

Finance

$$\pi^F_\sigma \, d\sigma/dz = -\pi^F/z \qquad\qquad (20A)$$

On the other hand, finance will prefer an interest rate that generates $z < 1$.

With Kaleckian Capital-Labor Relations and Speculative Finance, industrial capital will always prefer looser monetary policy than finance. With Enterprise Finance, the differences will not be so great. Both industry and finance will prefer loose monetary policy.

EMPIRICAL APPENDIX

I. Estimating capital-labor relations:

To determine whether capital-labor relations were Kaleckian or Neo-Marxian I estimated the Producers' Equilibrium line for the manufacturing sectors for eight OECD countries, over the period 1970–1985. If the PE line was estimated to be downward sloping, then I took capital-labor relations to be neo-Marxian. If the producers' equilibrium line was horizontal or upward sloping, I took capital-labor relations to be Kaleckian. Note that since I only have estimates for the industry share, I have implicitly assumed that the relationship between capacity utilization and the financial profit share does not alter the slope of the PE line.

To estimate the PE line, I used data compiled by Thomas Weisskopf, Wendy Carlin and Andrew Glyn (WCG) as well as data from the OECD National Accounts, (OECD) and the International Financial Statistics (IFS) for eight OECD countries:

Canada, France, Germany, Italy, Japan, Sweden, U.K., and U.S.,

The goal of the exercise was to estimate the slope of the PE line in z-σ space. To estimate the equation, I had to take into account the fact that the PE line is one equation in a simultaneous system. Thus, the PE and IS curves simultaneously determine z and σ.

$$PE = PE(z,\sigma) \qquad\qquad (1ea)$$

$$IS: IS = IS(z,\sigma, Exports, Imports, Government Expenditure) \qquad\qquad (2ea)$$

To estimate the PE line I used two stage least squares. As instruments I took the independent variables in the IS equation. The coefficient on the rate of capacity utilization in the PE equation is identified, though the coefficient of σ is not.

Moreover, given that I am just estimating manufacturing profits, implicitly I am assuming the benchmark case that capacity utilization does not alter the financial profit share.

In the estimating equation, I took the gross profit share of manufacturing as the dependent variable (WCG), and the rate of capacity utilization in manufacturing (WCG) and real rate of interest (IFS) as independent variables. As instruments I used the real rate of interest (IFS), Real Government Expenditures (OECD), Real Exports (OECD). All variables except for the real rate of interest were in natural logs. I estimated the equations over the period 1970–1985.

If the sign on z was negative and significant, I assigned the capital-labor variable a 1 (Neo-Marxian). If it was positive or insignificantly different from 0, I assigned it a 0 (Kaleckian). See Table 1.

A basic problem with these estimates is that they were rather unstable. Further research is necessary to identify the slope of the PE line.

II. Sources for Data in Table 4

Central Bank Independence:
The index of central bank independence was created by Epstein and Schor (1986), building on the work of Bade and Parkin (Robin Bade and Michael Parkin, 1980, "Central Bank Laws and Monetary Policy", mimeo, University of Western Ontario.) Bade and Parkin developed an index of central bank independence based on governing statutes. We adjusted their index to take into account practice as well as statute (Epstein and Schor, 1988). We also took account of institutional changes, such as the so-called Divorce of the Bank of Italy and Treasury in 1981 which increased the Bank of Italy's independence.

Finance Industry Relations:
Bank Share of non-financial corporate liabilities; stocks, except for Canada, for which stock data are not available. France's measure was adjusted with national data. Averages of available data, 1975–1983. Source: *OECD Financial Statistics*, part 3, 1983, 1984.

Capital Labor Relations:
See part I above.

Energy Imports:
Energy imports as a percentage of merchandise exports, 1981. Source: World Development Report, 1984. World Bank., p. 233.

GNP Gap:
GNP Gap = (potential GNP/Actual GNP) − 1 (Or GDP)
Calculated by the OECD. Average of 1970–1983. Source: Patrice Muller and Robert W.R. Price, "Structural Budget Deficits and Fiscal Stance", OECD Working Paper, Economics and Statistics Department, 1984.

REFERENCES

Bade, Robin and Michael Parkin. 1980. "Central Bank Laws and Monetary Policy," mimeo, University of Western Ontario.

Block, Fred. 1977. "The Ruling Class Does Not Rule: Notes on the Marxist Theory of the State," *Socialist Revolution* 33:6–28.

Boddy, Raford, and James Crotty. 1975. "Class Conflict and Macro Policy: The Political Business Cycle." *Review of Radical Political Economics* 7(1):1–19.

Bowles, Samuel and Robert Boyer. 1989. Labor Discipline and Aggregate Demand. *American Economic Review*. 78(2): pp. 395–400.

———. 1990. "A Wage-Led Employment Regime: Income Distribution, Labor Discipline, and Aggregate Demand in Welfare Capitalism." In *The Golden Age of Capitalism: Lessons for the 1990s*, Stephen Marglin and Juliet B. Schor (eds.). New York: Oxford University Press.

Bowles, Samuel, and Herbert Gintis. 1982. "The Crisis of Liberal Democratic Capitalism: The Case of the United States." *Politics and Society* 11(1):51–93.

———. 1986. *Democracy and Capitalism; Property, Community, and the Contradictions of Modern Social Thought*. New York: Basic Books.

Bowles, Samuel, David M. Gordon, and Thomas Weisskopf. 1989. "Business Ascendancy and Economic Impasse: A Structural Retrospective on Conservative Economics, 1979–1987." *Journal of Economic Perspectives* 3(1):107–134.

Bryant, Ralph C., et. al. 1988. *Empirical Macroeconomics for Interdependent Economies*. Washington: The Brookings Institution.

Carnoy, Martin.1984. *The State and Political Theory*. Princeton: Princeton University Press.

Crotty, James, 1985. "The Centrality of Money, Credit and Financial Intermediation in Marx's Crisis Theory." In *Rethinking Marxism*, S. Resnick and R. Wolff (eds.), pp. 45–82. New York: Autonomedia.

———. 1993. "The Rise and Fall of the Keynesian Revolution in the Age of The Global Marketplace." In *Creating a New World Economy; Forces of Change and Plans for Action*. Gerald Epstein, Julie Graham, and Jessica Nembhard, for the Center for Popular Economics (eds.) Philadelphia: Temple University Press.

Duck, Nigel W. 1988. "Money, Output and Prices: An Empirical Study Using Long-Term Cross Country Data." *European Economic Review* 32: 1603–1619.

Dymski, Gary. 1990. "Money and Credit in Radical Political Economy: A Survey of Contemporary Perspectives." *Review of Radical Political Economics*. 22(2/3): 38–65

———. 1992. "Controlling Labor by Controlling Credit: Inflation, Unemployment, and Monetary Policy." Mimeo, Department of Economics, University of California, Riverside. May.

Dymski, Gary, and Robert Pollin. 1992. "Hyman Minsky as Hedgehog: The Power of the Wall Street Paradigm," In *Financial Conditions and Macroeconomic Performance: Essays in Honor of Hyman Minsky*, S. Fazzari and D. Papadimitrou, (eds.) Armonk: NY: M.E. Sharpe, pp. 27–61.

Edwards, Richard. 1979. *Contested Terrain: The Transformation of the American Workplace in the 20th Century*. New York: Basic Books.

Epstein, Gerald. 1981. "Domestic Stagflation and Monetary Policy: The Federal Reserve and the Hidden Election," In *The Hidden Election*, Thomas Ferguson and Joel Rogers, (eds.). New York: Pantheon Press.

———. 1982. "Federal Reserve Politics and Monetary Instability," In *The Political Economy of Public Policy* Alan Stone and Edward J. Harpham, (eds.). Beverly Hills: Sage Publications.

———. 1991. "Profit Squeeze, Rentier Squeeze and Macroeconomic Policy under Fixed and Flexible Exchange Rates", *Economies et Societes*, Serie "Monnaie et Production", MP No. 8, Nov-Dec, pp. 219–257.

———. 1993. "Monetary Policy in the 1990's: Overcoming the Barriers to Equity and Growth", In *Transforming the U.S. Financial System: Equity and Efficiency for the 21st Century*, Gary Dymski, Gerald Epstein and Robert Pollin, (eds.), Armonk, NY: M.E. Sharpe.

Epstein, Gerald, and Thomas Ferguson. 1984. "Monetary Policy, Loan Liquidation and Industrial Conflict: The Federal Reserve and The Open Market Operations of 1932," *Journal of Economic History*, Vol. XLIV, No. 4, December, pp. 957–983.

———. 1991. "Answers to Stock Questions: Fed Targets, Stock Prices and the Gold Standard in the Great Depression", *Journal of Economic History*, March 1991.

Epstein, Gerald, and Herbert Gintis. 1992. "International Capital Markets and the Limits of National Economic Policy", In *Financial Openness and National Autonomy*, Tariq Banuri and Juliet B.Schor (eds.), Oxford: Clarendon Press.

Epstein, Gerald, and Juliet B. Schor. 1986. "The Political Economy of Central Banking". Harvard Institute for Economic Research, Discussion Paper No. 1281.

———. 1988. "The Determinants of Central Bank Policy in Open Economies", In *Monetary Theory and Central Banking*, Bruno Jossa and Carlo Panico (eds.), Naples, Italy: Liguori Press.

———. 1989. "The Divorce of the Banca D'Italia and the Italian Treasury: A Case of Central Bank Independence," In, *State, Market and Social Regulation: New Perspectives on the Italian Case*, Peter Lange and Marino Regini (eds.), New York: Cambridge University Press.

———. 1990a. "Corporate Profitability as a Determinant of Restrictive Monetary Policy: Estimates for the Post-War U.S.", In *The Political Economy of American Monetary Policy*, Thomas Mayer, (ed.), New York: Cambridge University Press.

———. 1990b. "Macropolicy in the Rise and Fall of the Golden Age", In *The Golden Age of Capitalism: Reinterpreting the Postwar Experience*, Stephen Marglin and Juliet Schor (eds.), New York, Oxford University Press.

———. 1992. "Structural Determinants and Economic Effects of Capital Controls in the OECD", In *Financial Openness and National Autonomy*, Tariq Banuri and Juliet B. Schor (eds.), Oxford: Clarendon Press.

———. forthcoming. "The Federal Reserve-Treasury Accord and the Construction of the Postwar Monetary Regime", *Social Concept*.

Epstein, Gerald and Herbert Gintis. 1992. "International Capital Markets and the Limits of National Economic Policy", In *Financial Openness and National Autonomy*, Tariq Banuri and Juliet B.Schor (eds.), Oxford: Clarendon Press.

Faux, Jeff. 1988. "The Austerity Trap and the Growth Alternative." *World Policy Journal*, Summer, pp. 367–413.

Federal Reserve Bank of New York. 1986. *Recent Trends in Commercial Bank Profitability*. New York: Federal Reserve Bank of New York.

Glyn, Andrew and Bob Sutcliffe. 1972. *British Capitalism, Workers and the Profit Squeeze*. Harmondsworth, UK: Penguin.

Greider, William. 1987. *Secrets of the Temple; How the Federal Reserve Runs the Country*. New York: Simon and Schuster.

Hall, Peter A. 1984. "Patterns of Economic Policy: An Organizational Approach." In, *The State in Capitalist Europe*. S. Bornstein, D. Held and J. Krieger (eds.) London: Allen and Unwin.

International Bank for Reconstruction and Development. 1984. *World Development Report*. New York: Oxford University Press.

Jacobs, Michael. 1984. "Financial Instability: A Comparative Analysis of Some OECD Countries." Mimeo, New School for Social Research.

Kalecki, Michael. 1971. "Political Aspects of Full Employment." Reprinted in *Selected Essays on the Dynamics of the Capitalist Economy, 1933–1970*. Cambridge: The University Press.

Kurzer, Paulette. 1987. "Do Banks Matter? Economic Integration and Social Democracy in Four European Countries." Mimeo, Harvard Center for International Affairs.

————. 1988. "The Politics of Central Banks, Austerity and Unemployment." Mimeo, Harvard Center for International Affairs.

McCauley, Robert N., and Steven A. Zimmer. 1989. "Explaining International Differences in the Cost of Capital: The United States and United Kingdom Versus Japan and Germany," Federal Reserve Bank of New York Research Paper, No. 8913.

Magdoff, Harry, and Paul Sweezy. 1987. *Stagnation and the World Financial Explosion*. New York: Monthly Review Press.

Marglin, Stephen A., and Amit Bhaduri. 1990. "Profit Squeeze and Keynesian Theory." In *The Golden Age of Capitalism: Lessons for the 1990s*, Stephen A. Marglin and Juliet B. Schor (eds.), New York: Oxford University Press.

Mayer, Thomas, ed. 1990. *The Political Economy of American Monetary Policy*. New York: Cambridge University Press.

Mead, W. R. 1989. "The United States and the World Economy, parts I and II." *World Policy Journal*, Winter, Summer.

Minsky, H. 1982. "Central Banking and Money Market Changes," In *Can It Happen Again? Essays on Instability and Finance*. New York: Armonk, NY: M.E. Sharpe.

————. 1986. *Stabilizing an Unstable Economy*. New Haven: Yale University Press.

Mott, Tracy. 1989. "The Structure of Class Conflict in a Kaleckian-Keynesian Model." Mimeo, Jerome Levy Institute.

Panico, Carlo. 1987. *Interest and Profit in the Theories of Value and Distribution*. London: Macmillan.

Przeworski, Adam. 1988. "The State and The Economy Under Capitalism." Mimeo, University of Chicago.

Radecki, Lawrence J., and V. Reinhart, 1988. "The Globalization of Financial Markets and the Effectiveness of Monetary Policy Instruments." *Quarterly Review*, Federal Reserve Bank of New York, 13(3):18–27.

Rowthorn, Bob and Andrew Glyn, 1990. "The Diversity of Unemployment Experience Since 1973." In *The Golden Age of Capitalism; Lesson for the 1990's*, Stephen Marglin and Juliet Schor, (eds.). New York: Oxford Unviversity Press.

Schmitter, Philippe C. 1986. "Neo-Corporatism and the State." In *The Political Economy of Corporatism*, Wyn Grant (ed.) London: Macmillan.

Schor, Juliet B. 1985. "Wage Flexibility, Social Wage Expenditures and Monetary Restrictiveness." In *Money and Macro Policy*, Mark Jarsulic, (ed.), pp. 135–154. Boston: Kluwer-Nijhoff.

Schor, Juliet B., and Samuel Bowles. 1987. "Employment Rents and the Incidence of Strikes," *Review of Economics and Statistics* 59(4):584–592.

Wachtel, Howard. 1987. *The Money Mandarins*. New York: Pantheon.

Weisskopf, Thomas. 1988. "The Analysis of Neo-Marxian Crisis Theory." *The Economic Review* 39(3):193–208.

Willet, Thomas D. ed. 1988. *Political Business Cycles; The Political Economy of Money, Inflation, and Unemployment*. Durham, N.C.: Duke University Press.

Zysman, John. 1983. *Government, Markets, and Growth; Financial Systems and the Politics of Industrial Change*. Ithaca: Cornell University Press.

CHAPTER 10

Saving, Finance and Interest Rates: An Empirical Consideration of Some Basic Keynesian Propositions

*Robert Pollin and Craig Justice**

1. Introduction

In pre-Keynesian mainstream analysis, the saving rate was regarded as a central variable determining the pace and level of overall activity. According to this perspective, high saving rates produced an ample supply of loanable funds at relatively low interest rates, providing the financial means for the growth of investment. Correspondingly, low saving rates created a scarcity of loanable funds and high interest rates that discouraged new investment. James Meade aptly characterized the pre-Keynesian model as one in which "a dog called *saving* wagged its tail labelled *investment*," (quoted in Bridel 1987a, p. 161). This perspective can be traced through various incarnations, beginning with Smith, advancing through Ricardo and Say, and closing with Marshall and the Marginalists.[1]

A major thrust of the Keynes-Kalecki revolution, of course, was to reject the notion that saving determines the rate of investment activity through its impact on loanable funds supply and the interest rate, and indeed, to establish the independence of investment from saving: to shift, again in Meade's words, to a model in which "a dog called *investment* wagged its tail labelled *saving*." In the Keynes-Kalecki view, firms' investment decisions are made on the basis of their profit expectations. The interest rate at which they can borrow is only one factor, and probably only a secondary one, in establishing investors' profit

*We acknowledge the constructive comments on this or related work by Fred Block, James Earley, Gary Dymski, two anonymous referees, and participants at the September 1992 Levy Institute Conference on Employment, Distribution and Markets.

1. Bridel 1987a is an excellent analytic history of the development and transformation of ideas on savings, investment and macroeconomic activity from Marshall to Keynes. Bridel 1987b offers a brief overview of a much longer span of pre-Keynesian thinking on savings and investment.

expectations. More important, Keynes and Kalecki argued that any growth of activity, initiated through investment spending and propagated through the multiplier, would raise both the level of total income and, in particular, the level of saving. Two major implications flowed from such reasoning: that saving is a passive variable, fluctuating along with aggregate income, whose changes in turn are determined by the level of investment; and that increases in investment are self-financing, in that, through the multiplier, investment growth generates an amount of saving commensurate with a given increase in activity.[2]

But within this analytic framework, one major question still needed to be addressed before the independence of investment from saving could be established: How was the activity-initiating increase in investment, occurring during the interregnum period before the completion of the multiplier, to be financed if not by a prior increase in saving? Keynes and Kalecki both argued that the banking system—private institutions as well as the central bank— was itself capable of financing the investment growth during the interregnum, regardless of the preceding pattern of saving flows. Keynes in particular emphasized a central institutional fact here, that private banks and other intermediaries, not ultimate savers, are responsible for channeling the supply of credit to nonfinancial investors. The central bank can also substantially encourage credit growth by increasing the supply of reserves to the private banking system, thereby raising the banks' liquidity. But even without central bank initiative, the private intermediaries could still increase their lending if they were willing to accept a temporary decline in their liquidity. The reason this liquidity decline would only be temporary is that liquidity would rise again after the interregnum–that is, after the multiplier process has generated an increase in saving commensurate with the level of investment growth. It is through this chain of reasoning that Keynes concluded that "in general, the banks hold the key position in the transition from a lower to a higher scale of activity" (1973, p. 222).

What becomes clear from this analysis is that to establish the independence of investment from saving—and more fundamentally, to develop macroeconomic analysis in the tradition of Keynes and Kalecki—it is necessary to first develop understanding of the institutional relationships within financial markets and between financial institutions and nonfinancial investors. Pursuing such questions, of course, has been at the heart of Hyman Minsky's work throughout his distinguished career, and as such, Minsky has made basic contributions to the advance of Keynesian macroeconomics. Although Min-

---

2. Thus, as Joan Robinson wrote (1962, pp. 82–83), it is "the central thesis of the *General Theory* that firms are free, within wide limits, to accumulate as they please, and that the rate of saving of the economy as a whole accommodates itself to the rate of investment that they decree."

sky has not written extensively on the saving/investment nexus per se, he has explored in depth the more general issue of the role of financial intermediation for understanding macroeconomic outcomes.

In particular, Minsky has made a penetrating contribution on the question of money supply endogeneity in which he shows how, through financial innovation, the velocity of circulation can rise without engendering equivalent increases in interest rates (1982). As a result, a given amount of base reserves can be used to finance an increasing amount of investment spending without necessarily raising interest rates. In short, Minsky's work shows how financial institutions may well lead "the transition from a lower to a higher scale of activity" independent of households' saving decisions, and even, to a significant extent, of central banks' strategic interventions.

Minsky's work on finance, investment, and macroeconomic activity has been a high point in the rather schizophrenic development of macrofinance after Keynes. The early postwar years saw a burst of creative research on macrofinance, including, in addition to Minsky, contributions by the Radcliffe Commission, Gurley and Shaw, and the early Tobin. However, mainstream Keynesian research veered away from such concerns by the late 1960s, perhaps in part because of the growing acceptance of the framework of discussion—if not the results themselves—advanced by Milton Friedman and associates.[3]

Recently, discussion of the link between saving, finance, and investment among mainstream economists, even the self-professed Keynesians, has reverted to the pre-Keynesian position, stressing that individual saving decisions and monetary expansion by the central bank—exogenously controlled money—are the only two possible sources of loan funds. Thus, the prominent mainstream Keynesian Lawrence Summers writes that "the allocation of resources between present and future consumption or saving is perhaps the most

---

3. Earley 1985 is a superb, if unfortunately unpublished, survey of what Tobin then called the "new view" of monetary theory and macrofinance. Earley attributes the rapid demise by the mid-1960s of this approach within mainstream thinking to several factors: (1) the influence of Keynes' *General Theory*, which put aside the insights on financial intermediation of his *Treatise on Money*; (2) the rising interest in long-run growth theories, leading to the neglect of cyclical and other "short-run" influences; (3) a focus on stocks rather than flows in the modeling of financial market activity; (4) the inherent complexity of the new approach, which required examination of intersectoral flow relationships rather than simply aggregate stocks and (5) the most important factor in Earley's view: the rise, led by Milton Friedman, of the new quantity theory, which offered a much simpler set of theoretical propositions, which in turn were much more amenable to econometric modeling. In addition to these factors, we would also suggest that another important influence was the link forged by Friedman and associates between the new quantity theory and the idea that free market economies were inherently self-correcting equilibrium systems. This was the idea, after all, that underpinned Friedman and Schwartz's highly influential, market-exonerating explanation of the causes of the Great Depression.

fundamental choice facing any economy. . . .The rate of saving determines the rate of growth a country can enjoy". (1986, p. 65).

Within the post-Keynesian school to which Minsky belongs, a recent attempt to seriously grapple with the relationship between saving, finance, and investment is a widely cited paper by Asimakopulos (1983). The paper's basic argument is that Keynes and Kalecki had in fact exaggerated the independence of finance from saving, and thereby of investment from saving.

Asimakopulos charges that Keynes and Kalecki neglect the fact that unless an increase in saving precedes investment, the initiating investment financed by intermediaries will normally involve an increase in interest rates and an upward shift in the yield curve. The level of interest rates will rise because the intermediaries will have to reduce their liquidity position during the interregnum when they use liquid assets to purchase investors' bonds. Long rates will rise in particular because intermediaries are assuming the risk that they can profitably sell the bonds they have purchased to initiate the investment activity. Thus, according to Asimakopulos, to the extent that the new investment is not preceded by an increase in saving, interest rates, particularly long rates, should rise during the interregnum, and such a rise may discourage investment growth.

According to Asimakopulos, the Keynes-Kalecki argument covering the interregnum, claiming that new investment remains independent of saving even in this initial period, is a special case. The Keynes/Kalecki position can hold only when intermediaries already have an excess liquidity position and are willing to part with liquidity without raising their interest rates. The general case, according to Asimakopulos, is one in which the initiating investment will entail higher interest rates and a rising yield curve unless an increase in saving precedes the rise in investment. Thus, in the general case, to the extent that the rising interest rates will discourage investment in the interregnum, Asimakopulos concludes that investment is not independent of saving— that is, higher saving rates will encourage investment in the interregnum by allowing new investment to occur at lower interest rates.

The purpose of this paper is to attempt to achieve greater clarity on this central, but clearly still unresolved, question in Keynesian macroeconomics. Amid a highly sophisticated and still-developing theoretical literature on this issue,[4] it is curious that little effort has been made to try to advance understanding by bringing an empirical dimension to the discussion. This paper attempts to begin to filling that lacuna by presenting evidence on the relation-

---

4. An important debate emerged between Asimakoupulis and various critics following publication of Asimakoupulis' 1983 paper. The basic critical interventions are Snippe 1985, 1986, Terzi 1986, Richardson 1986, Kregal 1986, and Skott 1988. Replies by Asimakoupulis include 1985, 1986a, 1986b, and 1986c. Pollin and Justice 1991 provides a brief survey of this literature.

ship between saving, lending and interest rates for the postwar U.S. economy. It is significant that we are considering the U.S. economy only. If we believe that institutional structures matter, we are forced to acknowledge that findings for one country may not be generalizable beyond that specific case. This study, then, cannot be interpreted as providing adequate evidence to confirm or refute any of the competing theories. At best, it will provide one useful platform on which, through further research, a set of general principles may emerge at a later time.

Section 2 reviews some major analytical issues in the debate on saving, finance, and interest rates. We do not seek to obtain definitive answers from this literature; instead we formulate a set of questions that we may then subject to formal empirical modeling.

Section 3 then briefly considers accounting questions associated with the measurement of saving and lending. This will provide the foundation for our empirical specifications, which are introduced in the next section. Section 4 presents results on two types of tests: the relationship between saving and lending, and how divergences between saving and lending flows affect both interest rate levels and the yield curve.

The concluding section summarizes the findings and considers them in the broader context of the literature on saving, finance, and investment. One of the important findings is how prescient Hyman Minsky's work has been in helping to shed light on the questions at hand.

2. Theoretical Issues in Dispute

Asimakopulos's critique of Keynes and Kalecki draws heavily on a 1939 paper by Kaldor, "Speculation and Economic Activity", (reprinted in Kaldor 1960). Kaldor argued that the Keynesian theory during the interregnum was a special case because it relied on the assumption that "speculators"—i.e. financial intermediaries and investment banks—had to be willing to purchase additional long-term securities at prevailing, rather than falling, prices. In addition, the speculators would themselves have to borrow short term from banks in order to purchase the securities prior to an additional flow of saving being generated by the multiplier. When the speculators purchased bonds at prevailing prices, they would therefore also bear the risk that short-term rates would rise in the near future, increasing the burden of their short-term obligations and discounting the value of their bonds. Kaldor claimed that there was no reason for speculators to accept these conditions and therefore no reason for them to purchase bonds at prevailing prices. But Kaldor also assumed that in most real-world situations the demands on speculative resources would be small relative to the aggregate resources of the financial market, and therefore any upward interest rate pressure from financing investment in the interregnum would be negligible. But Asimakopulos argues that the real-world conditions to which Kaldor was referring apply primarily to slack, deflationary economies, such as those prevailing in the 1930s. According to Asimakopulos, the Keynesian special case would not normally hold under contemporary economic conditions, in which inflationary expectations prevail. Rather, we would normally expect that interest rates would rise to finance the initial increase in investment, unless an increase in saving precedes the growth of investment.

In the debate surrounding Asimakopulos's paper, and in post-Keynesian discussions about finance and saving generally, there is little dispute that, all else equal, an initial increase in investment will exert upward pressure on interest rates. The debate is over how much prior saving flows can counteract this upward interest rate pressure, and whether financial variables—central bank policy, the liquidity preferences of intermediaries and the public, and the innovative capacity of financial intermediaries—will not have greater influence than saving in determining the interest rate response to the rise of investment.

Consider first a given financial structure, that is, with no allowance for innovation. There are three ways in which financial variables can influence how much interest rates will rise with an increase in initial investment. The first factor, of course, is central bank policy. As Asimakopulos acknowledges, Kalecki made clear that a "credit inflation"—by which he meant expansionary central bank policy—was the precondition for an increase in investment, both to provide the investment funds and to meet the higher transaction demands resulting from the consequent increase in economic activity and prices. Central banks may be constrained—for example, by concerns over inflation, the exchange rate, or rising wage levels—in their capacity to accommodate the rising demand for credit associated with the initiating investment increase. In addition, central banks have greater control over short-term rates than over the long rates at which investment will be financed: long-term rates are more influenced by supply and demand factors in the private market. Nevertheless, the central bank always has some power to influence both the quantity of credit and interest rates, and to the extent it does, as Kalecki recognized, it can influence the rates at which new investment is financed.[5]

---

5. Crucial to Kalecki's theory of investment finance is his distinction between the three stages in any investment project: investment orders, production of investment goods, and deliveries of finished equipment (1971). Though Kalecki does not develop his argument fully in this area, he suggests that increased investment will require provision of finance only insofar as (1) payment for the purchase of investment goods precedes the delivery of finished equipment, and (2) an increase in demand for money emerges due to the increase in aggregate production. These factors alone will generate the need for new financing—"credit inflation"—prior to the completion of the multiplier. How important are these factors? To answer that, a recent contribution by

A second factor is the banks' liquidity preference schedule, specifically whether intermediaries would be willing to accept this reduction in liquidity without raising their interest rates. This will depend on general economic conditions and each intermediary's specific circumstances. For example, intermediaries would be more willing to accept reduced liquidity if they were confident they could readily replenish liquid funds either through central bank open market purchases or by borrowing from the central bank or the private financial system. These factors in turn may be, but need not be, influenced by prior saving flows.

The third factor is the liquidity preference schedule of the public, that is, nonfinancial businesses and households. As Keynes argued, private sector liquidity preferences could be driven by expectations alone, for example, the expectation that rising bond prices brings lower liquidity preferences at present. But the growth of private saving may also be a determinant of private agents' liquidity preferences. Mott (1985), for example, has argued, following Robinson and Kalecki, that businesses' liquidity preferences should fall after an increase in profits, which in turn increases their internal funds as well as their ability to obtain external funds. And within such a framework, the relationship between saving and the provision of credit becomes complex, since increased corporate saving (internal funds) both decreases the need for corporate borrowing and simultaneously increases their access to external sources.[6]

In addition to central bank policy and private sector liquidity preferences within a given institutional environment, another factor that will influence outcomes in the interregnum is *changes in the institutional environment.* Minsky's 1957 paper (1982) has addressed this issue in a particularly illuminating way. The paper considers a situation in which loan demand is strong but the central bank is pursuing restrictive reserve growth policies. This situation can be easily extended to the directly relevant one in which there is no increase in saving flows to counteract the central bank's restrictiveness.

The paper makes two central points in considering this restrictive envi-

---

Messori (1991) argues that Kalecki's model needs to be supplemented by distinguishing the demands for investment financing from those of production financing. Investment financing involves "the monetary flows required to finance an increase in capital goods," whereas production financing involves "the monetary advances required to finance the purchase of working capital" (p. 301). In Messori's view, the demands for investment financing are more flexible than those for production financing, in which payrolls must be met on a consistent basis within relatively short time intervals. Thus, the needs for credit inflation within a Kalecki model would seem to stem primarily from the increment of production financing associated with new investment projects.

6. We are grateful to an anonymous referee for formulating this point clearly in his or her report. A basic reference on the relationship between corporate internal funds and the provision of credit is Fazzari, Hubbard, and Peterson 1988.

ronment. We assume that private intermediaries will normally want to accommodate increased loan demand. As such, when loan demand exceeds the central bank's willingness to increase reserve growth, the response of private intermediaries will be to circulate existing reserves more efficiently. This means raising the velocity of circulation of the given reserve supply. The private market's motivation for increasing reserve velocity is that intermediaries will receive higher interest rates for inter-institutional reserve lending than for holding idle reserves.

But Minsky's second point is that this rise in interest rates will also create inducements for financial innovation, specifically, new techniques of raising velocity without encouraging still further increases in interest rates.

The innovations Minsky wrote about in the 1957 paper were the development of the Federal Funds and Repurchase Agreement markets. Since then, we would also include such developments as the Eurodollar market, the commercial paper market, and money market mutual funds as innovations that have allowed private resources to be circulated more efficiently. The innovative momentum, in addition, was closely interrelated with the process of deregulation beginning in the early 1980s, as innovative circumventions of legal restrictions encouraged the elimination of ineffective laws, which in turn created a freer environment for further innovation.[7]

Minsky portrays this relationship between velocity, interest rates and innovation as a step function. Figure 1 is a variation on the Minsky model, in which we include both aggregate reserve levels (required and excess reserves, which are equal to borrowed and nonborrowed funds from the central bank) and saving flows as variables along the horizontal axis, but we assume both variables to be constants. Thus, each vertically sloping line represents the relationship between velocity and interest rates within a given institutional environment. The rise in velocity leads to a movement up the curve until interest rates are sufficiently high to induce an innovative response. The shift to a new curve signifies a shift to a new institutional environment, in which additional gains in velocity occur without further increases in interest rates.

Overall, we see that the determination as to whether an initial increase in investment drives up interest rates depends on the willingness or ability of the

---

7. The innovative/deregulatory environment has deepened the market for reserves, which in turn has increased competition and reduced transaction costs for short-term lending among intermediaries. Thus, through such reductions in their own cost of funds, intermediaries are then able to reduce their lending rates while maintaining a constant interest spread. Pollin (1991) presents evidence on the effects of financial innovation in the United States. For example, the loan/reserve ratio for private banks in the United States rose from an average of 3.7 over the 1953.3–57.2 business cycle to 25.5 from 1980.1–88.4. Virtually all of this change can be attributed to the rise of innovative financing. Good descriptions of financial innovations in the United States and other advanced economies are presented in De Cecco 1987 and Harrington 1987.

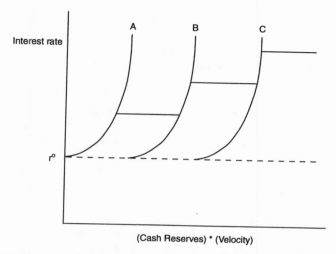

Fig. 1. Interest rates, velocity and innovation in a restrictive environment.

central banks, the public, and private intermediaries to supply liquidity, and on the impact of innovations on financial market practices. Each of these variables can induce an increase of loanable funds independent of flows of new saving into the financial market, and as such they represent the basis for Keynes's "most fundamental" conclusion in this area of analysis: "The investment market can become congested through a shortage of cash. It can never become congested through a shortage of saving" (1973, p. 222).

At the same time, it is clear that decisions by central banks, intermediaries, and the public are not themselves completely independent of the level of saving available in the financial market. For one, the central bank would not have to finance an increase in investment through as expansionist a monetary policy if financial markets were already well supplied with liquidity through a prior increase in saving. This may be a significant consideration when a central bank perceives substantial barriers to the pursuit of expansionist policies.

Liquidity preferences for intermediaries and the public are a function of the opportunity cost of holding money rather than of higher-yielding assets. Thus, it will normally require higher interest rates on nonliquid assets to induce intermediaries and the public to accept a lower liquidity posture. But initial increases in saving, depending on the form in which savings are held, may allow the satisfaction of liquidity preferences without forcing interest rates higher. In addition, as Minsky's model implies, the incentives for innovation would be weaker if an inflow of saving were to increase the supply of reserves—indeed, Minsky's model implies that increases in reserves either through central bank accommodation or increased saving are *substitutes* for increases in velocity through innovation.

In short, though the proximate cause of any "clogging" of the investment market remains the decisions by financial market participants, the flow of saving will influence those financial decisions. That is, the interest rate is a function of central bank policy, the liquidity preferences of intermediaries and the public, and the state of the financial structure. But each of these determinants of the interest rate is, at least partially, a function of saving flows.

If this is correct, the most basic question then becomes an empirical one: *How much* influence does saving have on the availability of credit and interest rates? This is the question that we pursue in the rest of the paper, by addressing the following questions in the context of the U.S. economy: First, what is the observable relationship between saving and lending, that is, to what extent are lending flows independent of saving? Second, how do deviations between saving and lending flows affect the level of interest rates? Theory suggests that interest rate levels will rise when lending grows more rapidly than saving; to what extent do we observe this to be true? Moreover, are these basic relationships affected, as Minsky's model suggests, by financial market innovations? Finally, following Kaldor's discussion, how will the yield curve be affected when lending and saving grow at differential rates? Kaldor's discussion suggests that long-term rates will rise when savings are inadequate to finance new investment. But we may also consider another possibility, that the rise in velocity within a restrictive environment, as described by Minsky, might induce short-term rates to rise in relative terms.

3. Measurement Issues

We confront numerous accounting issues in trying to understand the empirical relationship between saving, lending, and interest rates. To begin with, there is an extensive literature on the measurement of saving itself. The NIPA, for example, measures saving as the difference between income and spending, whereas the Federal Reserve defines saving by adding up financial assets. For our purposes, we will utilize the residual method. This is because saving is almost always considered a residual in theoretical and policy debates about its macroeconomic role—specifically, saving is considered as the act of abstaining from current consumption to provide the funds for investment spending.

We focus on gross private saving—that is, we include economic depreciation allowances in measuring business saving. The most important reason is that, from the perspective of the financial market, depreciation allowances constitute a substantial source of funds, mainly short-term deposits for intermediaries. They therefore contribute to the lending capacity of intermediaries, just as would deposits from any other source. In addition, depreciation allowances are not employed simply to replace worn-out plant and equipment. Rather, they are used primarily to finance investment in capital stock that represents some advance over previous vintages. Therefore, even from the viewpoint of the nonfinancial firm, depreciation funds contribute to growth, not merely replacement. Still, even though we regard gross saving measures as most appropriate here, we also report findings that utilize net saving measures.

We will also decompose the gross private saving figures into their business and personal saving components. Business saving accounts for roughly $^2/_3$ of gross private saving and is thus the primary determinant of the movement of aggregate private saving.

Finally, we must distinguish between saving and the provision of credit, or lending, in theoretically meaningful ways. One could reasonably argue that these concepts are identical—opposite sides of the same activity that generates a net increase in financial assets and liabilities. Thus, we now need to establish what distinguishes lending from the various concepts of saving.

Defining lending as a financial asset acquisition is the proper starting point. As such, if we were to consider strictly the lending of persons and businesses in this category, then lending would be identical to the saving of these units, minus their holdings of nonfinancial assets.

But our concerns are clearly different. We wish to measure how the structure and behavior of financial institutions influence the provision of credit, and specifically, the extent to which, through financial market practices, the provision of credit may become independent of the supply of private saving.

This leads us to define lending in a way that incorporates the lending by financial intermediaries as well of nonfinancial units. Our measure of lending therefore includes, first, the direct lending of private savers—their purchase of financial assets from nonfinancial units. It also includes the lending of domestic intermediaries to ultimate borrowers. To avoid double counting, this definition of lending would then have to exclude the lending by private units to intermediaries.

We now have a measure of aggregate lending by private domestic units. Foreign lending, of course, has been left out of the equation thus far. Our approach is to include foreign lending as a separate independent variable in the model. This allows us to specifically test the extent to which *domestic* saving constrains lending to domestic units. The inclusion of the foreign lending variable will then show how much this additional factor contributes to weakening the link between lending and saving.

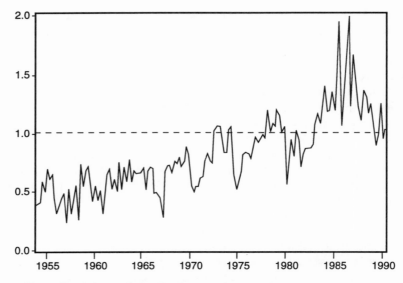

Fig. 2. Total domestic lending/gross private saving
Sources: U.S. National Income and Product Accounts; Flow of Funds
Accounts of Federal Reserve System

4. Empirical Findings

Our empirical investigation covers the period 1954.2–1990.3. The two endpoints are both identified as cyclical troughs by the National Bureau of Economic Research; our coverage thus ranges over seven full business cycles. We
begin with 1954.2 because it is the first trough covered in the Flow of Funds
Accounts quarterly data.

As is evident from figure 2, the relationship between lending and our
broadest measure of saving is not stable. Both, of course, are growing through
time, but as figure 2 shows most clearly, their rates of growth vary both
cyclically and over the trend.

The trend variation is most dramatic. To consider some rough indicators,
from the beginning of our period until the late 1960s, lending averaged 58
percent of saving, and the range of values for the lending/saving ratio (hereafter LSRATIO) was between 25–89 percent. Over the 1970s, lending rose, on
average, to 87 percent of saving—the mean value for the 1970s was nearly
equal to the peak figure through the late 1960s. The range of values over the
1970s was 51–121 percent, with lending exceeding saving for the first time in
1972.4.

From 1980.1 to the end of our period, lending exceeds saving on average—the mean value for the full period is 116 percent, and the range of values is 58–199 percent. That is, at the full-period peak in 1986.4, domestic lending was almost twice as much as private domestic saving. The ratio does fall sharply thereafter. However, even the lowest point after 1986.4 is still considerably above the peak levels of the early 1970s.

Our aim in what follows will be to employ more formal tools of analysis to explore this shifting relationship between lending and saving.

4.1 Cointegration

Cointegration tests measure whether long-term equilibrium relationships exist between variables. This is an important test for our purposes, since we are seeking to determine the extent to which lending flows are linked to, or, alternatively, independent of, prior saving flows.

Briefly, the logic of the test is as follows: two variables may be nonstationary—$I(1)$—but if a linear combination of them is $I(0)$, that is, stationary, the variables are said to be cointegrated. The linear combination of the variables can be expressed as:

$$U_i = Y_i - \alpha - \beta X_i,$$

which, of course, is a simple rearrangement of a bivariate regression equation. However, the rearrangement highlights that the disturbance term of the equation is a linear combination of Y and X. The test for cointegration thus becomes a test of stationarity for U_i. If U_i is $I(1)$, then X and Y will tend to drift apart without bound, and the relationship between them is out of equilibrium. If U_i is $I(0)$, any divergences in the time paths of X and Y will be limited; this suggests the presence of an equilibrium relationship between the two variables.[8] The specific test reported here is that developed by Engle and Granger (1987). With this procedure, one first runs what is called a cointegrating regression:

$$Y = \alpha + \beta X_t + U_t.$$

One then runs stationarity tests (Augmented Dickey Fuller, or ADF, tests) for the U_i term:

$$\Delta U_t = \beta_1 U_{t-1} + \Sigma \beta_i \, \Delta U_{t-i}.$$

---

8. Pindyck and Rubinfeld 1991 offers a clear introduction cointegration. An illuminating symposium was presented in the August 1986 issue of the *Oxford Bulletin of Economics and Statistics*, which was guest edited by David Hendry.

TABLE 1.   Cointegration Test of Real Private Domestic Lending with Real Private Saving (Variables Deflated by GNP Deflator) Quarterly Series, 1954.2–1990.3

Variable	Equation Specification	ADF t-Stat
Measures of Saving		
Gross Private	T,2	−3.18
Gross Business	T,1	−3.53
Net Business	C,0	−2.01
NIPA Personal	C,2	−2.18

*significant at 10%
**significant at 5%
***significant at 1%

The cointegrating regression will include an intercept and, if appropriate, a time trend variable. The test regression may include any number of lagged first differences. Thus, the "equation specification" column of table 1 reports whether a trend variable was used in the cointegrating regression, and the number of lagged first differences used in the test regression. Significance tests are based on MacKinnon critical values rather than standard t-tests[9].

Table 1 reports the results of cointegration tests for the real lending variable with each of the measures of real private saving. The findings are unambiguous: none of the measures of saving are cointegrated with lending at even a 10 percent level of significance. According to the cointegration test then, there is no long-run equilibrium relationship between lending and saving, at least over the period we are addressing.

Darnell and Evans (1991) have questioned whether such cointegration tests provide an adequate measure of long-run equilibrium relationships. They point out that cointegration cannot control for the stability of the long-run environment affecting both X and Y. Thus, with results such as those in Table 1, we cannot distinguish between two quite different situations—an unstable relationship between lending and saving in a stable overall environment, or a stable lending/saving relationship in an unstable environment.

This criticism is generally valid. Nevertheless, for our purposes, it is meaningful to know that lending and saving are not cointegrated, regardless of whether the source of their unstable relationship is the environment or a long-run disequilibrium between the variables. Further analysis will enable us to specify further the nature of this nonequilibrium relationship.

---

9. The standard t tables are inappropriate here because the Y variable would be nonstationary under the null hypothesis. MacKinnon, following Dickey and Fuller, provided a set of critical values appropriate for stationarity and cointegration tests (see Pindyck and Rubinfeld 1991; Hall, Johnston, and Lilien 1990).

4.2 Causality and Regression Tests

The Granger causality test is a measure of the sequential priority between two variables, and it indicates "causality" only in the sense that changes in one variable consistently precede those of the other variable. It is well established that sequential priority does not demonstrate causality in any fuller substantive sense; however, such a test of sequential priority is appropriate for our purposes. We want to know precisely whether changes in saving precede those of lending, and what the implications are should this be the case.

Because the cointegration tests show no equilibrium relationship between lending and saving, we would not expect strong Granger-causal links to exist between them. Still, the Granger tests will provide greater detail about the nature of their relationship.

We use first differences of our real lending and saving variables, ΔL and ΔS, in these tests to ensure their stationarity. We then perform the Granger tests in two steps. For the first step, we regress ΔL against lagged values of ΔL and ΔS:

$$\Delta L = \Sigma \alpha_i \Delta L_{t-i} + \Sigma \beta_i \Delta S_{t-i} + \epsilon_t$$

which is the unrestricted regression.

We then perform a restricted regression, ΔL against only lagged values of itself:

$$\Delta L = \Sigma \alpha_i \Delta L_{t-i} + \epsilon_t.$$

We then use the sum of squared residuals from each regression to calculate an F statistic, testing whether the group of coefficients $\Delta S_{t-1}, \Delta S_{t-2}. \ . \ . \ \Delta S_{t-p}$ is significantly different from zero. If it is, we can reject the hypothesis that changes in saving do not Granger-cause changes in lending.

As a second step, we test whether changes in lending do not Granger-cause changes in saving, by performing the same two regressions but switching the placements of the ΔL and ΔS variables in the two equations. To conclude that saving Granger-causes lending, we must both reject the "saving does not cause lending" hypothesis and accept that "lending does not cause saving."

The number of lags for such tests is arbitrary, so we perform the tests using lag structures of four, eight, and twelve quarters. Confidence in the results obviously increases if the results are robust over the various lag structures.

The results from the Granger tests are presented in table 2. As we can see, the reported F-tests show that, with each of the measures of saving, Granger causality does flow from saving to lending. But we also see that the results become less robust as we increase the number of lags, suggesting that additional past data about saving actually reduces our understanding of current lending patterns. Nevertheless, the overall results are sufficiently strong as to conclude that changes in saving flows do Granger-cause changes in lending.

Table 3 presents the full results for each four-quarter lagged unrestricted equation with lending as the dependent variable. It also presents results for equations

$$\Delta L_t = \alpha_i + \beta_1 \Delta S_t + \Sigma \beta_i \Delta S_{t-i} + \epsilon_t$$

that is, i.e., those excluding the lagged ΔL variables and including contemporaneous ΔS on the right-hand side. This enables us to obtain greater detail as to the Granger-causal relationship.

Depending on the measure of saving, we first see that either the first or second quarter lagged values are exerting the primary positive influence on lending, and that later lagged values contribute much less explanatory power. This is consistent with the broader finding that F-statistics declined in the

TABLE 2. Granger Causality Tests between Changes in Real Private Domestic Lending and Real Saving (Deflation through GNP Deflator) Quarterly Series, 1954.2–1990.3

Measures of Saving	Saving Causes Lending F-Stat	Lending Causes Saving F-Stat
Gross Private		
4 Lags	5.35***	2.06*
8 Lags	2.73***	1.13
12 Lags	2.23**	1.00
Gross Business		
4 Lags	5.85***	0.65
8 Lags	4.07***	0.62
12 Lags	2.63***	1.20
Net Business		
4 Lags	7.05***	0.96
8 Lags	4.59***	0.63
12 Lags	3.15***	0.75
NIPA Personal		
4 Lags	3.78***	1.17
8 Lags	2.68***	1.59
12 Lags	1.89**	1.28

*Significant at 10%
**Significant at 5%
***Significant at 1%

Granger tests as the number of lags increased. In addition, contemporaneous values of ΔS exert no significant influence on ΔL. Finally, the cumulative independent explanatory power of the ΔS variables is relatively low. Thus, $\bar{R}^2$ values range between 27 and 35 percent in the unrestricted equations but only between 3 and 15 percent in the equations using ΔS variables only. Not surprisingly, moreover, all of the equations that exclude lagged ΔL values on the right-hand side suffer from significant first-order serial correlation.

From this we can conclude that though concurrent saving does not exert any significant influence on lending, past saving flows are significant. However, their degree of explanatory power is relatively low. This result is consistent with the view we developed in section 2: prior saving flows do contribute positively to lending flows. But the channel of influence is through the more immediate determinants of lending—central bank policy and the liquidity preferences of businesses and individuals. The effects are therefore mediated by additional, and sometimes counteracting, influences. The impact of saving flows on lending is therefore relatively weak.

TABLE 3. Regression Equations
Dependent Variable Is Change in Real Private Domestic Lending
(t-statistics in parentheses)

Independent Variables, Summary Statistics	Gross Private Saving		Gross Business Saving		Net Business Saving		NIPA Personal Savings	
$\Delta L(-1)$	−0.50	—	−.60	—	−0.61	—	−0.45	—
	(−5.89)		(−7.19)		(−7.33)		(−5.31)	
$\Delta L(-2)$	−0.28	—	−0.42	—	−0.44	—	−0.22	—
	(−2.98)		(−4.44)		(−4.64)		(−2.31)	
$\Delta L(-3)$	−0.15	—	−0.24	—	−0.25	—	−0.11	—
	(−1.65)		(−2.49)		(−2.58)		(−1.17)	
$\Delta L(-4)$	0.08	—	0.05	—	0.05	—	0.09	—
	(0.94)		(0.66)		(0.60)		(1.03)	
ΔS	—	−0.46	—	−0.29	—	−0.07	—	−0.62
		(−1.15)		(−0.31)		(−0.08)		(−1.40)
$\Delta S(-1)$	0.31	0.22	2.36	2.28	3.01	2.72	−0.31	−0.35
	(0.85)	(0.52)	(3.08)	(2.50)	(3.93)	(2.96)	(−0.75)	(−0.73)
$\Delta S(-2)$	1.71	1.63	1.64	0.23	1.34	−0.53	1.24	1.45
	(4.56)	(3.91)	(2.07)	(0.26)	(1.64)	(−0.58)	(2.84)	(3.02)
$\Delta S(-3)$	0.20	−0.57	1.02	0.08	0.82	0.03	−0.32	−0.83
	(0.49)	(−1.39)	(1.27)	(0.09)	(1.00)	(0.03)	(−0.72)	(−1.76)
$\Delta S(-4)$	0.21	−0.06	1.87	1.08	1.72	1.16	−0.38	−0.45
	(0.54)	(−0.14)	(2.31)	(1.15)	(2.14)	(1.24)	(−0.87)	(−1.00)
$\bar{R}^2$	.30	.15	.35	.03	.36	0.04	.27	.13
D-W	1.97	2.78	2.03	2.83	2.02	2.83	2.00	2.79

4.3 Lending, Saving, and Interest Rates

The issue we explore here is the extent to which interest rates respond to deviations in the flows of lending and saving. It is not controversial to assume that, all else equal, interest rates should rise when lending increases relative to saving. The more interesting question is, *how much* will interest rates rise for a given increase in the lending/saving ratio, and what factors may counteract such interest rate pressure? Along similar lines, Kaldor and Asimakopulos argued that long-term rates will normally rise relative to short rates when an increase in investment financing is not preceded by an increase in saving flows. We consider that issue as well.

We ran regressions using two dependent variables, changes in the average level of interest rates (hereafter ΔI) and changes in the yield curve ($\Delta YIELD$ hereafter). The average interest rates were defined as the average of the rate on three month U.S. Treasury bills and the composite rate on Treasury notes of over 10 years. The yield curve is the 3-month bill rate divided by the composite note rate. ΔI is then the first difference of the average rate and $\Delta YIELD$ is the first difference of the yield curve.

The basic explanatory variable is the lending/saving ratio, LSRATIO. We generated a series of such ratios, using each of the measures of saving as a denominator. We also performed tests using a series of lagged values of the LSRATIO. We constructed these lag structures after observing the results from the Granger tests that the primary influence of saving on lending comes after a lag of one or two quarters. The LSRATIOs with lags did generate significant results. But because these results were almost identical to those obtained with unlagged LSRATIOs, we report here the findings with unlagged LSRATIOs only.

In addition to the LSRATIO, we included five control variables, which we expect would exert independent influence on ΔI and $\Delta YIELD$ in equations with LSRATIO.

The first is the rate of change in real GNP, which aims to capture the role of broad business cycle influences on interest rate levels and the yield curve. In general, interest rate levels will vary directly with the business cycle. This is both because the demand for credit will itself peak near business cycle peaks and because the Federal Reserve will tend to tighten credit at business cycle peaks to prevent accelerating inflation.

Yield curve fluctuations should also be influenced by the business cycle. Near cyclical peaks, short-term rates will rise relative to long rates, flattening the yield curve. This is due to expectations that the interest rate level is high relative to lower points in the cycle. Lenders will therefore seek to lock into high long-term yields and will require a premium to lend short. At the same time, borrowers will want to avoid long-term commitments and will pay a premium to borrow short.

These business cycle forces could even explain much of the deviation between lending and saving—that is, lending exceeds saving as part of the general financial overreach that occurs during business cycle upturns. It will therefore be important to include the cycle control variable to test the extent of influence exerted by the LSRATIO independent of general business cycle fluctuations.

The second control variable is the inflation rate, measured as changes in the GNP deflator. We include the inflation rate as an independent variable rather than simply deflating interest rates themselves to obtain a measure of real rates, since we did not want to prejudge whether the LSRATIO should affect real or nominal rates.

The third control variable is the amount of foreign lending in U.S. credit markets, measured as the ratio of foreign to total loans. As is well known, the U.S. financial market has become increasingly integrated since the development of the Eurodollar market in the late 1960s. Thus, the average proportion of foreign lending to U.S. borrowers was 1.5 percent between 1954.2–69.4, rose to 5.7 percent over the 1970s, then increased again between 1980.1–90.3 to 6.4 percent.

The fourth and fifth control variables are dummy variables, attempting to measure the broad effects of structural change in financial markets on the saving, lending, and interest rate relationship. We saw earlier that the lending/saving ratio has itself undergone significant changes over our period, with the values for the ratio shifting upward first over the 1970s, then again in the 1980s. Internationalization of the markets is one element of structural change, and perhaps this factor will be captured through the dummy variables as well as the foreign lending ratio itself. But more generally, as noted earlier (see section 2 and note 6), we have observed a dramatic increase in financial innovation since the late 1960s, and a substantial deregulation of the markets beginning with the 1980 Monetary Decontrol Act, which provided further opportunities for innovation.[10]

We have included two dummy variables, one through 1970.1–1979.4 and the other over 1980.1–1990.3. These are convenient decade breakpoints, but this is not the primary reason for setting the dummies over these periods. More important, we observe substantial increases in standard errors in the

---

10. We also considered controlling for structural change through piece-wise spline functions (see, for example, Suits, Mason, and Chan 1978). The problem with such an approach is that it attempts to capture the effects of structural change within a single variable—LSRATIO in this case. We are arguing that the effects of structural change in the financial market have emerged from a range of sources and reverberated broadly throughout the market. We therefore concluded that the dummy variable technique, through which we force an intercept shift without specifying any variable that either causes or best reflects that shift, was more appropriate for our purposes. This choice of technique is also consistent with our interpretation of the cointegration results that the source of disequilibrium between lending and savings is the broad structural environment rather than the specific lending/savings relationship.

residuals of bivariate regressions with ΔI and the LSRATIO beginning in the 1970s, and again in the 1980s. Using the gross private saving measure of LSRATIO, for example, 1970.4–1971.1 is the first period in which residuals exceed one standard error for two successive quarters. Then, 1980.2 and 1980.4 are the first quarters in which residuals exceed two standard errors. To evaluate these breakpoints more formally, we conducted breakpoint Chow tests for these two data points from the residuals for the bivariate regression with ΔI and the gross saving LSRATIO. This generated an F statistic exceeding the one percent critical value, confirming these as appropriate breakpoints for measuring structural change.[11]

Interest Rate Levels
To begin with, the results vary sharply according to the measure of saving one uses. Not surprisingly, the results for gross business saving most closely resemble those for aggregate private saving, since gross business saving is the largest component of the aggregate, and the one whose movements are most strongly correlated with the aggregate measure.

With the aggregate measure and gross business saving in the denominator of LSRATIO, the most basic result we obtain is the expected one—that increases in lending relative to saving exert upward pressure on interest rates. Is also clear, however, that one has to account for structural change to get a meaningful measure of the significance of this effect.

In table 4, we see that LSRATIO is positive but insignificant in regressions 1–4. Among the control variables, ΔGNP exerts a highly significant influence on interest rate levels, and the growth of foreign lending also has a significant negative, but weak, influence. For our purposes, the key observation is that without allowing for structural change through including the dummy variables, the explanatory power of LSRATIO is negligible. Note also that the Durbin-Watson statistics for regressions 1–4 demonstrate either positive serial correlation or are within the indeterminant region, but for regression 5, the 1.97 D-W enables us to reject the possiblity of serial correlation.

The picture changes, however, when we account for structural change. Regression 5 reports the results using the two dummy variables along with the three other control variables and LSRATIO on the right-hand side of the equation. This result is similar to specifications that did not include all three control variables.

In regression 5, we see that both dummy variables are highly significant and carry negative signs. This suggests that the two phases of structural

---

11. The test consisted of measuring whether residuals from the two dummy variable subsample periods in the bivariate ΔI/LSRATIO regression were significantly different from the residuals for the full period. The high F statistic means that the subsample residuals were significantly different from those for the full period.

**TABLE 4. Effects of Lending/Saving Ratio on Interest Rate Levels
Dependent Variable is Change in Level of Average Interest Rates
(t-statistics in parentheses)
(1954.2–1990.3)**

Independent Variables, Summary Statistics	Gross Private Saving				
	(1)	(2)	(3)	(4)	(5)
Constant	−0.17	−0.29	−0.27	−0.12	−0.79
	(−1.08)	(−1.94)	(1.62)	(−0.79)	(−4.21)
LS Ratio	0.26	0.20	0.19	0.31	0.71
	(1.46)	(1.21)	(1.08)	(1.77)	(2.87)
ΔGNP	—	0.22	—	—	0.24
		(4.13)			(4.43)
Inflation	—	—	0.03	—	0.09
			(1.63)		(3.82)
Foreign Funds	—	—	—	−2.20	−0.29
				(−2.16)	(−0.27)
Dummy 70	—	—	—	—	−0.56
					(−2.88)
Dummy 80	—	—	—	—	−0.69
					(−3.18)
$\bar{R}^2$	0.01	0.11	0.02	0.03	0.22
D-W	1.56	1.66	1.62	1.60	1.94

change—which we have associated with the initial burst of financial innovation in the 1970s and the second wave, encouraged by deregulation, in the 1980s—are both distinguishable as distinct influences on interest rate levels. When we account for structural change in this way, the LSRATIO is shown as a significant positive influence on interest rate levels. A 1 percent increase in LSRATIO will raise interest rates about 7/10 of a percentage point (70 basis points); however, the effects of structural change will more than counteract the upward interest rate pressure from a rising LSRATIO.

Both dummy variables push interest rates downward by about 0.6 of a percentage point. The net impact of two decades of structural change is thus to counteract nearly twice over the effects of the rise of the LSRATIO.[12] These results are consistent with the Minskian argument that the effect of structural change in financial markets is to allow increases in the provision of credit without additional increases in interest rates.

---

12. It is also interesting that the increasing degree of risk in financial markets in the 1980s—as measured, say, by the sharply increasing rates of business and bank failures—does not appear to contribute to the observed rising level of interest rates, as one might anticipate (see Pollin and Dymski, this volume). Yet it is also likely that a single dummy variable for the 1980s will not satisfactorily capture all major elements of structural change for one period.

Considering the other control variables, both ΔGNP and inflation are shown to exert a highly significant influence on interest rates. Business cycle forces, which would include Federal Reserve policy over the course of the cycle, are thus shown to clearly affect interest rate movements in predictable ways. However, these more familiar explanations for interest rate movements do not negate the independent influence of both the LSRATIO and the effects of structural change.

Finally, we see from the $\bar{R}^2$ in regression 5 that this specification explains only 22 percent of the total variation in the average interest rate. A more thorough explanation for interest rate behavior is obviously needed. Still, for our purposes, the results are sufficiently strong to allow three important conclusions: increases in the lending/saving ratio will exert significant upward pressure on interest rates; the extent of such pressures can be properly evaluated only within a context of structural change in financial markets; and structural changes will tend to exert a countervailing downward influence on interest rates, thereby allowing the lending/saving ratio to increase without also forcing interest rate levels to rise commensurately.

Table 5 reports tests in which gross business rather than gross private saving is used in the denominator of the LSRATIO. We see from regressions 6

TABLE 5.   Effects of Lending/Saving Ratio on Interest Rate Levels
Dependent Variable Is Change in Level of Average Interest Rates
(t-statistics in parentheses)
(1954.2–1990.3)

Independent Variables, Summary Statistics	Gross Business Saving	
	(6)	(7)
Constant	−0.25	−0.87
	(−1.44)	(−4.30)
LS Ratio	0.26	0.64
	(1.79)	(3.03)
ΔGNP	—	0.24
		(4.45)
Inflation	—	0.09
		(3.54)
Foreign Funds	—	0.09
		(−0.09)
Dummy 70	—	−0.63
		(−3.09)
Dummy 80	—	−0.70
		(−3.30)
$\bar{R}^2$	0.02	0.23
D-W	1.57	1.93

and 7 that the results are essentially the same as those for the bivariate and full multivariate tests (regressions 1 and 5) with gross private saving.

Regressions 8–11 in table 6 present results when net business and NIPA personal saving respectively are included as the denominator of the LSRATIO. The results with net business saving (8–9) suggest that LSRATIO has no significant influence on the interest rate level, even in a model controlling for both cyclical and structural change. At least in this situation, financial markets are apparently not making a distinction between depreciation allowances and other forms of business saving.

With personal saving (10–11), we see LSRATIO emerging as a negative, though insignificant, influence on interest rates. This suggests that personal saving, a relatively small component of aggregate saving, exerts little influence on interest rates independent of the larger sources of funds.

Yield Curve Regressions

The results of yield curve regressions are presented in table 7. They resemble the findings for interest rate levels in several ways. First, the results with gross private saving and business saving are quite similar to each other, whereas those with net business saving and NIPA personal saving are divergent.

TABLE 6. Effects of Lending/Saving Ratio on Interest Rate Levels Dependent Variable Is Change in Average Level of Interest Rates (t-statistics in parentheses) (1954.2–1990.3)

Independent Variables, Summary Statistics	Net Business Saving		NIPA Personal Saving	
	(8)	(9)	(10)	(11)
Constant	0.10	−0.43	0.19	−0.13
	(1.08)	(−3.12)	(1.55)	(−0.45)
LS Ratio	−0.01	0.01	−0.37	−0.49
	(−.78)	(0.85)	(−1.35)	(−1.43)
ΔGNP	—	0.28	—	0.25
		(5.15)		(4.53)
Inflation	—	0.09	—	0.09
		(3.49)		(3.51)
Foreign Funds	—	−0.85	—	−0.74
		(−0.79)		(−0.70)
Dummy 70	—	−0.35	—	−0.38
		(−1.90)		(−2.05)
Dummy 80	—	−0.37	—	−0.39
		(−1.62)		(−2.08)
$\bar{R}^2$	0.00	0.18	0.01	0.19
D-W	1.63	1.91	1.60	1.95

TABLE 7. Effects of Lending/Savings Ratio on Yield Curve. Dependent Variable Is Change in Yield Curve (t-statistics in parentheses) (1954.2–1990.3)

Independent Variables, Summary Statistics	Gross Private Savings		Gross Business Savings		Net Business Savings		NIPA Personal Savings	
	(12)	(13)	(14)	(15)	(16)	(17)	(18)	(19)
Constant	-0.02	-0.07	-0.02	-0.08	0.007	-0.04	0.03	0.03
	(-1.02)	(-2.37)	(-1.21)	(-3.44)	(0.72)	(-2.35)	(1.96)	(1.34)
LS Ratio	0.02	0.07	0.02	0.06	-0.001	0.002	-0.06	-0.10
	(1.26)	(2.38)	(1.43)	(2.77)	(-0.58)	(1.37)	(-1.99)	(-2.56)
ΔGNP	—	0.02	—	0.02	—	0.03	—	0.02
		(3.82)		(3.79)		(4.61)		(3.63)
Inflation	—	0.004	—	0.003	—	0.003	—	0.003
		(1.47)		(1.22)		(1.21)		(1.20)
Foreign Funds	—	0.18	—	0.20	—	0.14	—	0.16
		(1.50)		(1.71)		(1.18)		(1.42)
Dummy 70	—	-0.04	—	-0.05	—	-0.03	—	-0.03
		(-1.99)		(-2.32)		(-1.36)		(-1.68)
Dummy 80	—	-0.06	—	-0.07	—	-0.04	—	-0.05
		(-2.53)		(-2.83)		(-1.74)		(-2.50)
$\bar{R}^2$	0.01	0.13	0.01	0.14	0.00	0.10	0.02	0.13
D-W	1.60	1.89	1.61	1.90	1.60	1.81	1.64	1.90

With the aggregate saving measure and gross business saving, we also see that the LSRATIO exerts upward pressure on the yield curve. But here again, we must consider the effects of LSRATIO within a framework of structural change for this to be clear. Thus in regression 12, a bivariate test, LSRATIO has a positive but insignificant impact on the short/long ratio—raising short relative to long rates. When we include the two dummy variables in regression 13 along with the other three control variables, we see that LSRATIO is still positive, but now significant. And once again, the effect of structural change is to counteract the influence of variation in the LSRATIO. That is, we can interpret the negative signs for the two dummy variables in regression 13 as meaning that structural change will tend to counteract the relative increase in short-term rates associated with the rising LSRATIO.

As before, ΔGNP is the most influential additional control variable, indeed the only significant one in the yield curve regressions. This confirms the influence of cyclical factors—the desire of lenders to lock into long-term commitments at cyclical peaks and of borrowers to pay premia for short-term loans, and for the reverse patterns to hold during cyclical troughs. Once again, however, regression 13 suggests that the tendency of a rising LSRATIO to raise short rates disproportionately, and the tendency of structural change to counteract this effect are independent of cyclical influences. Still, the force of all these effects appears relatively weak, as the $\bar{R}^2$ for regression 13 is only 13 percent.

In short, there is no evidence here to support the Asimakopulos-Kaldor contention that long-term rates will rise relative to short rates when lending increases prior to increases in saving flows. One could rather interpret these findings as broadly, if weakly, consistent with the Minskian approach. The process Minsky describes is a rising demand for innovative methods, such as liability management, to increase the supply of credit. Such processes initially call for increased demand for short-term funds, since intermediaries will borrow short-term funds among themselves to meet the increased credit demand.

The results with net business saving in the denominator of the LSRATIO (regressions 16–17) are similar to those with interest rate tests. They suggest that LSRATIO has no significant influence on the yield curve, even in a model controlling for both cyclical and structural change.

When personal saving is the denominator of LSRATIO, we observe, as with the interest rate level tests, that the signs for LSRATIO are negative. Here however, the coefficients are also significant. One may want to interpret these findings as providing weak support for the Kaldor-Asimakopulos position. Before doing so however, it would be necessary to explain how personal saving affects the yield curve in a fashion opposite to that of business saving, a task beyond the aims of this paper.

5. Conclusions

What is the relationship between saving flows, lending flows, and interest rates? The first finding of this study is that the answer to this question depends substantially on how one defines saving.

We argued in section 3 that, for our purposes, gross private saving—that is, NIPA private saving—is the most appropriate saving measure, and we therefore focused on this measure in the formal testing reported in section 4. But we also performed tests and reported results with other saving measures. One finding that emerged was that the results generated using gross business saving were similar to those using aggregate private saving, whereas tests with gross personal saving produced divergent results. This is not surprising, given that business saving is by far the larger component of the aggregate saving measure. But it nevertheless raises some questions about personal saving: why are discussions about saving policy focused so heavily on this category? If personal saving carries more importance than its relative magnitude would suggest, what are the channels through which these effects operate?

Four basic conclusions emerged from the econometric tests themselves:

1. Saving and lending are not cointegrated. This result was robust across the saving measures. We can interpret this to mean that the relationship between saving and lending is capable of varying without bound, which is the specific meaning of a "long-run disequilibrium" relationship derived from the Engel-Granger cointegration test. As Darnell and Evans make clear, we cannot determine from the cointegration test whether this relationship is unbounded because of the relationship between the variables themselves, or because the broader environment is unstable. Our overall findings suggest, that changes in the broad environment have been instrumental in affecting the lending/saving relationship.

2. Even though the relationship between saving and lending is not cointegrated, the evidence shows that changes in saving flows do Granger-cause subsequent changes in lending flows. More precisely, though concurrent saving will not affect lending, increases in saving will contribute to lending growth after a lag of one or two quarters. The impact of this effect, however, was shown to be weak. Still, these results were robust across the saving measures.

The weakness of this influence of prior saving on lending helps to explain how there can be statistically significant Granger causality flowing from saving to lending even though the two variables are not cointegrated. In addition, the fact that Granger causality but not cointegration exists between the variables lends further support to the notion that the source of disequilibrium between lending and saving is the broader economic environment more than the relationship between the two variables. It would be difficult to explain how any degree of Granger causality could exist between saving and lending if there were no long-term relationship between them.

Finally, the weak causality finding is consistent with the view that saving can influence lending, but only through indirect channels: by influencing central bank policy, the liquidity preferences of intermediaries and private wealth holders, or pressures for financial innovations that shift the relationship between saving and the provision of credit.

3. Deviations of lending from saving flows will affect interest rates in a positive direction, as theory would anticipate. But this effect has to be observed within a framework that takes account of structural change. This is the interpretation we place on the regression results showing a high degree of significance for dummy variables whose purpose is to capture the innovative and deregulatory thrusts in financial markets over the 1970s and 1980s. Once we allow for the effects of these structural changes, we then see that increases in lending relative to saving will exert upward pressure on interest rates on a nearly one-for-one basis. At the same time, we see that structural change can almost fully offset upward interest rate pressure. This is one way in which we clearly observe how a changing environment can allow for a potentially unbounded growth of lending relative to saving.

4. The interest rate tests also suggest that short-term rates rather than long rates will tend to rise more quickly when lending growth exceeds that of saving. We interpret this as resulting from the initial activation of the market for short-term funds among intermediaries that accompany any growth in lending that is not matched—either through central bank policy or increased saving flows—by an equivalent increase in the markets' cash reserves. In other words, an initial increase in velocity should tend to flatten the yield curve. However, the explanatory power of the regressions generating this result was quite low, even after accounting for the effects of structural change through the dummies. Clearly, other factors have a greater effect on the final slope of yield curves.

As mentioned at the outset, one must be circumspect in drawing broad implications from these findings because the data are for the U.S. economy only. Thus, one obvious implication is that additional insights will be gained through conducting similar studies with data from other countries.

Nevertheless, we can tentatively attempt to draw out some broader theoretical points. A first important implication is support for the view that lending and saving are discrete and only weakly related activities. James Earley has expressed this view aptly: "We should recognize that in a fundamental sense the process of saving takes place in a different *terrain* from the process of lending and borrowing. . . . It would not be correct to say that saving and lending have no connections. It is simply that the connections are very loose" (1983, p.9; see also Earley, Parsons and Thompson, 1976).

The "loose connections" we observe between saving and lending are, in turn, supportive of Keynes's "most fundamental conclusion in this field": that it is the relations of "finance"—the decisions of central banks, private intermediaries, and the wealth-holding public—not the flow of saving, that can "congest" the investment market. This is not to say that saving flows are irrelevant to the determination of lending capacity; Keynesians and Keynes himself have overstated their case when they imply as much. The point is that institutional relationships within the financial market—the role of the central banks and private intermediaries in particular—are much more important than saving for determining how much lending may occur at any given time. Moreover, as most disputants in this field will agree, any liquidity shortages associated with the initial thrust of lending will recede in importance once the multiplier process has begun.

The general approach of Hyman Minsky's work on money supply endogeneity is also supported here. Indeed, one measure of that work's power is that it does not specifically address the relationship between lending and saving, but it nevertheless illuminates that debate. Unlike Keynes in *The General Theory*, Minsky is concerned to integrate the role of financial innovation into the very foundations of monetary theory. The results here suggests that Minsky's concerns are warranted. And once that basic insight is recognized, the weaknesses of mainstream monetary analysis appear glaring.

The findings here also carry more direct policy implications. Our results stand as a challenge to those who would argue that increases in saving flows are a basic precondition to raising fixed investment and productivity. Which saving rate needs to be raised? What effect will such an increase have on the provision of credit? A case needs to be made for "tight connections" between lending, saving, and interest rates before a persuasive analytic argument can be mounted for such a policy approach.

An alternative policy path is also implied by these findings. That is, to encourage the financing of productive investment, we need to better understand the major institutional relationships within financial markets. If the financing of productive activity is deficient, this is not because the flow of saving is too low. It is rather that financial institutions are inadequate to the tasks at hand.

REFERENCES

Asimakopulos, A. (1983) "Kalecki and Keynes on Finance,Investment, and Saving," *Cambridge Journal of Economics*, 7, 221–33.
——— (1985) "Finance, Saving and Investment in Keynes's Economics: A Comment," *Cambridge Journal of Economics*, 9, 405–7.

———— (1986a) "Finance, Investment and Saving: A Reply to Terzi," *Cambridge Journal of Economics*, 10, 77–80.

———— (1986b) "Richardson on Asimakopulos on Finance: A Reply," *Cambridge Journal of Economics*, 10, 199–201.

———— (1986c) "Finance, Liquidity, Saving and Investment," *Journal of Post Keynesian Economics*, 9, 79–90.

Bridel, Pascal (1987a) *Cambridge Monetary Thought: Development of Saving-Investment Analysis from Marshall to Keynes*, New York: St. Martin's Press.

———— (1987b) "Saving Equals Investment," in Eatwell, J., Milgate, M., and Newman, P. (eds.) *The New Palgrave: A Dictionary of Economics*, New York: Stockton Press.

Darnell, Adrian C., and J. Lynne Evans (1991) *The Limits of Econometrics*, Hants, U.K.: Edward Elgar Publishing Limited.

De Cecco, Marcello (1987) *Changing Money: Financial Innovation in Developed Countries*, New York: Basil Blackwell.

Earley, James S. (1983) "The Relations between Saving and the Supply of Loan Funds," in *Essays on the Credit Approach to Macro-Finance* Working Paper #1, Department of Economics, University of California, Riverside.

———— (1985) "Money, Credit, and Financial Intermediation: The Need for a New 'New View,'" manuscript, Department of Economics, University of California, Riverside.

Earley, James S., R. J. Parsons and Fred A. Thompson. (1976). *Money, Credit, and Expenditure: A Sources and Uses of Funds Approach*. New York: New York University School of Business Administration, Center for the Study of Financial Institutions.

Engle, Robert F. and C. W. J. Granger (1987) "Cointegration and Error Correction: Representation, Estimation and Testing," *Econometrica*, 55, 251–76.

Fazzari, Steven, Glenn Hubbard, and Bruce Petersen (1988) "Financing Constraints and Corporate Investment," *Brookings Papers on Economic Activity*, 1, 141–95.

Hall, Robert E., Jack Johnston, and David M. Lilien (1990) *MicroTSP User's Manual*, Irvine, CA: Quantitative Micro Software.

Harrington, R. (1987) *Asset and Liability Management by Banks*, Paris: OECD.

Hendry, David (ed) (1986) *Econometric Modelling with Cointegrated Variables*, a special issue of *Oxford Bulletin of Economics and Statistics*, 48, (3).

Kalecki, Michal (1971) *Selected Essays on the Dynamics of the Capitalist Economy*, London: Cambridge University Press.

Kaldor, Nicholas (1960) "Speculation and Economic Stability," (1939) in *Essays on Economic Stability and Growth*, London: Gerald Duckworth & Co. Ltd., 17–58.

Keynes, John Maynard (1973), "The 'Ex Ante' Theory of the Rate of Interest," (1938), in *The Collected Writings of John Maynard Keynes*, vol 14, London: Macmillan.

Kregal, J. A. (1986) "A Note on Finance, Liquidity, Saving and Investment," *Journal of Post Keynesian Economics*, 9, 91–100.

Messori, Marcello (1991) "Financing in Kalecki's Theory," *Cambridge Journal of Economics*, 15, 301–13.

Minsky, Hyman P. (1982) "Central Banking and Money Market Changes" (1957), in

Can "It" Happen Again? Essays on Instability and Finance, Armonk, NY: M.E. Sharpe, 162–78.

Mott, Tracy (1985) "Towards a Post-Keynesian Theory of Liquidity Preference," *Journal of Post Keynesian Economics*, Winter, pp. 222–32.

Pindyck, Robert S., and Daniel L. Rubinfeld (1991) *Econometric Models & Economic Forecasts*, third edition, New York: McGraw-Hill.

Pollin, Robert (1991) "Two Theories of Money Supply Endogeneity," *Journal of Post Keynesian Economics*, 13, 366–96.

Pollin, Robert and Craig Justice (1992) "Saving, Finance and Interest Rates," Working Paper 92–8, Department of Economics, University of California Riverside.

Pollin, Robert and Gary Dymski (1993) "The Costs and Benefits of Financial Fragility: Big Government Capitalism and the Minsky Paradox," this volume.

Richardson, David R. (1986) "Asimakopulos on Kalecki and Keynes on Finance, Investment and Saving," *Cambridge Journal of Economics*, 10, 191–98.

Robinson, Joan (1962) *Essays in the Theory of Economic Growth*, London: Macmillan.

Skott, Peter (1988) "Finance, Saving and Accumulation," *Cambridge Journal of Economics*, 12, 339–54.

Snippe, J. (1985) "Finance, Saving and Investment in Keynes's Economics," *Cambridge Journal of Economics*, 9, 257–69.

——— (1986) "Finance, Saving and Investment in Keynes's Economics: A Reply," *Cambridge Journal of Economics*, 10, 373–78.

Suits, Daniel B., Andrew Mason, and Louis Chan (1978) "Spline Functions Fitted by Standard Regression Methods," *Review of Economics and Statistics*, 60, 132–39.

Summers, Lawrence H. (1986) "Issues in National Saving Policy," in Adams, G. F., and Wachter, S. M. (eds.) *Saving and Capital Formation*, Lexington, MA: Lexington Books, 65–88.

Terzi, Andrea (1986) "Finance, Investment and Saving: A Comment on Asimakopulos," *Cambridge Journal of Economics*, 10, 77–80.

Part IV
Exploring Analytic Interconnections

CHAPTER 11

Minsky, Keynes and Sraffa: Investment and the Long Period

*Edward Nell**

For more than a decade Hyman Minsky played a central role in the summer meetings in Trieste, calling attention to financial institutions in the business cycle and infusing macroeconomics with the spirit of Keynes. Yet he found himself at odds with those who drew on Sraffa's work for inspiration in reconstructing economic theory, and like Tom Asimakopulos and Paul Davidson, he could never support the project of developing a Keynesian theory purged of marginalism and resting on modern classical foundations.

Minsky's own theory of investment, however, suggests that the classics were correct to emphasize the competitive pressure to pull rates of return together. Further, when a surprising gap in his approach is filled, we can see how a post-Keynesian approach can determine a set of prices compatible with the classical equations. This provides an interpretation of those equations, but it requires questioning "convergence to long-period positions" (LPPs), at least for advanced economies.

1. Rejecting the Classical Revival

Post-Keynesians commonly cite three reasons for rejecting the classical revival as a foundation for Keynesian thinking. First, Sraffa and the modern classicals determine prices and the rate of profits in long-period equilibrium, independently of demand. Although this leaves room, in a mechanical sense, for a Keynesian analysis to determine outputs, the Keynesian world is dynamic, full of uncertainty and speculation, with no room for any sort of long-period equilibrium. The assumptions and objectives of the two approaches are inconsistent (Asimakopulos, in Bharadwaj and Schefold 1989).

Second, the uniform rate of return on capital is central to the classical revival. This implies a high degree of competition. But in the post-Keynesian

*Thanks to Geoff Harcourt, Heinz Kurz, Hy Minsky, and the editors of this volume for helpful comments.

picture of the world, firms will set prices at levels that will establish a markup which will justify their present or desired financial obligations. This implies a high degree of market power, apparently ruling out uniformity of the rate of return on capital. Moreover, financial institutions also possess market power and actively promote projects that will enhance such power and improve their earnings. Activist finance will increase the likelihood of multiple rates of return.

Neither of these points is regarded as decisive by proponents of rebuilding Keynes on neo-Ricardian foundations. The "long period" can be defined in ways that allow for the effects of uncertainty, and uniformity is not required in the rate of profit, so long as the differentials are stable.[1] But a third argument is more troublesome.[2]

This argument holds that, in reality, there is no such thing as the "long run;" it is merely a logical constuct. Yet it is not even a useful one; in actual fact, prices, output, employment, and investment will be determined in the short run, reflecting the influence of current conditions. This short run will

---

1. The classical long period requires only settled conditions in regard to "benchmark" or normal prices. Minsky, like other post-Keynesians, needs to take such prices as given, as a basis for forming the aggregates, whose quantitative relationships are the subject of the theory of aggregate demand. As for the nonuniform rate of profit, it is easy to see that if the differentials are stable, there is no formal difference between the following two cases: First consider

$$Ap(1 + r) + lw = p$$

where A is the input-output matrix, p the price vector, l is labor and w the real wage, and r the uniform rate of profit.

This can be converted to

$$A*p(1 + r_i) + lw = p$$

where the subscript indicates the differentiated profit rate for each particular industry. Given that $\times$ is a vector of percentage deviations from the uniform rate of profit and i is the unit vector, then if

$$x\ i(1 + r) = 1 + r_i$$

it will follow that $A* = Ax\ i$

For any differentiated profit rate, so long as the differentials are stable, there will be a corresponding uniform profit rate and an input-output matrix adjusted to include "compensating costs."

2. Minsky adds his own particular challenge. In a Keynesian world, he contends, the flow of profits can be calculated and reliably projected, but, by contrast, the rate of profits cannot be projected, in principle. It can only be known ex post. Ex ante, however, it cannot be formulated, even though the expected flow of profits can be reasonably forecast, because the denominator of the ratio cannot be given a unique value. "Capital," ex ante, is inherently ambiguous. It can either refer to the expected maintenance and replacement cost of the firm's various projects, or it can refer to the value of the expected stream of earnings. Each of these ideas is useful for certain purposes, but since there is no way of choosing between them, it is impossible to form *the* rate of profit. Economic analysis must therefore discard the notion and content itself with the more useful notion of the expected flow of profits. As we shall see, however, this argument is not consistent with Minsky's own theory of investment.

blend into the next, and that into the following. The actual long run will be a succession of short runs, in each of which economic variables will be determined by factors reflecting the current conditions of the respective period. Over such a succession of periods accidental or temporary influences may cancel out, revealing the persistent, "long run" forces. But they may not; what seem to be temporary influences may have lasting consequences. The issue should not be prejudged. So the long run must be considered as a succession of short runs, not as a separate category. What the classical equations supposedly describe, a long-run equilibrium, can not exist in a Keynesian world.

2. "Long run" vs. "Long period"

But if, as suggested, we distinguish the "long run," a stretch of time comprising a number of short runs, from the "long period," a theoretical construct (Harcourt 1992), the argument no longer bites. For the classical approach rests on the long period, the theoretical notion. Even if the actual passage of historical time takes place as a succession of short-run positions—a point that still requires demonstration—it could still be the case that these short runs gravitate towards, or around, or otherwise depend on, a "long-period position"—LPP—as defined by classical theory.

3. Minsky's Theory of Investment

Minsky's own approach to investment sits uneasily in the company of the strong post-Keynesian emphasis on uncertainty and the short run. Minsky defines two "prices" of capital assets, neither of which is strictly speaking, a price, as understood in the theory of markets. Both are composites, and neither is directly determined by market processes. Both are idealized and smoothed out, rather in the manner of long-period variables; nevertheless they are suited to the roles prescribed for them in investment decisions. They are designated, respectively, P_K and P_I. Each is considered a function of the level of investment. P_I is the supply price of the investment project. This is a composite figure made up of the normal prices of the investment goods and the normal cost of installing them and preparing the project for operation. It is the cost that the investor has to bear in order to be in a position to earn returns, and in the future it will be considered the project's historical cost. By contrast, P_K is the demand price of the project, the capitalized value of the expected stream of quasi rents from the project.[3]

---

3. Clearly these two "prices" correspond closely to the two concepts of capital, which supposedly create a difficulty in defining the rate of profit.

It will be profitable to invest as long as the demand price is greater than or equal to the supply price.[4] Aggregating over firms and investors, at higher levels of investment, the supply price can be expected to rise, as more pressure is put on suppliers. On the other hand, at higher levels of investment, earnings can be expected to fall, as more projects compete with one another. Increasing risk for borrowers and lenders will intensify the fall and rise, respectively, of the curves. Hence on normal assumptions they will cross once, determining the level of investment and its normal earnings. (Of course, at this point the two concepts of capital are equal; hence any ambiguity vanishes.)

Moreover, this procedure determines a rate of return on invested capital. For the supply price is just the capital cost, and the demand price is the capitalized value of the stream of earnings, capitalized at the going rate of interest. Another way of calculating, however, would be to find the rate of return that would equate the anticipated stream of quasi rents to the supply price. This will be the rate of return of the project, and investment should be carried out until this has fallen to the level of the rate of interest.[5] Hence Minsky's procedure identifies a rate of return on invested capital and requires it to be made equal to the rate of interest on money.

But this is surely the rate of return at the margin; will not intramarginal units be making higher rates? That would be a mistaken interpretation of the function showing investment decisions. Following the logic of q-theory, at the equilibrium level of investment the supply price has risen for all projects; similarly, risk has increased, so all projects are now riskier. All compete with one another for demand, so all are more uncertain. P_I risen and P_K has fallen for all projects. The two are therefore equated for all projects, and there are no projects with high intramarginal earnings. Indeed, if there were projects earning higher rates of return, investors would abandon lower-earning projects in favor of them. All new projects compete with one another, and new projects compete with old.[6]

---

4. This, of course, is very close to Tobin's "q-theory" of investment. Tobin (1969) defines q as the ratio of the market price of a capital project divided by the production price of currently produced capital goods. When $q > 1$, investment is called for. Since the production price of capital goods reflects the current rate of profit but the stream of future returns is discounted at the rate of interest, this is equivalent to saying that investment will take place as long as $r > i$. Minsky differs from Tobin in introducing lenders' and borrowers' risk into the calculation, and he stresses uncertainty more; he also explains current profits differently. But in important respects their view of investment is the same.

5. It is well known that the equation may have multiple roots. Also, seemingly small or simple changes in accounting periods may have large effects on the resulting values.

6. Keynes observed that "there is no sense building up a new enterprise at a cost greater than that at which a similar existing enterprise can be purchased (on the Stock Exchange)." Lionel

Exactly the same calculation can be made by an existing firm, with respect to the investment of its depreciation funds. At any given moment, the replacement cost of exhausted equipment plus the historical cost (and maintenance charges) of the plant still operating will be the supply price; the demand price will be the expected stream of earnings, and the rate of return will be the discount factor that equalizes them.[7]

If this rate of return is less than the rate of interest earned by depreciation funds, it will clearly not be worth the firm's while to make the replacement. If it is less than could be earned from an altogether new investment in a different line, it would be worthwhile to shift depreciation funds into the new line, rather than to continue replacing equipment. Thus funds will be shifted from relatively unprofitable lines into more profitable ones, precisely by the calculation described by Minsky. Such arbitrage will cease when the rates of return in all lines have been brought into equality with the rate of interest, allowing, of course, for imperfections, market power and barriers to entry, and bearing in mind that all calculations regarding the future are uncertain—the anticipated streams of quasi rent are just that: anticipated.[8] But the picture is drawn on the basis of long-run expectations, removing the influence of temporary aberrations.

Of course, arbitrage among existing assets will be restricted by the normal rate of amortization; only the funds set aside for depreciation can be taken out of a project and shifted elsewhere—unless the project is scrapped altogether. But in an era of rapid write-offs this need not be a severe limitation. Nor need the arbitrage tend toward a stable target; as innovations come on line, profitability may be changing in different industries, and the overall or average rate of profit may be changing as well. Nevertheless, arbitrage will be tending to form a uniform rate, even if that rate is changing over time.

Robbins (1930) noted the difficulty caused by the rate of return on existing capital in connection with an examination of Schumpeter's theory of interest; he held that the net yield of the existing stock of capital must be considered the reward for abstaining from consuming that capital. Schumpeter, however, wanted to determine the rate of interest by the interaction between saving and investment, that is, in the market for new capital only. There appeared to be two different mechanisms determining the rate of interest. Minsky's q-theory approach stresses the competitive pressure to bring these rates together.

7. A more sophisticated calculation would consider the stream of expected replacement costs as machinery wears out, minus the interest earnings from depreciation funds while accumulating, in relation to the stream of anticipated quasi rents.

8. In recent years a degenerate form of arbitrage has emerged, where raiders can obtain control of a corporation, pay themselves large fees and salaries, and sell off its assets to pay large dividends and financial charges. In effect the raiders liquidate the company's assets, on the grounds that they are worth more separately than combined.

4. A Rate of Return in the Short Run?

Keynes himself was quite clear about the impact of arbitrage:

> The owner of wealth . . . can lend his money at the current rate of money interest or he can purchase some kind of capital asset. Clearly in equilibrium these two alternatives must offer an equal advantage to the marginal investor in each of them. This is brought about by shifts in the money prices of capital assets relative to the prices of money loans. The prices of capital assets move until, having regard to their prospective yields and account being taken of all those elements of doubt and uncertainty, interested and disinterested advice, fashion, convention and what else you will which affect the mind of the investor, they offer an equal apparent advantage . . . (1973, p. 117)

Elsewhere Keynes wrote,

> . . . if r is the money rate of interest (i.e. r is the marginal efficiency of money in terms of itself) and y is the marginal efficiency of capital asset A in terms of money, then A will exchange in terms of money at a price such as to make $y = r$. (1973, p. 102)

(Minsky quotes this (1975, p. 100) apparently without noticing the implied formation of a general rate of profit, though that implication was emphasized by Keynes in the following paragraph.)

The two concepts of capital, far from creating difficulties in defining the rate of profit, are the two components—supply and demand, respectively—of the decision to invest. The investment decision, generalized, includes replacement, which is to say, the decision to continue in a line of business. The level of investment is determined by equating the supply and demand prices, a procedure that implicitly defines a rate of return. Arbitrage then implies that capital will be shifted from project to project, until (allowing for imperfections, market power, and barriers) rates of return in all lines are equalized and equated to the normal rate of interest. Surprisingly, therefore, Minsky's approach actually implies a tendency toward a general rate of return.[9]

---

9. A further implication is that policy will have a different kind of impact on the economy according to whether the central bank pegs the interest rate or fixes the money supply. If M is fixed, then r and i and the MEC will adjust to one another, and the economy will (other things being equal) reach its short-run equilibrium. The fact that the potential rate of profit cannot move in the short run does not matter. But if the rate of interest is pegged, it is likely that the economy will settle into a persistent disequilibrium. Suppose $i < r$: the economy would tend to a persistent expansion, the immediate effect of which would be to raise the actual rate of profit; funds will

This does not bring him very close to the neo-Ricardians, however. Their rate of profit is long run and real, that is, based on the adjustment of relative prices of goods, whereas Minsky's is short run and financial, based on monetary valuations of assets.[10] Minsky's arbitrage takes place through the movement of funds, seeking the best return, in the context of given plant and equipment; it will not smooth out the real nonuniformities embodied in the current capital stock. Yet this is precisely what is of interest to the neo-Ricardians, who hold that in the long run the movement of real capital from sector to sector establishes the prices corresponding to uniformity in the rate of profit. Neither, however, requires that the rate of return actually reach uniformity; the tendency is enough.[11]

Yet the fact that Minsky's approach rests on arbitrage over rates of return may suggest some common ground between the post-Keynesians and the classical revival—more, indeed, than either side might welcome! Yet this appearance may be deceptive, for it results from Minsky's theory of investment, which appears to be at odds with the post-Keynesian emphasis on uncertainty.

5. Keynesian Investment

Even more important, the conception of investment in the q-theory is out of touch with Keynes. For the q-theory regards investment as a movement toward equilibrium; the marginal product of capital—or something like it—must be brought down, by raising the capital stock to its long-term, steady-state level. Once it reaches this level, investment will cease (or will only continue to keep pace with the exogenous growth of the labor force). Investment is basically treated as a disequilibrium phenomenon, not at all what Keynes had in mind.

flow to business and to equity markets, without any tendency to bring profits down. Quite the reverse would occur; the high level of demand might very well encourage a high rate of productivity growth, so that even if real wages drifted up, r would stay high. Suppose $i > r$: funds will tend to desert the active sphere, creating a tendency to persistent recession. Ultimately r could be raised only by compressing real wages, but though unemployment might eventually drive down money wages, real wages might not decline if prices were also falling.

10. Minsky's short run is not that short; he suggests a period of "six months, one or two years" as appropriate for the study of utilization of existing capacity (Minsky 1978, p. 9). During this period the aggregate quantity of specific plant and equipment is taken as fixed. This provides plenty of time for shifting funds about in search of the highest financial rate of return. It is long enough for businesses and/or items of existing equipment to be bought and sold, depreciation funds and working capital placed, takeovers and mergers executed.

11. The tendency to establish a uniform financial rate of return creates a problem for conventional macroeconomics—the current rate of profit on the existing stock of capital need not equal the rate of interest established by the IS-LM interaction (Nell 1992a, pp. 612–14 and 1992b). The system of equations is therefore inconsistent.

In most conventional theory, investment is understood to be the adjust-ment of the actual to the desired capital stock. Hayek (1941) is particularly clear that net investment—capital accumulation—is simply the process of moving toward the final, stationary equilibrium (chapters 19 and 20, espe-cially pp. 263 and 268). During the process the stock of capital may have a rate of return different from that expected on investment, but the equilibrium rate, toward which all will move, will be that on the stock of capital in the stationary state. Haavelmo (1960, pp. 3–7) also contrasts the idea of invest-ment as movement to equilibrium with "Keynesian" investment. Investment as understood in Keynesian and post-Keynesian growth theories (and in the Marxian system) is *not* a movement to some envisioned final position; it is a stage in an activity that could be expected to continue indefinitely. Accumula-tion, like progress itself, has no final destination. Capitalists invest, just as consumers consume—because it is their nature. They compete for wealth and power, and investment is the means to both.[12]

This is a different vision from that underlying q-theory. Minsky's basic approach is Keynesian; investment is the activity of capitalists, driven by profit, and taking place under uncertainty. This leads to a theory of arbitrage; there will be pressure for investment until rates of return, appropriately ad-justed for risk, are equalized all around. Since general equalization will never be realized, there will always be pressure for investment.

This helps to explain the allocation of investment—but it does not go so far as to explain the level. Minsky's adoption of q-theory has led to too mechanical a conception. Everything depends on the schedule of the marginal efficiency of capital—but in a post-Keynesian world that in turn depends on how well new technology will work, how avidly markets will take to new products, how fast new markets will open up, and, as noted, the course of wages and prices in the future, something that firms themselves will, in part decide. Firms in Minsky's world, as in the real, have substantial power to make decisions about prices, and they can be expected to make their invest-ment decisions and their price-setting decisions together, on the basis of the best judgments they can make about the future.

6. Prices, Investment and the Rate of Return

This brings to the fore a curious oversight in Minsky's treatment of invest-ment. On the one hand he dismisses the neoclassical theory of perfect compe-tition as a "fairy tale;" but on the other he assumes that the problem firms face

---

12. To be sure, Keynes thought it possible that, in a few generations, the marginal effi-ciency of capital might fall to zero—bringing "the euthanasia of the rentier." But this was by no means certain, nor was it the destination toward which the system was necessarily heading. Quite the contrary; were this to happen, it would be a new kind of world, requiring new patterns of behavior.

in regard to the future is simply one of correctly foreseeing their stream of quasi rents. Foresight is needed, to be sure; but there is more to it. Firms have the power to set their prices; they cannot be considered price takers. In an earlier era firms established themselves at their optimal size and remained at that level, producing whatever output maximized their profits at the prices they accepted from the market (Robinson 1931). But Minsky's firms are modern corporations; they retain profits and reinvest them to grow. They have no "optimal size;" the issue for them is the optimal rate of growth. They do not accept prices from the market; they cultivate the market and are able to set their prices, doing so in ways that will block entry, while encouraging market growth. So the size at any time, and the distribution over time, of the quasi rents from a project will depend on the prices the firm sets. Unfortunately, Minsky offers us no guidance as to how these prices will be determined.

Post-Keynesian theory, however, has put forth the argument that firms set their investment and pricing plans together.[13] They plan for prices that will justify their financial obligations and at the same time underwrite the capital construction they consider necessary to maintain or achieve their desired market position. It is well established that the size of market will be partly a function of the prices being charged; the new idea is that the rate of expansion of a market depends on the price. A price must be found that will permit the financing of the rate of expansion that this price will induce in the market. According to this approach, there will be a positive relation between price and the profit that will finance the investment, but a negative relation between price and the size of the required investment, for higher prices will inhibit the development of the market.[14] By balancing these two, firms can choose the prices that will maximize their rate of growth. This will in turn be reflected in their planned rate of profit.[15]

These long-run pricing decisions provide benchmarks for investment

---

13. The case has been argued by Eichner on the basis of industry studies, but with an eye to providing foundations for macreconomics; Wood and Harcourt present different models, but both seek a better basis for the theory of growth (Eichner 1976; Wood 1976; Harcourt and Kenyon 1976). There are technical difficulties in these models, but a coherent account of this approach can be established, (Nell 1992c, chapter 17).

14. This requires an explanation of the growth of demand; most demand theory, to date, has concentrated either on the aggregate level of demand or on explaining relative demands for different categories of goods. Yet modern businesses are greatly concerned with the question of the potential growth of their markets (Nell 1992c, chapter 17).

15. For each firm the planned rate of profit will be determined as a byproduct of the joint determination of prices and the rate of growth. As we have seen, financial arbitrage, interacting with investment planning, will tend to pull these rates together. Nevertheless, significant differences may persist, reflecting different expectations of market development and different degrees of market power. Still, expected growth in markets will influence prices and markups, which in turn determine potential profits. Causality runs from growth to profit. This approach will not find favor with many Sraffians, who reject the determination of profits by growth and argue that the money rate of interest is the crucial factor.

planning and constitute targets that current operations should realize, in order to generate the funds required for investment. But current conditions—supply and demand—may not be in balance; if there is excess demand, it is traditionally argued that prices will deviate from the target levels. Post-Keynesian theory adopts a skeptical attitude toward this. Many studies show that prices of manufactured goods tend to remain fairly steady over the business cycle, changing primarily with costs. Simple optimizing models have shown that, in modern conditions, holding prices steady in the face of changing demand is the best strategy in most circumstances (Nell 1992c; Eichner 1976).[16]

There are two kinds of decisions made by firms. Short-run decisions are based on current conditions and concern current prices, output, and employment; long-run decisions concern capital values (including prices), capacity, and market development. Long-run decisions set the context and provide the guidelines for current decisions, and in particular they determine benchmark prices. Long-run decisions set the parameters for the short run. But notice that long-run decisions are made in the short run! And, consequently, they are remade every succeeding period. Indeed, both Minsky and Keynes state explicitly that investment decisions and the corresponding pricing plans are formulated and execution is begun in the same period in which utilization is determined. Long-run decisions are made and revised regularly, in each short period.

These ideas provide more than the determination of prices required for Minsky's scheme; they also explain the level of investment—it is that level required to provide the capacity to service the new demand that will be forthcoming at the planned prices. All that remains of the q-theory is the emphasis on the competitive pressure to pull rates of return together.

Once the prices are settled the anticipated stream of quasi rents can be capitalized and compared with costs. As we have seen, at this stage projects will be scrapped if their anticipated returns are not high enough, and potentially high-earning projects will attract funds. Revisions of plans may call for reevaluating projects, if, for example, it appears that there will be more competition than previously estimated (Keynes 1973, pp. 101–102).

Firms will not invest or remain in industries in which the anticipated growth provides a return less than the rate of interest. Firms will try to get into faster-growing lines of activity; but precisely because of this crowding in,

---

16. For example, a "customer attraction function" can be defined, showing the numbers of additional sales that would be attracted from rivals by a price cut of a certain size (relative to the benchmark price). The shape of this function will depend on the costs of changing buying habits and on the degree of attachment between buyers and sellers. Given its shape and the firm's profit function, the optimal price-cutting strategy can be determined. It can be shown that sticking to the benchmark—no price-cutting—is optimal under a wide variety of conditions (Nell, 1992c, chapter 17).

returns in these lines are likely to be reduced. Informally, this suggests a tendency toward a uniform rate of return. Prices, meanwhile, will be set to cover the capital costs of the investment needed to serve the markets, where the growth of those markets will be a function of the prices set. Such prices are part of the firm's investment plan and will serve as benchmarks for marketing, inventory control, and in negotiations over finance.[17]

Minsky's analysis implies a short-run tendency to form a uniform rate of return on financial assets and the financial counterparts of real assets. A defect is his neglect of long-run pricing, which his theory requires, but the basics of a suitable approach can be found in the post-Keynesian literature. The determination of prices is thus conjoined to the competitive pressures tending to form a uniform rate of return, as Keynes says. This differs from Sraffa in that Minsky, like Keynes, considers short-run arbitrage in regard to returns on financial assets, and pays no attention to the pressures on real capital. But the post-Keynesian money prices/markups imply a set of relative prices, even if these have not been analyzed, and the competitive pressures operating on financial values in each short period imply a persistent pressure for capital to seek the highest return—a pressure that continues through the succession of short periods. How exactly is this to be interpreted? Is this approach consistent with the prices and rate of profits in neo-Ricardian theory?

7. Benchmark Prices or Centers of Gravitation?

Adam Smith advanced the idea that market prices gravitate toward natural prices. Market prices are a function of the ratio of demand in money terms to

---

17. The connection is clearly established by Keynes, who wrote: "Thus the price system resulting from the relationships between the marginal efficiencies of different capital assets including money, measured in terms of a common unit, determines the aggregate rate of investment." He went on to reflect on this: "These propositions are not . . . inconsistent with the orthodox theory, or in any way open to doubt. They establish that relative prices (and, under the influence of prices, the scale of output) move until the marginal efficiencies of all kinds of assets are equal when measured in a common unit; and consequently that the marginal efficiency of capital is equal to the rate of interest. But they tell us nothing as to the forces which determine what this common level of marginal efficiency will tend to be" (1973, pp. 102–103). Investment and relative prices are determined together by the arbitrage that establishes a common rate of profit on capital. Minsky has failed to bring this out. For Keynes, as for Minsky, the level of investment so determined—by the rate of interest—will set the scale of output. The problem here is that Keynes has run together two distinct problems, investment decisions and investment spending. These are determined by separate forces and pose different analytical problems. Investment decisions depend on long-run factors, but investment spending deviates from what has been planned according to the influence of the current state of the economy. Keynes fails to separate these two concepts of investment (analogous to the distinction between "benchmark" and "market" prices), and Minsky makes the same mistake. This will prove important in interpreting "the long period."

current supply on the market, and are subject to all sorts of temporary influences and particular pressures. Natural prices, on the other hand, reflect permanent and persistent forces, the deep structure, underlying the market. As Ricardo argued and as the Sraffian equations of today claim to show, natural prices are independent of supply and demand, and they depend only on the selection of the best-practice coefficients of production and the rate of profits (or the real wage), for a given set of outputs. They are determined by the pressures of competition and are thus unaffected by the temporary influences impacting the market and so provide a "center" around which market prices gravitate. The idea is that "there would be underlying tendencies for the system to move toward the dominant methods of production and toward uniformity of the rate of profit" (Bharadwaj 1989, p. 235). This seems to imply that market prices will gravitate toward, that is, tend to converge on, natural prices and, in so doing, bring together divergent rates of return.[18]

It is this approach against which Asimakopulos, Davidson, and Minsky have argued, following Joan Robinson. The neo-Ricardian equations are written in "real" terms, so that exchanges are barter trades, and prices are determined on the assumption of given, and therefore fixed, quantities. In spite of considerable effort, all attempts to demonstrate dynamic convergence, or "gravitation" have either discovered instability or have rested on special and unjustifiable assumptions. (In particular, the most promising route, drawing on "cross-dual" dynamics, rests on unacceptable assumptions regarding pricing and on an unjustifiable approach to investment. Moreover, the pricing and investment behavior both conflict with Keynesian premises. See the appendix.)

Post-Keynesians do not consider the long-period position a useful abstraction, on the grounds that it will be undermined by the forces actually at work in the long run. In the long run technical progress will occur, new products will be introduced, institutional changes will take place, learning will happen, and preferences will develop or alter. Moreover, these developments will be inseparable from the competitive process. Even if a long-period position could be defined toward which the system could be shown to move, changes along the way would alter the initial data, so that the target would move as well. The LPP could turn out to be unattainable in principle. Robertson foresaw, and attempted to forestall, this objection, writing, "It may be that the long-run equilibrium is NEVER attained. It is the state of affairs which would be attained if all the forces at work had time to work themselves out" (1957, pp. 92–93). But this permits nonattainment only as the result of insufficient time. It cannot be the case that "the forces at work" include forces that cause the LPP to shift or to change character. Nor can they include forces

---

18. Market prices could oscillate around natural prices, however, without any tendency to converge on them, no matter how long the period.

whose working would tend to cause patterns of movement driving the system away from the LPP. Yet in the long run just such forces are at work, in the opinion of post-Keynesians.

In any case, the long period *barter* position cannot be relevant to a Keynesian economy. Neo-Ricardians have never explained their system in terms of money; indeed, the core equations are not behavioral at all![19] They are designed to calculate the exchanges needed to accomplish reproduction and distribution in accordance with the law of one price, a uniform wage to labor, and a uniform rate of profit. The equations state results of action, but no behavior—choice or market strategy—is modelled on the part of anyone. There is a degree of freedom, which the Keynesian approach could conceivably close. But how can a short-run monetary answer apply to a long-period barter question?

Garegnani (1983) and, following his lead, Eatwell and Milgate (1983) have convincingly shown that the appeal to LPPs characterized not only the classics, but also the early neoclassicals. Indeed, the long-period equilibrium was usually thought of as a stationary position toward which the economy moved by means of investment. This was abandoned for the temporary equilibrium approach only in the 1930s and 1940s, the first comprehensive presentation being that of Hicks in *Value and Capital* (1939). One reason for the change was that the neoclassical system faced difficulties analyzing capital as produced means of production on which a rate of profit is formed. This is surely correct (Garegnani 1983, Eatwell and Milgate 1983, Nell 1992c) yet non-neoclassical economists—most notably Kalecki and Joan Robinson, but including most Keynesians—also came to set aside the long-period method (Kalecki 1990, pp. 534–537).

This may well have been influenced by changes in the economy, arising from the development of modern technologies, which call into question as-

---

19. Panico (1980) and, more comprehensively, Pivetti (1991), have advanced the theory that the rate of interest, controlled by the monetary authorities, governs the ratio of money wages to prices—and hence the actual rate of profits on the money value of capital will be ultimately determined by the rate of interest, subject to a number of qualifications concerning the role and power of trade unions, monopolies, etc. This is intended to complement a set of Sraffian price/profit equations. But it is open to serious objections (Nell 1989, 1992c; Steindl 1990). It treats policy as independent of the economy, but policy makers are sensitive to economic variables, and monetary policy is seldom pursued consistently over long periods. Discrepancies between the rate of interest and the rate of profit are supposed to affect the ratio of money wages to prices, but the effect on investment and growth is neglected, although if the rate of growth affected equity values, as in "growth stocks," it would impact on the bond market. In general, equity is assumed to behave exactly in line with bonds; if this assumption is dropped, then the prices and rate of profit determined will not be Sraffa's (Nell 1988). But the assumption is not tenable. Nevertheless, the argument does successfully demonstrate the weaker conclusion that a discrepancy between r and i should not be analyzed only in terms of investment; if prolonged it may also affect the relationship between money wages and prices.

pects of the LPP.[20] Compared to the world of the classical economists, firms have become much larger in relation to their markets; moreover, technical improvements are now a matter of competitive effort, and hence best-practice methods change regularly. Firms no longer plan to achieve an optimal size. They retain earnings and reinvest them in improvements and in new and superior equipment. Once technological advance became a part of competition, firms could no longer continue to operate their initial plant unchanged. Nor could they permit new firms to enter with new and superior plants and equipment. To remain competitive, existing firms had to plan investment to expand in pace with the growth of the market, adding enough capacity to service the new customers each period. Thus each firm has come to operate a mix of equipment of all vintages.

The implication is that, under modern conditions, best-practice techniques do *not* by themselves govern prices; that is, prices are not forced by competition to the levels implied by lowest-cost methods. Since each firm operates all vintages, prices will tend to the level that will provide the required profit on the *average* level of costs, that is, on the average level of productivity of all vintages still operating, weighted by the normal percentage of output each vintage produces. No firm can force the price down since all continue to operate old equipment, as well as new. (If a newcomer tries to enter, employing only new equipment, it would have to attract customers from existing firms, a difficult task, even at lower prices, since existing firms build to match demand growth, and have invested in customer relations, and, moreover, will adopt strategies to block entry.) Benchmark prices will not be set on the basis of best-practice coefficients. They will earn the profit required by the company's financial and investment plans, on the costs of all vintages kept in operation. (Best-practice productivity, along with wages, will be important in determining the scrapping margin.)

---

20. Hoffmann (1958), Chenery (1960), Chenery and Taylor (1968), and Sutcliffe (1971) have all surveyed the patterns by which the advanced countries developed industrially, showing that in the early stages there were large agricultural sectors in relation to manufacturing, high ratios of traditional and personal services to modern business services, and high ratios of consumer goods to capital goods in manufacturing. The early stages can be described as employing craft-based technologies, whereas in the later stages the technology shifts to mass production (Nell 1992c, chapters 16 and 17, and 1993). In both stages, capitalist firms hire workers for money wages and earn profits. But the craft-based system is relatively inflexible in the face of variations in demand; when production is based on teams of skilled workers, using water or steam power, it is difficult to change employment and output quickly; cost curves are U-shaped and prices are therefore flexible, varying with demand. By contrast, an economy operating mass production technology with electrical power and internal combustion engines will be more easily able to adapt output and employment to changing demand. A typical cost curve in such a system will have a long flat section (flat enough to allow prices to be independent of running costs), so that prices will be relatively stable at the benchmark levels (Hansen 1950).

8. Keynesian Investment and "Long-Period Positions"

The chief factors undermining the long period, considered as a position toward which the economy is moving, arise from investment. The movement of the economy toward the LPP cannot be separated from its movement in the process of accumulation (Caminati 1990). This gives rise to a dilemma: if investment were the movement from the actual, current capital stock to that desired in the stationary state (or along a steady growth path with only disembodied technical progress), then it would make sense to consider such investment as part of the movement toward the LPP, and it would have no disruptive influence. But such an assumption would also preclude a union of classical (Sraffian) theory with Keynes. On the other hand, if investment is conceived in the Keynesian manner as an ongoing, perpetual activity, driven by competition and grounded in uncertainty and therefore highly volatile, then its effects are likely both to be disruptive and to change the desired LPP. Such investment will be disruptive because it is not tending to a definite endpoint, and so, from period to period, the direction as well as the amount of investment may fluctuate. Thus, sectors will tend to expand disproportionately. Moreover, since competitive pressures operate on technical progress, each period's new investment may embody superior techniques or produce superior products, so that from period to period, the best-practice position will shift—without, however, moving in a determinate direction. (It cannot be assumed, for example, that costs will always fall—they could rise, while quality rose more. Yet quality might well be hard to measure.) Once a Keynesian conception of investment has been adopted (which, as we shall see, may depend on the stage of economic development), it is no longer possible to claim that the economy is always moving toward a determinate destination, and the long-period method becomes problematical.[21]

Consider a standard "marginal efficiency" calculation, writing out, now, in year 1, the yields—$(pq - wn)$—for each of the years in project 1's expected lifetime, and discounting the sum of them to equal the supply price. Let one year pass. Now—a year later—the firm will undertake another pro-

---

21. Roncaglia (1990) appears to agree with this when he writes, "Whenever the current and normal degree of capacity utilization differ, . . . realized profits will be affected, and this will affect financing conditions, which in turn may affect investment expenditure, . . . , as well as technology both through embodied technical progress and through cumulative 'learning' processes; on the other hand, the current level of investment expenditure will affect aggregate demand, and hence . . . current . . . capacity utilization." Roncaglia's concern is to criticize the notion that Sraffa's equations define a "stable or persistent" position representing "an average of booms and slumps," about which the economy in some sense gravitates. This appears consistent with the argument in the text, which claims that Keynesian investment precludes an interpretation of the classical equations as representing the position toward which the system tends.

ject, project 2; but because of technical progress project 2 will very likely improve in certain ways on the previous year. These improvements may render part or all of project 1 obsolescent; or they may complement it and improve its efficiency and/or the quality of its product. Consequently project 1's yields after the first year must be rewritten, and its MEC recalculated. In the following year the firm will again invest, and project 3 may compete with or complement either or both of the earlier ones, again requiring rewriting their yields and recalculating their MECs, and so on. Once firms engage in technical research and invest in expanding and improving their own activities, long-term expectations will shift continually, in ways that cannot be anticipated reliably.

Indeed Garegnani tries to tame the unruly behavior of investment by arguing that, whatever the pattern of fluctuations, the course of investment "inevitably describes a trend" (1992, p. 347), which it is the aim of theory to explain. This cannot be accepted; a trend can always be constructed ex post, but in an advanced economy no trend can be established ex ante. Nevertheless his argument provides an important clue, when he refers to observed short-term fluctuations as standing to long-term trends in the same relationship the classical economists described as holding between market prices and natural prices. His claim is questionable,[22] but the natural-market relationship may offer solid ground for theory in the sea of Keynesian uncertainty. Natural prices are explained by technology and distribution; market prices are based on natural prices but deviate from them in accordance with current conditions. This suggests that there should similarly be two appropriately related accounts of investment, dealing separately with long-term factors and with the modifications introduced each period by current conditions. The first would ex-

---

22. At a certain point (1992, pp. 345–347; 1989, pp. 355–357) Garegnani appears to advance a new argument: that the relation between actual, observed magnitudes and theoretical ones is the same as the relation between market and natural prices, as these were understood by Adam Smith and the classical economists. This must be considered problematic. Actual, observed magnitudes are empirical reports, based on the rules of observation and evidence. These rules provide the ways of relating the observations to the appropriate theoretical constructions. The first question to be answered is always, are the observations relevant, that is, are they instances of the theoretical concepts? If not, then, of course, they cannot confirm or disprove any theoretical propositions. Actual magnitudes are therefore related to theoretical concepts as particular to general—they are instances, usually very imperfect ones, and the rules of evidence are designed to tell us when these imperfections are so great that the observations no longer count. By contrast, "market price" is itself a theoretical construct, related to "natural price" by a relationship that states the market price diverges from natural price according to the current ratio of demand to supply. (In the early Classics, market prices were not well defined, but even there the rule relating them to natural prices was clear. See Roncaglia 1990.) Natural prices are independent of current demand and supply; thus the relation between the two concepts is not that of the particular to the general, but rather of a current or market theory to a natural or capital theory, in which specific, theoretically defined current variables determine the divergence of market values from natural ones.

plain the investment plan, the second, the actual implementation. The account of the plan would lay out the influences determining the construction of capacity, finance, and the pricing policies, in the light of technological innovation and the anticipated growth of the market, and the second would take into account the influence of current sales and earnings, and current financial conditions on the rate at which investment plans are carried out (Nell 1992c).

This is exactly the kind of theory previously outlined. Investment plans and benchmark prices are determined together; arbitrage in financial markets generates a persistent pressure pulling rates of return together; and current investment expenditure will deviate from the plan in the light of current conditions, in particular, current interest rates and the level of aggregate demand. Although investment plans will be subject to frequent revision and will not tend to move toward a determinate position, investment spending may be quite determinate in a given short period, though sometimes fluctuating sharply from period to period. Market prices, however, will not deviate that much from benchmark levels, because modern technology produces with constant variable costs. But though at any time there is a long-run plan, there is no long-run position toward which the system is moving, and the plan itself is continually changing, so there is no established trend, either. There is a relationship between current decisions and capital, or long-run decisions; but there is no long-run position to gravitate toward.[23]

9. Implications for Benchmark Prices

Thus none of the arguments rejecting gravitation imply a similar rejection of benchmark prices, corresponding to investment calculations by firms.[24] The

---

23. The discussion suggests that there are circumstances in which convergence to a LPP might be plausible. Consider an economy operating craftlike technology, in which there is little or no regular technical change and in which the development of new markets can be clearly foreseen, perhaps on the basis of population growth; on these assumptions new investments set up new firms that replicate existing ones. Firms are established at, or quickly grow to, their optimal size. The trend of investment will be clearly defined, and current investment spending can be expected to gravitate around it. Since technical change is occasional, irregular, and unforeseen, and since each firm operates plant and equipment of only one vintage, competition will tend to drive prices to those corresponding to the best-practice technique. It is plausible that investment will iron out differences in profitability between sectors. No investment will be made that does not pay at least the rate of interest; areas of investment that return more will attract capital, and competition will drive prices and earnings down. Over time, accidental variations will average out, and the system will more closely approximate the long-term position. The crucial assumptions are no technical change, "regular" investment, and prices determined by supply and demand on the basis of rising marginal costs (Nell 1992c, chapter 16).

24. Benchmark prices are calculated by firms, but they will hold industrywide in two cases: where there is price leadership by a dominant firm, and where there is strong competition and all firms are similar.

rates of return relevant to the firm are those expected, respectively, from new investments and from existing operations. The prices are those not only expected, but planned for—they are the prices the firms plan to charge, in light of their competitive circumstances, and those they have good reason to think will lead the market to grow at a rate that will justify the construction of the capacity they plan to build. (Benchmark prices are industry prices, for the prices planned by an individual firm must be consistent with its competitive position in the industry.)

Moreover, these prices are based on the average productivity of plant and equipment, which changes slowly as new investment introduces higher-productivity equipment. Similarly, invested capacity will shift from line to line only slowly, as depreciation funds are accumulated and reinvested. Hence benchmark prices, though subject to change, will change slowly, and so will provide a reliable set of valuations for macroeconomic purposes.

Rather than as centers of gravitation, benchmark prices should be considered as guideposts, determined as part of the investment plan, and serving as the standard or target to be reached in marketing. They are long run because they result from capital decisions; market prices are short run because they reflect current decisions, which modify the long-run plan in light of current conditions. But it can be shown that even when demand and other conditions vary considerably, it will still be optimal for firms to keep their prices at the benchmark levels.

Benchmark prices are designed to earn the required rate of return on the average value of the firm's invested capital, the rate required by the firms' financial position and investment targets. This rate states what firms plan to achieve, as they begin operations. They begin from the benchmark, and as long as conditions remain within a certain range, the optimal strategy will be to stick with them. Thus benchmark prices will be the relevant prices for the analysis of the short run and will tend to remain steady as other variables change.

Centers of gravitation are the endpoints of a dynamic process; by contrast, benchmark prices provide a starting point. But as the process unfolds, from short period to short period, the plans and the benchmarks themselves will be modified, often in unpredictable ways, although the changes (based on averages) will normally be small. At any time, however, there will be a plan providing guideposts and setting standards for current decisions. What is the relation of this plan, and the benchmark prices, to the classical system?

10. The Meaning of the Classical Equations

If there are no centers of gravitation, what do the classical equations describe? It can be argued that the classical equations set the stage for the short-run drama of effective demand by providing a framework connecting benchmark prices and normal quantities—a framework that makes aggregation possible. But if this framework is not the position to which the economy moves in the long period, what exactly is it, and how does it underpin the working of the system in the short run?

If we abandon "convergence" and consider benchmark prices as providing stable values on the basis of which current activities can be mounted, we can present an interpretation of the classical equations, as defining a LPP in a very different sense. Benchmark prices are charged on current activity to generate funds for investment, to build the capacity to serve the market that is expected to grow as a consequence of those prices. Investment/pricing plans are based on current capacity, current wages, and the techniques currently in use. The ensemble of investment, production, and pricing plans at any time draws on the same data that figure in the classical equations. But the classical system is designed to analyze interdependence, and to do this it must set aside not only accidental and irrelevant influences but the particularities of the current situation. These must be peeled away, and the structure remaining— the skeleton of the economy, as it were—is expressed by the classical equations. It is in this sense that they represent the long-period position underlying the short run.

11. The Long Period as Hypothetical Full Adjustment

This interpretation draws on a further traditional meaning of the "long period;" in the long run, according to Marshall, all processes have time to work themselves out. The LPP, then, is the theoretical position in which the full unfolding of the true and important influences is exhibited, allowing us to see temporary disturbances, which might capture our attention momentarily, for the distractions they are.

But the reference to time is really misplaced here. The point is to visualize the system free from extraneous influences, temporary inhibitions, and accidental blockages, so that all causal factors exert their influence in undiluted form. This sense of "long period" is purely hypothetical; it is how the economy would work, if. . . . There is no requirement that actual values converge to this position in the long run. Moreover, short-run processes—in which capital equipment is held constant—can be analyzed this way, too. The sense is that all relevant adjustments are fully worked out and that all factors being considered have exercised their influence without interference.

So the long-period position need not be interpreted as the point toward which the system is heading. It could be understood as how things would be if all irregularities were removed and all processes worked ideally, abstracting not only from disruptive influences but also from current conditions. This allows the theorist to shift focus from the particular situation of firms to the general interdependence of industries and sectors and to consider the changes in the values of aggregates such as capital and income, when prices change. In this respect the assumption of uniformity in the rate of profit should be seen as a simplifying assumption, justified by the fact that pressure toward such uniformity exists. But there is no need to contend that the system is actually about to establish a uniform rate.

The classical equations abstract, as well, from aspects of the economy that for one reason or another should be examined by a different kind of theory. In particular, proponents of the classical revival have argued persuasively that the equations of value and distribution describe a core of central and defining relationships constitutive of capitalism, which hold even through changes in other aspects of the system, such as the institutions governing money and finance, or household demand. Hence, it is argued, these core relationships should be studied independently from the rest of the economy. This has an important advantage. If, as suggested, Keynesian problems developed as technology and institutions became more advanced, the classical equations will be applicable to both the earlier, pre-Keynesian, and the later Keynesian eras. They could therefore provide a basis for studying the transition.

In this light Sraffa's equations can be understood as the abstract, normal form of the core value system, showing how wages, prices and profits *would* be related, abstracting from money and demand, if all industries operated all processes on the basis of their average coefficients, charging their benchmark prices, with all irregularities smoothed out. (Stable nonuniformity in the rate of profit can be handled as suggested in note 1.) The purpose of such equations, on this interpretation, would be to reveal interconnections and dependencies, to study the structure of the system, not to analyze behavior. The behavior studied in the theory of effective demand could then be understood as taking place in the context whose structure is presented in Sraffa's equations. For these equations show the connections between benchmark prices in the different sectors; changes in markups or prices of basics are changes in costs for other producers. Changes in real wages disrupt the rate of profit and call for price changes (Steedman 1991). The equations also show the linkages between the outputs of given sectors and the inputs required, directly and indirectly, from all other sectors. Such connections provide the opportunities and constraints facing the agents of the system, and therefore are the background to the study of behavior. Under such an interpretation—which is not the classical position, but is not so far from it—the objections of Asimakopulos, Davidson and Minsky would have no bite, and the Sraffian equations would describe the setting in which the drama of effective demand is played out.

APPENDIX: A CRITIQUE OF CONVERGENCE:
EARLY VS. ADVANCED TECHNOLOGY

A number of models have been presented purporting to demonstrate convergence to long-period positions, but all appear to have major defects. The basic cross-dual model is unstable; it can be stabilized by assuming demand substitution, but this is unrealistic when techniques are embodied in fixed capital. Further, the assumptions required to assure convergence to a long-period position appear to rule out variations in effective demand, while requiring prices to be demand sensitive rather than cost-determined (Flaschel and Semmler 1990).

Dumenil and Levy (1987, 1990) provide a good example: their model converges to a uniform profit rate with homothetic growth, provided the starting set of prices is "not too far" away from the final. Although the model is one of long-run dynamics, it rules out technical progress, increasing returns, and variability in demand, all of which certainly occur in the long run. There is no accelerator. Investment responds only to profit rate differentials, and it is tacitly assumed that all savings are invested— anything produced will find a market at some positive price, thereby ruling out Keynesian problems. Prices are adjusted in light of inventory movements—raised when inventories fall, and lowered when they rise. Prices are therefore demand-sensitive. Yet there is no demonstration that this is either a profit-maximizing strategy, or required by competition. (Dumenil and Levy address some of these issues in later works.) A more plausible investment function would upset the convergence, as would a different pricing strategy.[25]

Flaschel and Semmler (1986), following Mas-Collel, have shown that cross-dual dynamics (Goodwin 1967), when the reaction functions are augmented by responses to rates of change of key variables, will provide a very general stability, meaning that market prices will revolve around, and return to, the long-run "natural" prices, and the uniformity of the rate of profit will be restored if upset. The basic idea is that the change in prices in any industry depends on excess demand for that industry's products, and the change in outputs in any industry depends on that industry's level of profits. The augmentation terms then add that the more prices change, the greater is the change in excess demand, and the more outputs change, the greater is the change in profits.

There are three problems here. First, there is a general question concerning the linkages in the causal sequence: prices change because of excess demand, a current market relationship. This changes current profitability, creating profit rate differentials, which in turn leads to changes in investment, as capital shifts to the most profitable sectors. But investment is a long-term commitment. Is it reasonable to change long-

---

25. Concerned over the exclusion of Keynesian issues, Dumenil and Levy have proposed a revised model, in which questions of "proportion" are distinguished from questions of "dimension," the latter referring to aggregate activity levels; however, their model still has prices depending on supply and demand, and technical progress is still excluded. And from a Keynesian point of view the model rests on unacceptably restrictive assumptions about investment—the aggregate level is fixed and independent of aggregate demand, capitalists are mainly concerned with allocation of capital between industries, etc. (Dumenil and Levy 1990; Cartelier 1990).

term commitments on the basis of current market relationships? Surely not; investment depends not on current profitability, but on expected future profitability, to which the current state of the market is a weak and unreliable guide. This objection applies to all cross-dual models.

Second, cross-dual models assume that in the process of adjustment prices are demand sensitive, though governed classically in the long run by technology and the rate of profit. This does not make good economic sense. If there are constant returns in the long run, why not in the short? But if returns (costs) were constant in the short run, would prices respond to demand changes? Very likely not, as most studies have shown. Post-Keynesians argue that prices tend to remain steady, while outputs adjust to demand—and though this gives rise to interesting patterns of dynamic adjustment, such models take the set of prices/markups/profit rates as given at the outset.

Finally, there is a problem in the interpreting the "augmented" relationships. Investment is treated as independent of demand, current or future. Hence it would be possible to have a situation in which excess supply existed, but because profits were positive, investment would still take place. Excess supply would drive down price, but the expansion of output would lower the marginal product of labor, hence leading to a lower real wage. Thus profits would not necessarily contract, and investment would continue! Even under the augmented system, investment could continue although there is excess supply. This does not make sense.

Cross-dual models are the preferred representation of what has come to be called "the classical adjustment mechnism." But they are based on patterns of behavior that are not rationally justifiable under conditions of short-run constant costs (prices independent of demand), competitively driven techncial progress, market power and Keynesian investment. Other patterns of behavior tend to produce unstable or nonconverging results (Caminati 1990; Boggio 1990). These may be interesting in themselves, but they cannot justify the idea that the classical equations represent the position to which the economy tends.

Convergence in Early Capitalist Economies

Nevertheless, "convergence to LPPs" need not be wholly discarded. Consider an economy in which prices are responsive to changes in demand, technical progress is sluggish and occasional, and investment, averaged over several years, is governed by changes in the labor force and in per capita income, where the latter, in turn, also grows at a stable exogenous rate. We can define such investment as "regular;" note that regular investment does not necessarily imply full employment, even in the long run. The fact that a moving average of investment is a stable function of growth in the labor force and per capita income merely means that the capital stock expands pari passu; it does not imply that the expansion is large enough to employ all additional workers. Regular investment implies a determinate trend, and it excludes multiplier-accelerator effects.

But these cannot be excluded by fiat. If investment depends on income growth, as it surely does, then a multiplier change in income will affect investment. Investment can only be regular if there are no multiplier effects. Fortunately a condition can be found that, based on technology and cost behavior, divides economies into those that do have multiplier relationships in aggregate expenditure and those that do not. This condition also implies that in economies without a multiplier, prices will be responsive to demand.

Consider a proportional change in autonomous investment, dI/I: with a fixed multiplier, m, classical savings behavior and no price changes, this will result in an equi-proportional change in consumption, dC/C. Hence the elasticity of consumption with respect to investment, CdI/IdC, equals +1. With classical savings behavior and employment fixed by technologicial rigidity (firms face only two choices: to produce with all hands working, or to shut down), a proportional change in investment spending, dI/I, will (given certain further assumptions) change prices in the same proportion. Since short-run employment is fixed, money wages will not come under pressure; hence the real wage will change negatively in the same ratio, and so, therefore, will consumption. Hence in this extreme case the elasticity of consumption with respect to autonomous investment will be −1 (Nell 1992c, chapter 16).

These two cases correspond to two extreme forms of an aggregate production function embodying a given technique. The first case is a straight line from the origin to the maximum employment and output; the second is a reverse L-shape, connecting the only two feasible points, the origin and the maximum. But technology can clearly take other forms, for example, as traditionally assumed, a curved line exhibiting diminishing returns, connecting the two points. This curvature will give rise to a falling marginal product/rising marginal cost curve. Economically, this means that for employment to increase, demand pressure must bid up prices (lower the real wage), since additional workers will add a smaller increment of output.[26]

Now consider a falling marginal product curve with an elasticity of −1. This implies that the proportional decline in the real wage (proportional rise in price, equal on certain assumptions to the proportional increase in investment spending) will just be balanced by an equal proportional increase in employment. Consequently there will be no change in consumption spending. Hence the elasticity of consumption with respect to investment will be zero. So when the elasticity of the marginal product curve is less than unity, the elasticity of consumption will be negative, and when it is greater than unity, the elasticity of consumption will be positive. In the first case, there is no multiplier, and the nearer the value to −1, the more fully fluctuations in investment will be offset by an opposite movement in consumption. The curvature of the production function will be considerable, implying a sharply rising marginal cost curve. In the second case—elasticity of consumption positive—there will be a multiplier, that is, a change in investment will bring a change in consumption in the same direction. The nearer the value to unity (the flatter the marginal cost curve), the less sensitive prices will be, and the larger the multiplier effect (Nell 1992c).

Arguably, modern technologies are more flexible, in that they allow for changing levels of output and employment while keeping productivity and costs constant. So the

---

26. Notice that though this may be Marshall or Pigou (Hicks 1989, p. 36), it is not Wicksell/Walras. The real wage changes as a result of demand pressure, and the variation in the marginal product results from changing the employment offered by unchanged plant and equipment. There is no change of technique. This is not the "true" neoclassical theory (Hicks 1932, pp. 20–21). Moreover, the changes in employment, although "governed" by marginal productivity, are driven by effective demand (Nell 1992a).

more advanced the technology, the more likely that short-run costs will be constant; hence prices will be insensitive to demand, and a multiplier relationship will exist, so that investment cannot be assumed regular. Convergence is therefore out of the question. But when the technology is inflexible, as in underdeveloped regions or in earlier eras, cost curves will be U-shaped, prices will depend on demand, and fluctuations in autonomous components of aggregate demand will tend to generate offsetting movements in consumption. Investment therefore could be regular (this would not be a post-Keynesian world). Under these conditions (always assuming limited technical progress) convergence might well be plausible—although the inadequacy of the investment theory implied in cross-dual analysis means that the case still remains open.

REFERENCES

Asimakopulos, A. 1992. "Keynes and Sraffa: Visions and Perspectives," in Bharadwaj and Schefold, ed., *Essays on Piero Sraffa*, London: Routledge.
Bharadwaj, K. 1989. *Themes in Value and Distribution*, London: Unwin Hyman.
Bharadwaj, K. and Schefold, B. 1992. *Essays on Piero Sraffa*, London: Routledge.
Boggio, L. 1990. *Special Issue: Convergence to Long-Period Positions*, in *Political Economy: Studies in the Surplus Approach*.
Caminati, L. 1990. "Introduction," *Special Issue: Convergence to Long-Period Positions*, in *Political Economy: Studies in the Surplus Approach*.
Dumenil, G. and Levy, D. "The Dynamics of Competition: A Restoration of the Classical Analysis," *Cambridge Journal of Economics* vol. 15, no. 2.
———. 1990. *Special Issue: Convergence to Long-Period Positions*, in *Political Economy: Studies in the Surplus Approach*.
Eatwell, J. and Milgate, M. 1983. *Keynes's Economics and the Theory of Value and Distribution*, London: Oxford University Press
Eichner, A. 1976. *The Megacorp and Oligopoly*, Cambridge: Cambridge University Press
Flaschel, P. and Semmler, W. 1986. "The Dynamic Equalization of Profit Rates for input-output Models with Fixed Capital," W. Semmler, ed. *Competition, Instability, and Nonlinear Cycles*, Berlin: Springer-Verlag.
———. 1990. *Special Issue: Convergence to Long-Period Positions*, in *Political Economy: Studies in the Surplus Approach*.
Garegnani, P. 1983. "On a Change in the Notion of Equilibrium in Recent Work," in Eatwell and Milgate, *Keynes's Economics.*
———. 1989. "Some Notes on Capital, Expectations and the Analysis of Changes," in Feiwel, ed. *Joan Robinson and Modern Economic Theory*, London: Macmillan.
———. 1992. "Comment on Asimakopulos," in Bharadwaj and Schefold, *Essays on Piero Sraffa.*
Goodwin. R. 1967. "A Growth Cycle," in Feinstein, C.H. ed. *Capitalism, Socialism, and Economic Growth*, Cambridge: Cambridge University Press.

Hansen, A. 1950. "Cost Functions and Full Employment," in Clemence, R. *Readings in Economic Analysis*, vol. 2, Addison-Wesley: Cambridge, MA.

Haavelmo, T. 1945. *A Study in the Pure Theory of Investment*, Chicago: University of Chicago Press.

Harcourt, G. and Kenyon, P. 1976. "Pricing and the Investment Decision," *Kyklos*, vol. 29.

Hayek, F.A. 1941. *The Pure Theory of Capital*, London: Routledge.

Hicks, J. 1939. *Value and Capital*, Oxford: Clarendon Press.

Kalecki, M. 1990. In Osiatynski J., ed., *Collected Papers*, vol. 1, Oxford: Oxford University Press.

Keynes, J. M. 1936. *The General Theory of Employment, Interest and Money*, London: Macmillan.

———. 1973. "The Theory of the Rate of Interest," in *Collected Works*, vol. 14.

Minsky, H. 1975. *John Maynard Keynes*, New York: Columbia University Press

———. 1978. "The Financial Instability Hypothesis: A Restatement," Thames Papers in Political Economy. London: Thames Polytechnic.

———. 1986. *Stabilizing an Unstable Economy*, New Haven: Yale University Press.

Nell, E. J. 1988. "Does the Rate of Interest Determine the Rate of Profit?" *Political Economy*, vol. 4, No. 2.

———. 1992a. "Keynes, Marshall and Sraffa: Macroeconomics and Marginal Productivity," New York: Jerome Levy Economics Institute of Bard College.

———. 1992b. "The Old Trade Cycle and the New," New York: New School For Social Research.

———. 1992c. *Transformational Growth and Effective Demand*, London: Macmillan

———. 1993. "Transformational Growth and Learning: Developing Craft Technology into Scientific Mass Production," in Thomson, ed. *Learning and Technical Change*, London: Macmillan.

Panico, C. 1980. "Marx's Analysis of the Rates of Interest and Profits," Cambridge Journal of Economics.

Parinello, S. 1990. *Special Issue: Convergence to Long-Period Positions*, in *Political Economy: Studies in the Surplus Approach*.

Pivetti, M. 1991. *An Essay on Money and Distribution*, London: Macmillan.

Robertson, D. 1957. *Lectures on Economic Principles*, London: Fontana.

Robinson, E. A. G. 1931. *The Structure of Competitive Industry*, Cambridge: Cambridge University Press.

Roncaglia, A. 1990. "Is the Notion of Long-period Positions Compatible with Classical Political Economy?" *Special Issue: Convergence to Long-Period Positions*, in *Political Economy: Studies in the Surplus Approach*.

Steedman, I. 1991. "Questions For Kaleckians," Manchester University

Tobin, J. 1969. "A General Equilibrium Approach to Monetary Theory," *Journal of Money, Credit and Banking*, vol. 1, no. 1.

Wood, A. 1976. *Theory of Profit*, Cambridge: Cambridge University Press.

CHAPTER 12

Joseph Schumpeter: A Frustrated "Creditist"

*James S. Earley**

> All forms of credit, from the bank-note to book credits, are essentially the same thing, and in all these forms credit increases the means of payment . . . The external form of the credit instrument is quite irrelevant . . . *if it actually circulates.*
> —Schumpeter, *The Theory of Economic Development* (emphasis added)

> Money-of-Account . . . is the primary concept of a Theory of Money. A Money-of-Account comes into existence along with Debts and Price-Lists. . . . Something which is merely used as a convenient medium of exchange on the spot may approach to being Money. But if that is all, we have scarcely emerged from the state of Barter.
> —J. M. Keynes, *Treatise on Money*, p. 3

I. Introduction

Joseph Schumpeter is an important but neglected figure in what I call the "credit approach" to macroeconomics, which Keynes, himself a "creditist," called "monetary economics."[1] The credit approach to macroeconomics is, in my view, a "dynamic" monetary theory in Schumpeter's sense of dynamics—

*I gratefully acknowledge the help of my UCR colleagues, Robert Pollin and Carl Uhr. Bob has helped substantially in the chapter's formulation and editing. Carl kindly translated for me portions of Barbela Naderer's new work in German on Schumpeter's theories of money and credit.

1. The approach began in the early nineteenth century with Henry Thornton and the so-called banking school. Its subsequent votaries in England include such notables as J. S. Mill, Walter Bagehot, D. H. Robertson, R. G. Hawtrey, J. R. Hicks, and, preeminently, J. M. Keynes. Noted American followers, in their business cycle theory, include such otherwise diverse economists as Irving Fisher and Wesley Clair Mitchell. On the European continent, the approach was first taken by Knut Wicksell, the leader of the Stockholm School. In central Europe, Schumpeter and Albert Hahn were the pioneering creditists.

that is, it deals with the motion of a pecuniary economy rather than its equilibrium positions.

All those who follow the credit approach are not necessarily "creditists" in a full sense. For example, Irving Fisher used a credit approach in his business cycle theory but gave almost no attention to credit in his basic book on money (Fisher 1911). He therefore would not be considered a creditist.

What then is a creditist? It is someone who views the behavior of credit—i.e. the volume of borrowing and lending—to be the fundamental financial variable determining the behavior of the macroeconomy. In this sense, a creditist is opposed to a "monetarist," who considers the stock of money—the means of payment—to be the fundamental financial variable and who sees credit behavior of secondary importance. In this sense, Schumpeter was unquestionably a creditist. Throughout his works he stressed the importance of credit and was consistently anti-monetarist (Earley 1981a).

Another definition of a creditist is someone who uses a "credit theory of money." Such a theory views money itself as an endogenous variable whose behavior is determined by the behavior of credit. Schumpeter would have preferred a credit theory of money to the then prevalent "monetary theory of credit," but for reasons that we will discuss, he was unable to embrace it fully. Hence I call him a frustrated creditist.

Hyman Minsky is perhaps the leading present-day U.S. representative of the credit approach. In the prefaces to two of his books Minsky names Schumpeter, his professor at Harvard until Schumpeter's death in 1950, as one of the economists who most influenced him. No doubt it was Schumpeter, along with Keynes, who stimulated Minsky to develop his Wall Street view of monetary economics, which is thoroughly creditist.

2. Why Schumpeter's Creditism Has Been Neglected

That Schumpeter leaned towards creditism is indicated by the following passage from his *History of Economic Analysis* (1954a, hereafter *History*):

> "Credit" operations of whatever shape or kind do affect the working of the monetary system; more important, they do affect the working of the capitalist engine—so much so as to become an essential part of it without which the rest cannot be understood at all. (p. 318)

Why then was his creditism neglected? The most striking feature of Schumpeter's economics, of course, was his introduction of *innovation* into economic theory, and most attention has naturally been on this aspect of his work. The brilliance of Schumpeter's contribution on innovation cast his credit analysis into the shadows. Little attention was paid to Schumpeter's work on finance, and thus little literature developed around it.[2]

A second explanation is that Schumpeter's business cycle theory has been widely interpreted as following monetarist precepts. Most economists have viewed Schumpeter's notion of the banking system—the "banker" in his analytic model—as being essentially a vehicle for creating and destroying money.

There is indeed much justification for this interpretation. Despite Schumpeter's strong opposition to monetarist tenets—including the theoretical foundation of monetarism, the quantity theory of money—his uncertain and ambiguous handling of money and credit makes it possible to interpret his work within the broad boundaries of monetarism. Specifically, one can legitimately conclude that Schumpeter, consistent with monetarism, held that credit can be expansionary only when it originates with banks and involves the creation, and subsequent circulation, of new "monetary" instruments.

Unfortunately, Schumpeter's theory of credit, and especially his view of the way in which credit expansion stimulates spending, was fatally defective. As a result, Schumpeter stood to the end of his life with one foot in the creditist camp and the other in traditional monetary theory. His difficulty with money and credit was his greatest professional frustration.

3. Schumpeter the Revolutionist

Schumpeter saw himself, in his major theoretical work *The Theory of Economic Development* (1934, hereafter *Development*), as taking first steps toward a "fundamental overhaul" of the tools of economic theory. He proposed to shift the focus from economic theory's traditional "statics" and "comparative statics" to "dynamics," the temporal analysis of *endogenous* change.[3]

Development was studded with readily admitted "heresies." Not only did it introduce innovation into economic theory, but in its perhaps central chapter, "Credit and Capital," Schumpeter confessed to two monetary heresies:

2. I have dealt critically with the neglect and misinterpretation of Schumpeter's writings on money and finance in Earley 1981a, 1983 and 1987. See also chapter 8 of Reclam 1984, which summarizes the views of economists writing in English and German of Schumpeter's work on money and credit. Minsky's brilliant paper "Schumpeter: Finance and Evolution" (1990) presented to the 1988 meeting of the newly founded International Schumpeter Society, is one of the few exceptions to the broad neglect of Schumpeter's contributions to monetary economics. Minsky and I have proposed that an entire meeting of the society be devoted to financial aspects of Schumpeter's work, but, as of this writing, the proposal has not been taken up.

3. Much later, in *Capitalism, Socialism, and Democracy*, he declared that a stationary capitalism is a contradiction in terms.

first that money profoundly affects the behavior of the economic system and second that "other means of payment" (i.e., credit) does too (p. 95).

The new analytical "tools" he introduced were (1) the analysis of endogenous changes as departures from a static "circular flow" of spending, production, and consumption; (2) the inclusion of credit in economic analysis; and (3) "monetary" concepts of capital and interest to replace the traditional "real" concepts.[4] Unfortunately, his analysis of credit was defective, and, quite possibly in consequence, he made almost no later use of his key analytic concepts of capital and interest.

4. Schumpeter and Money: A Long, Unhappy Ordeal

An important part of the "thorough-going overall" of economic theory sought by Schumpeter was to get money onto what he called the "ground-floor" of economic theory. Sadly, he failed in this effort.[5] He dealt with money, in one way or another, in all of his major economic works, but in only two, his 1918 monograph, translated as *Money and the Social Product* (1956) and his posthumous unfinished *Das Wesen des Geldes* (1970), did he deal primarily with money.

The 1918 monograph dealt mainly with two matters: first, the appropriate concept of money and the source of its value; and second, the manner in which money courses through the "circular flow."

On the concept and value of money, Schumpeter lined up with the heretical "cartelists" against the then dominant "commodity theorists." In opposition to the latter, cartelists view money as a "token" or "ticket," rather than a commodity, and they view its value as explained by its functions and its scarcity, rather than by the value of the substance from which it is made. With this the revolutionary Schumpeter emphatically agreed.

Characteristically, however, Schumpeter put forth his own variety of cartelism. He saw money as primarily a "claim" on the social product, either a "claim receipt", (if the product had already been produced), or a claim on future product, in the case of credit extended to the entrepreneur. In either case, if the claim is also an obligation of a financial intermediary, such as a bank, it is also a claim on "money," that is, on legal tender. Schumpeter saw this latter claim as less important than the first.

The other part of the monograph was an analysis of the way in which these "claims" (both money and claims on money) circulate through the circular flow,

---

4. Later, in *Business Cycles* (1939, hereafter *Cycles*), he sought to introduce also the tools of economic history and statistics.

5. See *Cycles*, especially p. 129, and *History*, pp. 277–79. Swedberg, in his biography of Schumpeter, writes "Throughout his life it was always Schumpeter's ambition to produce a major work in the theory of money" (1991, p. 80).

which Schumpeter identified with the social product. Here the novel feature is Schumpeter's special concept of velocity. He chose to call it "efficiency," because it measures the "effectiveness" with which money carries out its primary function, which to Schumpeter is acting as a means of payment. This concept later became known by other economists as "circuit velocity."

A notable feature of the monograph is the absence of any dynamic treatment of money, such as the treatment credit had received in *Development*. All the analytical features of the monograph lie within the context of Schumpeter's "stationary" circular flow. It must be presumed that Schumpeter the revolutionist planned to get on to the dynamics of money in a later publication.

This intended sequel finally appeared more than fifty years later in *Das Wesen des Geldes*. The long sad history of this unfinished work traces Schumpeter's major professional frustration.

He began writing the book in the mid-1920s, when he resumed academic life following intervening years spent in public life and private banking. His painful experience with it is dealt with in both recent biographies (Allen 1991 and Swedberg 1991). Additional documentary evidence has recently come to my own attention.

Schumpeter worked intensively, even frantically, on this book from 1925 through most of 1930. In August 1928 he wrote Keynes, whom he had earlier visited in Cambridge, "My book on money does not proceed well. I wonder whether my difficulties cluster around the same points as those you told me you had still to grapple with." Concerning an international meeting they were expected to attend shortly thereafter, at which Keynes was to be honored, Schumpeter wrote, "I hope you will excuse me in case I feel too tired to go."

Two years later, in September 1930, he again wrote Keynes: "I am leaving [for a year's visit to Harvard and Japan] under a cloud, having not succeeded in finishing the ms. of my book on Money, which will have to wait now for another year, upsetting all my plans of further work."[6]

Despite his discouragement, which must have become even sharper when Keynes's successful *Treatise on Money* appeared in 1930, Schumpeter resumed work on what he called his "money book" when he moved from Bonn to Harvard in 1932. He later told a colleague that his first year at Harvard had been almost ruined by his troubles with the book (Swedberg 1991, pp. 213–14). He appears to have given up working on it in 1933 to turn to *Business Cycles*.[7]

The *Cycles* contained a short section, "Some Propositions on Money"

---

6. Mark Perlman kindly provided me with copies of these two letters, which he secured from Donald Moggridge from unpublished papers of Keynes.

7. That Schumpeter did very little, if any, work on the book after 1933 is evidenced by the

(pp. 544–48), introduced with a footnote reading, "The writer hopes to provide the background and to develop the theoretical structure of which these propositions are fragments, in his treatise on money." The "propositions" presented some of the monetary ideas he had earlier expressed in *Development* and in *The Social Product*, along with some others. As in his earlier works, the propositions were quite heretical. He questioned the reality of both the supply and the demand for money as conventionally conceived. He stated that the concept of velocity of money would have a quite different meaning under "dynamic" than under "stationary" conditions, defining dynamic velocity as the proportion of the total supply of money that is actually "circulating" (p. 546). He also declared that credit instruments should not be considered as a "substitute for money" but as *additions* to the volume of money.

Schumpeter's "money book" continued to trouble him to the end. When I started research on his theories of money and credit in 1981, I received a response to my inquiry about the book from Arthur Smithies, Schumpeter's closest Harvard faculty friend in his last years. Smithies wrote, "Schumpeter often talked about his difficulties with it," and added, "Schumpeter never seems to have got his ideas on money straightened out to his own satisfaction."

5. What Is the Nature of Money?

Schumpeter's "money book," an unfinished manuscript in German, was published in Germany as *Das Wesen des Geldes* in 1970. Despite its erudite scholarship, the book was a professional failure.[8]

Reclam (1984) reports that on the technical side there was little distinctively new in *Das Wesen*. Disappointingly, it did not expand appreciably on the heretical "propositions" included in the *Cycles*. But the work did carry an important new theme, namely that the *nature* of money evolves with the economy in which money is used. In a simple economy, money is correspondingly simple; the hand-to-hand transfer of coins is sufficient to carry out the monetary function. In a well-developed economy, however, money plays a complex role. One of its important functions is to act as a "unit of account," thus performing an important social bookkeeping function.

Schumpeter sees the unit of account not only as a bookkeeping device but also as a concrete thing. He writes, "these accounting units (*Rechenpfen-*

---

fact that all of the manuscript was written in German. Well before the 1930s, Schumpeter could write in English with facility, and all his later published work, I believe, appeared in English. He toyed with the idea of writing a *short* book on money late in his life, but nothing came of it.

8. Michael Reclam, a native German, originally planned to translate the book into English and write an analytical introduction as his Ph.D. thesis. After he had examined the book carefully and we had consulted several Schumpeter scholars and potential publishers, it became clear to us that it would not be worthwhile to translate it. Reclam used it instead as background and a portion of his thesis. My characterization of the book depends primarily on Reclam's 1984 thesis.

nige) exist, either physically or in a bookkeeping account. *These units of account we call money"* (his emphasis).[9]

Much the most important thing about *Das Wesen* was this recognition of "money" as an *evolving institution.* In this respect Schumpeter was here dealing with the "dynamics" of money, toward which he had been groping since he wrote *Development.* This evolutionary theme was carried further in Schumpeter's *History* (1954). Here he devoted much attention to the evolution of monetary institutions and doctrines.

Note the evolution he observed in the monetary institution was from simple commodity money to highly complex "credit money." Schumpeter observed that credit had become an integral part of the modern monetary system. He lamented that the literature of money and banking failed to reflect this evolution. He wrote,

> Even today . . . the huge system of credits and debits, of claims and debts, by which Capitalist society carries on its daily business . . . is built up [in the literature] step by step by introducing claims to money or credit instruments that act as substitutes for legal tender . . . but do not oust it [legal tender] from its fundamental role in the theoretical picture of the financial structure. Even when there is very little left of this fundamental role in practice, everything that happens in the sphere of currency, credit, and banking is construed from it, just as the case of money itself is construed from barter. (p. 717)

He continued,

> *The credit structure—which was incessantly developing—was the thing to be explored and to be analyzed.* . . . It is by no means clear that the most useful method is to start from [legal tender] . . . in order to proceed to the credit transactions of reality. It *may be* more useful to start from these in the first place, to look upon capitalist finance as a clearing system that cancels claims and debts and carries forward the differences—so that "money" payments come in only as a special case without any particularly fundamental importance. In other words: practically and analytically, a credit theory of money is *possibly* preferable to a monetary theory of credit. (p. 717, emphasis added)[10]

---

9. *Das Wesen*, p. 224. The English translation is taken from Reclam 1984 p. 254. It is interesting to compare Schumpeter's "unit of account" with Keynes's "money-of-account," which, Keynes declared in the first sentence of his *Treatise on Money*, is "the primary concept of a Theory of Money" (1930, p. 3).

10. Schumpeter appended a footnote to this sentence, reading "I hope this sentence is self-explanatory. It will, however, be illustrated [in a later chapter] by a discussion of one of the consequences of economists' failure to go through with the idea adumbrated above." The chapter

It is evident from what Schumpeter wrote in this final work that he had come close to embracing a credit theory of money. I call special attention to the sentence in which he criticizes a long line of theorists who directed their energies to deriving credit from money, saying that "the credit structure—which was incessantly developing—was the thing to be explored and to be analyzed." He proposed that analysis *start* with the credit structure rather than with money.

Notice, however, the words "may be" and "possibly" in the final sentence of the passage. They indicate that Schumpeter remained uncertain and hesitant. Although he clearly rejected the "monetary theory of credit," he seemed not fully prepared to embrace a "credit theory of money."

6. Why Schumpeter Was Hesitant

Apart from a possible loss of confidence suffered from his losing battle with his "money book," there are, I think, two substantive explanations for Schumpeter's hesitation to adopt a credit theory of money. The first was doctrinal, the second a matter of the time in which he lived and worked.

A credit theory of money conflicts sharply with the view of the monetary process that Schumpeter had acquired in his early years. He was a faithful follower of what has been termed by Arthur Marget the "Quesnay-Walras conception" of the monetary process (Marget 1951, p. 62). According to these physiocrats, money circulates through the economy as blood circulates through the human body. This vision became part of Schumpeter's own, and it stayed with him to the end.[11]

Leon Walras, Schumpeter's theoretical idol, reinforced Schumpeter's "circulating" view of the monetary process. Marget, a close professional associate during Schumpeter's later years, wrote that Schumpeter "acknowledged Walras as his master in the field of monetary theory as in the field of economic theory generally (1951, p. 63). In the *History* Schumpeter did express his great admiration for Walras's monetary theory but added, in significant italics, "*so far as monetary statics is concerned.*" Schumpeter was more interested in finding a "dynamic" theory of money.

---

referred to (pp. 1074–1138) contains equally sharp criticism of the literature of banking and credit and the "monetary theory of credit" that underlies it. The "consequence" he referred to was the refusal of many economists to recognize that banks "create" deposits by their loan activity.

11. In his early historical treatment of economic theory, *Economic Doctrine and Method* (1954b), Schumpeter hailed the physiocrats as the discoverer of "the circular flow of economic life," which he took as the point of departure for his theory of economic cycles and development. Schumpeter also credited the physiocrats with originating two other conceptions that, Schumpeter said, "assumed the greatest importance for economics" (p. 52). The first of these was "circulation," the second that of the "social product." Schumpeter saw money as circulating around the economy to form the money value of the social product.

His one direct criticism of Walras's monetary theory was his acceptance of the "cash balances" form of the quantity equation. Schumpeter strongly disapproved of this "money sitting" type of monetary theory, declaring in the *Cycles* that there was no "demand to hold money" in goods and services markets. He stated that Walras's *encaisse desiree* "is harmless only in the analysis of stationary states" (1939, p. 547), implying that it was not acceptable for "dynamic" monetary analysis. [12]

Unfortunately, Schumpeter carried his "circulatory" view of the monetary process into his treatment of credit. The circulatory conception of the monetary process does little harm in analyzing a simple economy in which there is no credit. It is not seriously misleading if credit is between only nonfinancial units. But it is fatally deceptive when dealing with credit extended through financial intermediaries, as in Schumpeter's theory of economic cycles and development.

Although Schumpeter first declared in *Development* that "all forms of credit, from bank notes to book credits, are essentially the same thing," and "in all these forms credit increases the means of payment" (1934, p. 99), he soon retreated from this position and held that credit is expansionary only if it creates a credit instrument that "circulates." Schumpeter stated this latter position explicitly in *Development* (p. 109) and clearly implied it at several places in *Cycles*. Schumpeter's settled view of the credit process was that credit expansion adds "credit means of payment" to "money," but that the credit money must "circulate" if it is to expand spending. [13]

The second substantive reason Schumpeter was not ready to accept a credit theory of money is that he had a conception of financial intermediation that is now obsolete. His conception reflected late-nineteenth and early-twentieth century commercial banking practice. At that time banks financed their operations mainly by issuing (that is, borrowing upon) bank notes, or by crediting (and thus borrowing upon) "checkable" deposit liabilities. In both

---

12. There are two widely differing views of the central function of money. One is that it serves primarily as the means of payment for goods and services. This is the traditional view, which Schumpeter accepted, apparently for dynamic as well as static monetary theory.

The other view is that developed by Keynes in the *General Theory*, namely that money's major function is to provide "liquidity." In this view, money primarily affects interest rates and other credit conditions. Providing a means of payment is secondary, perhaps simply an important byproduct of the credit system. This view fits a credit theory of money. It is ironic that Schumpeter criticized the particular feature of Walras's monetary theory that led eventually, with Keynes, to a monetary theory suitable for dynamic economics.

13. Consonant with his view of the monetary process as circulatory, Schumpeter also held that credit, to be expansionary, must be spent on goods and services rather than used for "financial" purposes. He also held that the chief, if not the sole, function of money is to act as a means of payment for goods and services. In one important article (1951, p. 37), he went so far as to say "to serve as means of payment . . . is the *only* function of money" (emphasis added).

these forms, bank credit does create a "credit means of payment" that does "circulate" in a meaningful sense.

But these methods of financing bank operations are no longer representative. Private bank notes have virtually disappeared. Banks still do extend most of their credit by crediting the checkable deposit accounts of their borrowers. But the main *source* of funds that finance banks has become the issuance of debts that do *not* circulate. Presently, banks and other depository institutions secure most of their funds, and virtually all of their incremental loan funds, by borrowing in forms that are *not* means of payment, and do *not* circulate.

The buyers of these nondemand debts pay for them by debits to their checkable deposit accounts at banks, and the borrowing banks normally use the funds to make loans. But since the debits to accounts at banks offset the credits to the borrowers' accounts, the banking system as a whole creates no net circulating media by this process. The banking system is simply enabled to expand its total earning assets by funding its operations with liabilities that require lower reserves than do checkable deposits. Credit expands, but "money" does not.[14]

A monetary system of this type is essentially one of debiting and crediting liability accounts of banks as envisioned by Schumpeter in the *History*. In fact, in the present-day financial system neither money nor credit "circulates" in the sense Schumpeter had in mind. All transactions, except the most trivial, are settled by debits and credits on the books of financial intermediaries. The money system and the credit system have become welded into one.

These radical changes in the funding of banks began only in the mid-1960s. Schumpeter could not be faulted for not analyzing a credit system that developed only after his death. He was in fact a keen analyst of banking and finance during the times he wrote. Had he been writing in the 1970s and 1980s, he would have seen the implications of the veritable revolution that has occurred in financial practices during recent decades.

But whether he could have escaped from his view that money is a *thing* that *circulates* is more questionable. The notion that money circulates is

---

14. For example, if Bank A sells certificates of deposit to customers of Bank B, Bank B now has lowered demand deposit liabilities. If Bank A lends the borrowed funds to a customer, its demand deposit liabilities rise by the same amount that Bank B's demand deposit liabilities have fallen. The banking system as a whole has unchanged demand deposit liabilities, but its total loans have risen. The volume of "money" has not changed, but the banking system has been enabled to increase its total lending because CD liabilities require much lower reserves than do demand liabilities.

This does not mean that the modern banking system does not "create credit." It means only that to create credit, each individual bank, and hence the banking system as a whole, must find creditors willing to hold their obligations. In this case, these obligations take a nonmonetary form.

extremely difficult to slough off. And Schumpeter was unusually unable to change his views of the economy. Yet only by doing so could he have developed the credit theory of money that he envisioned.[15]

7. What a Credit Theory of Money Would Have Done for Schumpeter

Schumpeter's suggested credit theory of money in the *History* inspired me, some years ago, to construct a "credit model" of the U.S. monetary and financial system to assess the relative merits of "monetarism" and the "credit approach" (Earley, Parsons, and Thompson 1976). My model abstracted completely from paper currency and commodity money. All transactions were "cleared" by debits and credits to demand deposit accounts of banks.[16]

The sources and uses of funds technique used to analyze the model was suggested by Schumpeter's masterstroke of macrofinancial analysis, his use of the circular flow as the springboard from which to launch macroeconomic analysis. In the circular flow, the sole source of funds to finance expenditure is the goods and services spending of microunits. There are no "financial" sources of funds. The result is unchanging aggregate spending. But any expansion of aggregate spending requires injection of funds from financial sources, the "banker" in Schumpeter's model.

Schumpeter reached these sound conclusions intuitively, without the help of a credit theory of money, although use of one would have permitted him to prove them rigorously (see Earley, Parsons, and Thompson 1976 1976, p. 4). But a credit theory of money would have led him to correct answers to two questions he answered erroneously. These are (1), by what *process* does credit expand spending; and (2) what *kinds* of credit are expansionary?

Schumpeter's view of the process by which credit expands spending was that credit adds a "credit means of payment" to the supply of "money," and that it is their *circulation* that expands total spending. His answer to the question of what *types* of credit are expansionary was that, for credit to be expansionary, it must (1) create a "credit instrument," which (2) is used as a

---

15. The nature of modern credit money is well illustrated by bank credit cards. What they do is to plug their holder into the credit and payments mechanism. If one's card begins to "circulate," one had better call the bank hotline quickly.

16. Two colleagues and I empirically tested the model against the flow-of-funds data of the Federal Reserve System for the period 1952–1973. We found the major statistical explanation of the changes in aggregate spending during the period to lie in the net changes in the credit being extended by banks and nonbank financial intermediaries to the nonfinancial sectors of the economy. Changes in the supply of "money," (that is, demand deposits) were not significantly related to changes in aggregate spending.

means of payment for goods and services, and which (3) subsequently circulates through the economy.[17]

A credit theory of money would strike each of these limitations. First, much credit that is clearly expansionary (such as most trade credit and much consumer credit) creates no credit instrument, being evidenced only by entries on the account books of the parties. Since no credit instrument is created, it obviously cannot circulate. Of course many credit instruments are traded on organized exchanges, and in this sense they do circulate. But they are not used as a means of payment.

Moreover, a large proportion of credit—probably most of it in the United States presently—is not extended to finance spending on goods and services but to finance the operations of the financial intermediaries that do finance the spending. This "financial" credit includes the huge funds lent to banks and other intermediaries by nonfinancial institutions. I have shown (Earley 1981b) that buoyancy of such financial credit is especially strategic in expanding spending in today's economy.

In short, Schumpeter's limits on the kinds of credit that are expansionary are unacceptable. A credit theory of money would substitute relevant matters for these irrelevant ones. It would shift the focus from the "credit instrument" created, if any, to the net effects of credit extension on the combined spending of the borrowers and lenders. And it would abandon the notion that credit circulates.

A credit theory of money finds that credit is expansionary if the added spending engendered by the borrowers exceeds any contractionary influence on the spending of the lenders. If the direct creditor is a nonfinancial unit, this latter may be substantial. But if, as in most current cases, a financial intermediary does the lending, the contractionary influence is negligible at most.

A credit theory of money would also have required Schumpeter to abandon his position that his "banker" creates credit ad hoc. Sources and uses analysis, which is the analytical backbone of my own credit theory of money, shows there must be a source of funds for every use. As a practical matter, banks and other financial intermediaries cannot expand their lending without securing additional funds from other parties. They normally take the initiative in their lending, and in this sense they initially "create" credit ad hoc, but they must find creditors willing to hold their liabilities in order to finance their lending on a sustained basis.[18]

---

17. Of these requirements, it was credit's "circulating" that was vital in Schumpeter's view. In *Development* he wrote "The external form of the credit instrument is quite irrelevant . . . if it actually circulates" (p. 109).

18. Ironically, Schumpeter's unsound position that the banker produces credit ad hoc was motivated by his very sound position that credit expansion is not financed by saving. One of Schumpeter's insightful heresies was that conditions in financial markets are only very loosely

There is a more important matter about which a credit theory of money might have persuaded Schumpeter to change his mind. In consistently rejecting monetary theories of the business cycle, he argued that money and credit have no mechanism of their own to generate business cycles. A credit theory of money would have shown him that, though this is true of money, it is not true of credit.

Hyman Minsky finds this mechanism in the progression, in an economic upswing, from "hedge" to "speculative" borrowing and on to "Ponzi finance." My own work also implies a cyclical credit mechanism. Increased borrowing expands aggregate expenditure and thereby expands receipts and incomes. These in turn improve the prospects of higher profits and other incomes, and lead to further credit expansion. But the *quality* of credit deteriorates as the process continues. Eventually the weakening of the financial strength of borrowers—and perhaps lenders as well—creates conditions in which credit expansion slows or is even reversed. A scenario of this general type was also envisioned by a notable American creditist of a past generation, Wesley Claire Mitchell.

Finally, a credit theory of money would have provided Schumpeter with the dynamic monetary theory he was groping for all of his professional life. Without realizing it, he had been dealing with the dynamics of money in his treatment of credit in the *Development*, for credit is the dynamic aspect of money.

It was most unfortunate that Schumpeter could not rid himself of the view that credit must circulate. This view is based on a medium-of-exchange concept of money's function. A mere medium-of-exchange concept of money is incompatible with dynamic analysis, as Marx, before Schumpeter, and Keynes, later, recognized. As Keynes observed, an economy in which money is used only as a medium of exchange "has scarcely emerged from the state of barter." The chief function of money in the Keynesian world is to satisfy liquidity needs. Acting as a medium of exchange is only a byproduct of the credit system.

Although a credit theory of money could have enabled Schumpeter to fulfill his life-long ambition of creating a dynamic theory of money, a dynamic theory of money could not in itself have fulfilled Schumpeter's other life-long ambition, which was to "put money on the ground-floor of economics." To do this requires radical change in the nature of economic theory. An economic theory with money on its ground floor is a very different thing from any theory with which Schumpeter was familiar. It is the theory of what Keynes labeled "monetary economics."

---

tied to decisions regarding spending and saving. Keynes later emphasizes this point in the *General Theory*. It also emerges in my work. (See the discussion by Pollin and Justice in this volume.)

A theory of monetary economics makes use, as did Keynes, of Schumpeter's pioneering monetary concepts of capital and interest, which, as Schumpeter rightly declared (1939 p.129), opens a suitable door to put money on the ground floor of economics. But a monetary economy is also characterized by uncertainty and unstable expectations, and therefore so must its theory be characterized. Schumpeter, unlike Keynes, was unwilling to abandon the Walrasian world. He cherished too greatly the static achievements of his intellectual forebears.

Schumpeter's revolutionary efforts were directed toward creating an *evolutionary* economics, not the short-run dynamics that interested Keynes. It would not be correct to conclude that Schumpeter's economics were less revolutionary than Keynes's. It was simply directed towards a very different objective.

REFERENCES

Allen, Robert Loring. 1991. *Opening Doors: The Life and Work of Joseph Schumpeter*. New Brunswick, NJ: Transaction Publishers.
Earley, James S. 1981a. "Schumpeter as 'Anti-Monetarist,'" paper presented at the Annual Meeting of the History of Economic Society.
———. 1981b. "What Caused Worldwide Inflation: Excess Liquidity, Excessive Credit, or Both?" *Weltwirtschaftliches Archiv*, Band 17, Heft 2.
———. 1983. "Schumpeter's Theories of Money and Credit: A Second Approximation," paper presented at the Annual Meeting of the History of Economics Society.
———. 1987. "Schumpeter's Theory of Credit and his Concepts of Capital and Interest," paper presented at the Annual Meeting of the History of Economics Society.
Earley, James S. and Gary Evans. 1982. "The Problem is Bank Liability Management," *Challenge*, (January/February).
Earley, James S., R. J. Parsons and Fred A. Thompson. 1976. *Money, Credit, and Expenditure: A Sources and Uses of Funds Approach*. New York: New York University School of Business Administration, Center for the Study of Financial Institutions.
Fisher, Irving. 1911. *The Purchasing Power of Money*. New York: Macmillan.
Keynes, J. M. 1930. *A Treatise On Money*. New York: Harcourt, Brace and Company.
Marget, Arthur. 1951. "The Monetary Aspects of the Schumpeterian System." In Seymour E. Harris, ed., *Schumpeter, Social Scientist*, Cambridge: Harvard University Press.
Minsky, Hyman P. 1990. "Schumpeter: Finance and Evolution." In Heertje, Arnold, and Mark Perlman, eds. 1990. *Evolving Technology and Market Structure*. Ann Arbor: University of Michigan Press.

Naderer, Barbel. 1991. *Die Entwicklung der Geldtheorie Joseph A. Schumpeter*. Berlin: Duncker & Humbolt.

Oakley, Allen. 1990. *Schumpeter's Theory of Capitalist Motion*. Aldershot: Edward Elgar Publishing, Ltd.

Pollin, Robert and Craig Justice. This volume. "Saving, Finance, and Interest Rates: An Empirical Consideration of Some Basic Keynesian Propositions."

Reclam, Michael. 1984. *J. A.Schumpeter's 'Credit' Theory of Money*. Ann Arbor: University Microfilms International.

Schumpeter, J. A. 1914. *Economic Doctrine and Method*. London: George Allen & Unwin Ltd.

———. 1934. *The Theory of Economic Development;* trans. Redvers Opie. Cambridge: Harvard University Press.

———. 1939. *Business Cycles*. New York: McGraw-Hill Books Co.

———. 1942. *Capitalism, Socialism, and Democracy*. New York: Harper Brothers Publishers.

———. 1951. *Essays of J. A. Schumpeter*. Cambridge: Addison Wesley Press, Inc.

———. 1954. *The History of Economic Analysis*. New York: Oxford University Press.

———. 1956. *Money and the Social Product*; trans. Arthur Marget. In Alan T. Peacock, Wolfgang F. Stolper, Ralph Turvey and Eilzabeth Henderson eds., *International Economic Papers*, Vol. 6.

———. 1970. *Das Wesen des Geldes*. Edited by Fritz Karl Mann. Gottingen: Vandenhoeck & Ruprecht.

Swedberg, Richard. 1991. *Schumpeter: A Biography*. Princeton: Princeton University Press.

CHAPTER 13

Marx, Minsky and Monetary Economics

Arie Arnon

1. Introduction

Hyman Minsky's influential writings on the complicated processes through which modern capitalism evolves belong, naturally, more to Keynes than Marx. Minsky's roots in Keynesian thought are explicit and well documented (see, for example, Minsky 1975) As for Minsky's intellectual relationship with Marxian thought, the picture is more complicated. The relationship has to draw more on implications and interpretations than on direct references by Minsky himself. Minsky has never written on Marx in a way that would shed light on the scope and depth of their common ground.

The reader might wonder whether the project of examining Minsky's connections to Marx is simply an empty and artificial exercise, like that of "The Elephant and the Jewish Question." This is not the case. To begin, both Minsky and Marx emphasized in their methodologies the importance of processes as opposed to moments in time. This emphasis, common in Marx's lifetime, was relatively rare when Minsky was writing. For Minsky and Marx abstract economic reasoning is not just true or false but right under the (historical) circumstances. Minsky writes mainly about capitalism as it has developed after World War II, focusing his analysis on the 1960s and after, whereas Marx of course dealt mainly with early capitalism. Nevertheless, Marx's writings obviously include observations relevant to modern capitalism, and Minsky refers to early capitalism, so we may seek fruitful parallels.

In addition, Minsky was intellectually influenced by Marxian thought and was personally involved in socialist circles. He was introduced to economics by Oscar Lange. (Minsky 1985, p. 215). Lange was visiting at the University of Chicago in 1939, and Minsky, who as a student there was politically involved both on campus and outside, went to downtown Chicago to listen to a series of talks given by Lange to the Socialist Club of Chicago on "The Economic Theory of Socialism." These talks were based on his papers in the Review of Economic Studies[1] An incidental meeting with Lange on "a windswept elevated train platform" proved to be crucial to Minsky's career; coincidence and uncertainty were to remain crucial also in his economic theories. Lange apparently suggested that he should look into majoring in economics instead of mathematics and physics, which Minsky found unsatisfying.

Lange was also instrumental in introducing Minsky to Abba Lerner, who became a life-long friend. This meeting took place in a political/social gathering organized by the Socialist Club at Professor Paul Douglas's apartment.[2] Forty-six years later Minsky remembered this evening:

> Lange introduced me to a friend of his, a British visitor who seemed equally ill at ease. As a result, I spent most of the evening talking to Abba Lerner who had just come from Mexico, where he had apparently tried to convince Trotsky that Marxism needed to be revised in the light of the new insights due to Keynes.

Trotsky, who was murdered a year later, did not revise Marxism in this light, but Lange and Lerner were struggling to redefine socialist thinking, trying to build a bridge between Marxian analysis and modern economic theory. Both rejected mainstream interpretations of Marx, including the then sacred labor theory of value and the Soviet-style command economy. But they also held to some of the basic Marxian messages, including class analysis and the dismal future of capitalism. Where did Minsky stand on these issues in later years?

I will try to shed some new light on Minsky's relationship to Marx through examination of the two thinkers' views on several issues. First I will discuss their views on crises in a capitalist system, examining whether they thought this phenomenon to be unavoidable and, if not, what means they believed could prevent such waste. Considering this issue will then lead me to compare their positions on the government's role in a capitalist economy.

A second, and related, topic will be their analyses of money and finance in developed capitalism. Here we will turn to their own arguments as well as their place in the history of monetary theory. I will argue that, concerning this heatedly debated topic, Marx and Minsky share some roots. They both held many of the conclusions of the anti-quantity theory of money tendency as

---

1. These famous papers by Lange were published in book form in Lange and Taylor (1938).
2. Paul Douglas is known for the famous Cobb-Douglas production function. However, when Doutlas was a professor, Minsky remarks, "[he] was not an ordinary neo-classical theorist," and in "his various courses he often enthused about the Utopian visions of Robert Owen and he took bargaining theories of wage determination—such as the Webbs put forth—seriously," (Minsky 1985, p. 216). Douglas later became a liberal senator from Illinois.

formulated by the banking school. Thus, their somewhat similar approaches to money and credit have deeper roots than is usually assumed.

In the second section I will briefly present Marx's positions on crises, money and finance, and the role of government. In particular, I will discuss possible influences of earlier thinkers on Marx. This will lay the ground for establishing some influences common to both Marx and Minsky. The third section will deal with Minsky's views on these issues. Since Minsky's views are presented quite extensively in this volume and elsewhere (for example, Taylor and O'Connell 1985 and Jarsulic 1988), I will concentrate only on the most relevant of these issues. The fourth section will compare Minsky's and Marx's views. In this section I will also elaborate on their common historical roots in the writings of past thinkers, in particular those of the banking school.[3]

2. Marxian Views on Crises, Finance, and Social Philosophy

A clear distinction must be drawn between the view of Marx and what can be described as Marxian economics, particularly on issues relating to money and finance. Marxian economics, especially as it was perceived in the "red thirties", when Minsky studied economics, put much weight on the real side of the economy. This emphasis was the result of the simplistic and narrow interpretation of Marx that became influential during this period. It had its roots in Marx's own writings, but it neglected important lessons that could have been drawn from them. Official Marxian economics of the period held the view that the major characteristics of capitalism can be understood through "real" analysis. What was this real analysis?

The point of departure for any Marxian analysis of the capitalist economy was the abstraction called value. Value, and the famous process that explains the creation of surplus value through the unequal exchange of labor power, was the focus of Marx's writings that were published during his lifetime (Marx 1859, 1867). These came to be treated as the canonical Marx. Most Marxians were satisfied with the analysis contained in them, to which one should add the elaboration concerning value when the composition of capital is different in the various branches, found in volume III of *Capital* (Marx 1894). Few Marxians put much weight on the analysis of money and credit that can be found in the same volume.

Thus, there were three common explanations of crises in Marxian circles, all based on Marx's real analysis (see, for example, Foley 1986). One,

---

3. Crotty 1986 is an earlier useful attempt at considering the analytical links between Marx, Keynes, and Minsky.

crises occur because of the tendency of the rate of profit to fall. This tendency is treated sometimes as a law, meaning that the forces behind it are too strong to be fought and the tendency, in spite of certain counterpressures, will sooner or later be manifested in the economy. Two, crises are the result of unbalanced growth, where there is not enough demand for some goods and too much demand for others. This type of explanation is sometimes labeled the disproportionality explanation, the result of the anarchic, unplanned character of capitalism based on uncoordinated markets. Third is the "underconsumptionist" school, which emphasizes the structural lack of effective demand.

Minsky, like Lange and Lerner, rejected altogether the validity of the Marxian real analysis based on the value category. He started his analysis from prices and did not worry about their relationship to any more abstract concepts. As a result he also implicitly rejected the order of determination so common in the Marxian literature, whereby some concepts represent more fundamental forces than others and "determine" their basic processes. Thus, analysis on the abstract level of value is "stronger" than that carried out on the less abstract level of production prices, and the latter is dominant in relation to market prices.

One further distinction must be made with respect to crisis theory. In the first volume of *Capital*, Marx analyzed the movement of the capitalist system with the aid of two circuits, that in which money-capital was translated into commodities and then back to (more) money-capital (m-c-m'), and the one where commodities were exchanged for more money and money for (the same value) of commodities (c-m-c). This analysis abstracted from modern money and banking phenomena and handled only the most basic form of money: commodity money.

Marx knew better than this, however. He was aware of complications caused by the more advanced forms of money and by the existence of a developed banking and financial system. He studied the financial systems of his time, speculated about future systems, and was well informed about the most advanced theories regarding money and banking. But Marx decided, consciously it seems, to leave those issues for future publications that he never completed. The reason for this decision was his belief that there is an order of determination also concerning the dichotomy between "real" and the "monetary" analysis , to use the classical distinction. For Marx the order was clear. The real is more fundamental than the monetary. There is no autonomy of the monetary circuit and processes: they are the result, not the cause. However, those who read the chapters in Volume III, where Marx elaborated on these issues, found that there was plenty of room left for what can be described as the "relative autonomy" of the monetary circuit. Thus, developments in the monetary circuit concerning money, credit, and financial institutions can affect the real processes. This important lesson was lost by Marxian economics in the 1930s.

Marx's views on money, credit, and the economy drew on his reading and understanding of the classicals. When his positions were finally shaped, it was clear that he rejected mainstream classical positions and adopted, to some degree, the famous critique of the banking school. The latter was based on an elaborate analysis of the various functions and forms of money and credit and their changing roles in the economy. It included an explicit rejection of the famous quantity theory and of Ricardo's monetary analysis.[4]

These issues are discussed in *Contribution to the Critique of Political Economy* (1859) and in *Capital* volume 1 (1967), but, a detailed discussion appeared only in volume III (1894).[5] There Marx drew on the works of Thomas Tooke and John Fullarton, the banking school advocates, who did not start the analysis by mechanically placing commodities on one side and money on the other. The banking school's position thus led to an important distinction between coins, notes, and deposits, and to a rejection of the quantity theory. Both were essential in the development of Marx's own analysis. Instead of the mechanical approach characteristic of Ricardo, the correct approach to money and credit, for Marx, had its starting point in a general theory of money and in an analysis of the different moments in commodity exchange.

A general theory of money fits any economy where commodities, that is, products for exchange, exist and the exchange is not barter. For Marx, money is the general equivalent, a commodity standing against all others but at the same time set apart from them. With the development of capitalism, however, many forms of money, functioning in various capacities, came to play important roles in the economy. Unfortunately Marx did not depart from an analysis based on commodity-money, but his analysis became increasingly less abstract and was capable of shedding some light on the actual monetary circuit.

In volume 3 of *Capital*, for instance, Marx describes gold as the reserve on which four different functions depended: "payments of bills in the interior business"; "currency"; "world money"; and "guaranteeing the convertibility of bank notes" (1894, pp. 536–37). Each of the functions of gold reserves had to be analyzed to draw a valid picture of the monetary process. Moreover, in times of crisis the various demands for the different forms of money change, but not necessarily in the same direction. This is the result of the complicated relationship between the liquidity needs of those involved in transactions between dealers and consumers, as opposed to those involved in transactions between dealers and dealers. During times of crises, the dealer/dealer demand for liquidity increases, since credit usually collapses; the dealer/customer

---

4. On Marx's theory of money and its development see Arnon 1984; de Brunhoff 1976; Foley 1982a, 1982b, and Harris 1976. More will be said on the classical school's approach in section 4.

5. This volume was edited by Engels, who described the section on money as in need of much editing; however, the text was written before the publication of volume 1 of *Capital*.

demand for liquidity, on the other hand, falls along with the collapse of spending. Thus, crises have an impact on the monetary circuit, which, in turn, may then influence the real side of the economy, exacerbating the crisis.

Thus crises, which have their roots in the real processes, may be influenced by the monetary circuit, and under certain circumstances, the monetary circuit can either trigger or prevent a crisis. Certainly this is not how orthodox Marxism in the 1930s perceived the role of the monetary circuit in crises.

3. Minsky on Crises, Finance and Social Philosophy

Minsky's interpretation of Keynes's work emphasized the latter's departure from the basic ideas of the classicals in his revolutionary work of 1936. The classicals' focus was the self-correcting mechanisms in decentralized capitalism. In their view, the market itself pushed the economy to rational exploitation of its resources. Unemployment was, then, a temporary problem that need not worry society, since the forces that would cure it are found within the system itself. On a more ideological level, the same assumption took the form of an "invisible hand" approach; nobody, certainly no authority, should take upon itself the unnecessary task of intervening in the economic process with some benevolent purpose in mind.

This opposition to molding the economy referred to any instrument, to use modern terminology—including, for example, money—as an interventionist tool. Money had no influence on the real economy according to this popular analysis, and at most determined "nominal" magnitudes.

Minsky, in the first chapter of his book on Keynes, summarized Keynes's position in 1936 as follows:

> His [Keynes's] analysis yielded the result that money was not neutral. In contrast to the quantity theory, his theory showed that real variables depend in an essential way on monetary and financial variables; that the price level does not depend solely or even mainly on the quantity of money; and that the transitional processes are such that a decentralized, unplanned, capitalist economy—one in which economic policy did not intervene in an appropriate manner—was not a self-correcting system that tended toward a stable equilibrium at full employment. In Keynes' new view full employment, if achieved, was itself a transitory state. (1975, p. 3)

The historical background was, of course, the Great Depression. High rates of unemployment, for a long period of time, put classical doctrines to a severe test. There were several attempts to formulate policies to counter the Depression, some in line with what was to become Keynesian thought, but those were not based on solid theoretical grounds.

One such attempt by Henry Simons of Chicago, a person admired by Minsky, was nevertheless criticized by Minsky for "dealing with symptoms rather than the causes of the then seemingly obvious flaws of capitalism" (Whalen 1988). On a theoretical level, the only alternative to traditional economics was offered by the Marxists. They saw the Great Depression as another proof of Marx's superior analysis of capitalism; the events were just another confirmation of their crisis theory. Keynes, in Minsky's eyes, was trying to develop a middle way. He was trying to understand capitalism and formulate policies that would make it workable, an unfeasible task in the Marxists' view and an unnecessary one according to traditional economists.

Keynes, of course, reached the basic conclusion in 1936 that a "visible hand" might work. The instruments may differ, but both monetary and fiscal policy can, in principle, influence the real economy. This conclusion, in favor of active interventions in the otherwise autonomous economic process, defined Keynes as an "alternative to the dismal views of the traditionalists and the Marxists" (Whalen 1988, p. 7). This important lesson—"that slumps are unnecessary and a waste of both human and nonhuman resources"—had become, almost everywhere, an "axiom guiding economic policy."

> However, this victory for Keynes' policy objectives and activist policy posture obscures the fact that implicit in his analysis is a view that a capitalist economy is fundamentally flawed. This flaw exists because the financial system necessary for capitalist viability and vigor—which translates entrepreneurial animal spirit into effective demand for investment—contains the potential for runaway expansion, powered by an investment boom. This runaway expansion is brought to a halt because accumulated financial changes render the financial system fragile, so that no unusual changes can trigger serious financial difficulties. (Whalen 1988, p. 12)

This is the reasoning underlying Minsky's oxymoronic term "destabilizing stability": as long as the capitalist process is driven mainly by animal spirits, there is no way to avoid the flaw. Stability, achieved through policy and fine tuning, cannot overcome the weaknesses in the capitalist process based on private interests and calculations. The only proposed solution, in Minsky's interpretation of Keynes, is the "socialization of investment"; that is, the application of different calculations and decision- making processes to the accumulation of capital.

Some may regard this as too radical an interpretation of Keynes; it is surely, as Minsky fully recognizes, well beyond what the mainstream has been willing to accept as Keynes's central message. From this interpretation, Minsky concludes that capitalism is doomed to face "stagnation and great depressions," unless it is replaced by "reformed capitalism . . . based on a dominance of social control over investment." This important conclusion is the outcome of his famous financial fragility thesis.

Investment decisions, according to this interpretation, involve future circumstances about which, as Keynes said, "we simply do not know" (1937, p. 214). The law of large numbers does not help in this case because economic agents will all be motivated by the same circumstances, and aggregation will not cancel individual deviations and create regularities. Thus, we have instead a bandwagon effect that will create irregularities.[6]

The Keynes/Minsky view is not simply that subjective factors might cause instability. Rather, subjective factors will *most probably* cause such instability. Since external finance is becoming increasingly important in the modern economy, the chain created as a result of the subjective revaluation of the future by producing firms is both shaped by the latter specific financial position and in turn influences the intermediary units. The change is then transferred to the rest of the economy through the intermediaries. It is important to emphasize that this cycle theory focuses on the firms' investment decisions, assuming throughout that the objective rate of profit does not change. The major driving force is the firms' subjective evaluation of future rates of profit; this is the unexplained black box that can, in principle, render any outcome possible.

When the economic system approaches full employment, the degree of fragility increases. Firms assume at some point in the upswing that future profits will be lower than before. This leads, through changes in the asset prices of existing capital goods relative to prices of new capital goods, to a decline in investment and, as a result, a depression. The beginning of a slump is magnified through its effects on the intermediaries. They cut their loans because they are worried about their survival during the coming difficult times. The chain reaction is clear. After an interval, fragility in the system decreases, and the decline stops when investment behavior changes; again, this change is a result of subjective change in evaluation of future profits.

Minsky's cycle theory does not, in short, depend at all on developments on the real side of the economy. Contrary to the Marxian approach, the objective rate of profit is not a key variable in this discussion. Neither is coordination a factor in his explanation. It is not clear why, if one accepts this theory, countermeasures cannot be taken. In principle, if a decline in investment is discovered, an increase in effective demand can be created, and the

---

6. Minsky emphasized Keynes's innovative discussion of uncertainty, particularly in his famous response to Viner's review of *The General Theory* (1937). There, the true revolutionary Keynes appeared most clearly. See the papers by Crotty and Dymski in this volume for further explorations on the issue of Keynesian uncertainty and investment. For more complete and rigorous treatments of Minsky's analysis of investment, finance and crisis, see Minsky 1975 ch. 6; Minsky 1982 chs. 4 and 5; the chapters by Taylor and Delli Gatti, Gallegati and Gardini in this volume; Taylor and O'Connell 1985; and Dymski and Pollin 1992.

chain reaction in financial markets can be fought through a managed credit system. Such views do in fact appear in Minsky's writings when he explains that the Great Depression will probably not happen again. However, as long as interventions are timid, and the hegemony in policy-making circles favors the more passive schools, the instability hypothesis is persuasive.

Minsky's position on monetary theory and policy narrowly defined—the quantity theory—deserves special treatment. Minsky does not believe that an active monetary policy can be successful in eliminating cycles. He believes that the financial and banking systems are basically demand determined, that is, the final users of the liabilities and assets determine their quantities. If the demand for 'money' increases, the various institutions will find the means to supply this growing demand, even if in the process the price of 'money' will increase. They will supply money through a more efficient usage of their existing resources (liability management), and through financial innovations. The conclusion is that sufficient liquidity will always be generated. Thus, Minsky clearly supports the notion that money is endogenous, a view he shared with Smith, Tooke, and Marx, among other classical writers.

This brings us to the question of social philosophy. Minsky's social philosophy can best be understood through his analysis of Keynes's approach to the matter, since he agrees with Keynes. According to Minsky, Keynes's social philosophy did not change with the appearance of the *General Theory* in 1936. Rather, Keynes's early classical economic theories were inconsistent with his social philosophy. After the *General Theory*, Keynes's social philosophy and economic theory harmonized. This means that his early social philosophy was based on intuition, beliefs, and values rather than on economic theory. This same pattern characterizes Keynes' views concerning policy. In Minsky's words:

> The face he set upon his policy views prior to the *General Theory* can be characterized as a flirtation with a humane, decentralized socialism, a flirtation which was tempered by the disciple of an economist. He could not accept the mechanisms the socialists put forth to achieve their common goals. (1975, p. 147)

For Keynes, the problem of any social philosophy was how to combine "economic efficiency, social justice, and individual liberty," (cited in Minsky 1975, p. 147) and Keynes' political stance on this triad put him neither with Labour nor with the Conservatives. He rejected traditional socialist thinking and believed that it should be replaced with something new that could be found among "constructive thinkers in the Labour Party and constructive thinkers in the Liberal Party" to which Keynes belonged. (Minsky 1975, p. 146) However, this search for a new theory was over, in Minsky's view, when Keynes wrote the *General Theory*. With it, "the traditional radical analysis and programs [became] both obsolete and unnecessary." (Minsky 1975, p. 147) Keynes believed, argues Minsky approvingly, that the "new theory rendered obsolete the muddle that he felt Marxist economics to be." (1975, 147).

For Minksy, the alternative economic order that best achieves the triad is a reformed capitalism where decentralized markets rule subject to interventions in distribution and, most important, in investment decisions. This is how Minsky interprets Keynes's notion of a "socialization of investment." Thus, regarding Minsky's social philosophy, his debt to Lange is clear. In Minsky's "Beginnings" article, an autobiographical essay dedicated to his first years in the profession, he wrote

> Lange was undoubtedly the major influence on my development during these [student] years. I like to believe that the research program I have been carrying out is consistent with the Lange of 1939–42."[7]

Was this research program, by any meaningful definition of the term, a Marxian research program?

4. Minsky in Light of the Economics of Marx

4.1 The Socialist Agenda

Minsky's attitude to Lange's work as it was formulated during the period 1939–42 is of great importance. At that time Lange was arguing for society's control over the anarchic economic process; this was his version of market socialism. More specifically, Lange was arguing for the socialization of monopolies and other large-scale activities, a view similar to Minsky's interpretation of Keynes's notion of the socialization of investment. This similarity between the radical Keynesians and some of the conclusions of Lange and other followers of market socialism plays a key role in understanding Minsky's own position. Both approaches reject the classical belief in the smooth functioning of decentralized capitalism and thus the need to replace it with a form of planning that is both more equitable and efficient than laissez-faire.

4.2 The Monetary Connection

Minsky was undoubtedly influenced by socialist thinkers, some of them Marxians. He always viewed capitalism as a system that is inherently flawed;

---

7. Minsky 1985 p. 221. Minsky's reference to the years 1939–1942 probably manifests his criticism of Lange's "compromise on ideology" in later years.

instability and crises are a part of capitalism that fine tuning will never be able to correct. However, the roots of this instability are to be found in the less fundamental monetary circuit. This should have put Minsky in a camp opposite to that of much of Marxian economics. But does it divorce him from the economics of Marx himself?

My answer is no. A serious reading of Marx on the issue of the relative autonomy of the monetary circuit will find his position consistent with that of Minsky. Marxian scholars should therefore find much that is illuminating in Minsky's approach to Keynesianism. Minsky managed to rescue important insights from his innovative reading of Keynes, challenging the conventional wisdom that has ruled throughout the post–World War II era.

The similarity between Marx's and Minsky's respective perspectives on monetary theories—specifically their rejection of the classical quantity theory and their consistency with the banking school approach—is significant.[8]

Classical monetary theory started from the analysis of commodity money. The approach was twofold: money was seen as a commodity, where the value categories applied; and also as a symbol of wealth and medium of exchange, where the quantity of money was of utmost importance. The tension between these two facets of money remained with monetary analysis as long as the basic form of money analyzed was commodity money. In this respect both Smith, who put more weight on the commodity aspect, and Ricardo, who emphasized the quantity of money, were genuine members of the classical tradition.

The historical rise of more complicated forms of money, and the increased sophistication of a developed financial system, made this approach obsolete. The need to understand forms of money that are divorced from any links to commodity money required a fundamentally new way of thinking. The banking school was a substantially successful attempt at providing such a new framework. They focused on the forms of money created by the financial system and treated them as having a life of their own. Thus, their understanding that deposits functioned exactly as does commodity money, though behaving according to different laws, was a path-breaking discovery.

The actual debate between the currency and banking schools was over a practical question: Should note creation become the exclusive responsibility of the Bank of England or should competitor banks also be allowed to issue notes? In the course of debate, the participants touched on the status of deposits and credit and on the appropriate means of controlling their quantity. The major conclusion of the Banking School was that the quantity of money, properly defined, was not the cause of changes in the price level *but its effect*.

---

8. See Arnon 1984, 1991 for discussions on Marx's monetary theory and the banking school, respectively.

That is, prices are determined independently of money, and, in Marxian terminology, the monetary circuit primarily reflects the real one.

Marx accepted the quantity theory conclusions as long as commodity money was the dominant form of money. However, when the system contained additional forms of money, such as inconvertible notes, deposits, and bills of exchange, he found the banking school approach to be superior. Marx's solution under these circumstances was somewhat technical. He treated the economy as if two parallel systems were at work: a gold (commodity-money) system and an inconvertible system. Prices, in gold, were then determined according to the laws governing commodity circulation while the price of gold itself, in terms of inconvertible forms of money, was determined by the simple quantity approach. Marx promised, but never fully completed, a treatment of the credit economy. Had he done so, Marxian economics might have found a better guide for integrating real and monetary analysis.

Minsky's contributions might be considered as helping to fill this lacuna in Marxian analysis. His perspective can be viewed as an analysis of the laws of motion of advanced capitalism in which the financial system is integrated with the real system. Thus, the monetary circuit and finance at large are no longer a redundant part of the system analyzed but an important factor in it. It is true that Minsky's analysis neglects an analysis of the real side of the economy. But combined with Marx, we now have an innovative and integrated approach in which crises can be caused by the monetary/financial circuit as well as the real economy.

Minsky clearly has never written in the Marxian tradition, as commonly defined. Neither the concepts nor the language he uses is Marxian. However the subject itself—a critical inquiry into the laws of motion of capitalism—is identical in the work of both authors. And, as we have seen, the explanations they provide for some basic features of the capitalist accumulation process are compatible and mutually reinforcing. How do we understand the role of money, credit, and finance in accumulation and, in particular, generating crises? Should public forms of control supplant the hegemony of market power? New light on these questions has already been shed through seeking a common ground between Marx and Minsky. Further explorations offer the promise of yielding significant new perspectives in the realms of both economic theory and progressive policy formulation.

REFERENCES

Arnon, Arie (1984), "Marx's Theory of Money: The Formative Years," *History of Political Economy*, 16, pp. 555–75.

———— (1991), *Thomas Tooke: Pioneer of Monetary Theory*, Ann Arbor: University of Michigan Press.

Crotty, James (1986), "Marx, Keynes, and Minsky on the Instability of the Capitalist Growth Process and the Nature of Government Economic Policy," in S. Helburn and D. Bramhall, eds., *Marx, Schumpeter, and Keynes: A Centenary Celebration of Dissent*, Armonk, NY: M.E. Sharpe.

de Brunhoff, Suzanne (1976), *Marx on Money*, New York: Urizen Books.

Dymski, Gary, and Robert Pollin (1992), "Hyman Minsky as Hedgehog: The Power of the Wall Street Paradigm," in S. Fazzari and D. Papadimitriou, eds., *Financial Conditions and Macroeconomic Performance: Essays in Honor of Hyman P. Minsky*, Armonk, NY: M.E. Sharpe.

Foley, Duncan K.(1982a) "On Marx's Theory of Money," manuscript, Department of Economics, Barnard College.

———— (1982b) "The Value of Money, the Value of Labor Power, and the Marxian Transformation Problem," *Review of Radical Political Economics*, 14, pp. 37–47.

———— (1986) *Understanding Capital: Marx's Economic Theory*, Cambridge, MA: Harvard University Press.

Harris, Laurence (1976), "On Interest, Credit and Capital," *Economy and Society*, 5, pp. 143–77.

Jarsulic, Marc (1988) "Financial Instability and Income Distribution," *Journal of Economic Issues*, 22, pp. 545–53.

Keynes, John M. (1936) *The General Theory of Employment, Interest and Money*, London: Macmillan.

———— (1937) "The General Theory of Employment," *Quarterly Journal of Economics*, 51, pp. 209–23.

Lange, Oscar, and Fred M. Taylor (1938) *On the Economic Theory of Socialism*, New York: McGraw Hill.

Marx, Karl (1859) *A Contribution to the Critique of Political Economy* [1970]. Moscow: International Publishers.

———— (1867) *Capital*, volume 1. Moscow: International Publishers.

———— (1885) *Capital*, volume 2. Moscow: International Publishers.

———— (1894) *Capital*, volume 3. Moscow: International Publishers.

Minsky, Hyman P. (1975) *John Maynard Keynes*, New York: Columbia University Press.

———— (1982) *Can "It" Happen Again: Essays on Finance and Instability*, Armonk, NY: M.E. Sharpe.

———— (1985) "Beginnings," *Banca Nazionale Del Lavoro Quarterly Review*, no. 154, pp. 211–221.

———— (1986) *Stabilizing an Unstable Economy*, New Haven: Yale University Press.

Taylor, Lance, and Stephen O'Connell (1985) "A Minsky Crisis," *Quarterly Journal of Economics*, 100, pp. 871–85.

Whalen, Charles J. (1988) "The Minsky-Simons Connection: A Neglected Thread in the History of Economic Thought," *Journal of Economic Issues*, 22, 533–44.

Part V
A Framework for New Macropolicy Approaches

CHAPTER 14

The Costs and Benefits of Financial Instability: Big Government Capitalism and the Minsky Paradox

*Robert Pollin and Gary Dymski**

1. Introduction

There is a provocative paradox at the center of Hyman Minsky's analytic work. On the one hand, Minsky, following Keynes, argues that capitalist economies are inherently unstable and that financial processes endogenously generate destabilizing forces. Minsky also claims, however, that interactive debt deflations such as the one in 1929–33 that led to the Great Depression, cannot "happen again."[1]

This paradox suggests two questions. Why can't debt deflations and depressions happen again? And if they can't happen again, what then are the consequences of the persistent tendency toward instability?

Addressing these questions requires an examination of the most important results of Minsky's theoretical framework. Equally, it demands a consideration of how, both within Minsky's framework and more generally, government policy interventions affect macroeconomic performance. Avoiding another Depression in the advanced capitalist countries is an accomplishment for which post–World War II government policies deserve some credit. But we need to better understand how macro-policies have attained this goal, and,

*The ordering of the authors' names is deliberately non-alphabetical but does not connote seniority. We are grateful for the constructive suggestions of Susan Carter, Joseph Duncan, Sarah Lane, Michele Naples, Mark Glick, Howard Sherman and two anonymous referees. All errors, unfortunately, remain our own.

1. We term this the "Minsky paradox" to acknowledge both the centrality of these ideas in Minsky's work and the importance of Minsky's work in reawakening economists' interest in financial instability. But we note at the outset that the first half of the paradox—the notion of endogenous financial instability—did not originate with Minsky, as Minsky himself acknowledges. Important predecessors include Marx, Keynes, and Wesley Mitchell. Two works that discuss Minsky's ideas within the context of earlier conceptions of financial instability are Mullineux 1990 and Wolfson 1986.

equally important, what have been the collateral effects of such policy interventions. In other words, if we accept Minsky's argument that capitalist
financial structures tend inexorably toward states of instability and crisis, we
need to examine both the *benefits* and the *costs* of preventing this inexorable
tendency from reaching its logical endpoint of full-scale depressions.

The question can also be fruitfully addressed from another angle. Although a 1930s-style depression has been avoided during the postwar period,
financial dislocations and stresses have not. Indeed, as Minsky and others
have observed, financial crises have become increasingly frequent and severe
since the mid-1960s. Entering the 1990s, the U.S. system of financial
intermediation—encompassing commercial banks, S&Ls, insurance companies, and other institutions—has been more vulnerable than at any point since
the 1930s. Neither the tightly regulated financial structure that was adopted in
the wake of the Depression nor the subsequent incremental dismantling of this
regulatory apparatus has reversed this secular tendency toward increased instability. Nor are alternative solutions evident on the horizon.

Moreover, the rise of financial instability has not been confined to the
United States or other advanced economies. Indeed, the most dramatic experience with destabilizing finance in the contemporary period has been the debt
crisis in the Third World. As of this writing, a decade has passed since the
crisis began in Latin America. But the Latin economies have still not begun a
renewed trajectory of stable and equitable growth (see Felix, this volume).
Meanwhile, the crisis has created severe hardship throughout Latin America,
while also inflicting damage on both the financial system and trade balance in
the United States.

This essay develops some elements of a historical perspective on the two
questions that emerge from Minsky's paradox: first, how are debt deflations
and depressions avoided in a system whose normal operations produce financial fragility, i.e. the precondition for debt deflation and depression; and
second, how are the unavoidable crisis-producing tendencies manifested when
depressions are prevented? We are particularly interested in the second question, since it will shed direct light on the array of problems besetting the
contemporary U.S. and international economies.

Indeed, we will argue that fundamental insights emerge by observing
contemporary conditions through the historical lenses provided by the Minsky
paradox. In particular, we believe that the current historical juncture is
unique. For nearly half a century, capitalist economies have possessed the
tools to avoid full-scale debt deflations but not the ability to prevent the thrust
toward fragility. Thus, the problems of fragility have deepened and the effectiveness of stabilization policies has declined. In other words, the benefits
associated with avoiding a depression are shrinking relative to the costs of
deepening fragility—so much so that, despite continued large-scale govern-

ment presence in capitalist economies, economic performance increasingly resembles that of earlier epochs in which government presence was minimal.

The policy implications of this historical observation are crucial. If indeed the costs of depression prevention increasingly approximate its benefits, then strong arguments are at hand for fundamentally shifting policy directions: either depression-prevention policies should be abandoned, as free market proponents advise; or new policy approaches should be pursued, which can lower the costs while maintaining—and perhaps increasing—the benefits of depression prevention.

The next section reviews the analytic arguments behind Minsky's paradox, emphasizing Minsky's own explanations of the causes of systemic fragility and of the consequences of avoiding depressions through government interventions. Section 3 then considers long-term trends in U.S. macroeconomic performance, contrasting in particular the movements of key aggregate variables within what we term the "small government" epoch, lasting through the 1930s depression, with a "big government" period beginning with World War II. In the concluding fourth section, we address the implications of our empirical findings for the future direction of macroeconomic policy.

2. Systemic Instability and the Limits of Stabilization Policy

Minsky argues that capitalist economies are inherently unstable because of the shift in expectations that occurs over the course of the business cycle and the way this shift is transmitted through the financial system.[2] At the trough of a business cycle, realized profits and profit expectations are both low. At the same time, the financial structure is robust, since the debt deflations that would have accompanied the previous downturn have brought a high proportion of overleveraged units to bankruptcy. As the economy moves up from the trough, profits begin to rise. But expectations are still low because of memories of the trough, and lenders' and borrowers' risk premia are correspondingly high. Financing patterns thus remain relatively cautious. However, as the upturn continues and realized profits exceed expectations, expectations

2. More detailed presentations of Minsky's conception of financial fragility and instability can be found in Minsky 1982, 1986 and in Dymski and Pollin 1992. Since the terms "financial fragility" and "financial instability" appear frequently in this paper, definitions of each are in order. As used here, financial fragility connotes a state of an economic system, and financial instability connotes a dynamic process affecting that system. An economy becomes more financially fragile as financial commitments rise relative to income flows, since smaller disturbances in income flows will then disrupt units' ability to meet repayment commitments. Financial instability occurs when disturbances in an economy's financial structure—such as a stock–market crash, major bank failure, or nonpayment of foreign debt obligations—affect the level of real activity in that economy.

shift upward. Animal spirits are now ignited, and firms become more willing to borrow in the pursuit of profit opportunities. In these circumstances, even more cautious firms feel pressure to either to pursue all apparent profit opportunities or to forfeit them to competitors.

As full employment is approached, "euphoric expectations" take hold. The growth rate of debt exceeds that of profits, since—for a given distribution of income between wages and profits—profit opportunities are constrained by the growth of productivity, whereas the extension of credit is not so constrained. The financial structure thus becomes increasingly fragile–that is, vulnerable to an interactive debt deflation that induces a downturn. In addition, banks and other lending institutions generally accommodate—and even aggressively promote—the growing demand for credit. Their expectations may have shifted upward as well. But more important, they do not generally refuse loan requests by large-scale solvent customers.

Minsky therefore concludes that a period of full employment is not a natural equilibrium point for a capitalist economy. It rather is a transitory moment in a cycle, one that in turn leads to overheating and increasing financial fragility. In the absence of government intervention, the market economy thus proceeds normally from a cyclical trough to an unsustainable boom characterized by speculative financial behavior. The cycle culminates in a debt deflation and depression. But the depression itself creates the conditions for a return to financial robustness and recovery. Thus, and here Minsky's position is perfectly consistent with that of Schumpeter and Marx, depressions are functional: they are the destructive but necessary mechanism—the "slaughtering of capital values," as Marx put it—that returns capitalist financial structures to balance. In other words, depressions bring benefits as well as costs to unregulated market economies. To recognize such benefits in no way minimizes the costs; that such "slaughtering of capital values" is necessary to control a free market economy's natural tendency toward fragility stands as a powerful indictment of the system.

In the wake of the most severe 1930s Depression, the challenge for economists—especially those, such as Keynes, who recognized capitalism's weaknesses but opposed its demise—was precisely to reduce the costs of controlling destabilizing financial market behavior, that is, to supplant the slaughter of capital values as a stabilization mechanism. Thus was born the post–World War II system of big government capitalism, with its accompanying instruments of macroeconomic management. Minsky argues that two policy instruments of big government capitalism have been extremely effective in preventing the recurrence of depressions. These are federal deficit spending and lender-of-last-resort interventions by the Federal Reserve.

Minsky argues that the effect of deficit spending during a downturn is to establish a floor for profits. He derives this by applying Kalecki's well-known accounting identity wherein, in a closed economy, profits equal investment plus the government deficit. Running deficits in the initial phases of a downturn will therefore stabilize profits. More favorable profit expectations in turn encourage investors' animal spirits, which should then break the downturn. At the same time, lender-of-last-resort interventions are able to counteract the liquidity shortages of distressed financial firms. It is through exercising these powerful policies that Minsky believes debt deflations and depressions are avoidable in contemporary advanced capitalist economies.

But here is the crux of Minsky's paradox. He argues that solving the problem of debt deflations by no means implies that interventionist policies can promote full employment equilibrium. Rather, Minsky claims that interventionist policies serve to validate the existing fragile financial structure: problems emerging out of the existing structure are allowed to continue and even deepen. It is therefore perfectly rational for market participants to pursue risky financial practices even as the level of financial fragility rises. This is because, through deficit spending and lender-of-last-resort interventions, the potential costs associated with risky financial practices are, to a considerable extent, socialized—government rather than private firms absorbs these costs. Indeed, the socialization of financial market risk promotes fragility since, as Minsky writes,

> once borrowers and lenders recognize that the downside instability of profits has decreased there will be an increase in the willingness and ability of business and bankers to debt-finance. If the cash flows to validate debt are virtually guaranteed by the profit implications of big government then debt-financing of positions in capital assets is encouraged. (1986, p. 213)

Thus, the effectiveness of depression-prevention policies will deteriorate over time: government policy is called on increasingly to bail out the fragile system and thereby avoid a depression, but this very policy encourages more fragility and thus increases the burdens placed on future policy interventions. Larger and more frequent interventions become necessary to fend off debt deflations and depressions: the costs of policy interventions rise while their benefits diminish.

Minsky's framework, in short, is permeated with dialectical tension. It is therefore not surprising that interesting parallels to the Minsky paradox can be found in the contemporary neo-Marxian literature on instability and crisis. Magdoff and Sweezy (1987), for example, have argued that advanced capitalist economies inherently tend toward stagnant growth owing to a secular tendency for profitable investment opportunities to diminish, which in turn produces a decline in investment growth and aggregate demand. But they argue that this inherent tendency can be mitigated through the demand stimuli provided by government spending, private wasteful expenditures induced through advertising, and the increasing reliance on borrowed funds to finance these activities. But again, Sweezy and Magdoff argue that the costs of such activities rise over time; they, like Minksy, have written extensively on the long-term rise of a fragile financial structure in the United States.

Another neo-Marxian approach is that of Bowles, Gordon, and Weisskopf (1986, 1991). They argue that capitalist economies can prosper only if surrounded by institutional structures that ameliorate the tensions generated by capitalism's inherently conflictual relations. In their view, institutional changes in the wake of the Great Depression—for example, the social wage derived from the federal governments' social spending, the stable labor relations acceptable to businesses and unions, and the Bretton Woods international monetary system—did significantly reduce conflict, and thereby, through the 1960s, promoted growth. But over time, the increasing stresses on the conflict-ameliorating institutions renders them less effective. This in turn weakens the economy's growth potential.

At a less theoretical level, it is evident that international economic integration has also weakened the stabilizing capacities of interventionist policies. Considering the U.S. experience, the presence of persistent trade deficits accompanying federal budget deficits has meant that a significant proportion of the demand stimulus from a given-sized deficit is exported to the U.S. trading partners. Correspondingly, globalization of financial markets has increased the difficulty of Federal Reserve interventions, affecting the behavior of private capital flows.

Given these considerations, what is important about the Minsky paradox is its robustness. One may find an alternative explanation for the rise of financial instability more compelling than that of Minsky, yet still draw substantially from Minsky's model for understanding the *implications* of instability. The insights that flow from the paradox are particularly illuminating, especially Minsky's explanation as to how the costs of financial stabilization policies can rise relative to their benefits.[3]

3. Small versus Big Government Capitalism: Long-Term Tendencies in the U.S. Economy

This section presents empirical evidence that illustrates two points: first, key aggregate variables behave differently in the "small government" and "big government" eras of capitalism; and second, over the 1980s, the movements

---

3. Pollin 1986 is one effort to develop an explanation for the rise of financial instability more consistent with Marxian approaches to declining profitability and stagnation, but Pollin nevertheless finds considerable compatibility between the Marxian and Minskian frameworks, especially with respect to the implications of instability.

of these same variables shift again, coming to resemble the patterns associated with the small government era.

If the government's role in reducing instability is as central as Minsky thinks, then the behavior of many data series should differ between the small government and big government eras. Further, the transition from one era to the other should involve a wide variety of institutional changes that reflect this new government role. A proper investigation of the significance of the small/big government disjuncture in U.S. economic history would be a formidable task, as both empirical and institutional changes would have to be carefully traced and interpreted.[4] Such a project is beyond the aims of this paper. We instead pursue a more limited investigation, examining the behavior of several key aggregate variables in these two periods. These include GNP growth and the unemployment rate, as measures of instability and the social costs associated with instability; the GNP deflator and the real interest rate, as indicators of price stability in both the product and financial markets; and the rate of business and bank failures, as indicators of the variable rate of "capital slaughtering" over time.

With one exception, our data for these time series begin in 1875, the period after the Civil War and Reconstruction, and carry through to 1989. The one exception is the unemployment series, which, because of data problems explained in Appendix B, we begin in 1890. The small government period lasts until World War II, that is, through 1941; and the big government period begins in 1942, with the United States full-scale involvement in the war. Federal government expenditures accounted for an average of 4.3 percent of GNP during the small government period and 21.1 percent of GNP during the big government era. We present both means and standard deviations of each variable as well as average movements over cycles for some variables.

3.1 Measurement Problems in Long Aggregate Time Series

Before investigating specific variables' behavior, it is important to consider three measurement problems associated with these long-term time series. The

---

4. We do not attempt to document all the ramifications of New Deal legislation regarding financial markets, though these of course were formidable, as the Roosevelt Administration undertook a complete restructuring of the financial system in the wake of the Great Depression. New Deal initiatives led to the segmentation of banking markets, specialization among financial intermediaries, a decline of deposit rates, virtual elimination of the threat of bank runs, and increasing power for the Federal Reserve, especially to intervene effectively in the face of incipient financial crises. We attempt to capture the basic effects of these changes through time series data. We also note that a more institutional and descriptive attempt to consider long-term financial history within a Minskian framework is Kindleberger 1978. Kindleberger's work differs from ours in that he considers Western European as well as U.S. history. In addition, his examination incorporates events as early as the 1720s.

first concerns the quality of data over the small government period. Christina Romer (1986a, 1986b, 1989) has argued that estimates of some aggregate variables over the pre-1930 period have been constructed using suspect methodologies, and this in turn has created distorted impressions of economic activity in this period. Romer has constructed alternative time series estimates for GNP, price level change, and unemployment; and she has used these estimates to argue that the U.S. economy exhibited considerably more stability in the pre-1930 period than had been previously believed.

Romer's work has initiated a substantial amount of recent literature responding to her findings. We have concluded from our review of this literature that the work of Romer's critics rests on a sounder methodological foundation. As a result, we use the data series generated by Balke and Gordon (1989) for GNP and price level, and that of Carter and Sutch (1992) and Weir (1992) for unemployment. Appendix B explains our reasoning on these issues.[5]

A second problem concerns the consistency of the data on business failure rates, especially in the recent past. The concern has arisen because of recent changes in bankruptcy laws and data collection methods. However, as we also discuss in Appendix B, our view is that the published data on failure rates provide an accurate indicator of the proportion of firms exiting over time either through bankruptcy proceedings or voluntary actions involving losses to creditors—that is, through measures bringing losses to creditors and thereby contributing to aggregate financial fragility.

The third data problem is how to control for extraordinary historical circumstances. Such outlier periods may so influence data averages as to create misleading impressions of long-term behavior. For example, both World War I and the Depression years are arguably aberrations within the small government epoch, and including them will skew results for this period. One could similarly argue that World War II distorts the figures for the big government epoch.

Given these concerns, we use several alternative measurements to present data for these eras. The small government era is measured in three ways: as ending before World War I in 1914, before the Depression in 1929, and in 1941. We then define the big government era as both inclusive and exclusive of World War II, that is, beginning both in 1942 and 1947, the year after the most dramatic effects of disarmament had been absorbed. Finally, we show figures for the 1980s as a separate category. This allows us to evaluate our central matter of concern: to what extent can we observe a decline in stability and overall economic performance during these later years of the big government era?

---

5. Appendix B also documents data sources for all series reported in the following discussion.

There is, of course, an element of arbitrariness in isolating the 1980s as a distinct period for observing the declining stabilizing powers of big government capitalism. Indeed, much of the work investigating the end of the postwar boom and the onset of stagnation and financial fragility, including that of Minsky and the neo-Marxists, would set the breakpoint between the robust and fragile phases of the postwar period as sometime during the late 1960s or early 1970s. But we are not primarily interested here in observing the beginning of the period of stagnation and fragility. Our aim, rather, is to consider the *effects* of the economy's having moved decisively into a fragile state. This is why, for our purposes, it is appropriate to set a later period, roughly the decade of the 1980s, as a separate unit of observation.

In addition to means and standard deviations of the time series data during the three separate phases of small government, big government, and the 1980s, we also consider average cyclical behavior of the variables during the three separate time series. We follow the basic approach just described in generating figures for average cyclical behavior in the small government and big government eras and the 1980s. In particular, we do not include the years surrounding either World War I or World War II in generating the average cyclical behavior. Details of our methodology are presented in appendix B.

3.2 Aggregate Economic Behavior in the Long Run.

For each variable, we first compare its means and standard deviations in the small government era, in the big government era, and in the 1980s. (Unless otherwise specified, all data are reported in Table 1.) We then present figures showing average cyclical movements in the three periods.

GNP Growth.

As general measures of performance, the GNP growth and per capita income figures convey a consistent picture, regardless of which time frame one uses to measure the two eras. Average income growth was slightly higher during the small government era; it ranges between 3.6 and 3.8 percent, depending on how one defines the period, as opposed to between 3.3 and 3.5 percent for the big government era. On a per capita basis, however, the big government era was slightly stronger, ranging between 1.9 and 2.1 percent, as opposed to between 1.7 and 1.9 percent for the small government era.

Despite these similarities in aggregate growth rates, the *stability* of the growth path was substantially greater in the big government era. After 1947 especially, standard deviations of growth are roughly half those of the small government era.

The 1980s represent an aberration from the big government era in that both average and per capita growth—at 2.7 and 1.2 percent respectively—are

TABLE 1. Aggregate Trends under Small and Big Government Capitalism

	Small Government Era:			Big Government Era:			1980s:
	1875–1941	1875–1929	1875–1941	1942–1989	1947–1989	1947–1979	1980–1989
Govt/GNP (%)	4.3 (3.9)	3.4 (3.6)	2.4 (0.3)	21.1 (6.3)	19.5 (2.9)	18.4 (2.3)	23.0 (0.9)
GNP growth Rate	3.6 (6.3)	3.8 (5.0)	3.8 (4.7)	3.4 (4.5)	3.3 (2.7)	3.5 (2.8)	2.7 (2.4)
Per capita GNP Growth Rate	1.9 (6.2)	1.9 (4.9)	1.7 (4.6)	2.0 (4.4)	1.9 (2.6)	2.1 (2.7)	1.1 (2.0)
Unemployment Rate*	7.7 (5.0)	6.1 (3.7)	6.6 (4.0)	5.3 (2.0)	5.7 (1.8)	5.1 (1.5)	7.3 (1.8)
Bank failures per 10,000 banks	165.9 (363.0)	104.8 (108.2)	89.4 (14.8)	19.5 (40.7)	21.2 (42.6)	4.0 (2.4)	78.1 (61.4)
Bus. failures per 10,000 firms	96.9 (26.3)	100.3 (22.5)	103.1 (20.6)	49.3 (27.7)	53.6 (26.0)	42.3 (11.5)	90.8 (26.1)
Inflation rate	0.7 (5.6)	1.0 (5.6)	−0.2 (2.6)	4.0 (3.9)	4.5 (3.0)	4.4 (3.1)	4.9 (2.6)
Real interest rate	4.4 (5.8)	4.2 (5.6)	5.3 (2.9)	1.8 (4.8)	2.6 (3.5)	1.2 (2.7)	7.2 (1.8)

Note: Figures in parentheses are standard deviations.
*Figures for unemployment begin with 1890.
Souces: See Appendix B.

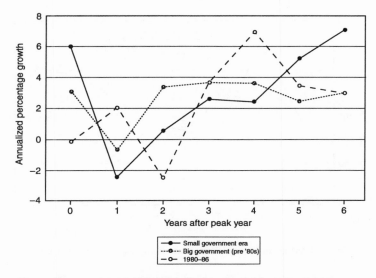

Fig. 1. Post-peak real GNP growth: Small vs. big government eras

significantly below historical trend levels. Standard deviations are within the range of the postwar period; but we would expect a lower standard deviation, since this relatively short time period contains fewer degrees of freedom for exhibiting instability.

Figure 1 provides additional perspective on the cyclical behavior of GNP growth over the three periods. The key observation is that the post-peak variability of GNP for the 1980s evinces a sharpness similar to that of the small government era, and much greater than that for the big government period.

Unemployment
The unemployment trends contrast with those for GNP, in that here we see improvements in both means and standard deviations during the big government era. Of course, the Depression years are a major factor raising the unemployment figures to a 7.7 percent average unemployment rate and 5.0 standard deviation for the full small government era. But even the figures for 1890–1929—a 6.1 percent rate and 3.6 standard deviation—are higher than for the pre-1980s big government era. In the 1980s, we see a reversion to small government levels of unemployment. The average rate of 7.3 percent is much higher not only than that of the big government years prior to the 1980s but also than that of the small government era before the Depression.

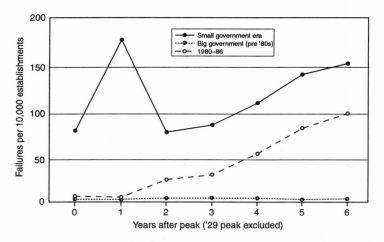

Fig. 2. Post-peak bank failures: small vs. big government eras

Business and Bank Failures

Both these series, measured per 10,000 enterprises, show dramatic improvements in the big government era. Comparing the small government era prior to the Depression with the postwar period to the 1980s, bank failures dropped from an average of 104.8 for the small government period to 4.0 for the big government era. More generally, we observe gains of similar magnitudes, for both means and standard deviations, regardless of how one divides up the two eras. In the 1980s, however, the bank failure rate rises precipitously, to 78.1 per 10,000, a figure which approaches that of the small government era.

Changes in the business failure rate exhibit the same general pattern, if to a less dramatic extent. The business failure rate falls by roughly half in the big government era relative to the small government era, from an annual average of about 100 to one of about 50 failures per 10,000 firms. In the 1980s, however, the rate rises to 90.8 per 10,000 firms—that is, an almost exact reversion to the small government failure level.

Again, the figures for post-peak performance provide another angle for observing these trends. Figure 2, giving cyclical patterns for the bank failure rate, shows that cycles simply did not occur in the pre-1980s big government era. But in the 1980s, the failure rate follows a pattern of increase closely corresponding to that of the small government era.

The pattern for business failures, shown in figure 3, is different. Here in the 1980s, we see a reversion to the level, but not yet the cyclical movements of the small government era. Indeed, figure 3 suggests that the rate of acceler-

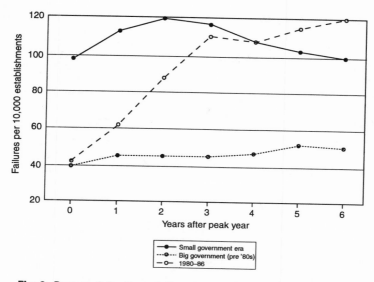

Fig. 3. Post-peak business failures: small vs. big government eras

ation of business failures over the 1980s far exceeds even the average experience of the small government era.

Inflation

The inflation figures present the most consistent patterns within each epoch. In the small government era, average inflation is very low, or even nonexistent. Prices actually *declined* by an annual average rate of 0.2 percent prior to World War I. Standard deviations, however, are large. This suggests that prices varied strongly in a classically cyclical pattern: inflation during a cyclical upswing matched by deflation in a downswing. Such a pattern emerges clearly in figure 4, which gives the average cyclical behavior of prices during the two eras.

An average inflation rate of 4.5–5 percent becomes a permanent presence during the big government era. Moreover, the relatively low standard deviations for average inflation in this era show that though the inflation rate varied, the price increases of one cyclical phase were never matched by declines in succeeding phases. This also can be seen in figure 4.

As for the 1980s, we do not in this case observe a reversion to the patterns of the small government era. Rather, as table 1 shows, the 1980s figures, as averages, resemble those for the full big government era. But from figure 4 we also see the strong disinflationary trend over the 1980s, this sustained disinflation being a unique feature of the 1980s period. Even with

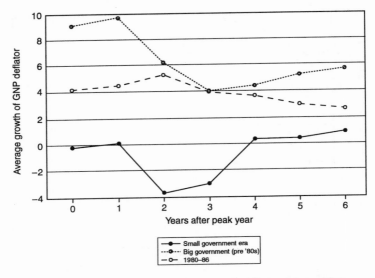

Fig. 4. Post-peak inflation rates: small vs. big government eras

this disinflation however, there has still been no time in the big government era during which the price level actually fell. Deflations, in short, have been eliminated in the big government era. Thus, the government's large economic presence in the 1980s continues to encourage inflation, even while the growth promotion and stabilizing effects of government—the tradeoffs for inflation—have deteriorated.

Real Interest Rates
The specific rate reported here is the long rate for corporate bonds. However, the patterns shown for this rate are basically in line with those for other rates.

We see in table 1 that the big government era prior to the 1980s achieved a dramatic drop in the average real long-term rate relative to the small government era. The patterns shown in figure 5 reflect these dramatic changes via average cyclical movements. This is true regardless of how one specifically periodizes the two eras: in the small government period, real rates vary between 4.2 and 5.3 percent, whereas the range for the pre-1980s big government era is 1.2–2.6 percent. Standard deviations are also consistently lower in the big government era. One could therefore argue that one of the achievements of the pre-1980 big government era was to create a stable enough environment to encourage long-term interest rates to fall by more than half the level of the small government period.

In the 1980s, the real rate rises to 7.0 percent—to a level substantially

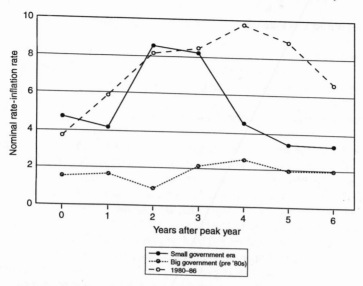

Fig. 5. Post-peak real interest rate: small vs. big government era

exceeding even that of the small government era. We also see from figure 5 that the post-peak upswing in the real rate during the 1980s also exactly tracks the first three post-peak years of the small government era. The difference is that in post-peak years 4–6, real rates fall much less in the 1980s than the small government era.

Overall the data suggest that this increase in real rates in the 1980s was a rational response to the sharp decline in overall stability in the 1980s. Indeed, the degree of riskiness in the 1980s may well be historically unique, in that it combines high and rising levels of instability with persistent inflation. But such a pattern is fully consistent with the Minsky paradox: big government continues to prevent deflations. But instability increases since debt deflation has been eliminated as the economy's self-corrective mechanism. A logical consequence is the sharp increase in real interest rates, reflecting the greater risks of lending money over the increasingly unpredictable long term.[6]

---

6. We are not claiming that rising riskiness can alone explain the unprecedented level of real rates during the 1980s. Other factors have surely played a role, including the high levels of aggregate credit demand by domestic nonfinancial borrowers—including households and nonfinancial corporations as well as the federal government—and the need to support the value of the dollar while the United States runs persistent trade deficits. As far as we know, however, there has been little, if any, consideration of the effects of rising riskiness over the 1980s on real rates, even though, in general, nothing is more elementary than incorporating the role of risk in interest rate determination. As one suggestive piece of evidence, the correlation coefficient between the business failure rate and the real interest rate over the full 1875–1989 period is a rather high .65.

4. Reopening the Question: Lessons from the 1980s

Although Minsky argues that a 1930s style debt deflation and depression cannot happen again, declining economic performance in the current big government era suggests the need for reconsideration.

4.1 Debt Deflation and Depression in Latin America

At one level, the proof is before us: depressions can and *have* happened in recent years, but they have occurred in the Third World rather than in the advanced capitalist economies. Considering only Latin America, what occurred over the 1980s, as measured by several indicators, was unambiguously a depression. Investment in Argentina, Brazil, and Mexico, the three largest economies in the region, fell by between 17 and 44 percent during 1981–1984. Per capita consumption fell by 5 percent between 1980 and 1987 for the region as a whole and open unemployment rose by 40 percent between 1980 and 1984. Even in 1992, a decade after the crisis began, real incomes on average were below 1981 levels and financial dislocations persisted.

To a significant extent, moreover, this depression followed a fairly predictable Minskian cycle. An enormous burst of international lending flowed into Latin America in the 1970s, as international banks became zealous loan merchants and the Latin countries equally ardent recipients of funds. The funds were channeled in several directions, varying by country according to the specific character of the elite groups in power. A substantial portion, if not the majority, of these funds were channeled to wasteful projects and capital flight.[7] It is thus not surprising that, over time, borrower countries' cash commitments outstripped their cash flows. Fragility thus deepened. A systemic shock then occurred when, in the depths of the 1982 recession, Mexico announced its intention of defaulting on its obligations. At that point, international financial institutions shut off further voluntary lending to the region. This converted much of the region, including Argentina and Brazil as well as Mexico—the three largest Latin economies—into what Minsky calls Ponzi units: entities that must increase involuntary borrowing just to meet interest payments (see, for example Diaz Alejandro 1984).

The preconditions for the debt deflation and depression were therefore in place. But here is where the recent Latin experience diverges so sharply from that of the advanced capitalist economies. The policy tools for preventing

---

7. Felix's chapter in this volume offers an excellent overview of both macroeconomic and social indicators in Latin America in the decade since 1982. It also is a serious attempt to analyze the situation within a Minskian framework. Other studies with broadly similar perspectives include Pastor and Dymski 1990, MacEwan 1990, Pollin and Zepeda 1987, and Pollin and Alarcon 1988. George (1988) provides a moving account of the human costs of the debt crisis.

such an incipient financial crisis from culminating in a debt deflation and depression were well known in 1982; however, an explicit decision was made *not to use these tools* to prevent a depression. Quite the contrary: macroeconomic policy, especially in the hands of the International Monetary Fund (IMF), was instead employed to impose severe government budget cuts and labor market austerity and to eliminate price controls. That is, it accelerated the contractionary spiral.

Thus, the 1980s Latin American depression was the first to occur since the toolbox for depression prevention was well known and available for use. It was therefore a *political* decision to forsake these tools and allow the crisis to proceed in its downward path.

4.2 Lessons for the U.S.?

This Latin solution, of course, has not occurred in the contemporary United States. Several obvious disparities between the United States and Latin American economies explain the divergent experiences. The first is the enormously greater stock of tangible and financial resources in the United States. From this flows the seignorage benefits that the United States enjoys by issuing what remains the world's leading reserve currency. These factors continue to promote foreign and direct investment in the United States, in both the financial and nonfinancial spheres, despite the United States economy's declining overall performance. In Latin America, by contrast, investment capital fled to advanced countries as the financial crisis unfolded.

It is also true that the continued attractiveness of the United States as an investment haven has been significantly bolstered—perhaps even decisively so—by high real interest rates and federally guaranteed deposits. But these factors must also be included among the costs to U.S. taxpayers and borrowers of avoiding a Latin-style depression. Finally, the economic disparities between the United States and Latin America lead to huge differences in political processes and outcomes. In the United States, economic policy is determined by domestic politicians, not the IMF. Thus, as long as the political costs of depressions are too high, no government will relinquish its ability to avoid one, regardless of prior rhetorical or even legal commitments.[8]

---

8. The history of the Gramm-Rudman-Hollings budget-balancing law makes clear that the government can always find ways of avoiding deflationary deficit reductions when the costs of budget balancing are perceived as being too high. The Gramm-Rudman-Hollings law, passed by Congress at the end of 1985, established that across the board budget cuts and tax increases would automatically result when the federal deficit exceeded a set ceiling. The ceiling was to fall annually, so that the budget would reach balance in 1991; however, the law never came close to achieving its intended aim. Its primary effect was rather to encourage creative deficit accounting procedures and measures to evade the law's guidelines.

U.S. policy makers can thus still deploy depression-prevention policies, even as costs rise and benefits correspondingly fall. But the present conjuncture raises obvious questions about the future of such policies.

For example, the ascendancy over the past fifteen years of free market economics becomes readily understandable within this framework. Free marketeers have been hammering at the failures of macro stabilization policies and their arguments are not baseless. Relying only on the data presented here, a free market proponent could legitimately argue that big government is no longer creating a more stable economic environment. Why not, therefore, abandon such policies and allow the government's involvement in economic management to contract to a minimum, perhaps the 4 percent level of the small government era. This, they could argue, would promote greater economic liberty, with no apparent loss of security.

The problem with this perspective is its short sightedness. It is true that overall economic performance in the 1980s—as measured by income growth, bank and business failures, unemployment, and real interest rates— approached that of the small government era. But the 1980s also represented the worst of the big government years. The evidence from the earlier phase of the big government era shows that results much superior to those attained either in the small government era or the more recent big government years are possible. Why should we accept the achievements of small government capitalism as a satisfactory standard; or even more, as the aspiration of future policy efforts? Questions such as these have been raised by mainstream Keynesians in recent years. And their position as well is not entirely baseless. Their point is that if only standard macroeconomic policies could be implemented more skillfully—i.e. as they presumably were in the 1950s through the mid-1960s—big government capitalism could return to its earlier phase of stable progress.

But this argument also founders, because it ignores the basic implication of Minsky's paradox—that depression-prevention policies produce costs as well as benefits, and that the costs rise with time as the fragile financial structure remains in place. What we observe over the big government period thus follows logically from Minsky's position: the impact of stabilization policies will be more favorable in earlier phases of their implementation. This means that the levels of stability achieved in the early big government era cannot now be replicated through relying on stabilization tools that worked in the earlier period.

Hence the quandary—indeed the historically unique dilemma—of the present period: conventional stabilization tools cannot return the economy to the early big government standard of performance, but abandoning these tools is likely only to reproduce the inferior performance of the small government era.

Are better alternatives possible? This seems improbable within the present range of acceptable policy discourse. But what our evidence suggests is that the range of discourse needs widening. The strategy of big government capitalism in the United States has been to keep in private hands the most basic decisions about the level and composition of finance and investment, but to socialize the costs investors face through either their own misjudgments or generalized economic downturns. The defining characteristic of a new direction should be to socialize the decision making and benefits of investment activity, not merely the costs of errors.

Specifically, what needs to be brought into discussion are new policy approaches that promote productive investment—that is, the creation of employment-increasing and productivity-enhancing assets, even if the short-term private rate of return from such expenditures is lower than for other types of investment, such as speculative asset transfers. By promoting productive over speculative investment, we counter the inherent tendency toward a increasingly fragile financial structure. This is because, at the most fundamental level, fragility emerges when debt commitments systematically outstrip income flows. Financing the creation of productive assets by its nature will, over the long term, increase the extent to which incomes rise in step with debt financing.

The question then becomes: what are appropriate policies for promoting productive over speculative investment? At a general level, this will require some form of democratic economic planning—following, in some fashion, Keynes's vague but alluring proposal at the conclusion of the *General Theory* for a "somewhat comprehensive socialization of investment." How this should be done is, of course, a profoundly difficult question, which perhaps is why Keynes himself almost entirely skirted it.

4.3 Rigging Markets and Socializing Investment

Minsky sketches some useful ideas in the concluding section of *Stabilizing an Unstable Economy* (1986). As a key organizing principle, Minsky makes the case for a strategy of "rigging markets" rather than relying primarily on regulations or controls to socialize investment activity. In Minsky's view, the problem with a regulation-centered strategy is that it requires far more administration of the details of economic activity, and thus invites inefficiency. One can make a similar argument for rigging markets relative to a heavy dependence on direct public expenditures. Relying on public expenditures for socializing investment would not only create large administrative demands but would also impose the additional burden of large budgetary outlays.

What then, are the most effective ways of socializing finance and investment without imposing detailed controls or excessive public expenditures? In the United States and other advanced capitalist economies, substantial successes have been achieved over the post–World War II period through credit allocation policies, such as loan guarantees, loan subsidies, asset composition requirements for intermediaries, the establishment of government-sponsored secondary markets, and discretionary discount window lending practices by central banks.[9]

In the United States, credit allocation policies have been used to support housing, education, agriculture, and exports. Probably the most dramatic success with credit allocation policies in the United States—and indeed one of the major economic policy achievements of the last 50 years—has been the establishment of a mass home mortgage market that provided non-wealthy households with unprecedented opportunities for home ownership. This was accomplished by requiring that S&Ls specialize in mortgage lending (that is, imposing an asset composition requirement on S&L's); creating a secondary market for mortgage loans; and indirectly subsidizing mortgage loans via interest payment deductions.

Other advanced economies have used credit allocation policies even more extensively in the past fifty years, Japan being the outstanding example.

The Japanese have relied on three basic credit allocation mechanisms. The first is control over small-scale individual savings. This was achieved through the post office savings system, through which the government directly received the deposits of small-scale savers. But the government also restricted private branch banking, thereby limiting the competition for post office savings. The second mechanism was the central bank policy of issuing short-term loans to commercial banks. Central bank lending to commercial banks in Japan is far greater than in the United States since it is able to lend post office savings as well as create new reserves. Moreover, discount window borrowing was used much more extensively than open market operations as a technique for creating reserves.

The other major instrument of credit allocation policy was the Ministry of Industrial Trade and Industry (MITI). MITI's primary function has been to channel credit to large firms and industrial sectors that it had earmarked for long-term growth. Thus, although Japan has never had a formal planning system, the extensive use of credit allocation policies meant that MITI, the central bank, and other government agencies became the de facto central planners.[10]

As a general principle, credit allocation policies are effective because they create a means of significant social control over major finance and

9. The following discussion on credit allocation policies draws on Pollin 1993.

10. The wave of speculative finance in Japan, culminating in the spring 1992 stock market crash, in no way diminishes the long-term achievements of these policies. Indeed, at least in part, the recent financial instability has resulted from the tendency to liberalize the state-directed allocation system, which began in the mid-1970s and accelerated in the mid-1980s.

investment activities, while still allowing considerable decision-making free-dom both for intermediaries and businesses. Private intermediaries are still responsible for establishing the creditworthiness of businesses and the viabil-ity of their projects. Businesses are still responsible for the design and imple-mentation of their investments. Indeed, businesses are still free to pursue nonpreferred projects, and banks can still finance them. Financing costs would just be significantly higher. It is, in short, a straightforward technique of rigging markets rather than relying on quotas and controls to socializing investment and finance.

Credit allocation policies would also carry with them the potential for deterioration over time, in which costs rise to a point where they would exceed benefits. Opportunities for mismanagement and abuse are evident. Indeed, credit allocation policies, if not properly designed and implemented, could easily degenerate into a rent-seeking free-for-all, in which the biggest winners become those who purchase the best lobbyists. Bad allocational decisions will also inevitably occur, even controlling for the influence of rent seekers. The only way to minimize these problems will be to build a high level of democratic accountability into the system—both to set and monitor performance standards and to guard against corruption. Markets will be nec-essarily be relied on for establishing one performance standard, among other possible indicators, just as they have been in all previous successful efforts—in the United States, Japan, and elsewhere—at public credit allocation.

Moreover, regulations in the form of quotas and controls would still be needed within a democratic planning model. Indeed, credit allocation and other market-rigging strategies could not work in an otherwise unregulated market. Regulations are needed both to monitor the viability of credit alloca-tion policies and also to establish a "level playing field" of incentives and constraints for all financial institutions.[11] In large measure, the demise of the old Glass-Steagall regulatory structure resulted through the emergence of an "unlevel playing field": traditional intermediaries faced significantly greater constraints on their activity than nontraditional financial institutions, and thus incentives for "disintermediation" emerged. A restructured financial system that intervenes to socialize investment will therefore have to establish consis-tent rules within the market—that is, a new system of regulation.

At present, the literature that develops a finance-oriented approach to socializing investment is admittedly relatively sparse.[12] This is in great con-trast to the large and mature analytic traditions supporting both small-

---

11. Dymski (1993) and D'Arista and Schlesinger (1993) discuss the issue of creating a regulatory environment that creates a "level playing field" among all intermediaries.

12. In addition to our own recent efforts cited in the previous notes, other useful discus-sions by colleagues are presented in Dymski, Epstein and Pollin 1993. Bardhan and Roemer (1992) develop a more micro-oriented but still finance-centric approach to socializing investment and market socialism.

government perspectives and the model in which big government acts primarily to limit downward instability. However, the burden of this paper is that neither the small government nor a traditional big government approach offers a satisfactory strategy for confronting the observed long-term problem of deepening financial instability. This circumstance alone creates a compelling case for developing stabilizing policies based on democratic planning and socializing investment.

As this tradition develops, it will benefit greatly by being forced to confront the challenge posed so sharply by the Minsky paradox, that is, how to design stabilizing policies whose collateral costs will not intensify with time. The importance of this challenge is but one measure of Minsky's contribution to contemporary political economy.

Appendix A: The Treatment of the Minsky Paradox in Contemporary Mainstream Macroeconomics

Both elements of the Minsky paradox—that capitalist economies have an endogenous tendency toward debt deflation and depression owing to financial fragility, and that this tendency is checked by institutional changes induced by economic outcomes—are completely absent from contemporary mainstream macroeconomics. This mainstream can be crudely divided into two opposing camps: the new classical and new Keynesian economists.

New Classical Perspectives.

Classical macroeconomics does not recognize financial instability. The new classical view assumes that aggregate variables represent equilibria in rapidly adjusting (and nearly continuously clearing) markets. Agents are driven by self-interested behavior to attain optimal risk/return tradeoffs and optimal lifetime consumption profiles. Market outcomes may be temporarily bumped away from equilibrium by unanticipated shocks, but price flexibility allows rapid adjustment back to long-term equilibrium levels. Technological progress is the sole factor that can shift these long-term equilibria permanently. So macroeconomic variables evolve independently of one another. In multiperiod macromodels characterized by rational expectations and precoordination, the evolution of variables is completely explained by recursive solutions. The value of any variable at any point in time depends solely on the model's initial conditions and on the parameters of the Euler equation that governs its motion.

Further, the notion that financial instability can produce significant structural changes in the economy, which then might affect levels of financial fragility, has not been acknowledged in contemporary classical macroeconomics. This theoretical approach takes the institutional context of economic activity as given, and not as evolutionary and time varying. Lucas's (1977) modern conception defines business cycles as simply deviations of aggregate real output from trend. This definition has, for many contemporary economists, replaced the older Burns/Mitchell notion of business cycles as sequences of expansions and contractions, occurring in a predictable order. Kydland and Prescott (1990) have extended Lucas's definition by suggesting that business cycles consist of covarying deviations from trends of different time series. The trend levels of aggregate variables have been hypothesized as sensitive only to exogenous shocks and to shifts in "policy regimes." What characterizes policy regimes is not a different institutional environment (such as the presence of deposit insurance or of a lender of last resort) but shifts in the rules under which government intervention will occur.

New Keynesian Perspectives

New Keynesians, by contrast, at least acknowledge that financial and "real" activities are distinct, and that financial relations may affect real outcomes. Rigid nominal magnitudes and nonclearing markets are viewed as common phenomena owing to the types of contracts and screening devices commonly used in markets. These phenomena, in turn, represent optimal responses to "flaws" in the market environment. These flaws stem from the costliness of market transactions and the uneven availability of information, leading to principal/agent problems among contracting parties. In credit markets, creditors may be reluctant to alter lending rates because they fear adverse selection among those queued up on the demand side, and creditors with imperfect information about borrower quality or intentions may ration credit on the basis of borrowers' collateral.

New Keynesian macroeconomists have developed numerous models demonstrating that "financial structure matters," largely by inserting asymmetric information and transactions costs as variables in their models (for example, Gertler 1988). But having a financial structure that matters is not the same as having a financial structure that endogenously drives the economy toward instability and crisis. Rigid lending rates and nonclearing markets are optimal micro arrangements, which can be arrived at in market equilibria. By implication, no endogenous drive toward financial instability arises from within the economy. Indeed, the economy's financial structure represents an optimal response to agents' information problems. An exogenous shock can have a heightened effect because it may be amplified in credit-market processes.

So contemporary Keynesian macroeconomics has, like classical macroeconomics, ignored the Minsky paradox. Theoretical effort has centered, as Fazzari (1992) observes, on demonstrating that rigidities and credit rationing are fundamental accompaniments of decentralized market economies. These demonstrations have typically deployed the simplest possible analytical elements—preferences, technology, information, and endowments. In part, this simplicity is owing to the difficulty in solving models of optimizing behavior with asymmetric information and/or costly exchange, and it has also facilitated comparisons with the results achieved in classical models of market economies.

However, this orientation to market dynamics in very simple models causes Keynesian theorists to miss any structural elements that might be at work at a more aggregated level. Some new work has begun to suggest the need for a more structural approach, to allow for the impact of changes in the financial system on macroeconomic variables. For example, Romer and Romer (1989, p. 163) have written,

Our results suggest that the effects of demand disturbances were both more rapid and less persistent in the interwar era than in the postwar period . . . an explanation of the change in the overall persistence properties of real output after World War II should be sought in changes in the mechanisms that determine the economy's response to a given type of shock, rather than in changes in the nature of the shocks themselves.

Appendix B: Data Sources and Methods

This appendix first discusses methodological issues in the construction of unemployment and GNP data. It then considers possible problems with the data for business failures. Next it describes the methodology employed in generating the cyclical patterns portrayed in figures 1–5. It finally documents the sources of the remaining data series reported in the main text.

Real GNP and Unemployment Estimates

The results presented in this paper depend on interpreting aggregate economic time series that date from the latter part of the nineteenth century. As discussed in the text, considerable controversy now surrounds aggregate time series data for real GNP and unemployment. (See, for example, Romer 1986a, 1986b, 1989, Balke and Gordon 1989, Weir 1986, 1992, Zarnowitz and Braun 1990 and Carter and Sutch 1992). Indeed, alternative estimates have been developed for two central time series, real GNP and the unemployment rate. We first explain here why the Balke/Gordon GNP series has been used instead of Romer's GNP series. We then discuss why, with unemployment data, we have used a combination of the figures generated by Weir and Carter/Sutch rather than those of Romer.

The controversy with long time-series data began largely as a result of Christina Romer's work, which developed alternative time series for unemployment, output, and price-level data.

GNP
Romer recalculated prewar real GNP data because of her concern that the previous estimates of pre–World War II GNP by Kuznets exaggerated the cyclical variability of GNP. The following passage captures her basic argument:

Annual movements in real GNP are derived by assuming that deviations from trend of GNP move one for one (or nearly so) with deviations from trend of commodity output. However, there is evidence that GNP actually moves much less over the cycle than commodity output; for the postwar era it is widely accepted that the noncommodity components of GNP such as services, trade and transportation are much less cyclically sensitive than the commodity component. (1989, p. 10)

Romer then derives new prewar GNP estimates by estimating the deviations from trend of real GNP and real commodity output "in a period when good data exist for both these series and then using this estimated relationship to form estimates of prewar GNP" (p. 14). But she then writes

> However, unlike Kuznets, I exclude the 1930s from the sample period of estima-
> tion because economic theory and empirical evidence suggest that the relation-
> ship between GNP and commodity output may be much different in a severe
> depression than during more stable periods (p. 14).

Of course, this wider deviation would also tend to mean that data points suggesting wider cyclical volatility earlier in the century would be thrown out of her estimating equation. Specifically, she estimates a linear regression of the form

$$GNP(t) - \text{Trend GNP} = f(\text{Commodity Output}(t) - \text{Trend Commodity Output})$$

for the time periods 1909–1928 and 1947–1985.

Balke and Gordon's rebuttal is as follows. They distinguish between two different approaches to building up estimates of aggregate variables when data are restricted: (1) the components approach, which requires detailed information about institutions forming a "component" of the aggregate in question (GNP); and (2) the indicators ap-
proach, which relies on the existence of variables that are correlated with the aggregate in question. Clearly, Romer relies on an indicators approach.

Gordon and Balke then argue that using an indicators approach (which necessarily involves a regression estimation method such as Romer's) is unsatisfactory in that it discards available detailed data. They then go on to come up with "available annual indexes of transportation and communication," expressing their "most surprising dis-
cover[y] that no previous study of real GNP has made any use at all of the copious data available" in these areas. They also use data on construction activity. This components approach leads to their own new estimates for real GNP.

Unemployment

Modern unemployment statistics began in 1940, when the Current Population Survey section of the Labor Department began interviewing a sample of households to ask whether anyone was unsuccessfully seeking a job. Romer's widely discussed paper (1986a) was a sharp critique of Stanley Lebergott's initial attempt (1964) at constructing a consistent time series on unemployment that would include the years before 1940.

Romer argued that Lebergott introduced significant spurious volatility into the pre-1940 data. This was because his method of estimation with the pre-1940 data generated a pro-volatility bias relative to the methods used with the official post-1940 data. Romer thus replicated Lebergott's methods with post–World War II data and found that unemployment volatility roughly doubled under this approach relative to what the official estimates measure. As Weir (1992) explains, Romer then revised Lebergott's estimate of the pre-1940 data "by a simple mathematical procedure that essentially moved each annual observation half the distance back toward the mean for the period", (p. 4).

But Weir found three basic errors in Romer's revision of Lebergott. The first is that Romer did not separate out trend increases in unemployment over the postwar period from the cyclical volatility of unemployment. According to Weir, a simple linear trend explains 43 percent of the variance of postwar unemployment, but from 1900 to 1930, the trend explains less than 1 percent of total variance.

Second, because Romer used an indicators rather than a components approach to estimation—just as she did with GNP statistics—she did not take account of structural differences between the prewar and postwar economies. In particular, Romer neglects the fact that the relative share of manufacturing, construction, and trade increased in the postwar economy.

By the same token, Weir argues that Lebergott's own methods also distorted the industrial distribution of employment. For the period 1900–1930, Weir's adjustment of Lebergott's method produced an increase in the relative size of the cyclically volatile sectors of the economy. But, according to Weir, Lebergott also substantially overstated the magnitude of unemployment for the 1890s, because for that decade only he assumed that total unemployment varied one-for-one with employment in manufacturing. This neglects the fact that employment in nonmanufacturing, notably in agriculture and self-employment, was far less volatile than output variations in manufacturing. Weir thus performs data adjustments in recognition of these changes in the relative proportions of the various sectors of the economy. Romer, however, did not recognize these errors in Lebergott's methods.

Weir constructs a consistent time series by making a set of adjustments to recognize the effects of the changing composition of industry. He also takes account of Darby's (1976) observation that government relief workers were classified as unemployed in the official data and by Lebergott, whereas modern definitions would count them as employed.

We have relied on Weir's revised figures for the period 1906–1989. For 1890–1905, however, we were persuaded by Carter and Sutch (1992) that adjustments in addition to those performed by Weir are necessary. Carter and Sutch found that previous researchers had neglected the effects of two factors influencing the aggregate unemployment rate in the 1890s. The first was unemployment created by industrial suspensions of operation in which an entire firm would close for periods ranging from several days to even months. The second was unemployment created by business failures. Carter and Sutch argue that the effect of these two factors becomes far less significant after 1905, so that neglecting them with more recent data does not create serious errors in estimation.

Finally, Carter and Sutch argue that because of the difficulty in obtaining reliable data on these two effects prior to 1890, it is "difficult, probably inadvisable, to estimate annual employment for the period before 1890", (p. 24). The series we report for unemployment, splicing together Carter and Sutch with Weir, thus begins in 1890. Our other series begin in 1875.

Business Failure Rates

The basic source of data on business failures is Dun and Bradstreet, which has been collecting data in this area since the 1870s. They define business failures as the exit of businesses either through court bankruptcy proceedings or through voluntary actions involving losses to creditors. As Lane and Schary (1991) note, this measure does not include the most common form of business exits, which is simple discontinuance—or the closure of a business without loss to creditors. Simple discontinuances are far more frequent than failures, but, according to Lane and Schary, there is a high correlation between failures and discontinuances. Moreover, for our purposes, the failure rate is a more meaningful indicator of business distress, since it involves loss to creditors and therefore contributes to macrolevel financial instability.

Two possible measurement problems have been raised regarding the failure rate series. The first is that it has been biased by changes in bankruptcy laws. In particular, one might expect that the 1978 revisions in corporate bankruptcy law, which, through chapter 11, allows significantly greater opportunities for debtors to undertake reorganization rather than liquidation (Glick 1992), will have created an upward bias in the failure rate.

In fact, however, it is unlikely that these bankruptcy law changes have biased the failure rate trend upward. Firms that seek protection and then successfully reorganize through chapter 11 should not qualify as business failures (some may be counted as such, but only because of errors in sampling methods). Indeed, by allowing firms greater opportunities to reorganize rather than exit, the 1978 revisions may well exert a *downward* bias on the failure rate. In any case, the proportion of chapter XI failures constitutes a small proportion of the aggregate number of failures, relative to those that exit through other bankruptcy routes or through voluntary actions involving loss to creditors.

The second concern with the Dun and Bradstreet series is the substantial change in their data sample beginning in 1984, when they increased their coverage of the service sector. According to Joseph Duncan of Dun and Bradstreet's economic research division (private communication December 1, 1992), this change in sampling does not affect the failure rate since both the numerator and denominator—the number of failures and the number of firms—are equally affected. However, if the firms newly incorporated into the sample are more susceptible to failures—that is, if service industry firms are more likely to fail than manufacturing and mining firms—then the aggregate failure rate would indeed rise with the increase in the data sample. Lane and Schary (1991) and others find that the single greatest determinant of changes in failure rates is prior changes in entry rates, since young firms are most susceptible to failure. Thus, if entry rates are higher for service industry firms, then it is plausible to expect failure rates to rise with the increased sampling of the service sector.

Lane and Schary argue that the change in sampling fully accounts for the rise in the failure rate after 1984. They reach this conclusion through econometric testing in which they represent the 1984 sampling revision as a dummy variable. However, they offer no substantive explanation as to why the data revisions should have so significant an effect. Moreover, this consideration cannot explain the fact that the post-1984 pattern is actually an extension of the upward trend in the rate beginning in 1978. In a private communication (December 1, 1992) Lane reports that she is pursuing a revision of her 1991 model and anticipates that her results may well alter through a more precise specification of the effects of the data revision.

Overall, the 1984 data revision may have created some upward bias in the data. But this is almost certainly not to the extent suggested in Lane and Schary's original estimate. Moreover, this upward bias may also be counterbalanced by a downward bias resulting from the 1978 changes in corporate bankruptcy laws. In short, we conclude that the data trend offered by the failure rate is preponderantly, if not entirely, the result of substantive changes in economic activity.

As for substantive explanations, Duncan of Dun and Bradstreet, in private communication, argues that the downsizing of corporations and increased use of unaffiliated suppliers associated with the restructurings of the 1980s encouraged an increase in firms, which then brought an increase in the failure rate. Moreover, the failures of large corporations in the 1980s, even though they are relatively few numerically, also contributed to the rise of the aggregate failure rate when smaller firms supplying the large corporations absorbed the impact of the large firms' failures. In a complimentary analysis, Naples (1990) argues that, over the 1980s, the decline in funding for income maintainance programs contributed to the acceleration of failures. This is because such transfer payments redistribute income from relatively prosperous to relatively depressed areas, sustaining demand in areas more heavily afflicted by downturns and thus helping to prevent failures. The arguments of both Duncan and Naples are clearly consistent with a broad Minskian perspective on the impact of increasing fragility and speculative finance over time.

Measuring Cyclical Behavior

Figures 1–5 portray the postpeak behavior of five variables: real GNP, the inflation rate, bank and business failure rates per 10,000 establishments, and the real long-term interest rate. Here a "peak" represents a value of real GNP greater than is recorded subsequently.

The computation of typical cyclical movements with annual data presents some methodological difficulties. First, we want to avoid the distorting effects of large wars on aggregate economic data. This leads us to exclude all cyclical peaks occurring just before, during, or after the outbreak of World Wars I and II.

Our second methodological difficulty was that though cyclical peaks are measured using quarterly data, long-term historical data have been computed only on an annual basis. This leads to two problems. First, a quarterly peak may not be reflected in annual data; that is, annual estimates of real GNP may not fall in the year after one in which a peak quarter has occurred. Second, depending on when in the calendar year a recession begins, the statistical impact of the onset of a cyclical downturn may be felt before, after, or during the year in which the peak quarter actually occurs.

Dealing adequately with the statistical problems posed in moving from quarterly to annual data would require a detailed exploration of cycle-dating methodology.[13] Here, we adopt a simple rule for defining peak years. The first characteristic of a peak is that it contains a cyclical peak month, as computed by the National Bureau of

---

13. The methodological and economic issues involved in business cycle dating are discussed in Moore 1983 and Sherman 1991.

Economic Research (NBER). We then exclude data that falls five years prior to or after the two world wars. Finally, we define as peak years only those in which real GNP falls between the year containing the peak month and the subsequent year.

This screening procedure thus uses NBER monthly datings of cyclical peaks as the basis of our estimated peak years; however, the year in which the peak month occurs is only accepted as a peak year if real GNP for the entire year is also at a peak level. Years that pass these screens are used as peak years in figures 1–5.

Five peak years are used for the small government era: 1873, 1887, 1893, 1906, and 1929. The year 1895 also satisfies our criteria but is not used as a peak year because it occurs so soon (two years) after an earlier peak. All of the remaining years containing NBER peaks in the small government era either overlap with World War I or occur in years in which real GNP, measured annually, does not subsequently fall.

In the big government era prior to the 1980s, four peak years are used: 1953, 1957, 1969, and 1973. The data for the 1980s use 1980 as a peak year because this calendar year contains a peak quarter. The year 1982 passes the screens for inclusion as a peak year, but it is not incorporated separately into the 1980s data because it occurs just two years after the 1980 peak.

For each variable, four observations—drawn from the four cycles included in the sample—lie behind each data point in the big government era, and five observations are used to generate each data point in the small government era. There are two exceptions to this: (1) the small government data for bank failures exclude the 1929 peak year because of the abnormally high number of bank failures in those years compared to historical experience; and (2) the small government data for real interest rates exclude the 1873 peak year, because our interest rate data begin with 1875.

We should note that we have examined numerous permutations of these data, varying both the peak years that are included in averages and the method of determining a peak year. Such alternative calculations do not alter the essential shape of the data as shown in figures 1–5: the 1980s data for these variables echo, more or less closely, data trends associated with the small government era.

Data Sources

Federal Government Expenditures
The figures from 1875 to 1939 are drawn from the *Historical Statistics of the United States* published by the U.S. Department of Commerce (1976). Subsequent figures come from the U.S. Council of Economic Advisors' *Economic Report of the President* (1992).

Real GNP
We rely on Balke and Gordon's (1989) method of estimation. The most recent figures based on these estimates are presented in appendix A of Gordon 1990.

Inflation Rate
The GNP deflator is used to indicate price levels. Data for this variable are also generated in Balke and Gordon 1989 and are updated in Gordon 1990.

Real Interest Rates
The data for the corporate bond rate are taken from appendix A of Gordon 1990.

Bank and Business Failures
The data for business failures are taken from the *Survey of Current Business*, May issues and *Statistical Abstract of the United States* (1992), both published by the U.S. Department of Commerce. The source of these data, as discussed above, is Dun and Bradstreet. The data for bank failures are drawn from the *Historical Statistics of the United States* (1976) and from the Federal Deposit Insurance Corporation's publication *Historical Statistics in Banking* (1992). Note that prior to 1933, bank failures per se are not recorded; instead, records were maintained on the number of suspensions of commercial and mutual savings banks. After 1933, bank failures were recorded directly for this same set of institutions.

The data for bank failures are for commercial banks only. Among financial intermediaries in the United States, commercial banks were established relatively early; hence a comparison that encompasses the nineteenth and twentieth centuries will be least distorted with the effects of industry development. Goldsmith (1958) considers the development of financial intermediaries in the United States in depth.

REFERENCES

Balke, Nathan S., and Robert J. Gordon. 1989. "The Estimation of Prewar Gross National Product: Methodology and New Evidence," *Journal of Political Economy* 97(1): 37–92.

Bardhan, Pradnab, and John E. Roemer. 1992. "Market Socialism: A Case for Rejuvenation," *Journal of Economic Perspectives* 6(3): 101–116.

Bowles, Samuel, David M. Gordon, and Thomas Weisskopf. 1986. "Power and Profits: The Social Structure of Accumulation and the Profitability of the U.S. Economy," *Review of Radical Political Economics* 18(1–2): 132–68.

———. 1991. *After the Waste Land: A Democratic Economics for the Year 2000.* Armonk, N.Y: M.E. Sharpe.

Carter, Susan and Richard Sutch. 1992. "The Great Depression of the 1890s: New Suggestive Estimates of the Unemployment Rate, 1890–1905," in Roger Ransom, ed., *Research in Economic History* 14, JAI Press, pp. 347–376.

Darby, Michael R. 1976. "Three-and-a-Half Million U.S. Employees Have Been Mislaid: Or, an Explanation of Unemployment, 1934–41;" *Journal of Political Economy* 84(1): 1–26.

D'Arista, Jane W., and Tom Schlesinger. 1993. "The Parallel Banking System," in G. Dymski, G. Epstein, and R. Pollin eds., *Transforming the U.S. Financial System*: Armonk, N.Y.: M.E. Sharpe, forthcoming.

Diaz Alejandro, Carlos. 1984. "Latin American Debt: I Don't Think We are in Kansas Anymore," *Brookings Papers on Economic Activity* 2: 335–403.

Dymski, Gary. 1993. "How to Remake the U.S. Banking System: Level the Playing Field and Renew the Social Contract," in G. Dymski, G. Epstein and R. Pollin, eds., *Transforming the U.S. Financial System* Armonk, N.Y.: M.E. Sharpe, forthcoming.

Dymski, Gary , Gerald Epstein and Robert Pollin, eds. 1993. *Transforming the U.S. Financial System: Equity and Efficiency for the 21st Century*, Armonk, N.Y.: M.E. Sharpe, forthcoming.

Dymski, Gary, and Robert Pollin. 1992. "Hyman Minsky as Hedgehog: The Power of the Wall Street Paradigm," in S. Fazzari and D. B. Papadimitriou, eds., *Financial Conditions and Macroeconomic Performance: Essays in Honor of Hyman P. Minsky.* Armonk, N.Y.: M.E. Sharpe, 27–62.

Fazzari, Steven. 1991. "Keynesian Theories of Investment: Neo, Post, and New," in S. Fazzari and D.B. Papadimitriou, eds., *Financial Conditions and Macroeconomic Performance: Essays in Honor of Hyman P. Minsky.* Armonk, N.Y.: M.E. Sharpe, 121–132.

Felix, David. 1993. "Debt Crisis Adjustment in Latin America: Have the Hardships Been Necessary?" This volume.

George, Susan. 1988. *A Fate Worse Than Debt.* New York: Grove Press.

Gertler, Mark. 1988. "Financial Structure and Aggregate Activity," *Journal of Money, Credit, and Banking* 20(3): 559–88.

Glick, Mark. 1992. "A History of Corporate Bankruptcy," manuscript, University of Utah.

Goldsmith, Raymond W. 1958. *Financial Intermediaries in the American Economy since 1900.* National Bureau of Economic Research, New York. Princeton: Princeton University Press.

Gordon, Robert J. 1990. *Macroeconomics.* Glenview, Ill: Scott, Foresman.

Kindleberger, Charles P. 1978. *Manias, Panics, and Crashes.* New York: Basic Books.

Kydland, Finn E., and Edward C. Prescott. 1990. "Business Cycles: Real Facts and a Monetary Myth," *Quarterly Review, Federal Reserve Bank of Minneapolis* 14(2): 3–18.

Lane, Sarah J. and Martha Schary, 1991, "Understanding the Business Failure Rate," *Contemporary Policy Issues*, October, 9(4): 93–105.

Lebergott, Stanley. 1964. *Manpower in Economic Growth; the American Record Since 1800.* New York: McGraw Hill.

Lucas, Robert E. 1977. "Understanding Business Cycles," in Karl Brunner and Allan H. Meltzer, eds. *Stabilization of the Domestic and International Economy*, ed. Karl Brunner and Allan H. Meltzer, Carnegie-Rochester Conference Series on Public Policy 5: 7–29. Amsterdam: North-Holland.

MacEwan, Arthur. 1990. *Debt and Disorder: International Economic Instability and U.S. Imperial Decline.* New York: Monthly Review.

Magdoff, Harry, and Paul M. Sweezy. 1987. *Stagnation and the Financial Explosion.* New York: Monthly Review Press.

Minsky, Hyman. 1982. *Can "It" Happen Again?* Armonk, N.Y.: M.E. Sharpe.

———. 1986. *Stabilizing an Unstable Economy.* New Haven: Yale University Press.

Mullineux, A. W. 1990. *Business Cycles and Financial Crises.* Ann Arbor: University of Michigan Press.

Naples, Michele I. 1990. "Transfers, Business Failures, and the Expenditure Multiplier: The Macro-Regional Consequences of Reaganomics," manuscript, Department of Economics, Monmouth College.

Pastor, Manuel, and Gary Dymski. 1990. "Debt Crisis and Class Conflict in Latin America," *Review of Radical Political Economics* 22(1): 155–78.

Pollin, Robert. 1986. "Alternative Perspectives on the Rise of Corporate Debt-Dependency," *Review of Radical Political Economics* 18(1–2): 235–65.

Pollin, Robert. 1993. "Public Credit Allocation through the Federal Reserve: Why it is Needed; How It Should Be Done," in G. Dymski, G. Epstein and R. Pollin, eds., *Transforming the U.S. Financial System* Armonk, N.Y.: M.E. Sharpe, forthcoming.

Pollin, Robert, and Eduardo Zepeda. 1987. "Latin American Debt: The Choices Ahead," *Monthly Review*, 38, 1–16.

Pollin, Robert, and Diana Alarcon. 1988. "Debt Crisis, Accumulation Crisis and Economic Restructuring in Latin America," *International Review of Applied Economics*, June, 137–154.

Romer, Christina D. 1986a. "New Estimates of Prewar Gross National Product and Unemployment," *Journal of Economic History* 46(2): 341–352.

———. 1986b. "Is the Stabilization of the Postwar Economy a Figment of the Data?" *American Economic Review* 76(2): 314–44.

———. 1989. "The Prewar Business Cycle Reconsidered: New Estimates of Gross National Product, 1869–1908," *Journal of Political Economy* 97(1): 1–37.

Romer, Christina D. and David H. Romer, 1989. "Does Monetary Policy Matter? A New Test in the Spirit of Friedman and Schwartz," *NBER Macroeconomics Annual 1989*. Cambridge, Mass. The MIT Press, 121–69.

Sherman, Howard. 1991. *Business Cycles*. Princeton: Princeton University Press.

U.S. Council of Economic Advisors, (1992) *Economic Report of the President*. Washington, D.C.: U.S. Government Printing Office.

U.S. Department of Commerce, Bureau of the Census, (1992). *Statistical Abstract of the United States*. Washington, D.C.: U.S. Government Printing Office.

U.S. Department of Commerce, Bureau of the Census (1976). *Historical Statistics of the United States, Colonial Times to 1970*. Washington, D.C.: U.S. Government Printing Office.

U.S. Department of Commerce, Bureau of Economic Analysis, *Survey of Current Business*, various May issues.

U.S. Federal Deposit Insurance Corporation, Bank Statistics Branch, Division of Research and Statistics (1992). *Historical Statistics in Banking: A Statistical History of the United States Banking Industry, 1934–1991*. Washington, D.C.: Federal Deposit Insurance Corporation.

Weir, David R. 1986. "The Reliability of Historical Macroeconomic Data for Comparing Cyclical Stability," *Journal of Economic History* 46(2): 353–65.

———. 1992. "Unemployment Volatility, 1890–1984: A Sensitivity Analysis." in Roger Ransom, ed., *Research in Economic History* 14, JAI Press, pp. 301–346.

Wolfson, Martin. 1986. *Financial Crises*. Armonk, N.Y.: M.E. Sharpe.

Zarnowitz, Victor, and Phillip Braun. 1990. "Major Macroeconomic Variables and Leading Indexes: Some Estimates of Their Interrelations," in Philip Klein, ed., *Analyzing Business Cycles: Essays Honoring Geoffrey H. Moore*. Armonk, N.Y.: M.E.Sharpe, 177–205.

Contributors

Arie Arnon, Department of Economics, Ben-Gurion University of the Negev, Beer-Sheva, Israel, and Research Department, Bank of Israel, Jerusalem, Israel 91007

James Crotty, Department of Economics, University of Massachusetts, Amherst, MA 01003

Domenico Delli Gatti, Dipartimento di Scienze Economiche, Catholic University, Milan, Italy

Gary Dymski, Department of Economics, University of California, Riverside, Riverside, CA 92421-0427

James Earley, Emeritus, Department of Economics, University of California-Riverside, Riverside, CA 92521-0427

Gerald Epstein, Department of Economics, University of Massachusetts, Amherst, MA, 01003

David Felix, Emeritus, Department of Economics, Washington University, St. Louis, MO 63130

Mauro Gallegati, Instituto di Scienze Economiche, University of Urbino, Italy

H. Peter Gray, Emeritus, Economics and Finance, Rutgers University, and Economics and Management, Rensselaer Polytechnic Institute, Troy, NY 12180

Jean M. Gray, Emeritus, Department of Finance, Rider College, Lawrenceville, NJ 08648

Laura Guardini, Instituto di Scienza Economiche, University of Urbino, Italy

Dorene Isenberg, Department of Economics, Drew University, Madison, NJ 07940

Craig Justice, Department of Economics, Chaffey College, Rancho Cucamonga, CA 91737

Edward Nell, Department of Economics, Graduate Faculty, New School for Social Research, New York, NY 10011

Robert Pollin, Department of Economics, University of California-Riverside, Riverside, CA 92521-0427

Lance Taylor, Department of Economics, Graduate Faculty, New School for Social Research, New York, NY 10011

Index